9
58

STUDIES IN THE
EARLY BRITISH CHURCH

STUDIES IN THE
EARLY BRITISH CHURCH

BY

NORA K. CHADWICK
KATHLEEN HUGHES
CHRISTOPHER BROOKE
KENNETH JACKSON

CAMBRIDGE
AT THE UNIVERSITY PRESS
1958

PUBLISHED BY
THE SYNDICS OF THE CAMBRIDGE UNIVERSITY PRESS

Bentley House, 200 Euston Road, London, N.W.1
American Branch: 32 East 57th Street, New York, 22, N.Y.

©

CAMBRIDGE UNIVERSITY PRESS
1958

Printed in Great Britain at the University Press, Cambridge
(Brooke Crutchley, University Printer)

Prefatory Note

This book contains five studies in the Celtic Church of western Britain and southern Scotland, and one study in the early Irish scriptoria. Our principal interest lies in the Church of the British- or Welsh-speaking area during the period between the 'age of the saints' in the sixth century and the changes brought about by the coming of the Normans and the medieval religious Orders. The object of our work is to widen the sources of our knowledge for the period. In the Introduction I have explained the principle and scope of our researches and the basis of the choice of our individual subjects.

The studies are the work of four contributors. I am responsible for the original conception and the plan, and for arranging the discussions which we have held from time to time, and also for the assembling and presentation of the completed work. I have allowed each contributor to be quite independent in regard to the views expressed, and have not thought detailed co-ordination necessary or even desirable.

We are grateful to the Syndics of the Cambridge University Press for their initial encouragement of our proposal and for their generosity in undertaking publication. We also wish to thank the staff for their care in the production of the book. I addition we are happy to acknowledge our indebtedness to Mr G. V. Carey for his willingness to make the Index, and for his help in the final stages of the proofs.

NORA K. CHADWICK

CAMBRIDGE
March 1958

Contents

Introduction

BY NORA K. CHADWICK

The object of this book is to offer some studies of the intellectual life of Early Britain after the departure of the Romans, more especially before the foundations of Saxon England. Our studies have, it is true, taken us down to much later times, and a large proportion of our book is concerned with documents and institutions of the Norman Period. Our primary concern, however, is not with the actual history of this later period, but with the light which its documents shed retrospectively on Celtic Britain in early historical times. In the early centuries of Celtic British history the intellectual life of the great majority of the population was carried on by means of oral tradition. Any written records were made by ecclesiastics; even the oral traditions were ultimately recorded by clerics. The period must have been one of great mental activity, because it is one of overlap and transition, racial, or national, linguistic, political. The Romans were still a living memory, and their organisation, political delimitations and military and official influence had left a still living tradition behind. The Celtic peoples, who had ruled our island for centuries before the Roman occupation, were once more, for a brief period of their history and our own, the rulers of the land, with their kings great and small, their wide undefined kingdoms of the west and north-west, and their combination of Roman traditional culture superimposed on their native heroic civilisation. The Church, in some degree no doubt a Roman heritage, in part a new institution introduced from the Mediterranean world, took root and grew within our period, bringing with it the Latin learning and outlook of Continental education and something of the mysticism of the East.

All these varied currents of thought would have combined to stimulate a keen intellectual life in Britain. And for our knowledge of all these currents of thought and their expression, whether in the native alphabets on stone, whether in the heroic poetry and genealogies preserved at the courts of the native chiefs by highly trained bards and genealogists, or whether in the contemporary Latin learning introduced from the Continent, we are ultimately dependent on the written records left us by the ecclesiastics trained in the contemporary Church. A study of the early British Church is the gateway to all our knowledge of early British thought, education and intellectual life generally.

Our aim has therefore been to make a series of brief studies of the early British Church, and our researches and our interests have concentrated rather on its intellectual life than on its theological or ritual aspects. Our evidence has led us to share in the desire expressed by Nennius to disprove the accusation of want of intellectual vitality among the British of the early Middle Ages. Certainly our work has led us to the belief that they were not guilty of the *hebetudo* with which they had been charged. It is true that relatively few documents have survived from the period; but this is in part due to the fact that as yet the great monastic scriptoria, which were destined to play so important a part in the production of manuscript materials of all kinds in the later period, had not come into being. A beginning had been made, notably at Llanbadarn, Llancarfan, and earliest of all at Glastonbury, probably also somewhere in Cornwall, and certainly in Brittany. It is to scribes of such early British scriptoria that we owe our earliest written records of the British language, some of them dating from the eighth century, such as our earliest glosses, and probably others from the ninth, e.g. poetry preserved in the *Juvencus* Manuscript in the Cambridge University Library (MS. Ff. 4. 42).

In view of the relative sparsity of direct evidence for the period, it has been found necessary to draw extensively upon indirect evidence, and, consequently, from a wide field. This will be obvious from the range of the various chapters in this book. It will also be apparent that the differing classes of evidence vary greatly in their nature from one area and from one period to another, even within the small compass to which we have restricted our studies. Experience has led us to the belief that before a survey or narrative can be made profitably for the period as a whole, it is essential to have before us studies by a number of individuals whose special interests lie within the field, but whose discipline and technique, and whose special field of research, differ widely from one another. It is hoped that in this way not only will new information become available for special areas, but various types of training and discipline, and a variety of approaches, while directed more especially to the subject with which the writer is himself directly concerned, may also suggest new methods and sources of information which may profitably be used in future for other fields.

We have therefore not attempted to make a comprehensive treatment of the early British Church, but each of us has made a special study of some aspect within the area and period in which our own special researches have lain. Professor Jackson has examined the sources and nature of the materials for the life of St Kentigern, the patron saint of the British ('Welsh')-speaking peoples of Cumbria and Strathclyde, his object being an inquiry into the nature of the materials used by the compilers of our extant *Lives*, and other materials, such as the Breviaries of Edinburgh and Aberdeen. St Kentigern is usually assigned to the sixth century, the 'age of the saints', and his obit appears in the *Annales Cambriae*, *s.a.* 612. No written contemporary records have survived from the British Church in this area, i.e. from Scotland south of the Firths of Forth and Clyde, or from north-western England; but all our secular traditions recorded later in Wales in both Latin and vernacular texts suggest that oral poetry and genealogical lore had been highly cultivated in the North British territory from the sixth century onwards, and there is evidently reason for believing that ecclesiastical sagas, and perhaps also genealogies, were to some extent cultivated in the same milieu.

Indeed our earliest extant source for the life of St Kentigern, the fragmentary *Anonymous Life*, composed about the middle of the twelfth century, claims that the author has made use, not only of 'material found in a little volume (or 'volumes', *codicell-*), but also of what was told him orally by trustworthy people'.[1] The nature of the material which was evidently preserved in this fragmentary *Life* suggests that the *codicellus* or its source has made use of local materials and oral traditions, partly Gaelic in character. But it had itself been based on an earlier Latin *Life* composed in the early eleventh century, in a Cumbric rather than a Gaelic context, possibly before the loss of the independence of Strathclyde following on the death of its last British king Owen. We have no evidence of written tradition earlier than this; but even so this takes us back almost to within living memory of the Battle of

---

[1] *De materia in virtutum eius codicell- reperta et viva voce fidelium mihi relata.*

Brunanburh and the period of the composition of the Welsh poem known as the *Armes Prydein*, the period when the patriotic and anti-English fervour were at their height in the Celtic countries further south, and when the oral traditions of the great heroes of the sixth and seventh centuries were revived and cultivated, and even in part recorded, at some centre as yet undetermined. It is possibly to this Celtic 'climax' further south that we owe the formulation of the cult of the principal North British (Strathclyde) saint, and the entry of his name in the *Annales Cambriae*, which we might almost call the North British roll of honour for this period. In the longer *Life* by Jocelyn, a monk of Furness Abbey in Lancashire-over-the-Sands, compiled probably *c.* 1180, a wider range of material has been employed, including both the *Anonymous Life* itself, and the lost *codicellus* used by its author; but we have no clear evidence of any early writings in the vernacular, and the historical value of these late Latin *Lives* and of the materials contained in the still later Latin Breviaries is necessarily slight.

There were indeed two periods during which the Roman Order of the Church in our islands collected and adapted such traditions of the early Celtic Church as still survived, in order to stimulate and encourage local cults, partly with a view to enlisting the sympathies and loyalty of the Celtic peoples, partly to bring them into line with the reformed Church. These two periods are the late seventh and early eighth centuries, the period of the union of the Celtic with the Roman Order; and the early twelfth century, the period of the reforms in the Scottish Church by David I, and more particularly his reorganisation of the diocese of Glasgow on Norman lines. From the first of these periods certain documents from Whithorn contemporary with Bede make it clear that about this time materials were collected and adapted relating to St Ninian, the apostle to the southern Picts; but a *Life of St Ninian* was again written in the twelfth century by Ailred, abbot of Rievaulx, in a style regarded as more in keeping with Norman requirements. The two earliest surviving narratives of the life of St Kentigern date from the same century, and were similarly composed to supersede earlier work which did not come up to Norman standards.

Of these two extant *Lives* of St Kentigern the earliest, of which a fragment only remains, was composed, so the author tells us, at the request of Herbert, bishop of Glasgow (1147–64), in emulation

4

of Symeon of Durham's *Life of St Cuthbert*. It was probably the work of a Norman priest in the following of David I, and his aim, in accordance with Bishop Herbert's intention, was to bring the former national Church of Strathclyde into line with other Norman dioceses by producing an up-to-date version of the legend of the patron saint, precisely as we find Lifris and Caradoc writing the *Lives* of St Cadoc of Llancarfan in South Wales *c.* 1100, and other hagiographers producing the *Lives* of Dubricius and Oudoceus for insertion in the *Book of Llandaff*. Some thirty years after the composition of the *Anonymous Life of St Kentigern*, a *Life* of the saint was written by Jocelyn, again for the bishop of Glasgow, avowedly with the intention of superseding the former work; and Professor Jackson's analysis of Jocelyn's work and its relationship to its sources shows how far the conception of hagiographical narrative had progressed from a local and localised tradition to an independent and more generalised class of story of the type which Professor Brooke classifies among the works, not of the local monk recording the traditions of his founder, but of the professional hagiographer, a member of a professional literary class. The MS. Cotton Vespasian A. xiv, the subject of one of Miss Hughes's studies, would seem to be a collection of such literary *Lives*.

For our knowledge of the Church of Wales in the 'age of the saints' contemporary with St Kentigern, our most important source is in fact the collection of *Lives* of Welsh saints contained in the MS. just mentioned. Almost all our important Welsh saints are represented in this collection except the group of what we may describe as the 'outward bound' saints, the traditional founders of the great Breton monasteries, such as St Samson, St Pôl de Léon, St Gildas, St Gurthiern, and others whose biographies were composed in Brittany, the country of their adoption. The collection of *Lives* contained in our text was probably compiled at Monmouth Priory. Its interest is, however, not primarily local, and the general interest of its varied and sustained narratives, beginning with the *Life* of St Cadoc of Llancarfan and including local saints of South and West Wales, and even Anglesey and the north coast, suggests that its aim is neither liturgical nor lectionary but literary, a collection of stories intended to interest at least as much as to edify. Like the two extant *Lives* of St Kentigern, these Latin *Lives* of Welsh saints are late compositions, the earliest being that of St David, written before 1100; but like the Kentigern *Lives*, they embody earlier traditions. The *Life of St Cadoc* in particular has preserved interesting allusions to secular stories and local traditions, some apparently relating to the North British territories. Still more interesting are its allusions to offices in the early Church, such as that to Cau the giant as Cadoc's *fossor*, which is one of the early Orders of the Continental Church. Hardly less interesting is the allusion in the same *Life* to the *famosus rethoricus* coming to Wales from Rome, bringing with him up-to-date Latin, the acquisition of which was eagerly sought as being smarter than the provincial Latin taught in the Irish schools. The selection of saints whose *Lives* are included in this collection, and the other contents of the MS. also, was doubtless dictated, as Miss Hughes has shown, by the interests of the Norman house at Gloucester. It is nevertheless by far our most comprehensive collection of information relating to Welsh saints of the sixth century.

Little information is available as to the circumstances in which these Welsh *Lives* were written. Undoubtedly a large part of the contents are derived from oral tradition, ecclesiastical and even in part secular saga. Yet the traditions which they record are valuable, however untrustworthy in detail. In general they present us with a picture of the Celtic Church in the 'age of the saints' which is consistent in itself; substantiated by such ecclesiastical writings as have come down to us from other sources; and in agreement with what we know from contemporary records of the Continental Church at this period and the one immediately preceding it. It must, of course, be freely admitted that we have always to allow for the fact that the ideals and usages of a later age will tend to colour the picture, as we have seen to be the case even in the testimony of Bede. If the material and literary records for all the Celtic countries be taken together, however, the picture which they present is consistent in its broad outlines. It is that of a monastic Church, with an ascetic discipline and a high spiritual standard, an organisation by no means negligible, but without central authority on a broad basis; a simple and austere way of life, architecture of the simplest, but not necessarily crude. The rarity of important Welsh scriptoria, due to the absence of wealth and the simplicity of the organisation in general, has been the cause of a corresponding scarcity of early records for the early Church in Wales, as in North Britain; and it is not impossible that the jealousy of the bards, the professional repositories of oral tradition with strong vested interests in both countries, may have held back the development of a written tradition in some measure. It is easy to recall stories of the hostility of the poets to book learning—in Irish saga Suibhne Geilt throwing St Ronan's sacred book into the water; in Welsh poetry Yscolan doing the same; in the Welsh poem *Armes Prydein* the poet himself pours out a malediction on the *llyfrawr*, which is surely a cut at the 'book-learned man'.[1] Yet despite our relatively meagre contemporary information for the period in Wales, the uniformity of the monastic system in the early Celtic Church, and the general consistency of our records, such as they are, allow us to assume that in this, as in many other respects, the Welsh schools would resemble those of Ireland, and Miss Hughes's further study of the Irish monastic scriptoria presents us with direct information, more or less contemporary, as to the circumstances in which the records of the early Celtic Church were composed, copied, and transmitted.

In a study of the 'Early Culture and Learning in North Wales' during the ninth century we have passed from the 'age of the saints' to the Viking age. The records are on the whole concerned primarily with secular matters; but it would seem that many writers of the Irish scriptoria met and exchanged ideas and matters of learned interest at the courts of the newly founded dynasty of Merfyn Vrych and his son Rhodri Mawr, 'the Great', in North Wales. From here they proceeded to the Continental centres of learning and culture, both secular and monastic, even journeying as far as to Rome itself, passing along the ancient pilgrims' route over the Alps, by way of the Irish foundation of St Gall, carrying their books with them. But North Wales was also in touch with the native North British oral traditions, and was familiar with the ancient native manner of transmitting history by saga and poetry, and oral genealogies; and, for whatever reason, these oral records of the past were cultivated by the court, and perhaps in some measure by the Church. Our records for Gwynedd, whether secular or ecclesiastical, are relatively few; but when we assemble the information contained in a variety of widely scattered sources, a picture emerges of an interesting and cultivated centre, judged by provincial standards, where conversation might be heard in the two principal Celtic languages, and where Celtic literary traditions

[1] Sir Ifor Williams would translate the word 'magician' (*Armes Prydein o Lyfr Taliesin*, Cardiff, 1955), 67.

7

and personal anecdotes met on an equal footing with the current Latin learning of the day, and even now and then with a touch of halting third-form Greek.

In our study of Llanbadarn Fawr we pass to a centre of clerical activity wholly monastic in character. The place is situated in west Wales, practically on the shore of Cardigan Bay, and the period is the late eleventh century. We are now under Norman rule; but the little world of Llanbadarn is still essentially a Welsh world, and the monastic organisation is neither Benedictine nor Cistercian, but that of the early Welsh *clas*, with its hereditary succession to the abbacy, its married clerks, and its fully developed family life. Here again, however, as in Gwynedd, we meet an interesting fusion of cultures, both Celtic and Latin. This time the Celtic element comes, not from North Britain, but from Ireland, and the milieu is wholly ecclesiastical. From one and the same school, even from the same family, we have, on the one hand, such writings as that of the *Life of St David*, which incorporates Irish hagiography and folk-tales; and, on the other, copies of Latin patristic and liturgical texts; or again personal and topical poems, grave, religious, or patriotic, composed in excellent Latin of almost classical quality. West Wales clung tenaciously to the organisation and ideals of the Celtic Church, and grievously lamented the loss of the country's independence; but there is no sign of rusticity in her patriotism, or of provincialism in her learning.

In the *Life of St David* by Rhigyfarch, the son of Bishop Sulien who had twice held the see of St David's, we are watching the closing phase of the Celtic Church in Wales. The claim that the seat of St David should be accorded metropolitan status is a prominent aim of the writer throughout, and indeed he does not scruple to claim that David had been archbishop of all Britain. Here, however, as at Rhigyfarch's own home at Llanbadarn, the Norman interests proved too strong. Canterbury would not cede her right to direct control of the Church of a conquered and occupied country. Professor Brooke, in his study of the arch-bishops of St David's, Llandaff and Caerleon-on-Usk, shows how, from the time of the establishment of the Norman castle of Pembroke, and we may add, of the compact between William I and the Lord Rhys, Dyfed became the strongest centre of English power in South Wales. The appointment of Bernard, the first Norman bishop of St David's, in 1115, was the direct implementation of a policy to make Dyfed a base from which to effect the transformation of the Church in South Wales from Welsh to Norman. The measure was eminently successful, and the early years of the twelfth century saw the conversion of the bishopric of St David's into a cathedral and a regular diocese, and the conversion of the former Welsh *clas* into a medieval chapter. Henceforth the Celtic form of monasticism gradually gave place to the European Orders, and the Celtic chapters were transformed into the chapters of the new foundations. The *clas* churches became parish churches in the modern sense. The Church of Wales, which had hitherto faced westwards for centuries, sharing with Ireland a common store of traditional usages and learning, must henceforth look to England, and take its place as a part of the wider organisation of the medieval Roman Church.

In one respect Bishop Bernard adapted himself to the traditions of his new home in a way not acceptable to his English colleagues, for our evidence suggests that he came near to establishing a primacy for St David's; but other forces were at work, more congenial to Norman interests. Llandaff never made any claim to independence of Canterbury or Norman rule or papal privileges; and Professor Brooke traces the struggle for precedence between these two principal South Welsh churches in the twelfth century, and the final establishment of the cathedral of Llandaff under its Welsh bishop Urban as the centre of a diocese based on Norman and Continental models. The growth in the conception of the primacy on the Continent, based as it was on the civil organisation of the Roman provinces, led to an effort, first on the part of Canterbury, and then of the other ancient religious foundations, to establish in the eyes of the Normans their rights to their ancient privileges and properties. Here, however, the scarcity of ancient data was a serious obstacle, and the eleventh and twelfth centuries saw a period of intensive historical research into old charters and ecclesiastical, including hagiographical, traditions, and of activity in creating new ones on traditional lines.

Something of the atmosphere in which these activities were carried on can be seen behind the brilliant pageantry of Geoffrey of Monmouth. The *Life of St David* by Rhigyfarch, with its reference to the lost documents of the Church of St David's, was unquestionably written to establish a claim for supremacy on the ground of its saintly founder. But the *locus classicus* and by far the

9

most important survivor of these pseudo-historical researches and writings, is the body of spurious hagiography and forged charters contained in the Gwysaney MS. of the *Book of Llandaff*. Professor Brooke's analysis of the genesis and growth of the *Book*—its aims and method, and the brilliant achievement of its unknown author —enables us to live again through the last days of the Welsh Church in the south of the country. We can trace, not only how the charters of the ancient Welsh church of Llancarfan were appropriated and transformed so as to subserve the community of Llandaff; but also how the community of Llancarfan itself supplied the knowledge, the experience and literary skill requisite to support the claims of the newer foundation. Even the great Bishop Urban himself belonged to this older Llancarfan *clas*. The Welsh *clas* of both Llancarfan and Llanbadarn are a lasting monument to the intellectual activity and singleness of purpose of the early Welsh Church. It was probably the very lack of early prestige and of national Welsh traditions that enabled Llandaff to succeed where St David's had failed. Rhigyfarch had done his work too well. But undoubtedly these two early Welsh dioceses drew their life-blood from the Welsh *clas* family communities of Llanbadarn and Llancarfan.

In order to be in a position to assess the value of our sources we must first try to ascertain so far as possible the circumstances in which they were made, their purpose, their background, and the political milieu in which they came into being, their immediate inspiration. At a time when the art of writing was restricted to a few scholars with a clerical education in a Latin tradition, and when materials were scarce and expensive, we may take it for granted that records would not be made except for a practical end, or in response to some urgent need. Looking back over the records with which our studies have been chiefly concerned I would suggest that their chief inspiration has arisen as a result of some national crisis which has given birth to an overwhelming sense of national consciousness. The patriotism which has given rise to the records was not a steady or continuous emotion, not felt alike throughout the Celtic lands, or alike in all periods. It sprang up from time to time in response to various causes, now local, now widespread; at one time military, at another political, or again religious.

The outline of Celtic history during the period which we are studying was such as could not fail to arouse a deep and lasting love of the country, the language, and the traditions in all the Celtic-speaking peoples. For many centuries before the coming of the Romans the Celtic languages had been spoken throughout our islands, and still today have left their traces under the palimpsest of our place-names. While much of the country had been conquered and under Roman rule for more than four centuries, most of Scotland and the whole of the Hebrides and Ireland had remained unconquered, and retain their unbroken Celtic traditions down to the present day. Even Wales, though an armed bastion of Roman Britain, was little affected in her economy by her military overlords. The influence of the Saxon invaders, while the results have been more permanent, was even more restricted in area. To this day the greater part of the British Isles, geographically speaking, has retained its Celtic languages and its Celtic traditions, its acute consciousness of being a separate race from those of the successive conquerors of our Islands—Roman, Saxon, Norman. It is on this note that Giraldus Cambrensis concludes the second edition of his *Itinerary through Wales*, unequivocally expressing the belief of the Welsh in the undying spirit of the nation and of their language. The speech which Giraldus attributes to the old man from Pencadair near Carmarthen to King Henry II is so well known that an apology is perhaps needed for repeating it here; but it is important for us as showing the value which the Celtic people of comparatively early times set on their native speech, and it expresses a world of thought not easily comprehended or realised by a conquering nation like ourselves.

This nation, O king, may now, as in former times, be harassed, and in a great measure weakened and destroyed by your and other powers... but it can never be completely subdued through the wrath of man, unless by the wrath of God also. Nor do I think that any other nation than this of Wales, *or any other language*, whatever may happen to the greater remainder of it [sc. of Wales? or of the world?][1] shall, in the day of severe examination before the supreme judge, answer for this corner of the earth.[2]

We may distinguish roughly three periods when the growth of national consciousness among one or other of the Celtic-speaking

[1] The meaning is not wholly clear.
[2] Giraldus Cambrensis, *Description of Wales*, II, 10.

peoples received a special impetus. The first was the period at the close of the Roman occupation and during the Saxon invasions, when for a brief period the Celtic princes were the dominant military and political power in Britain and ruled our country. This is the British Heroic Age, the period when the North British princes, known in our earliest records as the *Gwyr y Gogledd*, 'The Men of the North', 'fought strenuously', so the *Historia Brittonum* tells us, against the Saxon princes entrenched in Lindisfarne, the mysterious founders of the brilliant dynasty which was to transform Manau Guotodin and Bryneich into Bernicia and ultimately into Northumbria. This is the period, we are told, of Arthur, of Ambrosius or Emreis Wledig, and of the great Vortigern of unenviable fame and flamboyant power. It is the period to which we owe our finest early British literature, our most cherished British or Welsh traditions, preserved orally for centuries by professional bards under royal auspices.

Like most oral literatures it owes its preservation to the fact that much of it is composed in the form of poetry which could be readily committed to memory, and therefore accurately transmitted. Much of this poetry consisted of panegyrics on living princes, and still more of elegies of high quality. These are the primary records of the British Heroic Age. They tell in stirring verse and with matchless economy and vivid and telling phrase of the selfless devotion of the British princes, of Urien, prince of Rheged, greatest of them all, compared to whose valour the onslaught of his enemy Morgant was 'a mouse scratching on a rock'; of the hated English lying on the field after the battle, 'with the light shining on their eyes'. The elegies enable us to see how they fought a prolonged rearguard action against the slow but steady advance of the oncoming Saxons. Like the heroic poetry of the Serbs and the early Russians, the native heroic poetry of the Celtic peoples is that of a people in its defeat. It is probably to this sad fact that we owe its preservation by later generations, to whom its poignant memories served as a constant reminder of their splendid past, and a constant hope of a still greater future. In later ages its memories had a definite military and political value.

The second period of renewed vigour in Celtic patriotism is of somewhat longer duration and wider geographical range, embracing Ireland and Celtic Scotland in addition to Wales and southern Britain and even Brittany. This is the struggle between the adherents of the Celtic and the Roman Churches, the former clinging to the ancient native traditions inherited from the 'age of the saints'; the latter following appeals couched in a series of compelling letters from Rome, urging conformity of usage and inclusion in the Roman Order. This second period of renewed expression of national consciousness is not primarily military or political in inspiration, therefore, but cultural and ecclesiastical. The struggle between the old Order and the new is implicit in the ecclesiastical saga brilliantly recorded by Bede which relates the interviews of St Augustine with the British bishops, first at Augustine's Oak, and again later when they have had further consultation with their own people. The implications of the passage are not always clearly realised; but the significance of the attitude of the British bishops lies not so much in their emphasis on humility—a quality which Bede always rates very highly—as in the standard of the highest authority recognised by the British bishops themselves. The final appeal and the final judgement which were found acceptable to them are not those of their own seven bishops and all their most learned men, but that of a recluse, a hermit. The power and prestige of the great monastery of Bangor Iscoed with its abbot Dinoot and its bishops and monks is here deliberately and pointedly rated lower than that of an anchorite. Bede was writing at the height of the anchorite movement, and in this story, no less than his portrait of St Aidan in his defeat, Bede reflects unconsciously the atmosphere in which he had grown up, the atmosphere of Old Melrose and Lindisfarne, with their ancient Celtic traditions, inherited from the island sanctuary of Iona. It is noteworthy that when these Celtic monks found themselves forced to withdraw from Lindisfarne, they established themselves on another island sanctuary—that of Inishbofin off the west coast of Co. Mayo in Ireland. The island sanctuaries of the Mediterranean may well have affected Ireland from an early date; but our evidence suggests that the anchorite movement which began on a large scale in the seventh century and reached its height in the eighth, was a native movement within the Church in Ireland, and perhaps also in western Britain; and that its chief incentive was not the need of reform in contemporary monastic life, but a passionate clinging to the traditions and usage of the Celtic past, a strong reaction, or rather a constructive protest against conformity with the Roman usage advocated by Cummian and his party in the seventh century.

It is essentially a revival, revision and formulation of the ideals and traditions of the early Celtic Church in Ireland.

The fundamental and far-reaching nature of this great spiritual and intellectual contest between the Celtic Church and the adherents of Roman usage can hardly be overestimated. In Scotland the embassy from Nechtan IV, king of the southern Picts, to Abbot Ceolfrith of Jarrow, which Bede has recorded, doubtless from first-hand knowledge, must have had far-reaching aims and results, politically no less than ecclesiastically. When Nechtan sent the Celtic monks back across Druim Alban to Iona in 717 he was dividing Scotland virtually into two Churches, and it was not till after the death of St Columba's biographer Adamnán in 704 that Iona conformed to Roman usage, in 718. Even after the repeated sack of Iona by the Danes the head of the Celtic Church in Scotland was moved to Dunkeld in Atholl, *Athfhódla* ('The new Ireland'), and its closest ecclesiastical ally was the church of Kells in Ireland, whither the abbot of Iona had withdrawn when Iona was finally abandoned. It was not till the lifetime of David I that the abandonment of the ancient Celtic usage was virtually completed in the Scottish Church. On the other hand, by Nechtan's mission to Northumbria and acceptance of the Anglo-Roman Order, the southern Picts had become a part of the political and cultural world of England and of north-western Europe. The change in the whole point of view is fundamental, and the struggle between the two Churches and all that this implies is a predominating factor in the political struggle between the royal Houses of Dálriada, or Argyll, and of the southern Picts for the next century and a half.

In Ireland the transition was long and zealously contested. In the famous letter from Cummian, who was probably abbot of Durrow, to Segene, abbot of Iona, written as is believed *c.* 627, the writer says that he has made a careful study of the Roman dating of Easter and has also consulted his 'elders'[1] and called a synod at which five other religious houses were represented; but in the same letter he also tells us that a strong reactionary movement had taken place, whose leaders claimed that they themselves were adhering to the 'tradition of the elders',[2] but who, instead of creating the 'unity' to which Rome urged them, were creating

[1] *Successores videlicet nostrorum patrum priorum.*
[2] *Traditionem seniorum.*

diversity; and Cummian adds ironically: 'Roma errat; Hieroso-lyma errat; Alexandria errat; soli tantum Scoti et Britones rectum sapiunt.'

Even in southern Ireland, therefore, we can trace the clash of controversy, and it would seem that when the southern Irish, or a party among them, agreed officially to accept the Roman dating of Easter it was a decision of a minority which carried the day. Northern Ireland still held out for some sixty years, and at the turn of the century the dispute was still raging.

It is possibly to this controversy more than to any other cause that we may look for the source of the so-called anchorite reform which seems to have arisen in the seventh century and to have reached its peak in the eighth and to have still been active in the first part of the ninth centuries.[1] The impetus to the 'desert', which began in the East long before, and spread to the Medi-terranean islands during the fourth and fifth centuries, gave rise in the Irish Church to a religious movement referred to in the document called the *Catalogus Sanctorum Hiberniae* as the 'Third Order of Saints'. According to this text the First Order of Saints consists of those who belonged to the episcopal party founded by St Patrick, and these are said to be 'most holy'; the Second Order, of those who founded the great religious Houses of the sixth century, and they are only 'very holy'; the Third Order, of those described as 'living on herbs, and water and alms, and possessing nothing of their own', and they are said to be only 'holy'. These are the anchorites and recluses to whom we are presumably in-debted for the innumerable little island sanctuaries dotted around our coasts, with their dedications to the early Celtic saints.

The biased nature of this document will be obvious at a glance. It is clearly written in the shadow of the controversy which we are discussing, and there are good grounds for believing that, so far from being a contemporary work, its composition is not earlier than the ninth century.[2] It is, in fact, a piece of ecclesiastical pamphlet-eering, and voices the views of the Patrician party in Ireland, the adherents of the 'Roman' Order, by seeking to minimise the antiquity, the sanctity and the prestige of the anchorite movement.

[1] See the article by the late Dr Robin Flower, 'The Two Eyes of Ireland', in *The Church of Ireland A.D. 432–1932*, 66ff. (being the Report of the Church of Ireland Conference held in Dublin in 1932, and published in Dublin, 1932).

[2] See the edition and commentary by the Rev. Paul Grosjean in *Analecta Bollandiana* (1955), LXXIII, 197ff., 289ff.

The point of view is sharply opposed to that of the British Church as reflected in Bede's story of the British bishops long before; sharply opposed to that of the Columban Church of Iona, Old Melrose, and Lindisfarne, and their southern offshoots. Our two earliest memoirs of St Patrick, those by Tírechán and Muirchú, both written shortly before 700, are manifestly composed with the same object—that of upholding the *unitas*, the catholicity of the Patrician Church. But on the other hand the two following centuries have given rise to a whole literature springing directly from the 'anchorite reform'. Many, indeed most, of the Irish 'rules', penitentials, martyrologies and service-books are believed to have been compiled by adherents of this movement, and some can be shown to have been written at, or under the influence of the religious house of Tallaght near Dublin, with its founder Máelrúain at the head, or at other houses of the reform, such as Terryglass. These works were not in general in the nature of fundamental innovations. The scribes did not invent them. They recorded them from the earlier traditions of the Church of their forefathers, and we cannot doubt that the whole movement and its literary expression was directed to strengthen and extend the ancient Church of the Celtic people as it had been handed down by tradition from the past. The movement coincides with the Viking period, and it is reasonable to suppose that it played an important part in helping to keep alive the spirit of national consciousness throughout the enemy occupation.

The third period in the rise of national consciousness in Wales is undoubtedly that of the ninth century, and here our sources would lead us to the belief that it is primarily local and political in character, having no immediate connection with Ireland, and being directed to the building up of a united Wales, doubtless with a view to eastward expansion, and ultimately to anti-English aggression. During some four centuries the little Welsh kingdoms, most of them claiming—with what justification is open to question —to trace their ancestry to the sons of Cunedag in the fifth century, had enjoyed an unbroken history, registering little change in either their national boundaries or their reigning families. During the ninth century a new dynasty of uncertain origin, but claiming to be descended from the 'Men of the North', had arisen in Gwynedd, and by a series of royal marriages and a sound diplomatic policy had managed to unite the greater part of Wales into a single nation.

The deliberate nationalism of their policy can be seen in the way in which the ancient North British traditions were collected and recorded and even expanded in Wales during this period, and in the care with which early North British and Welsh royal pedigrees were collected and recorded and the collections of the ancient poetry of the North put together. These efforts, and their deliberate nationalistic, and still more anti-Saxon, inspiration reached their climax in the poem known as *Armes Prydein*, dating probably from early in the following century, which calls upon all the Celtic peoples to unite and drive the Saxons out of Britain.

It is interesting to speculate on what the history of Wales might have been if the greatest king of this new dynasty, Rhodri Mawr, Rhodri 'the Great', had not been killed in warfare against the Saxons. While he had been busy concentrating the little Welsh kingdoms into a united country his Saxon neighbour and rival, Alfred the Great, on the other side of the Border, had been concentrating on a precisely similar aim and policy in regard to the Saxon kingdoms. Rhodri had failed to win Dyfed (the Welsh kingdom which included rather more than modern Pembrokeshire), even though he had succeeded in hemming it in; and it was from this centre that Alfred managed to inaugurate a pro-English policy among the princes of South Wales, a policy which was to bear fruit in the alliance between Hywel Dda, Rhodri's grandson, and Aethelstan, Alfred's grandson, in the following century. It is in no way surprising that the English chronicler, set free from the terror of the Danes by Alfred's efforts, should be almost wholly preoccupied with his military successes against the enemies in the east. Nor would one look for a realisation, far less an appreciation, from a Saxon chronicler, of Alfred's support of the Celtic Church and of his relations with the Celtic countries. Yet his diplomatic activities in the west are hardly less remarkable than his military successes in the east, and perhaps we may associate his interest in St David's—a church and monastery of pronounced Irish character —with his contributions to the Irish Church of which we hear from Asser; possibly also with the visit to his court by the Irish anchorites reported in the Parker Text of the *Anglo-Saxon Chronicle*, *s.a.* 891, to have crossed the Irish Sea in a curragh and come ashore in Cornwall. Living on the Welsh border he can hardly have failed to realise that Wessex and Mercia, to say nothing of the rest of England, could never hope to remain permanently secure in time of invasion while they had a permanent and implacable enemy on their rear.

The death of Rhodri while Alfred was rapidly rising in power undoubtedly facilitated the task of uniting, first the south Welsh princes, and ultimately the whole of Wales, under the English king. But the spirit of Welsh patriotism and of Celtic racial pride, on which Rhodri had founded his wide and united kingdom of northern and central Wales, was never again to die out. We shall not perhaps greatly err if we attribute this, in part at least, to the fact that under this dynasty the poetry and traditions of the British Heroic Age were cultivated and recorded under the influence of an enlightened court which had learnt by intercourse with both Ireland and the Continent the value of learning and letters, and the importance of the written word. Henceforth the past, recorded in written form, could never again be forgotten. Its memories had become a permanent possession of bard and cleric alike, a rich storehouse of tradition and allusion to which both could turn whenever political or military crisis arose to awaken the sense of national consciousness among the Welsh people.

As the historian studies various aspects of the early Middle Ages he becomes aware that the period differs fundamentally from that of all later periods. Not only are the sources of our information relatively sparse, but if they are to be rightly understood they require to be approached in a different way. A different method has to be adopted, a technique specially adapted to a unique type of material, a technique rigorous, objective, yet elastic enough to be equally applicable, on the one hand to plausible Latin documents compiled under ecclesiastical auspices by writers educated in the tradition of early medieval scholarship, and on the other to traditions which have been handed down orally for centuries in varying milieus, and recorded in writing only in their last phase. Both classes of evidence tend to have been recorded in circumstances which have inevitably produced a bias, whether ecclesiastical or political, and more often than not the modern scholar is without direct information as to where and when the records were first made. In both these classes of evidence the historian of the period has to make use of a discipline—whether epigraphical, palaeographical, linguistic, or even archaeological—for which the normal historical approach offers no precedent or training.

A considerable change has come over the historians' attitude towards this early period during recent years, almost overnight. Even in our own generation the view is sometimes expressed, and even more commonly implied, by professional historians that the sources of early medieval history have been exhausted. This general attitude has reference chiefly to the works of Gildas and of Nennius; and the work for which Nennius is generally held to have been chiefly responsible, the *Historia Brittonum*, is regarded primarily as a collection of folk-tales rather than as a serious historical source or storehouse of historical material. Neither view is sound. It is the prime duty of every fresh generation to scrutinise the sources afresh in the light of added textual experience and of improved methods of interpretation, and above all in the light of our increasing knowledge of contemporary Continental history. But this is only a beginning. The range of our sources is also increasing with every fresh generation, and even in our own lifetime new light has been thrown on the written sources by our progress in archaeology, early art, philology, inscriptions, the study of place-names, perhaps most of all by the progress made by Irish and Welsh scholars in the study of early poetry, and by a better understanding everywhere of the nature and value of oral tradition and poetry relating to the earliest periods of British history.

In the following studies our own work has chiefly lain in the written sources, many of which have long been known. Our contribution lies, not in the discovery of new materials or new texts; it lies partly in the application to the familiar texts of these new fields of knowledge, and partly in the frank recognition that in our own generation a change has come about in our attitude to the sources with which we are already familiar. A generation ago it was felt that it was enough to ascertain which were the most reliable sources and then to follow them faithfully. A wholesome dread of a subjective interpretation acted as a deterrent from any departure from our best written authorities. 'Bede says' became a final judgment, and few ventured to question how Bede came by his materials, so different and so divergent in character and value. Perhaps our chief advance in this matter is that we have now learned to ask how the sources came into being at a given period— what was the motive which inspired the record, to what extent do the sources reflect not only the individual bias of the writer, but also the trend of thought, the events, and above all the controversies of his age. It will certainly be found that a large proportion of our Latin documents of the early Middle Ages have been recorded as elements in religious or political controversy. In later periods, when the creation of the prolific scriptoria of the monastic houses of the great religious Orders had developed book production and distribution on the grand scale, such motives do not necessarily form any part in the production of a document or *libellus*; but in the times with which we are here concerned such organisations were only in their initial stages, and in their early days they could only have come into being with the financial support of a secular prince or, at a later period, of the mother-house of a powerful religious Order. In such circumstances it is not unnatural that our sources often reveal to us even more about the people who wrote them and about the period and the atmosphere in which they were written than about the subject which they purport to record.

This change in our attitude towards our sources involves a change in the method of the presentation of the evidence. In well-documented periods, such as the more modern centuries of our history, the historian's work consists first of all in selection from the wealth of material available, and afterwards of synthesis. In the early Middle Ages selection plays hardly any part because our sources are so few that every scrap of material is precious. For synthesis we have to substitute the detective instinct, and seek to determine the importance of the significantly little. The method is intensive, and a training in the methods of Scotland Yard would be more relevant than a training in the history of the Napoleonic wars. The all-important element is the clue, and the use to which it can legitimately be put by means of the imagination, trained, disciplined, and rigorously controlled.

It follows that where so little material is available, and where our conclusions are necessarily tentative, the style of our presentation must lack the authoritative note which is legitimate in the writing of modern historians, who are frequently in a position to base their conclusions on demonstrable fact, and who can eschew the discursive method of which they stand in no need, and whose standards in deploying their material are those of rigid relevance. In our own studies the accepted canons of historical style require modification. Our basis of ascertained fact is relatively small, and we are aware of wide areas of related material without any certainty as to the exact nature of the relationship. Here the value of the interpretation often lies in the suggestion of the half-suspected fact, in the possible avenues which open up unexpectedly to the explorer. We may venture even further, and declare frankly that we cannot always afford to condemn out of hand the inclusion of a new interesting fact because its immediate relevance may not be strictly demonstrable. In a region where we ourselves are not as yet masters of our chart perhaps our wisest course will be, not to attempt demonstration, but to enlist the co-operation of the reader at every step, and to make our exploration jointly with him, conducting him in a spirit of humility rather than of authority.

Something has already been said of the new material which in our own generation has done much to throw light on the written Latin sources, and to increase the range of our knowledge of the period. Among these it is probably in the field of oral tradition that we may chiefly look for progress in the immediate future. This study should yield its most important results for the sixth and seventh centuries, which are only barely represented in our written annals, and in which oral traditions form the chief basis of such annals as we possess. These oral traditions were handed down in the Celtic-speaking countries of Britain in an artistic technique which was highly cultivated and guarded in a strict manner hardly imaginable in countries where records have been handed down for many centuries in a written form. Yet oral tradition is, or was until yesterday, the only form of historical record among the great majority of the peoples of the world. The value of such oral traditions can hardly be overestimated; but this value is difficult to assess, and tradition can only be safely used for purposes of history after very considerable experience in comparative oral literature, and after a careful study of the circumstances in which it is cultivated, and of the class of poets, genealogists and story-tellers responsible for its composition and the purity of its transmission.

Perhaps the most valuable of such traditions are panegyric and elegiac poems of whatever kind, because these in general retain the largest proportion of proper names, which appear and reappear often in a number of poems, and serve as a check and a supplement to one another. Forming a framework to the proper names, the original milieu of the characters and the personnel as a whole retains its integrity, and the metre and the poetical form ensure, on the whole, accurate memorisation at a relatively high level, and become, with appropriate reservation, a relatively valuable source of knowledge. Where the same person recurs frequently such traditions have a special light to throw on a bare name in a genealogy which could otherwise convey little to us. These oral poetical traditions are mostly personal and aristocratic records, as the monopolies of royal bards would lead one to expect. Except by inference they tell us little of a constitutional or political nature, or of institutions in the strict sense of the word. All these can only be very imperfectly inferred from the vivid narrative, the reported words of the characters, and the reflections of the poet himself. Even here we have to be on our guard against reposing too much faith in his single-mindedness. A heroic poet, inevitably attached to a small court or prince, will not feel free to report anything deleterious to his patron, or even lying outside the ready attention and comprehension of his audience. It is a serious mistake to impute to an age or phase of society the ultra-simplified conditions necessarily reflected in heroic poetry. Nevertheless such poetical records reflect, albeit in a highly simplified and stylised form, the conditions of the milieu in which they themselves flourish, and their references often clothe with flesh and blood the names otherwise known only from bare lists and genealogies. The traditional poetry of the *Gwyr y Gogledd*, the 'Men of the North', represents for us something like a Debrett and a gazetteer to Strathclyde and Cumbria in the British Heroic Age.

The earliest Irish poetry from Munster and Leinster,[1] much of it dating from the seventh century, some of it probably from the sixth, comprises innumerable proper names and allusions to events and exploits with which they were traditionally associated. Many of these poems predate our earliest Irish chronicles by at least a century, and our earliest Irish saga texts by still more, and their allusions offer a wealth of variant traditions and supplementary information for the earliest period of Irish history. Most of them are panegyric or elegiac in inspiration; but others, such as those attributed to the Leinster king, Find Fili, from whom all the Leinster kings claim descent, are virtually commemorative lists celebrating the long line of his ancestors, and thus serving to perpetuate what is, in effect, an oral dynastic record. If due

---

[1] For the texts see Kuno Meyer, 'Über die älteste irische Dichtung', *Abhandl. der Königl. Preuss. Akademie der Wissenschaften* (Berlin, 1913 and 1914); also his 'Bruchstücke der älteren Lyrik Irlands', *ibid.*, 1919.

allowance is made for poetic hyperbole, especially in the matter of round numbers, such as are beloved by all heroic poets, these early Celtic poetic records are in general sober and literal, and superhuman elements are very rare. The Irish *Annals of Tigernach* cite such poems frankly and freely, and a careful reading of the early Scottish *Chronicle of Dálriada* (the so-called *Pictish Chronicle*) enables us to detect the panegyric poems on which many of the entries are based, such as those relating to Kenneth mac Alpin, and to Brude mac Bile, 'favoured by Christ' at the Battle of Dún nechtain or Nechtanesmere, in which the Northumbrian king Ecgfrith met defeat and death.

Our earliest written authorities for the period have undoubtedly made use of such traditional material, and the results are clearly manifest, both in the nature of the writings based on them, and in the mistakes which can sometimes be traced directly to imperfect acquaintance with the conditions of oral transmission. One of the commonest errors of this kind is the duplication of a single historical event by an author who is often unconsciously following variant traditions. It is probable that the two visits to Britain which Constantius attributes to St Germanus, as against the single visit mentioned by Prosper, a contemporary authority, are to be accounted for in this way. It is to be suspected that Bede also occasionally falls into this error when he is making use of oral sources, as, for example, in his account of the two interviews between St Augustine and the British bishops; and again in his accounts of the western campaigns of Aethelfrith and Edwin. It is a curious fact that the first of these battles is related by Bede as a consequence of the obduracy of the British bishops and the threatening prophecy of Augustine. The whole narrative, with its vivid presentation of the scenes and the conversations reported verbatim can hardly have been derived by Bede from any written source. The whole is an elaborate, cautionary ecclesiastical saga, and it would seem by no means improbable that Bede or his informant has combined two variant versions of a single original story.

One point in which the research worker in the early Middle Ages differs fundamentally from the modern historian, and sometimes thereby incurs his censure, is in his tendency to identify unknown men of identical names in stories derived from oral sources. In this respect some of us, at least, are unrepentant, and the conditions of oral transmission weigh the balance of probability on our side, though it is not, and cannot be, claimed in the absence of further evidence that such identifications can have more value than that of probability. In general, however, it may be accepted that our earliest British records are derived from panegyric or elegiac or some such kind of personal poetry, composed by a professional bard who is supported by a chief in whose interest a given poem has been composed. It may fairly be claimed that at a given time, within a very limited area, there will probably not be many chiefs of the same name powerful enough or rich enough, or so outstanding as to have been celebrated simultaneously by bards who are dependent on their patronage and who have extolled them in a manner which has gained them a prestige in oral tradition lasting for many centuries.

Here a word of caution may appropriately be spoken with regard to an oral form which is of very frequent occurrence in our records, and which is frequently confused by modern scholars with genuine tradition. This is what, for want of a better description, I would refer to as 'inverted tradition', and it consists of antiquarian speculation, inference, and deduction, made already during a relatively early period. In the absence of a genuine tradition, the learned professional classes of the period before the age of writing sought to explain the present in terms of the past by using their reasoning powers and their antiquarian instincts and training, in the place of memory, or to eke out memory. This form of antiquarianism was especially in vogue among the Celtic peoples generally, and they have left us a vast literature relating to the origins of prehistoric monuments, fortresses and tombs of the dead, place-names and political institutions. They have sought to explain the original populations of our islands by a series of successive invasions, and the ultimate distribution of the population groups. Hardly any of this literature represents genuine tradition, that is to say a genuine oral record of a given event, registered in the memory from the beginning, and handed on by word of mouth till its final record in written form. On the contrary it is a speculation without antecedents, a more or less reasonable guess by men of antiquarian pretensions; or at best an inference, a tentative conclusion suggested to them by, but not necessarily proved or warranted by, the data; or a deduction, based logically on the facts before them. From the modern point of view such inverted traditions—traditions created to explain the present by the past—are

24

valueless for the period to which they are intended to refer. No serious scholar with a trained critical faculty now believes in the historicity of the so-called *Book of Invasions*, elaborated into an ambitious narrative in medieval Ireland, and represented in a briefer form at an even earlier period in the *Historia Brittonum*. Nevertheless such antiquarian speculations have a value as the record of the kind of intellectual matter popular among the pre-literate peoples of the British Isles, and indeed till the end of the Middle Ages; and the archaeological and place-name speculations in particular have been the means of preserving for us a large proportion of genuine tradition, despite its unhistorical and wholly irrelevant setting.

In addition to contemporary records and traditions carried on orally and written down at a later date, there is a third class of evidence, the importance of which we are coming to realise more fully than hitherto. This is what we may call retrospective in-ference, the value of Norman and later records for the light which they throw on the conditions of earlier periods.[1] As a result of the necessity felt by the Norman conquerors to govern and to tax, there arose a great wealth of records of all kinds which are of great value for information which they contain on matters for which we are without earlier knowledge. Among the most important are the inquisitions and assessments, which have the advantage of pre-cision because they were required for fiscal purposes. They also have the advantage of a considerable measure of consistency, because in general they are made in conformity with a central system. Many of our Norman and medieval records are official documents made by professional clerks working with an expert training, and a sense of responsibility to a higher authority. Almost equally valuable is the growing wealth of personal and official letters, especially between churchmen, such as those between the cathedral chapter of St David's and Canterbury; or again the surveys and itineraries, such as those made by Bishop Andrew of Caithness, or the *Itinerary through Wales* recorded by the prince of observers, Giraldus Cambrensis, as a result of his tour in the train of Archbishop Baldwin. In all these medieval documents, however, we have again to make a close scrutiny if we

---

[1] Reference may be made, for example, to the Lecture by Prof. J. G. Edwards, 'The Normans and the Welsh March', *Proceedings of the British Academy* (1956), 155 ff.

would not be cheated by racial and political prejudice. The danger is especially rife in regard to ecclesiastical writings. The failure of Bishop Reeves to detect and allow for the hostile bias of Scottish-Norman clerks in their reports on the Culdees in Scotland is an element with which we must always reckon in his otherwise invaluable work on the subject. We must not believe all that our sources tell us, however plausible they may appear.

One of the most difficult lessons which we have still to learn is the right use of negative evidence. In an age which made few written records the absence of records does not necessarily imply the absence of a given institution or of a given tradition. The termination of our list of the bishops of Whithorn in the early ninth century does not necessarily mean that the bishopric came to an end at that time. It may only mean that the records ceased to be kept or were lost. We have no list of bishops of Hoddom, to which late tradition assigned Kentigern as bishop; but the discovery near Hoddom of the top of a staff or crosier shrine, believed to date probably from the tenth century, and to have been preserved in the twelfth-century church of which the foundations still exist on the spot,[1] makes us hesitate to deny the existence of an earlier bishopric, even though we have no written evidence earlier than the twelfth century. The series of carved stones dating from the eighth century and continuing throughout the Viking age prove the continuous history of the later monastery.

Again, where our material is scanty we have to be on the watch for analogy, for what we can learn from contemporary custom. Much adventitious tradition about St Patrick, and the accumulated speculation of centuries, might be profitably swept away in favour of a closer examination of the genuine canon of his writings, or those accepted as such. Then, after a more humble study of what they actually tell us, we could interpret them, not in the light of later, but of contemporary records, especially those of the Continental Church, which are better preserved than our own, and in the light of the usages of the Continent, well known from the letters and other documents of the period. Our problems of St Patrick and his travels in the Tyrrhenian Sea, his consecration at Auxerre, and the whole confused chronology, would vanish if we could attach due weight to the fact that Patrick himself makes no

---

[1] See C. A. Ralegh Radford, 'Hoddom', *Dumfriesshire and Galloway Natural History and Antiquarian Society* (1954), XXXI, 177, n. 6 *a*; (1955), XXXII, 115 ff.

reference to these matters in circumstances where they could not have failed to give strength to his claims to recognition. Such foreign Continental consecrations are of a later time. Yet because Bede, writing nearly four centuries after the traditional period of St Ninian, claims that Ninian went to Rome to be consecrated *regulariter*, it is still today argued by serious historians that there is no reason why Ninian should not have gone to Rome. This is true. But the valid question is not whether he could have gone to Rome, but whether he would have been likely to go at a time when Gaulish consecrations were normally local, and Rome had as yet no authority beyond her high prestige. Bede not unnaturally drew his inferences from the customs of the early eighth century, as the word *regulariter* itself suggests. What, in short, is the value of Bede's statement that Ninian actually went to Rome for consecration? We must beware of accepting statements even on high authority, if they are inherently improbable, and relate to a period and conditions on which that authority is not in a position to have been well informed. The testimony of Nechtan's Pictish mission to Ceolfrith, which may well lie behind Bede's statement, would, on such a matter as this, have been no less biased and chronologically at fault than Bede himself.

In relation to our period work which concentrates exclusively on a narrow field cannot fail to lead to error, at least error of interpretation, if not of fact. In order to be able to estimate the precise significance of negative evidence, and to make a sound critical use of analogy, it is essential that the historian should have enough knowledge of the period as a whole, and in the widest sense, to enable him to make a valid suggestion as to what is lacking in our pattern of the evidence as we have it. The process is that of reconstructing a fresco from bits of wall-plaster, or a mosaic from a few scattered tesserae. We have no documents from the monastery of St David's in the Welsh kingdom of Dyfed till long after Asser's day; but from later writings relating to the monastery and to the saint himself we have every reason to believe that in the 'age of the saints' St David's was an ascetic centre whose closest relations were with Ireland. And these inferences are borne out by the early traditions, secular and ecclesiastical, and by the epigraphy and archaeology of the little mountain kingdom of Brycheiniog with which Dyfed was traditionally associated, and which help to explain its curiously Irish context.

Perhaps the most important function of the historian of our period is that of perceiving the significance of interlocking and interrelated evidence on a broad canvas; of the legitimate use of various types of evidence drawn from widely divergent disciplines. Here over-intensive and exclusive specialisation is especially crippling. Here, more than anywhere else, the mind of the research worker must move freely in a wide sphere. Here the use of the constructive imagination is especially essential in order to enable him to see in his sources, not only what they actually tell us, but perhaps even more what they intend to tell us, most of all what they would have told us had they been free from the hampering limitations imposed by the personal bias or preoccupations or prejudices incidental to the record. In the final stage we are dependent on the legitimate use of the imagination, conditioned and controlled by ascertained fact, for the interpretation of all our evidence.

I

Early Culture and Learning in North Wales

BY NORA K. CHADWICK

I. ANTIQUARIAN SPECULATION. ORIGIN LEGENDS

In or before the ninth century a number of ruling dynasties of the British Isles gathered about them stories of their origin which have come down to us in written form. In every case the ruling families are either themselves intrusive, or belong to a people who are described elsewhere as newcomers. At least one such story is related of each of the principal dominant peoples in our islands about this time, the Welsh, the Irish, the Gaelic peoples, and the Picts. The origin of these ruling dynasties is attributed in general to some period in the fifth century. In most if not all of these stories the founder of the incoming dynasty, or his sons, are eponyms of later kingdoms. This alone should put us on our guard against treating the traditions as genuine history. We are in a scholarly milieu—the milieu of antiquarian speculation, or of inference.

Thus we are told in an early survey[1] of the kingdom of Scottish Dálriada (early Argyll), which evidently dates at latest from before 843,[2] while Dálriada was still a separate kingdom, that the kingdom of Scottish Dálriada arose as the result of a movement from the Irish kingdom of Dálriada on the Antrim coast. The incomers consisted of Erc, son of Eochu, and his six sons, who took possession of lands in Dálriada or Argyll. Of these sons Loarn and his family are said to have occupied the district of Lorne in northern Argyll, while Fergus's share was divided between his grandsons, Comgall occupying the district of Cowall, which bears his name. It will be noticed that the eponymous element is present in this story, though not consistently developed.

[1] The document is called the *Senchus Fer nAlban* in the text. Published and translated by W. F. Skene, *Chronicles of the Picts and Scots* (Edinburgh, 1867), 308 ff. The same story can be traced in the Irish annals and in the *Chronicle of Dálriada*. See H. M. Chadwick, *Early Scotland* (Cambridge, 1949), 120 ff.

[2] 650–60 (M. Dobbs, *Scottish Gaelic Studies*, VII, 89); *c.* 670 (E. MacNeill, *Phases of Irish History*, 198); 'eighth century' (H. M. Chadwick, *Early Scotland*, 120).

Bede, writing in the early eighth century, relates how the Picts came from Scythia, first to Ireland, and later to the northern part of Britain.[1] He gives no details as to the precise part of Scotland which they occupied; but we have two surveys of Scottish provenance,[2] which, though contained in a document evidently dating from *c.* 1165, appear on internal evidence to represent the political geography of the ninth century, the first survey before 843, the second from between 850 and 950. In both these documents the country called *Scotia*, by which is evidently here meant the kingdom of the Picts, is divided into seven provinces. In the first survey *Scotia* is compared with the figure of a man, and the writer speaks of seven brothers by whom the country was divided into seven parts, the names of which are specifically given in pairs and correspond to the names of later provinces. In the second survey the natural boundaries of the provinces (here called 'kingdoms', *regna*) are given, but not the names.

It will be noticed that these surveys are territorial rather than genealogical in their present form; but a third and earlier survey is implied in certain texts[3] of the document generally known as the *Pictish Chronicle*,[4] or perhaps better the Pictish king-list, a Latin document thought to have been put together possibly about the middle of the ninth century, though our oldest version may be more than a century later. In this document we are told that Cruithne, the eponymous ancestor of the Picts, has seven sons who bear the names of the Pictish provinces and are clearly the seven brothers mentioned in the first of the two surveys referred to above, and who also correspond to the parts of the figure of a man with which the kingdom of 'Scotia' as a whole is compared. Thus Texts A, B, and C of the *Pictish Chronicle* contain the statement that:

Cruithne, son of Cing, father of the Picts who dwell in this island, reigned a hundred years. He had seven sons. These are their names...

after which follow their names, and these are the names of the Pictish provinces; and in certain texts these are followed by the

[1] *Hist. Eccles.* I, i (ed. Charles Plummer, Oxford, 1896).
[2] For the text, see Skene, *Chronicles of the Picts and Scots*, 135–7.
[3] See Chadwick, *op. cit.* 35 f., 81 ff.
[4] For the best text, see Skene, *op. cit.* 3 ff. See further K. H. Jackson in *The Problem of the Picts*, edited by F. T. Wainwright (Edinburgh, 1955), 144; M. O. Anderson, *Scottish Historical Review*, XXVIII (1949), 35 ff.; Chadwick, *op. cit.* 1 ff.

length of the reign of each. It is clear that, whether the 'provinces' are pictured as brothers or as sons reigning in succession, the idea of an eponymous family origin was held to account for the rise of the Pictish kingdom. Incidentally the reference to 'the Picts who dwell in this island', together with the names of the Scottish regions as Cruithne's 'sons', makes it clear, as M. O. Anderson has pointed out,[1] that this part of the document was composed in Britain.

In itself the document is related more or less closely to a group forming part of a development of antiquarian speculative literature in Ireland, and it is in Ireland that the type of antiquarian stories of origins with which we are here concerned is most fully developed and most richly represented. Here a whole series of legends of invasions and dynasties developed in the hands of learned pseudo-historians and 'synchronisers', known collectively in its most extended and elaborate form as the *Lebor Gabála*,[2] 'Book of Invasions' (lit. 'takings', 'seizings'), and in the oldest extant Irish version of this work, preserved in the *Book of Leinster*, the incursions of various races of Ireland are traced with fantastic speculation, the last being led by the sons of a certain Míl, the eponymous ancestor of the ruling families of Ireland in historical times, usually referred to as 'Milesians'.

This version of the *Lebor Gabála* is believed to date from the twelfth century;[3] but there can be no doubt that the story was in existence at a much earlier date, even in Ireland, while the earliest extant form of the series of invasions represented in the *Lebor Gabála* is that which is found in the *Historia Brittonum*,[4] a work

[1] See the *Scottish Historical Review*, XXIX (1950), 17, and the references there cited. There is some reason for believing that it may have reached its present form at Abernethy in Perthshire; but in fact the precise place of origin is a matter of uncertainty.

[2] Edited and translated by R. A. S. Macalister, *Lebor Gabála Érenn*, four parts (Dublin, 1938–41).

[3] See the note on '*Leabhar Gabhála* and the Book of Leinster' by Lucius Gwynn, *Eriu*, VIII (1916), 114ff. The first two volumes of the new edition of the *Book of Leinster* have been edited by R. I. Best, O. Bergin and M. A. O'Brien, Dublin, 1954. The original compilation is believed to have been made during the second half of the twelfth and the first half of the thirteenth centuries (see *ed. cit.* p. xvii). The MS. of the *Book of Leinster* would seem to have been completed early in the thirteenth century (*ibid.*).

[4] For the convenience of readers I have given references to the *Historia Brittonum* throughout in the edition by F. Lot, *Nennius et l'Historia Brittonum* (Paris, 1934). An English translation of the text and other documents contained in MS. Harleian 3859 has been published by A. W. Wade-Evans, *Nennius's History of the Britons* (London, 1938). Lot has based his texts on the edition by

which we shall discuss later, and which is generally thought to have been compiled in the early ninth century. Here also other eponymous rulers are found, e.g. Britto as ruler of Britain.[1] Again, therefore, we are brought back to the period at least as early as the early part of the ninth century[2] for the date at which the original story of these 'Invasions' was composed.

The 'origin' stories mentioned above all occur in more than one version, or at least receive partial corroboration from more than one source. Such antiquarian studies were evidently widely current about the ninth century. The story of Cruithne, son of Cing, eponymous ruler of the Picts, and his sons, has survived in at least three early variant versions.[3] The account of the foundation of the Scottish kingdom of Dálriada by the sons of Erc is known from a number of both Scottish and Irish authorities, and is implicit in the *Tripartite Life of St Patrick*,[4] itself also ascribed to the ninth century.

The remaining story which comes in for consideration here, and with which we are more directly concerned, related the foundation of the Welsh kingdoms. The first part of the tradition is contained in the *Historia Brittonum*, c. 62. According to this account Maelgwn's ancestor Cunedag and his eight sons left their home in the north in the region of Manau Guotodin and settled in Gwynedd 'one hundred and forty six years before Maelgwn reigned'; and they expelled the Irish from those regions with great slaughter so that they were never again able to settle in Wales. The second part of the tradition is embodied in a brief narrative at the end of the royal Welsh genealogies, and immediately preceding the catalogue of the 'cities of Britain' in the invaluable collection of early Welsh historical and antiquarian documents embodied in an important manuscript in the British Museum known as Harleian 3859, which will be discussed later. This brief narrative or note enumerates the sons of Cunedag, here stated to have been nine, of

Mommsen, pp. 112–42 (cf. p. 38 below), which is still the best edition and which I have consulted throughout; but Mommsen's Introduction requires to be supplemented in the light of more recent studies. See below.

[1] *Historia Brittonum*, c. 11.

[2] See a brief recent discussion by T. F. O'Rahilly, *Early Irish History and Mythology* (Dublin, 1946), 193 f.

[3] For a brief account of these, see Chadwick, *op. cit.* 120 ff.

[4] Edited and translated by Whitley Stokes, 2 vols. (London, 1887, Rolls Series); a more recent critical edition by K. Mulchrone, *Bethu Phátraic* (Dublin, 1939).

whom the eldest, Typiaun, is said to have died in the region called Manau Guotodin, and not to have come hither 'with his father and with his [aforesaid][1] brothers'. It is added, however, that Meiriaun his son divided the possession with Typiaun's brothers.[2] It is further added that their territory (*terminus*) reached from the Dee to the Teifi, and that they held very many districts (*plurimas regiones*) in the western district (*plaga*) of Britain.

It is to be observed that this note relating to the sons of Cunedag is no part of the text of the *Historia Brittonum*, and possibly offers a variant tradition. It is not easy otherwise to account for the mention of the death of Typiaun in Manau Guotodin unless there was some discrepancy which required to be smoothed out as regards the number of Cunedag's sons. But while this second account forms no part of the *Historia Brittonum*, it must also be emphasised that it is no part of the text of the pedigrees. It follows immediately after them with no break in the manuscript, just as the list of the 'cities of the Britons' follows immediately upon this note, also without a break. But the affinities of the note on Cunedag's sons are closer to the 'cities' than to the pedigrees. Both texts begin with the same formula: 'Hic sunt nomina'. The list of Cunedag's sons is, in fact, a mnemonic catalogue, like the 'cities of Britain' which follows it; the 'marvels of Britain', in the same MS.; and the list of Arthur's battles in the *Historia Brittonum*, c. 56. The list has all the appearance of being the speculation of antiquaries relating to eponyms in the pedigrees—notably nos. 1, 3, 17, 18, and 26—thought of as the founders of certain kingdoms which fall within the limits specified in the note, i.e. 'between the Dee and the Teifi'.

The weaknesses of this account are patent. There is a triad tradition that the Irish were expelled from Gwynedd by Cadwallon Llawhir, father of Maelgwn, who is said to have defeated them at the great battle of Cerryg y Gwyddel in Anglesey;[3] but this evidence is late. More important is the fact that the kingdoms said to have been founded by Cunedag's sons are not in general on the coast, and are situated for the most part remote from Lleyn, where the greatest Irish concentration in North Wales undoubtedly was. Most of the sons are eponyms of later Welsh provinces. Further, it is

---

[1] The word is incomplete. Editors seem to be agreed that it is an abbreviation for *predictis*. [2] *Inter fratres suos.*
[3] See C. Plummer, *Bedae Hist. Eccles.* III, i, and note *ad loc.*

important to note that the entire story is without corroboration from any other source, save that in c. 14 of the *Historia Brittonum* we are told that the descendants of Liathán—an Irish people from Munster—'settled' (*obtinuerunt*) in the regions of Dyfed, Gower and Kidwelly until they were expelled by Cunedag and his sons from all British districts. Even the *Annales Cambriae* make no reference to the story. It is presumably because several of the royal genealogies in Harl. 3859 and Jesus College, Oxford xx trace their ancestry from Cunedag's sons that the unsupported testimony of Nennius for this movement of Cunedag into Wales, some four hundred and fifty years earlier, has gained almost universal credence among modern historians. Yet the story belongs in all its essential features to the same class of eponymous origin stories as those related of the Picts and the rulers of Scottish Dálriada.[1]

It is a curious feature of our insular stories of the eponymous founders of kingdoms that, while most of our texts appear to have been recorded round about the ninth century, the stories themselves, in so far as they appear to have any relationship to historical times, relate for the most part to a period somewhere in the fifth century, that is to say, about the period of the close of the Roman occupation of Britain. A comparison of the evidence of the Irish annals with that of the *Tripartite Life of St Patrick*, the *Chronicle of Dálriada*, and the *Duan Albanach* suggests that the date (c. 464) given by the last is approximately correct for the foundation of the kingdom of Dálriada which is attributed to the sons of Erc.[2] Both the Pictish and the Irish antiquarian writers carry back the origins of their kingdoms to periods fantastically ancient, and their beginnings are impossible to compute on any sound chronological basis. For Ireland, however, the historical period is now generally believed to begin in the fifth century with the reign of Níall Noígiallach and the arrival of St Patrick; and the testimony of the genealogies is strongly in favour of this. Back to that date they are independent and valuable; but they all fork in the fifth century and before that they are not independent of one another, and are probably fabrications.

In the same way the date c. 450 favoured by the most recent

---

[1] Such eponymous origin legends are not, of course, confined to our islands, but are widespread in the Dark Ages and earlier. As an example relating to Gaul reference may be made to Ammianus Marcellinus, xv, ix, 6.

[2] See Chadwick, *op. cit.* 121 ff.

scholars for the invasion of Cunedag and his sons into Wales receives confirmation from the genealogies of the founders of those Welsh kingdoms claiming descent from his eponymous sons, all of which fork at a date somewhere in the fifth century. It is not without significance that the kingdoms of the northern Britons, and the Britons of Strathclyde and Galloway, seem to emerge as independent units about the same period, the two great founders of these later dynasties, Coel Hen and Dyfnwal Hen, having lived, so far as we can judge from the testimony of the genealogies, in and after the middle of the fourth century.[1] The evidence as a whole points to the conclusion that genuine historical tradition and genuine genealogies in Celtic Britain began to be preserved shortly after the close of the Roman Period. From then onwards both seem to have been preserved orally by trained bards and *filid* down to the period of writing. The high quality of this oral tradition, and the care with which it was preserved and transmitted, corroborate the view that a great Celtic revival was in progress about this period, a revival perhaps already begun and even fostered by the Romans themselves as a part of their frontier policy.[2] For some reason or other, about the ninth century a general desire made itself felt in all the Celtic countries to carry history further back, hence speculation was highly cultivated at this period to supplement tradition.

The general similarity in the essential features of these 'speculative origin stories'—the origin of kingdoms traced from an intrusive head of a family of eponymous sons who founded kingdoms and dynasties; the relevance of these stories to the fifth century; and the apparent agreement of the date of the actual records somewhere about the ninth century—would seem to place it beyond doubt that we are dealing, not with historical tradition in the strict sense of the word, but with antiquarian speculations of the native learned class—their attempts to account for the origin and distribution of the peoples and kingdoms of their own day. To

[1] For the evidence, see Chadwick, *op. cit.* 143; and cf. P. Hunter Blair, *The Origins of Northumbria* (Gateshead-on-Tyne, 1948), 29 ff. For a suggested earlier date, see Sir Ifor Williams, *Wales and the North* (Kendal, 1952), 77.

[2] I may refer, for example, to the apparent promotion of native Celtic families of the northern and perhaps the western frontiers of Britain from the fourth century onwards. See Collingwood and Myres, *Roman Britain and the English Settlements* (Oxford, 1936), 288 ff.; cf. Chadwick, *op. cit.* 150 f.

3-2

this end they used the best means at their disposal, the genealogies. And it is a striking fact that these led them consistently to the end of the Roman period. The reason for this is a matter of great interest in itself; but our present concern is not with the actual history of the fifth century and the developments which resulted from the cessation of Roman rule, but with the nature of our record.

It would seem that about the beginning of the ninth century a new intellectual impetus was at work throughout Celtic lands, resulting in the 'origin' stories discussed above. The effect of this new intellectual activity was the record of the native traditions and their expansion, by means of inference and speculation, with the aim of creating a great national past. But behind this intellectual ambition there undoubtedly lay a deeper emotional stimulus. The documents of antiquarian inference and speculation are the intellectual expression of the rise of national consciousness, of the emergence of the Celtic peoples as wider consolidated kingdoms, under rulers whose achievements in this growth of national pride have impressed themselves on later generations as those of great men. In Scotland this national consciousness seems to have begun with the union of the kingdoms of the Picts and Scots under Kenneth mac Alpin, and the emergence of 'Scotland' as a nation about the middle of the ninth century; in Ireland somewhat later, with the actual union of the northern and southern kingdoms under the title of the *ard rí*, the 'high-king', at the close of the Viking period; in Wales with the union of more than half the smaller Welsh kingdoms under Rhodri Mawr, 'the Great'. We may point to the beginnings of the *Saxon Chronicle* and the impressive sense of national consciousness which finds expression about the same time in England under Alfred 'the Great'. The rise to supreme power of Charlemagne ('Charles the Great') and his grandson Charles the Bald at this period, and the interest of the latter especially in antiquarian studies, may not have been without effect in our islands.

2. LATIN TEXTS OF WELSH PROVENANCE

Nennius and the 'Historia Brittonum'

It would be of great interest to know how far the various schools of antiquarian activity were in touch with one another. An equally important problem is the extent and nature of the debt of the compilers of the written Latin records to the oral transmitters of the ancient traditions and genealogies. These questions are part of the much wider problems connected with the sources and compilation of antiquarian literature, questions on which it is obvious that we cannot enter here. It will readily be agreed, however, that such a specialised form of intellectual activity as our British eponymous origin legends must have been concentrated in definite centres of learning. Among the southern Picts the early foundation at Abernethy has been suggested, but Brechin is not impossible.[1] In northern Ireland, Bangor in Co. Down was undoubtedly an early centre of historical studies; but there were also others, and southern Ireland may well have been ahead of northern Ireland in antiquarian studies.[2] The centre of Welsh antiquarian studies has not as yet been determined, but it is impossible to doubt that a local intellectual centre must have been in existence in the ninth century somewhere in western Britain, and moreover that this centre not only shared the general intellectual activity to which I have referred, but made its own contribution to the historical and antiquarian activity of the time. In view of the importance of the *Historia Brittonum*, and the prominence which it gives to the antiquarian stories with which we are here concerned, it is natural to suppose that this compendium of ancient traditions must have arisen in such an intellectual milieu. Unfortunately the exact provenance of the *Historia Brittonum* is as yet unknown. The part of Nennius himself in the authorship or revision of the book is equally uncertain. Indeed it may safely be said that no problem of the early Middle Ages presents greater difficulties than the origin and textual history of the compilation of the *Historia*.

---

[1] See M. O. Anderson, *Scottish Historical Review*, vol. XXVIII (1949), 35; XXIX (1950), 35, 38.

[2] This we are led to suspect from the extensive genealogical poems recording Leinster princely families, and believed to date from the seventh century, or even earlier. For the texts, translation (German) and some discussion see Kuno Meyer, *Über die älteste irische Dichtung*, parts I and II (*Königl. Preuss. Akademie der Wissenschaften*, Phil.-Hist. Classe, Berlin, no. 6, 1913; no. 10, 1914).

A detailed discussion would be impossible here. A few observations on the subject are, however, essential to our theme.

It will be well at the outset to state very briefly the nature of the contents of the *Historia* as we find them in our earliest and best text, MS. Harleian 3859 (see below). These may be enumerated as follows:

1. The Six Ages of the World (c. 1–6).
2. The History of Britain (c. 7–49).
3. The Life of St Patrick (c. 50–5).
4. The account of Arthur (c. 56).
5. The Anglo-Saxon Genealogies and northern matter (c. 57–65).
6. The computus (c. 66).

to which most manuscripts add:

7. The list of the cities of Britain (c. 66).
8. The list of the marvels of Britain (c. 67–76).

It should be added that c. 62 includes an early list of British poets and the account of the coming of Cunedag and his sons from Manau Guotodin to Gwynedd (North Wales) and of their expulsion of the Irish.

Among the many difficult problems which come in for consideration are the date of the original compilation; the original author; the relations of the various versions to one another; and the relations to one another of the various manuscripts. The last of these problems is the only one on which a certain amount of firm ground has been reached. The text is contained in some thirty-three manuscripts, and in 1894 Theodor Mommsen published his critical edition of Nennius based on an examination and classification of all the manuscripts.[1] These he divides into several groups, chiefly represented by the following:[2]

(1) MS. Harleian 3859 (H), a manuscript which is assigned to shortly before or after 1100 (cf. p. 39 below) and makes no reference to any known author of the *Historia Brittonum*. This is by far the best text. With this MS. is associated the closely related text K.
(2) The Chartres MS. (Z), a text written *c.* 900, which bears the heading: *Incipiunt Exberta fii Urbagen*, etc.

---

[1] *Historia Brittonum cum Additamenta Nennii. Monumenta Germaniae Historica: Auctores Antiquissimi*, XIII; *Chronica Minora, Saec. IV, V, VI, VII* (Berlin, 1898), pp. 111 ff.
[2] I have used throughout the letters adopted by Mommsen.

(3) The so-called Vatican MS. (M) of the eleventh century, which bears the heading: *Incipit istoria Brittonum edita ab anachoreta Marco eiusdem gentis sancto episcopo.* This text is related to the one contained in the Paris MS. of the twelfth century (N).

(4) The largest group (MSS. C, D, G, L, P, Q), consisting of some fifteen manuscripts or more, none of them earlier than the twelfth century. The majority of manuscripts of this group attributes the composition of the *Historia* to Gildas, which is a self-evident anachronism.

(5) A number of the manuscripts of group (4) attribute the composition of the *Historia* to Nennius. These manuscripts are ten in number, of which the two most important are Mommsen's D² and C, dating from the twelfth and thirteenth centuries. They are commonly referred to by scholars as the 'Cambridge group'. To these we must add the Irish version of Nennius, to be referred to more fully below. It thus becomes clear that no extant manuscript associates the name of Nennius with the *Historia Brittonum* before the twelfth century. The two manuscripts C, D² have before the preface: *Incipit eulogium brevissimum Britanniae insulae quod Nennius Elvodugi discipulus congregavit.* And the title prefixed to the text of this *libellus* itself is: *Incipit res gesta a Nennio Sapiente composita.*[1]

The best and most complete of these versions is the one contained in MS. Harleian 3859 (H), which is believed to have been compiled round about the year 1100 or 1110 (cf. pp. 46, 74 below) from an earlier exemplar. This is the only text which contains the whole of the *Historia* as this is generally believed to have been edited in its fullest form *c.* 800 by one Nennius, perhaps with an appendix added in a later 'edition', *c.* 828–9.[2] I would however stress two facts—first that the name Nennius occurs nowhere in this text; and second that the preface, in which Nennius claims to be the author, is lacking here and also in the Chartres and Vatican texts. The name Nennius, in fact, as already stated, does not occur in any extant version before the twelfth century.[3]

Apart from H our most interesting version of the *Historia* is contained in a manuscript at Chartres (Z), which is generally believed to be our oldest text and to date from *c.* 900 but may be somewhat later.[4] The text is badly transcribed and very incomplete—indeed deliberately selective, as its heading would seem

---

[1] Mommsen, 113, 125.

[2] See Sir Ifor Williams, 'Notes on Nennius', in *Bulletin of the Board of Celtic Studies*, VII (1935), 387.

[3] As regards the genuineness of the prefaces, however, see H. M. Chadwick, *The Origin of the English Nation* (Cambridge, 1907), 42, n. 3.

[4] See F. Lot, *Nennius et l'Historia Brittonum*, 31.

to imply. The complete heading runs: 'Incipiunt exberta fii [for filii] Urbagen de Libro Sci Germani inventa et origine et genealogia Britonum, De Ætatibus Mundi.' This is far from clear, but seems to suggest that what follows contains excerpts or selections made by a son of Urbagen or Urien from a *Book of St Germanus*, and there is no doubt that the *acta* of St Germanus rather than the history of the Britons are the principal concern of the compiler of the Chartres recension. We are told in both this text and H (c. 63) that it was a certain *Rum* (i.e. *Run*) son of Urien who baptised the Northumbrian king Edwin, christened according to Bede in 627. It is natural to suppose this is the son of Urien to whom the Chartres version is ascribed. We shall return to Run himself and also to the Chartres text later.

One other version of the *Historia* may be referred to here. This is contained in an eleventh-century manuscript now in the Vatican Library (Vatican Ref. 964) (M), which claims to have been written by 'Mark the anchorite, the holy British bishop',[1] in the fifth year of the reign of King Edmund. The composition of the text can therefore be securely dated in 943–4,[2] and since it makes reference to an English king it is natural to suppose that it was compiled by an Englishman. This version, however, contains certain comments on the sites mentioned in the list of Arthur's battles (c. 56) which are not found in any other version. I refer to the '*quae Bryttanice nominatur*' glosses, and the names which the glossator introduces by *quem nos appellamus*.[3] Thus in connection with *Breguoin* the commentator says '*quem nos Cat Bregion appellamus*'—'*We* call the battle at the hill of Breguoin by the name Cat Bregion'. These comments could only have been made by a Welsh speaker, and therefore not by the English compiler of M. They are not very likely to be later.[4] Could they not be the comments of the British bishop, Mark the anchorite himself? To Mark the anchorite also we shall return later. Meantime it is worth noting here that Thurneysen regarded this recension as based on the Harleian and the Chartres versions.[5]

---

[1] Text and translation by W. Gunn, *The Historia Brittonum*, London, 1819.
[2] Despite F. Lot, *Nennius et l'Historia Brittonum*, 13.
[3] 'Quae nominatur Brittanice Duglas. Quae Bryttanice Cat Coit Celidon nominatur. Quae Bryttanice Cair Lion dicitur. Quem nos Cat Bregion appellamus.'
[4] I am indebted to Professor Kenneth Jackson for calling my attention to these interesting glosses. [5] *Zeitschrift für celtische Philologie*, i (1897), 159.

It is now believed that no extant version represents the original form of the *Historia Brittonum*,[1] or even the precise form which it assumed in the hands of Nennius, who is generally regarded as its latest, or practically its latest redactor. Some twenty years ago a careful examination of the Irish MSS. was made by Van Hamel, who came to the conclusion that the text which approximates most closely to the original version is the so-called *Lebor Bretnach*,[2] an Irish translation three versions of which are contained in the well-known Irish MS. the *Book of Lecan*, written *c.* 1400. Of these Van Hamel regards version I (L¹) as the oldest, and as representing ultimately a lost original. It is noteworthy that L¹ is the only Irish version which lacks the prologue and the ascription to Nennius, whose name nowhere occurs in this version, though it occurs three times in the two remaining Irish versions, which are ascribed to Gilla Coemáin († not later than 1071), and in which Van Hamel believes this author to have incorporated material from the 'Cambridge recension'. Van Hamel's claim for the early date and high value of L¹ has not been accepted without question, and F. Lot, the most recent editor of the *Historia*, regards this version as a fragmentary abbreviation of Gilla Coemáin's edition.[3] This is not the place for a detailed examination of the arguments which have led our leading scholars to conclusions differing widely on this most difficult and complicated problem, but some observations on Van Hamel's views on the Irish textual tradition may be of help to us when we come to consider the Continental versions of the *Historia* at a later stage in the present article.

According to Van Hamel's argument, out of an original Latin version of the *Historia*, called for convenience the *Liber Britannicus*, grew our *Historia Brittonum* by the addition of a *Liber Sancti Germani*, and apparently of other British material. The earliest version of the Irish *Lebor Bretnach*, is derived, not from this primitive *Liber Britannicus*, but from a slightly enlarged recension, which also lies behind the 'Cambridge' group of the MSS. of the later *Historia Brittonum*. It is important to note, however, that the Harleian (H) and Vatican (M) groups are based, not on this later recension, but on the primitive *Liber Britannicus*. This is also true

---

[1] Cf. Mommsen, *ed. cit.* 133.

[2] Edited from all the manuscripts by A. G. Van Hamel (published by the Irish Manuscripts Commission, Dublin, 1932).

[3] *Ed. cit.* 135 ff. See also Thurneysen, 'Zu Nennius', *Zeitschrift für celtische Philologie*, xx, 108 ff.

of the Chartres text; but the latter is believed to be derived from a recension in which the *Liber Britannicus* and a *Liber Sancti Germani* had already been combined.

If, therefore, we could accept the conclusions of Van Hamel, the evidence of version L[1] of the *Historia* would support the evidence of the Harleian, the Vatican, and the Chartres texts that the association with Nennius appears at a late stage in the MS. tradition.

The *Historia Brittonum*[1] as a whole would thus appear to be in the nature of an organism rather than a composition as we usually understand the latter term. Opinions differ as to what constituted the original nucleus, but on the whole it would seem most probable that the work as we now have it has developed by the incorporation at different periods of a number of independent documents, most of them composite in character.

It is not easy to speak with any confidence of the part played by Nennius in the compiling of the *Historia Brittonum*. Mommsen, with most earlier editors,[2] believed that Nennius was only the last editor of an earlier anonymous work, dating from the seventh century, probably about the time of the downfall of the Northumbrian kingdom, between 679–85. Zimmer, from a comparison of the British recensions with the Irish version of Gilla Coemáin made in the eleventh century, denied the existence of an earlier composite *Historia Brittonum*, regarding Nennius as the original author, though he admitted the incorporation of a little Northumbrian historical 'tract', c. 57–65 referred to below.[3] More recently Liebermann has again denied the existence of any *Historia Brittonum* before 800, claiming that the composition is the work of Nennius about that date.[4] The arguments of Liebermann in this respect are unconvincing, and so far the work of Van Hamel seems to me to add weight to the arguments in favour of a small British nucleus of late seventh-century date on which a number of later recensions have been based; and in some of which other matter has

---

[1] For references to early editions, see Sir J. E. Lloyd, *History of Wales*, I, 223, n. I.

[2] See the elaborate study by Thurneysen, *Zeitschrift für deutsche Philologie*, XXVIII, 90–113.

[3] *Nennius Vindicatus* (Berlin, 1893), 78–105, 269.

[4] 'Nennius the Author of the *Historia Brittonum*', in *Essays in Medieval History presented to Thomas Frederick Tout*, edited by A. G. Little and F. M. Powicke (Manchester, 1925), 25 ff.

been included, such as the contents of a *Liber Sancti Germani*, and a *Vita Patricii*.

It would seem probable from internal evidence (cf. pp. 65 ff. below) that an important recension was made *c*. 800. The last Saxon king mentioned whose date is known is Ecgfrith of Mercia, who reigned for a brief period in 796. The archetype of most of the MSS., including H, was evidently transcribed by a man who speaks (c. 9) of Fernmail as ruling in his own day in the two regions of Buelt (modern 'Builth') and Guorthigirniaun, two districts on the Upper Wye; this version would seem to date, therefore, from about the year 800.[1] A later copyist indicates (c. 16) that he was writing in the fourth year of Merfyn Vrych, who probably came to the throne of Gwynedd in 825, or possibly 816 (cf. p. 79 below).

Reference has been made above to the preface found in the Cambridge group of manuscripts, dating in their extant form from the twelfth century, in which a certain Nennius or Nemnivus gives his own name and claims to have compiled the *Historia*, enumerating his sources categorically. They include the 'annals of the Romans'; the 'chronicles of the sacred Fathers, viz. Jerome, Eusebius, Isidore, Prosper'; the 'annals of the Irish and of the Saxons'; and 'the tradition of our ancestors'.[2] Nennius had a considerable fund of learning according to the standards of his time, and he evidently had access to a good library. His reference to the annals of the Saxons need not, of course, necessarily imply that the annals in question were actually compiled in the vernacular; but it may be mentioned here that the author of the *Historia*, whether Nennius or a predecessor, was certainly familiar with the Anglo-Saxon tongue.[3] The importance of this will become clearer as we proceed.

In this same preface Nennius claims that he is writing as the 'disciple' (*discipulus*) of one Elvodugus. His words are:

I, Nennius [or Nemnivus], disciple of Elvodugus, have been at pains to write some excerpts, which the dulness (*hebitudo*) of the British nation (*gentis Britanniae*) had passed by....

---

[1] According to the pedigrees contained in Jesus College MS. xx (see p. 75 below), Fernmail (Ffernfael) had a cousin *Brawstudd* married to Arthfael of Morgannwg (Pedigrees 9, 14), which would suggest a date for Ffernfael *c*. 800.

[2] 'Ex traditione veterum nostrorum.'

[3] For the evidence, see Chadwick, *op. cit*. 41 ff.; cf. Liebermann, *op. cit*. 39. Cf. also p. 44 below.

The Elvodugus in question is believed to be the Elfoddw who is credited in the *Annales Cambriae* (see p. 58 below), *s.a.* 768, with having emended the date of Easter among the Britons, thus including the British Church in the *Unitas Catholica*. In the year 809 the same annals enter the death of Elfoddw, there referred to as 'archbishop in the region of Gwynedd' who is in all probability the same person. The epithet 'archbishop' is, of course, merely honorific, for no archbishops existed in Wales at so early a date. His association with Gwynedd is important, however, and gives a presumption in favour of his association with Bangor in Arfon, traditionally the chief sanctuary in North Wales, believed to have been founded by St Deiniol in the 'age of the saints'. As a natural corollary to this, if we accept the preface referred to above as genuine, there would also be some ground for associating Nennius with the same area.

Zimmer claimed[1] that the *Historia Brittonum* was known under the name of Nennius to Cormac Mac Cuilennáin, the bishop and perhaps king of Cashel (†908), and that it was referred to by him in the lost *Saltair Caisil*. The original of this work is believed to have been compiled by Cormac himself about the beginning of the tenth century. The MS. was still in existence in 1453, when portions of it were copied into the MS. Laud 610, now in the Bodleian Library at Oxford. It is of interest, in view of the story relating to Nennius next to be considered, that Cormac is also credited with the composition of the *Sanas Cormaic*, 'Cormac's Glossary', a kind of dictionary of recondite and obsolete Irish words. Traditionally, therefore, his interests were to some extent pedagogic. But though Zimmer's claim was accepted by Mommsen[2] it cannot be said to be proved, and is not accepted by F. Lot.[3]

I have referred above to the familiarity of the compiler of the *Historia Brittonum* with Anglo-Saxon. This is noticeable in the form of the names in the Northumbrian tract on the Anglian genealogies, and also in the story of the Saxon invasion, which the late Professor Chadwick held to have been very closely related. Here, in the story of Hengest's treachery, Nennius gives the actual words in Anglo-Saxon: 'Eu Saxones, eniminit saxas', which he immediately translates into Latin: 'Cultellos vestros ex

[1] *Neues Archiv der Gesellschaft für ältere deutsche Geschichtskunde*, XIX, 436.
[2] *Op. cit.* 117.
[3] See F. Lot, *Historia Brittonum*, p. 128, n. 5.

ficonibus vestris educite' ('Saxons, draw your knives', etc.). Liebermann rightly observes[1] that this playing upon homophonous words ('Saxons', 'saxas', 'short swords') sounds like the pun, not of a Cymric folk-tale, but of a philological scholar, proud of his knowledge of the Teutonic tongue. Liebermann points further to the uncalled-for emphasis on the 'interpreter' Ceretic in the meeting between Hengest and Vortigern (c. 37), and he even goes so far as to suspect that Nennius himself held the post of interpreter at his prince's court near the English frontier. However that may be, we would stress the obvious knowledge which Nennius shows of the Saxon language, and his somewhat pedagogical use of it in his pun.

Now in a text of the *Liber Commonei* contained in an Oxford MS. (Bodl. Auct. F. 4. 32), commonly known, since Zeuss first called attention to it, as the *Oxoniensis Prior*, and written early in the ninth century, we are told that one Nemniuus[2] invented a Welsh alphabet on the spur of the moment in order to refute a Saxon scholar who had declared that the Britons had no alphabet of their own. He did this *ut vituperationem et hebitudinem deieceret gentis suae*. The words, as Sir Ifor Williams has pointed out,[3] recall those of the preface to the *Historia Brittonum* quoted above, in which Nennius remarks that he is writing some *exberta* (?'excerpts') *quae hebitudo gentis Britanniae deiecerat*, and there can be little doubt that the same sensitive patriot is the person referred to in both cases. Thurneysen was inclined to believe that *Oxoniensis Prior* was written by 'Nemnivus' himself;[4] Sir Ifor Williams, that the writer was rather a disciple and admirer of Nemnivus who had access to a manuscript written by Nemnivus from which he copied the faked alphabet. For us the interest of the story lies in its early date, and in its emphasis on Nennius as a scholar, and especially

---

[1] *Op. cit.* 39, 43.

[2] The reading of *Oxoniensis Prior* points strongly in favour of *Nemniuus* or *Nemnivus* as the true form. I have retained the more usual *Nennius* partly as being more generally familiar, and partly because I do not feel certain that it is unconnected with the name *Ninian*, in which case *Nennius* would be the more correct form.

[3] 'Notes on Nennius', *Bulletin of the Board of Celtic Studies*, VII (1935), 380 ff.

[4] *Zeitschrift fur celtische Philologie*, xx, 97 ff. The MS. also contains other pedagogic matter in addition to the alphabet of Nennius, e.g. notes on weights and measures, and a brief list of grammatical terms such as *protasis, aposiopesis, epentesis, paragoge, aphresis, sinagoge, apagoge* (*sic.* See Whitley Stokes, 'Cambrica', *Transactions of the Philological Society*, 1861, 206).

one who concentrated on alphabetical lore. We must not, however, accept literally the statement about the invention of the alphabet on the spur of the moment, for in fact the alphabet in question is still extant and is recorded immediately after the story, and each letter is accompanied by its Welsh name.[1] It has been shown to be derived directly from the Anglo-Saxon version of the runic alphabet. 'Nemnivus', in fact, constructed his alphabet on the basis of that of his Saxon traducer. Indeed the names given to some of his letters seem to show evidence of an actual knowledge of their Saxon names.[2]

It is a curious story. The avowed object of the Saxon was to belittle British culture, a matter which Nennius was apparently concerned to defend. We shall see presently (pp. 94 ff. below) that about the same time, that is to say, during the first half of the ninth century, an attempt was made, apparently by an Irish scholar at the court of Merfyn in Gwynedd, to put four Irish scholars out of countenance by facing them with a cryptogram requiring an elementary knowledge of the Greek alphabet for its solution. Like Nennius they rose superior to their detractors; but it is remarkable that in both cases the *casus belli* should turn on an alphabet.

3. THE ANNALES CAMBRIAE

(i) *The Irish Entries*

The questions of the milieu of the *Historia Brittonum* and of the part of Nennius in the work cannot be treated in isolation. They are closely connected with those of certain other texts which occur in relationship to the *Historia Brittonum* in the most important manuscript of the latter that we possess, namely British Museum Harleian 3859 which, as already stated, can be dated in its present form to within a few years before or after 1100, but which we have good ground for believing to have been based on a text dating from *c*. 950.[3] The most important of these texts are the British annals (in

---

[1] A facsimile of this page of the MS. is given by Sir Ifor Williams, *op. cit.*, facing p. 381.

[2] See R. Derolez, *Runica Manuscripta* (Bruges, 1954), 157f.; cf. also *ibid.* 159, 'There can be no doubt that Nemnivus knew the O.E. *futhorc* and derived his Welsh alphabet from it.' I shall refer to this work throughout as Derolez[2] to distinguish it from a slightly earlier work by the same author to be discussed later, to which I shall refer throughout this chapter as Derolez[1].

[3] See Wade-Evans, *Nennius's History of the Britons* (London, 1938), 13.

Latin), commonly referred to by modern writers as the *Annales Cambriae*, and the genealogies of the Welsh and North British princes. The last entry in the *Annales* relates to *c.* 955, and they are regarded as having been drawn up not later than 956[1] though the original composition probably took place much earlier,[2] and the compiler has certainly made use of earlier written records, as we shall see.

The genealogies would seem, on internal evidence, to have been drawn up in the same milieu and about the same period as the *Annales*.[3] Both bear a close relationship to the contents of the *Historia Brittonum* in its present form, and were presumably drawn up in the same milieu.[4] To this subject I shall return later; but I may mention here the common interest shown by both the *Historia* and the *Annales* in Arthur, in the princes of northern Britain, and in their victories over the Saxons—information not found elsewhere. I may point also to annal 626 in the Harleian MS. of the *Annales Cambriae*, which relates the baptism of the Northumbrian king Edwin by *Run filius Urbgen*, a statement also found in the *Historia Brittonum*, c. 63, in contrast to the statement in MS. B (see p. 48 below) of the *Annales* and in the remaining groups of MSS. of the *Historia*, which, in agreement with Bede, state that Edwin was baptised by Paulinus, bishop of York. The genealogies show a comparable interest in the northern princes, and are apparently aware of a tradition of some Arthur or other, though they mention only the name, which is entered in the genealogy of the princes of Dyfed.[5]

The first two genealogies give the paternal and maternal descent of Owen, son of Hywel Dda. Owen reigned in south-west Wales from *c.* 950 to *c.* 988, and the annals come to an end in the early years of his reign. There can therefore be hardly any doubt that the compendium from which our MS. Harleian 3859 was copied

[1] Loth, *Les Mabinogion*, II, 370. Lloyd would place their composition somewhat later in the century (*History of Wales*, I, 159). Cf. also Chadwick, *Growth of Literature*, I (Cambridge, 1932), 149. Cf. also p. 273, n. 1.

[2] See Chadwick, *Growth of Literature*, I, 147.

[3] Chadwick, *op. cit.* I, 149, 151. Loth and some other scholars believe that the *Annales* and the genealogies have been drawn up by the same person. See further Wade-Evans, *op. cit.* 32.

[4] See Chadwick, *Growth of Literature*, I, 151.

[5] In the maternal ancestry of Owen, son of Hywel Dda. See Pedigree 2 of MS. Harleian 3859; and Pedigree 12 of Jesus College MS. xx, the latter published in *Y Cymmrodor*, VIII (1887).

was compiled in the second half of the tenth century. It represents, so to speak, Owen's family archives.

The *Annales Cambriae*[1] have been preserved in two later MSS. in addition to the text (A) contained in Harleian 3859. Both these later texts (B and C) were written in the thirteenth century; both form a continuation of a chronicle of which the first part is based indirectly on Isidore of Seville's *Origines*; both contain additional entries, some relating to general ecclesiastical history, others derived from Geoffrey of Monmouth. The first of these texts (B), written without title or preamble on certain fly-leaves of an abridged copy of Domesday Book in the Public Record Office,[2] is of considerable interest in its own right, since it does not appear to be derived directly from either A or its prototype, and sometimes offers a better reading than either this manuscript or MS. C next to be discussed.[3] MS. C[4] also forms a part of a chronicle derived from Isidore's *Origines*, and has incorporated some additional matter, its general contents agreeing closely with those of the preceding manuscripts, especially B.[5]

In MS. Harleian 3859 the genealogies[6] follow immediately on

[1] The printed text has been edited for the Rolls Series by J. W. ab Ithel (London, 1860). The editor has based his text on MS. Harl. 3859, but has in general printed variant readings in the footnotes. This Harleian version was published by M. Egerton Phillimore in *Y Cymmrodor*, IX, 152 ff., and has been reproduced by J. Loth in *Les Mabinogion*, II (Paris, 1913), 370 ff.; an English translation was published by A. W. Wade-Evans in *Nennius's History of the Britons* (London, 1938), pp. 84 ff. [2] MS. E. 164, vol. I.
[3] To mention one or two instances: annal 573 has a detailed note on the protagonists in the battle of Arthuret; annals 584 and 606 have the correct form *depositio* for the erroneous *dispositio* of Harl.; annal 601 has the correct *David Menevensis episcopus obit*; in annal 626 the baptism of Edwin is attributed to Paulinus, bishop of York, and no reference is made to the *Run filius Urbgen* of Harl.
[4] British Museum, Cotton MS. Domitian A. 1, fo. 139 ff.
[5] A study of the MSS. (more especially MS. Record Office E. 164, vol. I) from the point of view of the early chronological system and its relationship with that of the Irish annals has been published recently by Professor James Carney, *Studies in Irish Literature and History* (Dublin, 1955), 324 ff. See especially the 'Additional Note on the *Annales Cambriae*', 371 ff. The present writer, like Professor Carney, has found it necessary to consult all three MSS., and is in complete agreement with him as to the urgent need of a new and complete critical edition. Indeed as early as 1889 Henry Bradshaw, in speaking of the *Annales Cambriae* and the genealogies which follow them in MS. Harl. 3859, expressed the view that the whole volume (i.e. Harl. 3859) ought to be photographed. See his *Collected Papers* (Cambridge, 1889), 467.
[6] The genealogies of MS. Harl. 3859 have been published by J. Loth, *op. cit.* II, 326 ff., and by A. W. Wade-Evans, *op. cit.* 101 ff.; those of Jesus College

the *Annales Cambriae*. There are thirty-one, most of which are found also in other MSS. Of these the most important is Jesus College, Oxford, MS. xx, which contains fifty-one genealogies; and MS. Hengwrt 536, which contains only twelve, all these twelve relating exclusively to the North British—i.e. the Strathclyde and Cumbrian—princes, generally referred to as the 'Men of the North'. The two latter texts are assigned to the fourteenth century, and the language has been modernised, whereas that of the Harleian text is ancient. There are, however, instances where the Jesus text preserves earlier readings, notably in the Dyfed pedigree (Jesus xx).[1] In any case the genealogies, like the *Annales Cambriae*, have a history behind them, older than, and independent of, the great compendium Harleian 3859, and deliberate selection, and possibly accident also, has played an important part in our three principal collections, as we shall see. We shall consider the genealogies more fully later.

If now we turn to examine the nature of the entries of the *Annales Cambriae* down to, and including the early years of the seventh century, we notice that their contents are almost exclusively concerned with (1) one entry about St Patrick;[2] two entries about St Brigit and three about St Columba; (2) obits of five other Irish saints; (3) obits of Welsh saints and princes; (4) annals relating to the *Gwyr y Gogledd*, the princes of Strathclyde and south-western Scotland and north-western England; (5) two entries relating to Arthur. These two last entries are, in fact, the first two entries relating to Britain in the *Annales Cambriae*. The early entries in particular show a preoccupation with Irish ecclesiastical tradition. Entries relating to Wales before the middle of the seventh century are less prominent than we should expect. They are practically confined to the obits of three Welsh princes of Gwynedd and Powys (Maelgwn, Selyf ap Cynan and Iago ap Beli) and of some six Welsh saints, of whom SS. Cynog, Dewi and Dyfrig are the only ones of apparently Welsh origin. St Kentigern certainly, and St Deiniol probably, belong at least in origin to North Britain, while

MS. xx by M. E. Phillimore in *Y Cymmrodor*, VIII, 1887, IX, 1888; those of the 'Men of the North' from MS. Hengwrt 536 by W. F. Skene, *Four Ancient Books of Wales*, II (Edinburgh, 1868), 454f.; and by J. Loth, *op. cit.* II, 349f.

[1] Cf. Chadwick, *Growth of Literature*, I, 152.

[2] On this entry see the recent observations by Professor J. Carney in his *Studies in Irish Literature and History* (Dublin, 1955), 339ff. See more especially 347ff.

St Gildas has a Gaelic name, and a traditional northern ancestry.[1] The entries relating to North Britain will be considered later.

Let us consider the Irish entries first. The basis of their selection is not obvious. Patrick, Brigit and Columcille are, of course, natural enough. But the choice of Benén, Íbar, Ciarán, Brendan of Birr, and Cuimíne Fota requires explanation. Benén is St Benignus, St Patrick's youngest associate, and his successor in the see of Armagh, whose death is recorded in the *Annales Cambriae* in 468. Cuimíne Fota is the abbot of Clonfert in Co. Galway, whose death is recorded in 661. The deaths of the three remaining Irish saints in our list—Íbar, Ciarán and Brendan of Birr—are recorded in the *Annales Cambriae* in 501, 544 and 574 respectively. As the *Annales Cambriae* were in all probability compiled in the ninth century, some two hundred years later than Cuimíne, and at least three hundred later than the obits of the remaining saints, we may suspect that this selection was dictated, not so much by the prestige of these particular saints, as by the prestige of their monastic foundations, either in the compiler's own day, or in that of his source—more probably the latter. Reference to important monasteries by the name of their founders was already practised in Leinster by Cummian, the author of a famous letter to Abbot Seghene, in the seventh century.

The ecclesiastical foundations associated with our five saints are as follows. St Benén's associations are with Armagh. St Íbar was the traditional founder of Imblech-Íbair (anglicised *Emly*), the chief Munster sanctuary. St Ciarán was the founder of Clonmacnoise, the greatest monastic foundation in the west of Ireland. St Brendan of Birr is an older contemporary of the famous St Brendan of Clonfert in Co. Galway, the hero of the *Navigatio Brendani*, who may have been to some extent confused with him in later tradition.[2] Cuimíne Fota was the most famous abbot of Clonfert in the seventh century. It will be noticed, therefore, that the list includes some of the most important ecclesiastical foundations in Ireland, beginning with Armagh. The omissions are the more remarkable. We have for example no reference to St Comgall of Bangor; or to St Finnian of either Clonard or Moville. W eare

---

[1] For details of the traditions relating to the origin and parentage of St Gildas, reference may be made to my article in *Scottish Gaelic Studies*, VII (1953), 122 ff.

[2] See J. F. Kenney, *The Sources for the Early History of Ireland* (New York, 1929), 410, n. 140. For the obit of Brendan of Clonfert see *Annals of Ulster* in 577 or 583.

forced back to the question as to the basis of selection. What claim, for example, has Birr to be included in the list?

Let us leave aside for the moment the question of Birr and glance at two early lists of Irish monastic foundations. The first, which is very brief, occurs in an account of a synod which it is claimed had been held in Mag-Léna in the neighbourhood of Durrow in Leinster, to consider the question of reform in accordance with Roman usage in the reckoning of the date of Easter. Our authority is a letter from Cummian, probably abbot of Durrow, to Segene, who was abbot of Iona 623–52.[1] The letter is thought to have been written probably c. 632–3. The text is said to be much corrupted,[2] but the general tenor is clear. The writer states that he had made a careful study of the question of the Roman dating of the Easter cycle and had consulted his elders,[3] the coarbs of certain monastic founders, of whom he enumerates five who, he adds, assembled either in person or by deputy[4] at Mag-Léna, a plain in Offaly near Durrow. The synod may have been convened by the abbot of Durrow, possibly Cummian himself.[5]

The monastic institutions represented at Mag-Léna are enumerated by Cummian as follows, and in this order: Ailbe episcopus, Ciarán of Clonmacnoise, Brendan, Nessán, Lugid.

Armagh, it will be noticed, is not mentioned. Ailbe episcopus is, of course, the coarb of the great Munster sanctuary Imblech-Íbair, and so, with Ciarán and Brendan, would seem to correspond to the Íbar, Ciarán and 'Brendan of Birr' whose obits are entered in the *Annales Cambriae*, and in the same order. The two final names, in Cummian's list, Nessán[6] and Lugid, do not occur in the *Annales Cambriae*, but Lugid is clearly a reference to Mo-lúa, the patron saint of Clonferta-Molúa (†609). The Clonfert of Cuimíne Fota

---

[1] The text of the letter is published in Migne, *P.L.* LXXXVII, col. 969 ff. For some account of the letter see Kenney, *op. cit.* 220.

[2] So Kenney, *loc. cit.*   [3] 'Successores videlicet nostrorum patrum priorum.'

[4] 'Illi, congregati in unum, alius per se, alius per legatum suum vice sua missum, in campo Lene sanxerunt, et dixerunt', etc.

[5] See MacCarthy, *Annals of Ulster*, IV, cxli.

[6] According to Kenney (*op. cit.* 220, n. 184), following MacCarthy (*A.U.* IV, cxxxviii) he is probably Nessán of Mungarit, three miles south-west of Limerick. Cf. also Plummer ('Life of S. Ailbe', c. 42), *Vitae Sanctorum Hiberniae* (Oxford, 1910), I, p. xxxi, n. 3; 61. He is probably to be identified with the *Monessóc* of west Munster who figures as a guarantor in a west Munster synod, traditionally held in the sixth century, of which we have record in the tract contained in MS. Laud 610 (fo. 102*a*) published in the *Zeitschrift für celtische Philologie*, VIII, 315.

in Co. Galway in the *Annales Cambriae* has perhaps been sub-stituted for Clonferta-Molúa of the earlier list owing to its greater fame, and the great fame of its abbot Cuimíne Fota in the seventh century. It has already been mentioned that Cuimíne is nearly a century later than the other Irish saints in the *Annales Cambriae*.

The lists can hardly be wholly independent of one another, but their exact relationship is not clear. The foundations referred to by Cummian are, as one would expect, all in southern Ireland, including Clonferta-Molúa, i.e. Clonfertamulloe, now Kyle in Leix, whereas in the *Annales Cambriae* Clonfert in Co. Galway has taken its place, and Armagh heads the list with St Benén. Cummian's list in fact represents the monasteries which were concerned with him in establishing the new dating of Easter, which in southern Ireland was settled in favour of Rome shortly after 632 or 633; whereas the *Annales Cambriae*, showing knowledge of St Benén, Patrick's successor in Armagh, and Cuimíne Fota of Clonfert in Co. Galway, are in touch with northern Ireland, which did not conform till some sixty years later. Cummian's list, therefore, cannot have supplied the original of the *Annales Cambriae*.

It is, however, not improbable that other lists of signatories and religious foundations taking part in this controversy were drawn up at the time, for we learn from this same letter of Cummian that soon after[1] the synod of Mag-Léna a strong reactionary movement took place, under the leadership of a certain *paries dealbatus* ('a whited wall')[2] who claimed to adhere to the tradition of the Fathers,[3] but who 'instead of unity created division'.[4] The reference would seem to be to another synod of which we have some account in the *Life of St Fintan or Munnu*, c. 26 f.[5] This synod is stated to have been held in Mag-Ailbe,[6] near Slievemargy, on the borders of the present counties of Kildare and Carlow and is described as *magnum concilium populorum Hiberniae*. It is said to

---

[1] For a note on the relative chronology of the two synods see Plummer, *Vitae Sanctorum Hiberniae*, I (Oxford, 1910), p. lxxxv; cf. MacCarthy, *loc. cit.*

[2] Cf. Acts xxiii. 3.

[3] 'Traditionem seniorum servare se simulans.'

[4] 'Qui utraque non fecit unum, sed divisit.'

[5] The text of the *Life* is given by Plummer, *op. cit.* II, 237.

[6] *In campo Albo.* Is there a pun between the *paries dealbatus* and the *campo Albo*? Is Cummian referring to Munnu as *dealbatus* for having raised a barrier (*paries*) at this synod of *Mag-Ailbe*?—perhaps *dealbatus*, 'whited' i.e. deceptive, as in Matt. xxiii. 27.

have met to hear a discussion between Laisrén or Molaisse (†629), abbot of Leighlin or Leithglenn, Co. Carlow, who advocated the new order 'recently introduced from Rome',[1] and Fintan or Munnu (†635), abbot of Taghmon, Co. Wexford, who defended the old order. Evidently there was more than one synod held on this vexed question in southern Ireland, and the adherents of the Roman party appear to have been in the minority[2] despite their ultimate victory.

We noted above the curious fact of the inclusion of Brendan of Birr in the *Annales Cambriae*. In fact Birr became widely known towards the close of the eighth century for a synod held there, apparently in connection with a later phase of this same Easter controversy. It was at Birr that Adamnán of Iona is said to have held the important synod in 639 at which the *Cáin Adamnáin* claims to have been promulgated.[3] The text[4] in which the *Cáin* has been preserved is a composite one, clearly comprising a number of originally distinct documents. Its primary claim is to set forth the freedom of women from the bondage to which they had formerly been subjected by Irish law and custom, and at the close of the enactment (*forus*) of this *Cáin* is subjoined a list of 'the men of Ireland and of Alba' on whom it is said to have been enjoined at Birr. Immediately after the list, however, we are told that all the holy churches of Ireland, together with Adamnán, have besought the unity (*óentaid*) of the godhead of the Father and of the Son and of the Holy Spirit, that whoever fulfils this 'Law' and exacts the necessary claims and levies may be exalted in Heaven and earth. Similar ambitious claims implying unity in the Church of Ireland are made also later in the document, and this and other considerations, notably the names in the list referred to above, and the subsequent history of the Irish Church, have led to the conclusion

[1] For Laisrén see Kenney, 450f. He is thought to have been the principal advocate of the Roman Easter in southern Ireland in his day.

[2] See MacCarthy, *Annals of Ulster*, IV, cxliiff.

[3] For a brief reference to Adamnán's activities in Ireland see Bede, *H.E.* v, xv. The long and bitter Easter controversy has left many obscure traces in addition to much documentary material. To mention one example only, the island of Aran Mór in Galway, though its patron saint is Enda, is dominated by the little church of St Benignus (Benén), on a height visible from far out to sea, while a grave-slab in the churchyard of the same island bears the significant inscription: 'To the VII *Romani*', i.e. perhaps to martyrs who may have perished in the Anglo-Roman controversy.

[4] The *Cáin Adamnáin* was edited and translated by Kuno Meyer, Oxford, 1905.

that this was in reality the synod which finally brought about the acceptance of the Roman Order by the north of Ireland.

His list of names is of great interest, the most striking being those of Adamnán, abbot of Iona, and Bishop Ecgberht of York, the latter the representative of the Anglo-Roman party, and its chief promoter, first in Ireland, and later in Iona. This list, which opens with the abbots and their monasteries, then passes successively to bishops and other ecclesiastics, and finally to kings. The most interesting and significant of the latter is Brude Derile's son, king of the southern Picts in Scotland, whose death is recorded in the *Annals of Ulster* in 706, and whose brother, Nechtan IV, king of the Picts of Angus, wrote the famous letter to Abbot Ceolfrith of Jarrow as a preliminary to joining the Roman Order,[1] and who, according to the same *Annals*, banished the Columban clergy from his kingdom in 717. As Kuno Meyer, the most recent editor of the *Cáin Adamnáin*, observes, it is a most valuable historical document independent of the *Annals*, and contains names of the chief members of the Romanising party among the Gaelic clergy of Ireland and Scotland, including Flann Feblae, the bishop of Armagh, who is known from other sources to have accepted the new Order. It may be added that all the subscribers to this synod, so far as the dates of their deaths are known, were alive in that year.[2] Yet surely the occurrence of the name of Brude Derile's son should be enough in itself to warn us against supposing that the signatories were necessarily present at the synod in person.

Now if we compare the list of religious foundations represented by the obits of their patron saints in the Irish entries in the *Annales Cambriae* with the list of ecclesiastics and the foundations which they represent in the *Cáin Adamnáin* we find in the latter all the foundations represented in the former, and in the same order. The list in the *Cáin* is, of course, very much longer; but apart from its greater length there is no actual discrepancy. Clonferta-Molúa here corresponds to Cummian's list, and occurs in the same relative position. Clonfert-Brenainn is actually mentioned much later in the list, but among the fifteen 'sages' or ecclesiastics who follow the list of abbots and bishops; and there it is merely entered to indicate the place to which the *Faelán* mentioned in the list belongs, and not in its order of precedence.

[1] Bede, *H.E.* v, xxi.
[2] See Kuno Meyer's Introduction to the *Cáin Adamnáin, ed. cit.* p. viii.

For the sake of clarity I give here a list of the corresponding entries in the three documents in the order in which they are there given, but omitting intermediate names in the *Cáin Adamnáin* with which we are not concerned.

Annales Cambriae	*Cummian's Letter* *c.* 632–3	*Cáin Adamnáin*
Benén (468. *Armagh*)	Ailbe ep. (*Emly-Íbair*)	*Armagh*
Íbar (501. *Emly-Íbair*)	Ciarán (*Clonmacnoise*)	*Emly-Íbair*
Ciarán (544. *Clonmacnoise*)	Brendan of ?	*Clonmacnoise*
Brendan (574. *Birr*)	Nessan (*Mungarit*)	*Birr*
Cuimíne Fota (661. *Clonfert* in Galway)	Lugid (*Clonferta-Molúa*)	*Clonferta-Molúa* (*Clonfert Brenainn,* i.e. in Galway).

The absence of Armagh from Cummian's letter is readily accounted for by the time and circumstances in which he was writing. The substitution of Clonfert in Co. Galway in the *Annales* for Clonferta-Molúa in the other lists may be accounted for by the enhanced prestige which the former had attained under its great abbot Cuimíne Fota, who, as we have seen, is almost a hundred years later than the other saints represented in the list. It has also been noted that there is reason to believe that Brendan of Birr and his younger and more famous contemporary Brendan of Clonfert (in Co. Galway) have been to some extent confused in hagiographical tradition, and this may have helped towards the substitution of the more famous Clonfert of Cuimíne for the Clonfert of St Lugid in the older records.

The correspondence between these three lists can be accounted for only in one of two ways. Either the compiler of the *Annales Cambriae* or his source had a copy of the *Cáin Adamnáin* or of Cummian's *Letter to Segene* before him; or he had a copy of a list similar to theirs. The correspondence of the two latter would seem to be too close to be independent, while the substitution in the *Annales Cambriae* of Clonfert in Galway, the church of Cuimíne Fota, for the less well-known Clonferta-Molúa of the two earlier lists, and the substitution also of St Benén for Flann Feblae, abbot of Armagh in Adamnán's list, as well as the omission of Bangor, Co. Down (which figures high in Adamnán's list), all suggest that the Welsh compiler or his immediate source was using and perhaps

55

modifying an earlier list than the latter. There can in any case be little doubt that lists of the principal Irish abbacies, probably in order of precedence and the dates of their foundations, and the sides which they had favoured in the Easter controversy, were in circulation in the Irish scriptoria between the late seventh and the ninth centuries. The drawing up of such a list would be one of the earliest steps in the claim of Armagh to the primacy; but it had in all probability originated at a still earlier date in the south, perhaps in response to the requirements of the see of Rome.

If, as we shall see reason to suspect, the *Annales Cambriae* acquired their present form in Gwynedd, about the time when Bishop Elfoddw was inducing his Church to accept the Roman Order, it is not difficult to understand the importance which these synods, and the burning questions there debated, would have for the compiler. It is not improbable that copies of such enactments as that of Adamnán's synod, with its list of ecclesiastics, would find their way into the scriptorium of Elfoddw's community. This would help to account for the fact that the early entries in the *Annales Cambriae* consist of a number of somewhat curiously selected Irish saints. But the entries themselves were probably not directly copied from such lists. They have probably been selected and derived from some intermediate source, which has itself drawn its material from some such early lists as those which we have been discussing.

It is generally assumed, and on the whole the assumption is probably correct, that the immediate source of the Irish hagiological entries in the *Annales Cambriae* is a lost Irish source on which the earliest Irish annals are based. A comparison of the entries under discussion contained in the *Annales Cambriae* with the dates roughly corresponding in the *Annals of Inisfallen*, of *Ulster*, and of *Tigernach*, shows that all our early Irish entries in the *Annales Cambriae* are also found in these three collections from the time when *Tigernach* begins in 488. Of the three entries before this date in the *Annales Cambriae* the birth of St Brigit occurs in both the *Annals of Inisfallen* (*s.a.* 455) and the *Annals of Ulster* (*s.a.* 452) in identical words: 'Some say Brigit was born.' The correspondence is too close to be fortuitous and makes direct derivation from a common source certain—perhaps not the identical source used by *Annales Cambriae*, since no such qualification is entered there. The entry *s.a.* 457 in the latter, recording the death of Patrick, is not found in the *Annals of Inisfallen*, but an entry occurs *s.a.* 496. On the other hand the earliest entry of all in *Annales Cambriae*, *s.a.* 453, relating to the change in the date of Easter by Pope Leo, bishop of Rome, is absent from the *Annals of Ulster*, but recorded in the *Annals of Inisfallen*. It would seem, therefore, that the exemplar of the lost Irish annals which was used by the *Annales Cambriae* was in all probability a Leinster composition, drawn up after Leinster had accepted the Roman Order, and before the acceptance of the Roman Order and the development of the cult of St Patrick by northern Ireland, i.e. between 632 and 697. Other features, positive and negative, support this hypothesis of a Leinster provenance. We may point to the prominence of Brigit and Columcille on the one hand; and to the absence of reference to north Irish mainland saints, such as Comgall of Bangor and Finnian of Moville on the other. The absence of Finnian of Clonard is also striking. As to the centre of learning which produced these original Irish annals it is impossible to be more precise, though Durrow is not improbable, Kildare not impossible. The importance of our conclusions for our present purpose is that this exemplar was probably not an Ulster composition. Bangor in Co. Down seems to be out of the picture.

Whatever the precise relationship of these Irish entries in the *Annales Cambriae* to such Irish lists as those of Adamnán and Cummian, and to the entries in the lost Irish annals, there can, I think, be little doubt that their inclusion in the *Annales Cambriae* was originally stimulated by the Easter controversy, and directly from southern Ireland. Though the marginal annal numbers of the *Annales Cambriae* begin in A.D. 445 the first entry is *s.a.* 453 which records that Easter is changed 'on the Lord's Day' by Pope Leo, bishop of Rome. Apart from this, and with the exception of the two entries about Arthur *s.a.* 516 and 537, and a reference to a pestilence in Britain and Ireland *s.a.* 537, we have only seven entries for the first hundred years, and all relate to Irish saints—Brigit (birth), Patrick, Benignus, Ebur (Íbar), Columba, again Brigit (death), and Ciarán, in this order. After the opening entry of 453 relating to the changing of the date of Easter by Pope Leo, the only entries relating to the Continent till the eighth century are the record of the conversion of Constantine in 589, and the death of Pope Gregory in 601. There is no entry relating to the Anglo-Saxons till the conversion by Augustine, here entered *s.a.* 595.

There can be no doubt that the eyes of the original compiler were turned westward rather than eastward, and that his chief interests, and his chief sources of information, related to the Irish Church. The nature of these sources, already discussed, and his first entry about Pope Leo and the change of the date of Easter, point to a direct stimulus by the Easter controversy, followed by the acceptance by Ireland *c.* 697 of the Anglo-Roman Order. This conclusion is confirmed by the entry *s.a.* 768: 'Easter is changed among the Britons, Elbodugus, the man of God, correcting it.'[1]

(ii) *The North British Entries*

However one views the immediate impetus which inspired the Irish entries in the *Annales Cambriae*—our classes (1) and (2) as defined on p. 49 above—it is obvious that their relationship to Irish ecclesiastical affairs, as well as to Irish annalistic writings, is very close. We have seen that comparison of the Irish entries in the *Annales Cambriae* with those of the earliest Irish annals (Inisfallen, Ulster, and Tigernach) places it beyond doubt that the majority of these entries are derived from a common source. On the other hand, none of the Irish annals contains any references to the material comprised in our classes (4) and (5)[2] of the *Annales Cambriae*, and virtually nothing of our class (3). These Welsh entries of class (3) cause no difficulty, being of more or less local provenance.[3] But the all-important question is, where could the common source behind the Irish annals have been united with the British annals of classes (4) and (5)?

It is obvious that the source of the entries relating to North Britain must lie in some lost northern annals, relating chiefly to Strathclyde, and to southern Scotland and north-western England. Where and in what milieu could these local annals have been drawn up? If we could find the answer to this question we should be in a position to hazard a fair guess as to where they could have been united with the lost Irish annals by the compilers of the *Annales Cambriae*.

The complete absence of early written records for the British

---

[1] 'Pasca commutatur apud Brittones, emendante Elbodugo homine dei.'

[2] The *Annals of Tigernach* have some obscure references to an Arthur apparently in association with Kintyre; but these appear to be wholly unconnected with the entries in the *Annales Cambriae*.

[3] For St Kentigern cf. p. 298 below.

Church of southern Scotland and northern England has been commonly thought to rule out Cumbria and Strathclyde. Iona, it may be argued, would be in a favourable geographical position for obtaining information relating to the *Gwyr y Gogledd*, of whom the Irish annals know nothing; and moreover Adamnán has given us our earliest information about a historical Arthur, the son of Aedán mac Gabráin, the king of Dálriada contemporary with St Columba, who may be the Arthur referred to in the *Annales Cambriae*, *s.a.* 516, 537, possibly also in two entries in the *Mirabilia*.[1]

In spite of these considerations, however, there are serious difficulties in the way of assigning the annals in question to Iona, of which perhaps the most important is its predominantly Irish and Gaelic interests. Adamnán tells us nothing of the British Church, mentions no British saint. He records a prophecy respecting the death of King Rhydderch, son of Tudwal; and he is aware that he was ruler of Allt Clud or Dumbarton,[2] but he betrays little knowledge of the Strathclyde princes, such as we should expect from a centre which produced the annals relating to the 'Men of the North'. He mentions the name of *Artur*, but betrays no knowledge that it was British, though he records his death in battle among the Miathi.[3] He relates the death of a monk whose name Brito[4] may indicate a British origin; and he mentions a Saxon monk in the monastery, Genere by name.[5] He refers indirectly to the war with Ecgfrith, and to his own visit to his *amicus*, his 'friend' King Aldfrith;[6] and he has a number of stirring stories of the intercourse of Columba with the northern Pictish king Brude on Loch Ness. But apart from these incidents the sphere of his narrative is almost exclusively bounded by Gaelic Scotland, the Inner Hebrides, and Ireland—Ireland most of all.

As no early written records have survived from the North British area, the Isle of Man or North Wales occurs to us as a possible area in which to seek the original centre of the North British annals; but for the Isle of Man we have no records whatever till a much later date, apart from stone inscriptions, which are

---

[1] For some discussion of this question reference may be made to my paper on 'The Lost Literature of Celtic Scotland: Cau of Pritdin and Arthur of Britain' in *Scottish Gaelic Studies*, VII (1953).

[2] *Life of St Columba*, I, c. 15.   [3] *Ibid.* I, c. 9.

[4] *Ibid.* III, c. 6.   [5] *Ibid.* III, c. 10.

[6] *Ibid.* II, c. 46. Aldfrith succeeded his brother Ecgfrith as king in Northumbria in 685.

usually confined to proper names. On the other hand we shall see that at a later period, during the ninth century in particular, Wales has recorded traditions of these northern princes; and in Wales also we find our earliest written references to King Arthur. Yet it would seem very improbable that these northern annals, which concentrate exclusively on British princes of the sixth and seventh centuries outside Wales, on their local contests among themselves, and their warfare against the Northumbrian kings, can have originated in Wales. We have little or no evidence that at so early a period the Welsh of Wales took any interest in northern Britain. We must look to a British source further north than Wales.

There is one early centre of learning in the North which should not be wholly overlooked in this connection. This is Whithorn. I have shown reasons elsewhere[1] for believing that Bede's account of St Ninian's episcopate[2] depends on traditions which are not much earlier than the eighth century; but it is clear from the native writings preserved from Whithorn itself that already in the latter part of the seventh century Whithorn was a centre of learning and culture; and Bishop Pecthelm, Bede's contemporary, had been educated in the Irish foundation at Malmesbury, and was in touch with both Aldhelm and Bede, the two greatest English scholars of his day.[3] The sculptured stones here and at Kirkmadrine in the parish of Kirkmaiden in the Mull of Galloway show that south-western Galloway had been for some time a Celtic ecclesiastical centre.

Moreover, a consistent body of later tradition represents prominent Irish saints of the fifth and sixth centuries as receiving their education at Whithorn, notably St Enda of Aran,[4] St Finnian of Moville,[5] Tigernach of Clones[6] and Eugenius of Ardstraw;[7] but

---

[1] 'St Ninian: a Preliminary Study of Sources', *Transactions and Journal of Proceedings of the Dumfriesshire and Galloway Natural History and Antiquarian Society. Whithorn Volume* (XXVII), 1950, 9 ff.

[2] *H.E.* III, iv.

[3] See W. Levison, 'An Eighth-Century Poem on St Ninian', in *Antiquity*, XIV (1940). Also N. K. Chadwick, *op. cit.* 24 ff.

[4] See the edition of the text of the *Vita* by Charles Plummer, *Vitae Sanctorum Hiberniae*, II (Oxford, 1910), 60 ff.; and for the late date, see *ibid.* I, lxif.

[5] See Plummer, *op. cit.* I, cxxvi. The only text of a Latin life is that of John of Tynemouth of the first half of the fourteenth century, abridged from some text now lost.

[6] See Plummer, *op. cit.* I, lxxxviii; II, 263. For further references, see Kenney, *op. cit.* 386 f.

[7] See Plummer, *op. cit.* I, cxxvi; Kenney, *op. cit.* 400.

most of these traditions are known to us in their present form from a period not earlier than the twelfth century, and their evidence is of extremely doubtful value. Even the earlier tradition recorded by a certain Conchubranus (*c.* 1000–50), the Irish biographer of St Mo-Nenna or Darerca,[1] founder of Killeevy near Armagh, in which it is claimed that 'Chilnecase [i.e. doubtless *Candida Casa*] in Galuueie [Galloway]' was the first of the churches founded in Scotland by this saint, carries back the traditional connection of the early Irish saints with Whithorn no further than to the tenth century, though it may possibly be derived from an earlier text.[2]

Whithorn is also represented as a centre of learning in a brief satirical narrative recorded as a preamble to the so-called *Hymn of Mugint*, a prayer in rhythmical prose, beginning 'Parce, Domine', contained in the *Liber Hymnorum*.[3] Abbot Mugint of Whithorn has 'books for copying', and hither not only Irish scholars such as Finnian of Moville, 'along with Rioc and Talmach and several others' resort, but Drusticc, the daughter of Drust the 'king of the Britons'—perhaps of Strathclyde—is also sent here to be taught reading. The period in which this humorous little story is set is the early sixth century;[4] and the story is interesting for its tradition of Whithorn as a famous monastery and school of learning. Indeed its position across the narrow seas from Bangor, Co. Down, would lead us to expect no less. It should be added that in the lists of mothers of saints preserved in the *Book of Leinster*, fo. 373a, Drustic (*Dustric*) figures as the mother of Lonán of Treoit, Talmach's son, whose name appears in the entry for November 1 in the *Martyrology of Oengus the Culdee*. In the notes to this contained in MS. Rawlinson (1), which is the best text, we read: 'Lonán, son of Talmach from Treoit in Bregia', i.e. in Ireland; but the Talmach here referred to is doubtless the pupil of Mugint referred to above and was so identified by the author of the notes

---

[1] See the text of the *Vita* and the Preface by M. Esposito, 'Conchubrani Vita Sanctae Monennae', in *Proceedings of the Royal Irish Academy*, XXVIII, section C, no. 12 (1910), 233. For *Moninne*, i.e. *Darerca*, and her pedigree, see the *Martyrology of Oengus*, edited and translated by Whitley Stokes (The Henry Bradshaw Society, XXIX, London, 1905), entry *sub* 6 July, p. 161, and notes, p. 166.   [2] See Esposito, *loc. cit.*

[3] Edited and translated by Bernard and Atkinson (London, 1897), I, 23; II, 112f. Cf. A. O. Anderson, *Early Sources of Scottish History*, I, 7ff.

[4] See Anderson, *loc. cit.* Drust is the name of a Pictish king. See Chadwick, *Early Scotland* (Cambridge, 1949), 12.

to the entry for 1 November of the Rawlinson (2) text of the *Martyrology*.[1]

A still earlier, though somewhat obscure tradition, would seem to represent monasticism as first introduced into Ireland by St Cairnech,[2] perhaps identical or confused with Cairnech, son of Saran, 'king of Britain',[3] i.e. it would seem of the British-speaking area in south-western Scotland which contained Whithorn.[4] Saran was succeeded by his son Lurig, and his other son Cairnech, Lurig's brother, was apparently the traditional ruler of a monastery at Whithorn. Cairnech belonged to the obscure period between St Patrick and the saints of the sixth century, and in the Irish story known as the *Aided Muirchertaig maic Erca* he and his brother Lurig are associated with the Irish high king Muirchertach mac Erca (†534 or 536).[5] In the Preface to the *Senchus Mór* Cairnech is associated with Patrick and Benignus in the revision of the Irish laws. In the version of the *Aided*, edited and translated by Skene from the *Book of Ballymote*, Cairnech is said to have been a bishop of 'Martin's House', and though this is said to have been at Tours, the 'Martin's House' at Whithorn is undoubtedly the original monastery to which the tradition has reference.[6]

The geographical position of Whithorn, no less than its ecclesiastical tradition, might seem to favour the suggestion that the original annals of the 'Men of the North' may have been compiled here. Unlike Iona, it is in an area which within historical times has been British rather than Gaelic. It is not far from Dunragit, which

[1] See *The Calendar of Oengus*, edited and translated by Whitley Stokes (London, 1905), 233, 239. See further the entry for November 1 in the *Martyrology of Donegal* (edited by Todd and Reeves, Dublin, 1864).

[2] See Kenney, *op. cit.* 180. St Cairnech was identified with St Carantoc at an early date.

[3] See Kenney, *op. cit.* 352f.

[4] The pedigree of one Saran is given in the notes to the *Martyrology of Oengus the Culdee*, February 11, p. 73 (edited and translated by Whitley Stokes, *Transactions of the Royal Irish Academy*, Dublin, 1880). See also Stokes's later edition, *The Martyrology of Oengus* (The Henry Bradshaw Society, XXIX, London, 1905), 73.

[5] The Irish text of the story of Saran and Lurig is contained in the *Book of Ballymote*, edited by Robert Atkinson and published for the Royal Irish Academy (Dublin, 1887). It was earlier edited and translated by Skene in his *Chronicles of the Picts and Scots* (Edinburgh, 1867), 52ff. Another text from the *Yellow Book of Lecan* and MS. H. 2. 7 in Trinity College, Dublin, was also edited by Whitley Stokes, *Revue Celtique*, XXIII (1902), 395f. Cf. further Kenney, *op. cit.* 351f.; A. O. Anderson, *Sources*, II, 4.

[6] See Skene, *Celtic Scotland*, II (Edinburgh, 1887), 46.

according to the *Martyrology of Oengus*[1] was the home of St Colmán Duib Chuilind. Colmán was associated, according to the same source, with St Comgall of Bangor, through whose virtue he was miraculously conceived from ink (see below, note 1), surely another hint of the traditional connection between the learning of Bangor, Co. Down, and that of the Rinns of Galloway. South-western Scotland was under the British rule of the royal house of Dumbarton, the descendants of Dyfnwal Hen.[2] On the other hand the second element of *Dunragit* has been thought to contain the same element as *Rheged*,[3] the name of the important though vaguely defined kingdom of Urien, the most powerful of the princes of southern Scotland and north-western England who seems to have lived in the latter part of the sixth century.

The centre of the kingdom of Rheged is generally believed to have been Carlisle,[4] and this is, I believe, a sound conclusion; but *Dunragit*[5] may have been a western outpost fortress of the kingdom, which seems to have consisted of the lands bordering the Solway. If so we may suppose both Galloway and Whithorn to have been within the sphere of influence of this descendant of both Dyfnwal Hen and Coel Hen, and the centre which would naturally be concerned to record in writing the traditions of these two great British dynastic families of southern Scotland, the 'Men of the North'. This is the area to which the 'poet' Llywarch Hen is believed to have belonged (cf. pp. 88 f. below); and we shall see the

[1] Entry for November 24. '*Colmán Duib Cuilinn*, i.e. black Colmán from Cuilenn', to which the notes in the text Rawlinson (1) adds, 'i.e. a mountain which is at Belach Conglais in Leinster'. Another text (Louvain F) adds: 'Colman of the ink (*duib*) of Cuilenn in the Renna [i.e. the Rinns of Galloway], i.e. from Dún Rechet; and from Belach Conglais in Leinster; and from other places. Congall of Bangor went to the house of Colmán duib Chuilinn's father, who had a barren wife. Then the cleric asks writing-ink of the barren wife. It is given (and she tastes it). Thereof Colmán is conceived. Hence he was called Colmán son of the ink of Cuilenn.' (*The Martyrology of Oengus the Culdee, ed. cit.* 246 f.)

[2] See the Harleian pedigrees 5, 6 and 7.

[3] The same element is conjectured to lie in the early form of *Rochdale*, which appears in *Domesday Book* as *Reced ham*. Rochdale may have been within the southern boundary of Urien's kingdom.

[4] See Sir John Morris Jones, 'Taliesin', *Y Cymmrodor*, XXVIII (1918), 67. This identification is generally accepted and receives strong confirmation from Sir Ifor Williams, *Wales and the North* (Kendal, 1952), 83 f. Cf., however, John MacQueen, 'Yvain, Ewen and Owein ap Urien', in the *Transactions of the Dumfriesshire and Galloway Natural History and Antiquarian Society*, XXXIII (1956), 110 f.

[5] For the suggested etymological connection see W. J. Watson, *History of the Celtic Place-names of Scotland* (Edinburgh, 1926), 156.

North Welsh dynasty of Merfyn Vrych and Rhodri Mawr in the ninth century claiming descent from him. If, therefore, the early northern annals which we have been considering were composed in the same area, at some centre such as Whithorn, it would not be difficult to see their special interest for this North Welsh dynasty,[1] and the means by which they came to be incorporated in the documents contained in Harleian 3859.

There are possible alternatives to Whithorn as the home of the northern annals. One of these is Hoddom in Dumfriesshire, today the beautiful little site of an early church, probably dating from c. 700, on the banks of the River Annan, near Ecclefechan. Hoddom is only some four miles north of the little town of Annan, which lies by the northern shore of the Solway. Annan is close to the Border and only about seventeen miles from Carlisle, and thirteen from Longtown, the latter the probable site of the battle of Arthuret, near Carwinelow, or *Caer Gwendoleu*, in the heart of our North British area and its princes. Here tradition placed the earliest seat of St Kentigern, the founder of the British Church of Strathclyde, before his consecration to the episcopal church of Glasgow under his friend and patron, Rhydderch Hen (Hael), the most illustrious of the descendants of the princes of the Dumbarton line, descended from Dyfnwal Hen. At the same time it is important to remember that, according to the fragmentary anonymous and earliest *Life of St Kentigern*,[2] the saint was a son of Owen (*Ewen*), son of Urien (*Erwegende, Ulien*)[3] of Rheged, in whose territory Hoddom almost certainly lies; and tradition represents the saint as treated with bitter hostility by a certain Morken, who is apparently a ruler in this region, and quite probably the Morcant referred to in the *Historia Brittonum* (c. 63) as having caused the murder of Urien from envy of his prowess and prestige.

[1] It is not impossible that the dynasty may have been dislodged and driven south by the westward expansion of the Anglians of Northumbria, in the seventh or eighth century.

[2] The text and translation of this version of the *Vita*, together with the—probably slightly later—*Vita* by Joceline of Furness, has been published by A. P. Forbes, *Lives of St Ninian and St Kentigern* (Edinburgh, 1874). Both are believed to have been compiled in the twelfth century from older material. For an exhaustive study of the sources for these *Vitae*, see the article by Prof. K. Jackson, pp. 273 ff. below.

[3] The earlier form of the name *Urien* was *Urbgen*, an older form of which appears in the Chartres text of the *Historia Brittonum* as *Urbagen*. See Sir Ifor Williams, *Bulletin of the Board of Celtic Studies*, VII (1935), 388. Cf. p. 284 below.

The hostility between Kentigern and Morcant would seem to take on the aspect of a blood feud. If it could be shown that any tradition of writing or of learning was attached to Hoddom it would be a natural place to which to look for the annals of our northern kingdoms, certainly more natural than Whithorn, of which the external associations, at least from the sixth century, would seem to be predominantly Irish. We have at Hoddom the foundations of a church of *c*. 700, and a number of fine crosses, some probably dating from *c*. 750,[1] and the series shows that an Anglian monastery survived here throughout the Danish period. We also have the top of a staff (or crozier shrine) from near Hoddom, probably dating from the tenth century, and its preservation in association with a church of the twelfth century would suggest an earlier bishopric. Nevertheless we have no certain evidence of any kind for its Celtic origin, and no written records have been preserved, no traditions of a scriptorium.[2] The puzzle remains, and Kentigern's later foundation, the church of Glasgow, throws no light on it. We must not lose sight of the fact that the important kingdom of Strathclyde was Christian, and must have had a Christian centre, and that the tradition incorporated in the *Life of St Kentigern*, late though this is, would favour a site at or near Rhydderch's capital at Dumbarton. Glasgow must surely have been a sacred site long before the revived bishopric was established there and a cathedral built in the twelfth century. Yet we have, in fact, no early traditions of Glasgow as a place of learning, and apparently no references to it under this name before 1122.[3]

4. INTERNAL EVIDENCE OF THE 'HISTORIA' AND THE 'ANNALS'

In view of the absence of external evidence which might throw light on the provenance of our northern annals of seventh-century date, let us turn to examine more closely the nature of their content, to see if any light is shed on our problem by their internal evidence. Extracts from these annals have been incorporated, as

[1] See the article on 'Hoddom' by C. A. Ralegh Radford in the *Transactions of the Dumfriesshire and Galloway Natural History and Antiquarian Society* (Third Series, vol. XXXI, 1954), 174 ff.

[2] For further cogent reasons against the Celtic origin of Hoddom, and against its early association with St Kentigern, see the article by K. Jackson, p. 320 below.

[3] See W. J. Watson, *History of the Celtic Place-Names of Scotland* (Edinburgh, 1926), 388.

we have seen, in both the *Historia Brittonum* and the *Annales Cambriae*, and they are, in addition, implicit in the genealogies of both the Jesus and the Harleian versions, while they form the exclusive content of the Hengwrt collection. Leaving aside the difficult and admittedly unsolved problem of Arthur, let us first turn to the notices relating to the *Gwyr y Gogledd* 'Men of the North' in the *Annales Cambriae*. It will be noticed that these constitute most of the references to Britain between the years 650 and 750, but in fact they begin in 574 and continue for more than two centuries. Those relating to the sixth and early seventh centuries relate to people and events celebrated in British heroic poetry, such as for example 574, the Battle of Armterid (Arderydd); 581, the death of Gwrgi and Peredur; 596, the death of King Dunawd. In 612 the death of St Kentigern is recorded (cf. pp. 58, 298). These point to the existence of written records among the North British of Cumbria or Strathclyde which can hardly be later than the seventh century; otherwise we might have expected to find traces of them in the Irish Annals.

Moreover, the personnel of these entries can be shown on the evidence of the genealogies of the 'Men of the North' (cf. p. 49) to be contemporary with Rhydderch Hael and Urbgen, who can be confidently ascribed to this period on the evidence of Adamnán and of Northumbrian history respectively. The absence of Rhydderch from the *Annales* is remarkable and perhaps not without significance, especially since the death of his patron saint, Kentigern, is entered, while his own pedigree and that of a collateral branch of the Strathclyde princes are given among the Harleian lines. The absence of an entry of his obit in the *Annales* would seem to be a hint that the interest of the compiler did not centre on Strathclyde but rather south on Cumbria. This conclusion would seem to be strengthened by the fact that we know from other early evidence that the nature of Rhydderch's death formed the material of an important saga. Annals and genealogies alike are interested in Cumbria rather than Strathclyde.

At this point the evidence of the genealogies is helpful. It is clear that their position in MS. Harleian 3859 immediately after the *Annales Cambriae* is not fortuitous. They fall almost entirely into two groups, first those relating to the family of the princes of Gwynedd and their wives, including their ancestors and descendants; and secondly those relating to the 'Men of the North'. It is particularly this last group which has manifestly been selected by the compiler of the Harleian compilation in close association with the contents of the *Annales Cambriae* and also with the *Historia Brittonum*. By the juxtaposition of these documents the compiler of the Harleian corpus evidently had a definite end in view. First let us look at the northern genealogies to see what light they may throw on the origin of our northern entries in the *Annales*.

The genealogies in question are nos. 5–12, which follow immediately on the genealogy of the princes of Strathclyde, and no. 19, which is a collateral line of no. 11, the missing names of which, earlier than Pappo Post Priten, can be supplied from Hengwrt MS. 536.[1] Of these Harleian genealogies nos. 11 and 12 are the genealogies of Dunaut, and of Gwrgi and Peredur, whose deaths are entered *s.a.* 596 and 581 in the *Annales Cambriae*. The names of Riderch, Urbgen, Guallauc, and Morcant, at the head of genealogies 6, 8, 9, and 10 respectively, are also the names of the four kings in the *Historia Brittonum*, c. 63, who fought against Hussa, apparently king of the Bernicians. The names are the same, and also, with one exception, the order, which may be significant. In the genealogies Rhydderch precedes Urbgen, probably because his genealogy is connected with the preceding one (no. 5), which is also a Strathclyde line. The *Historia Brittonum* may well have placed Urbgen first in the list with a view to the high prestige which this work accords to him, both in this chapter and elsewhere (cf. p. 71). Hengwrt genealogies and the poems agree in applying to Rhydderch the epithet *hael*, 'generous', in contrast to the epithet *hen*, 'the old', applied to him in the *Historia*. The close connection between the genealogies of the 'Men of the North' in Harleian 3859 on the one hand, and the *Annales Cambriae* and the *Historia Brittonum* on the other, becomes even more striking in view of the wide divergences between the two latter texts and the Hengwrt genealogies.[2]

We are now in a better position to form some idea as to where and when our lost northern annals took shape. We have seen that such evidence as we have perhaps favours Cumbria rather than

[1] Skene, *Four Ancient Books of Wales*, II (Edinburgh, 1868), 454; J. Loth, *Les Mabinogion*, II (Paris, 1913), 348.
[2] For a detailed comparison the reader may be referred to Chadwick, *Growth of Literature*, I, 151.

Strathclyde, and that the contents of these annals relate to heroes and events of the sixth century. It follows that our annals were almost certainly drawn up in the seventh century and probably, though less certainly, in Cumbria.

There are other considerations also which point to the seventh century as the period when our northern annals took shape. In the early part of the seventh century the Irish annals contain references to Britain which could not have come from English sources, but which the Irish annals have obtained from an Irish chronicle written not later than the opening years of the eighth century. They offer evidence for written records in Britain during the seventh century, and it can be shown that some of the entries in the *Annales Cambriae* cannot be later. An example is the account of the Battle of Chester, which has found its way into both Irish sources[1] and Bede,[2] and which is believed to be derived from British (Welsh) oral sources through a written intermediary, at least in so far as Bede is concerned.[3] Other examples could also be cited.[4]

At this point it is relevant to turn to the North British material at the close of the *Historia Brittonum*, to which reference has already been made.[5] It is now generally agreed that part of the material in the *Historia*, more especially c. 57–65, is a Cumbrian composition into which the Anglian genealogies have been interpolated. Here it occurs in two manuscripts only, viz. Harleian 3859 and one closely allied text (B.M. Cott. Vespasian, D. XXI), the latter ascribed to the twelfth century. It is chiefly on the ground of such northern matter in the oldest part of the *Historia* that some scholars, including F. Lot, would claim that the author of the *Historia* is not a Welshman but a Briton of Cumbria or Strathclyde.[6] The tract is usually ascribed to the seventh

[1] See *The Annals of Tigernach*, edited and translated by Whitley Stokes, *Revue Celtique*, XVII, 171.   [2] *H.E.* II, ii.
[3] See my additional chapter in H. M. Chadwick, *The Study of Anglo-Saxon*[2] (Cambridge, 1955), 82 f.; and cf. K. H. Jackson, *Language and History in Early Britain*, 55 n.   [4] See Chadwick, *Growth of Literature*, I, 148.
[5] See further K. Jackson, 'The Britons of Southern Scotland,' *Antiquity*, XXIX (1955).
[6] *Nennius et l'Historia Brittonum* (Paris, 1934), pp. 79 f. Lot's conclusion, it should be added, is based also partly on the northern location which he attributes to Arthur's battles—an argument which is not admissible, since the locality of these battles is, in reality, virtually unknown. Somewhat earlier Max Förster discussed the possibility that Nennius was an Irishman, but came to a negative conclusion. See his article 'War Nennius ein Ire?', *Heinrich-Finke Festschrift* (Marburg, 1925), 25–44.

century,[1] but the orthography of the English names appears to be that of the eighth century.[2] On the grounds of the selection of the royal houses represented in the pedigrees K. Sisam concludes that the genealogical tables of the Anglo-Saxon dynasties were incorporated into the *Historia Brittonum* at the end of the eighth or the beginning of the ninth century—which is the period of Nennius's activity.[3]

This northern document follows immediately on the account of Arthur. It consists (c. 57–61) of the genealogies of the Anglian royal houses, beginning with Ida (547–59), the founder of Bernicia, but excluding Lindsey and Wessex, and here and there the genealogies are expanded by the addition of notes on the persons recorded, for example the brief account of Ida's great-grandson Ecgfrith and his warfare against his cousin, the Pictish king Birdei at the 'battle of Lin Garan' which we know from Bede[4] to have been Nechtanesmere near Forfar. In c. 62 we have an isolated statement that Dutigern fought bravely against the Angles. Dutigern, or, better, Outigern,[5] is unknown elsewhere; but he was apparently one of the North British princes, for his name occurs on Harleian geneal. 10 (that of Morcant), as one of the ancestors of Coel Hen, which at least suggests that he belonged to the North, as do also Aneirin and Taliesin, and probably the three other British poets mentioned in the same chapter.

The northern concentration of the compiler of the *Historia Brittonum*, and his immediate concern with the interests of Gwynedd, seem to me best to account for the totally irrelevant introduction at this point of the name of Mailcunus (i.e. Maelgwn) as ruling in Gwynedd, and the account of the arrival of his ancestor, Cunedag, together with his eight sons from Manau Guotodin in the North. Then, in c. 63, we are back among the descendants and successors of Ida. Here we are told of one Hussa

[1] A passage in the Corpus text (c. 63) in which Nennius refers to Bishops Renchidus and Elbobdus as his teachers would also seem to suggest that this Northumbrian text came into Welsh hands before the death of Elfoddw, bishop of Bangor.

[2] See H. M. Chadwick, *Origin of the English Nation*, 44. Chadwick evidently regarded the account of the Saxon invasion as having come from the same source as the Anglian genealogies (*ibid.* 42–4).

[3] 'Anglo-Saxon Royal Genealogies', *Proceedings of the British Academy*, XXXIX (1953), 294; cf. 328. [4] *H.E.* IV, xxvi.

[5] For *Outigern* see the note by Sir Ifor Williams, *Bulletin of the Board of Celtic Studies*, VII (1935), 387f.

who seems to have been fifth in succession from Ida,[1] and against whom fought four kings (*reges*), who are apparently located in south-western Scotland and north-western England, for they include Riderc Hen and Urbgen and Guallauc and Morcant; and we are told of their siege of Lindisfarne, here given its British name *Metcaud*, and of the murder of Urbgen, here attributed to Morcant out of envy of his great prowess. From here to c. 65 the narrative is concerned with the history of the kingdoms of Bernicia and Deira, and their relations with Mercia, and concludes with the death of Penda (†655). Lot is emphatic that c. 63–5 are based fundamentally on Bede; and points to such items as the etymology of the name Bamborough; the story of the conversion of King Edwin of Northumbria and of his daughter Eanfled by Bishop Paulinus,[2] the contest between Oswald and Cadwallon, the victory of Penda, the recognition of Oswald as a *saint*; an expedition of Oswy against the town of Iudeu and his victory over Penda; the death of Ecgfrith and of St Cuthbert. In addition use is made, according to Lot, of North British heroic poems of the sixth and seventh centuries, and there can, I think, be little doubt that many of the picturesque details of the narrative[3] and the static epithets are of this origin. But we must not suppose that the compiler of the *Historia* was himself responsible for the task of welding these North British and Saxon elements. The entire conduct of the narrative rather suggests that the *Historia Brittonum* has incorporated an earlier set of annals in which the fusion had already taken place.

This is especially important in regard to the northern personal and place-names, of which there is a comparatively high proportion in these sections of the *Historia Brittonum*, and which are all British—and can only have come from a British source.[4] Instances are the epithet *Flesaur* applied to Æthelfrith, Ida's grandson

---

[1] For the chronology, see P. Hunter Blair, 'The Moore Memoranda on Northumbrian History', in *The Early Cultures of North-Western Europe* (Cambridge, 1950), 245 ff. See also F. Lot, *op. cit.* 74, n. 1.

[2] For references to various views on the source of this latter section, see Lot, *op. cit.* p. 72, n. 6.

[3] See, e.g., Lot, *op. cit.* 76 f.

[4] A possible exception is *Lin Garan*. *Lin Garan* may be Pictish; but this has probably passed through a British intermediary and though there is no reason in the actual form of the name to suggest this, it came in all probability from the same British source as the rest. On these British names see K. H. Jackson, 'The Britons in Southern Scotland', *Antiquity*, XXIX (1955), 77 ff.

(c. 57, 63); *Metcaud*, 'Holy Island', *Din Guaroy*, *Meicen*; and names of battles, e.g. *Catscaul* (c. 64), *strages Gai campi*, *Cocboy* (*ibid.*). Other references, such as that to the *Atbret Iudeu*, the 'Restoration of Iudeu', cannot have been derived directly from Bede. It has come through a British intermediary. The notice of the expulsion of Cerdic from Elmet in West Yorkshire must be derived from British sources, doubtless written.[1]

Internal evidence suggests that our text is derived from Cumbrian annals originally compiled in the seventh century, though some of the pedigrees continue into the eighth century. We have no reference to the *Adventus Saxonum*, and the English kings are not traced to the invaders, but might, from all we are told, be traced to native British stock. The British 'kings' appear not as fugitives, but as aggressors. The *Historia* narrative ends with Penda, and although the Mercian genealogy is prolonged to Offa (†796), Penda's son Wulfhere is not mentioned. The last battle recorded is that of Lin Garan, which was fought at Nechtanesmere near Forfar in 685 and in which Ecgfrith met his death. This is clearly a matter of importance and even jubilation to the annalist, for he tells us that with Ecgfrith fell all the strength of his army, and the Picts with their king remained victorious; and never again did the Saxons venture to levy tribute from the Picts from the time of that battle; and it is called *Gueith* ('the action') *Lin Garan* (c. 57). In a later section (c. 65) the annalist again says of Ecgfrith: 'It is he who made war against the Picts and perished there.'

We have already seen reason to believe that the so-called *Annales Cambriae*, which were probably compiled in their present form in the reign of Rhodri Mawr, have made use of a Cumbrian or Strathclyde document dating from the seventh century not known to us from any other source; and we have also seen that we are without clue as to the intellectual centre from which such a document could be derived. We now find ourselves in a similar position in regard to the document which has been incorporated into the closing chapters of the *Historia Brittonum*, and which broadly speaking would seem to have originated in the same area and the same period. The greatest hero in this last section is Urien, whose attack on *Metcaud* (Lindisfarne) is dwelt on, and his murder by the instrumentality of Morcant stated, and also Morcant's motive, which is here given as envy, 'because in him was above all

[1] Lot, *op. cit.* 77.

71

the other kings the greatest strength in the prosecution of warfare'. This looks like a derivation from heroic poetry; but it is an entry made by a partisan. In the elegy on Urien (cf. p. 88 below), which purports to be the work of his cousin Llywarch Hen, a different tradition is recorded, for here it would seem that he was slain in fair fight by a faction headed by Morcant and Pabo Post Prydein, though the panegyrist claims nevertheless that the attack of Morcant is merely that of 'a mouse scratching on a rock'.

The elegy has all the marks of a genuine piece of heroic tradition. Who, one wonders, has been interested, and who has had the education necessary to record the death of Urien and attribute it to treachery? Who has been interested to depart from the tradition of the elegy that he was slain in battle?

In all the principal texts of the *Historia* except Chartres we are told shortly after the passage on the death of Urien that King Edwin and his daughter and all her followers, and twelve thousand people, were baptised with the king; and we are told moreover that the person who baptised them was Rum map Urbgen. The Harleian and the Vatican texts leave it at that, whereas the other manuscripts add that this Rum was identical with Paulinus, bishop of York. We may perhaps dismiss this as a conjecture based on the writer's information from Bede that Edwin was, in fact, baptised by Paulinus of York; and it is important to note that the *Annales Cambriae* A. also record (*s.a.* 626) the baptism of Edwin by Rhun son of Urien in words which almost repeat those of the *Historia Brittonum*. Rum map Urbgen, then, according to the tradition recorded in these early versions of the *Historia*, must have been in holy orders. Is Rhun the author of our basic northern annals, and does this account for the annalist's unwillingness to admit that Urbgen could be overcome save by treachery? Does this account for the writer's statement that it was Rhun who baptised Edwin? We recall the heading of the Chartres text, which would seem to be best explained on the assumption that the son of Urien there referred to is Rhun, and that he was a man in orders, with access to books, at least claiming access to a *Liber Sancti Germani*. We have seen that the author of our closing annals had access to Bede, and other books.

But again, where did he write? There must have been some important ecclesiastical site on or near the Roman road running north from Ribchester through Carlisle into Scotland with the

Bewcastle Cross to the east of it, and the Ruthwell Cross to the west. Again one thinks of Hoddom, less because of its twelfth-century association with St Kentigern, than because of its wealth of stone crosses from the eighth century onwards; but this is slender evidence, and would argue equally strongly in favour of Whithorn, where also we have a wealth of much earlier crosses, and where, in addition, a tradition of a scriptorium has survived, with 'books for the purpose of copying'. On the whole somewhere in the neighbourhood of the head of the Solway would seem to be the more likely.

In the absence of better evidence elsewhere my mind dwells on Carlisle. Even as late as the seventh century, on the testimony of the anonymous monk of Lindisfarne, who may well have known Old Melrose, we learn of the splendid Roman structures still proudly displayed to visitors in this Roman city, where in 685 Ecgfrith's queen awaited the issue of the battle of Nechtanesmere (the *Lin Garan* of Nennius), and where St Cuthbert and his priests and deacons joined her, and passed the time 'looking at the city wall and the well formerly built in a wonderful manner by the Romans, as Waga the reeve of the city, who was conducting them, explained[1].'

This was the most important Roman centre in north-western England, and in the area which we think of as Rheged. Its culture in all probability had an unbroken history from Roman times, and its Christianity may also have had an unbroken record. Hints are not lacking in the life and writing of St Patrick that Roman culture and tradition and Latin education still lingered in south-western Scotland; and the technique of stone sculpture in western Britain, including the Solway area, is more likely to be a survival than an innovation. To me, despite the absence of early[2] ecclesiastical evidence, Carlisle seems the most likely centre at which the earliest records of Cumbria might have been written. If we might believe that the writer was indeed Rhun, son of Urbgen, and himself in orders, his father's city, Carlisle, would seem the most likely place in which to seek him. But this is, alas, at best a mere conjecture.

[1] *Anonymous Life of St Cuthbert*, c. VIII (B. Colgrave, *Two Lives of Saint Cuthbert* (Cambridge, 1940), 122, 123).
[2] See, however, the note on p. 120 below.

5. MS. HARLEIAN 3859 AND THE GENEALOGIES

Let us now return to a further consideration of the earliest document in which the so-called *Annales Cambriae* are incorporated. This is the collection contained in the British Museum MS. Harleian 3859. The MS. itself seems to have been written *c.* 1100 or *c.* 1110,[1] but the compilation appears to have acquired its present form in the time of Owen, son of Hywel Dda, about the middle of the tenth century; and there are good reasons for believing that its various contents were collected in the time of Hywel's grandfather, Rhodri Mawr, ruler of Gwynedd, who died in 877. The collection is, indeed, a historical document in its own right, for, as we have seen, the contents bear a certain relationship to one another. To recapitulate briefly, these contents are a text of Nennius's *Historia Brittonum*; the *Annales Cambriae*; some twenty-five genealogies of Welsh princes, beginning with those of Owen's father Hywel Dda and his mother Elen, daughter of Loumarch (Llywarch), son of Himeit (Hyfaidd) Hen, ruler of Dyfed; a list of *Mirabilia Britanniae*, two of which relate to King Arthur; and a few other texts with which we are not here directly concerned. We have seen that in all three of the principal texts (the *Historia Brittonum*, the *Annales Cambriae*, and the pedigrees) the northern heroes figure prominently, and in the first two King Arthur[2] also —in addition to the references to him in the *Mirabilia*. Here, then, in this collection, we have an extension of, and an emphasis on those elements (4) and (5) (pp. 49, 58 above) of the *Annales Cambriae* which are absent from the Irish annals. It is generally agreed, and indeed it is obvious, that the genealogies, the *Annales Cambriae*, and the *Historia Brittonum* in its present form, are closely related, and their relationship has been demonstrated with especial clarity in regard to the northern heroes. There can be no doubt that they have been brought together of set purpose by the original compiler of our collection—this purpose being to emphasise North British interests and traditions. The same purpose is a marked feature of the selection and assembling of the original contents of MS. Harleian 3859 as a whole.

[1] So Sir Ifor Williams, Introduction to *The Saga of Llywarch the Old*, by Glyn Jones and T. J. Morgan (London, 1955), 7; cf. also p. 39 above.

[2] It has already been mentioned (p. 47 above) that an *Arthur* figures on the Dyfed pedigree (of Elen, Owen's mother). Computing thirty years to a generation would give him a date *c.* 590; but such a date is, of course, very elastic.

When was this collection originally drawn up? Again the pedigrees come to our help. They fall for the most part into two groups, those relating to the 'Men of the North', which we have already considered; and those relating to the family of Rhodri the Great, including the pedigrees relating to his wives, and to some contemporary Welsh dynasties with which we are not immediately concerned, but which are probably ultimately connected with the latter. Now we have seen that in its present form the evidence of the pedigrees in MS. Harleian 3859 points to the lifetime of Owen, son of Hywel Dda. It seems clear, however, that they were originally drawn up much earlier.

Of the genealogies in Harleian only two (that of Owen, son of Hywel Dda, and perhaps that of the family of Dunoding) come down to the tenth century, and the contemporary kings of Gwynedd are lacking. The reason for the insertion of Owen's line has already been given. Of the rest at least seven end in the ninth century, and others at an earlier date, while the genealogy of the paternal ancestry of Merfyn Vrych is omitted. The later MS. of the genealogies contained in Jesus College, Oxford, MS. xx, would seem to offer both a more reliable guide and in some cases a better and earlier reading[1] than the pedigrees in Harleian; and though Jesus xx contains a number of later genealogies than Harleian, those which correspond to the longer Harleian genealogies do not come down to a later date. In this Jesus text the pedigrees focus, not on Owen, or Hywel, both South Welsh princes, but on Owen's great-grandfather, Rhodri Mawr, ruler of Gwynedd or North Wales from 844–77.

In these Jesus genealogies four lines of Rhodri's ancestry are given, and also a list of his sons and the genealogy of his wife Angharad, whose name here (Jesus pedigree 21) corresponds to that of her brother Gwgon the king of Cardigan in Harleian 3859 (pedigree 26). Jesus also gives some important additions. While pedigree 4 in Harleian 3859 ends (c. 750) with a man's name [I]udgual, the name of a woman Celenion occurs in this position in Jesus xx, 19, and the pedigree is continued through four succeeding generations to Rhodri (Elidyr,[2] Guriat, Merfyn, Rhodri). Thus it is one of Rhodri's paternal lines of ancestry, only joining the line recorded in Harleian 3859 at his great-great-grandmother. Further, Rhodri's direct line of paternal ancestry, omitted in Harleian, is

---

[1] Cf. p. 49 above. [2] Is this a family name? Cf. pp. 79, 120 below.

recorded in Jesus, pedigree 17, back through Llywarch Hen to Coel Hen. Most curious is the truncated pedigree Harleian 22 which in Jesus xx, no. 18 is extended at both ends, and constitutes the important pedigree of Rhodri's mother Nest and the royal line of Powys, back to the great Vortigern (Gwrtheyrn Gwrthenau), whose name is omitted in the Harleian pedigree. The other long pedigrees in Jesus MS. xx are those of princes contemporary with Rhodri. There can indeed be no doubt that the common source of the Harleian and Jesus pedigrees was drawn up in Rhodri's reign.

It will be noticed that the Jesus pedigree of Rhodri's mother Nest tacitly accepts the Powys royal pedigree of Eliseg's pillar, set up by King Concenn himself, in flat contradiction to the counter-claim of the *Historia* that the royal line of Powys was of servile origin. The reason for this omission in the Harleian pedigree is not easy to see; but it is surely deliberate, and directly connected with the report of the *Historia*. Is it a piece of editing on the part of the South Welsh princes to support their seizure of Powys on Rhodri's death by discrediting his mother's ancestry? It is surely significant that they also omit his paternal line, whereas Jesus, as we have seen, includes it (no. 17). It is difficult to avoid a suspicion that the Harleian pedigrees have been tampered with in the interests of the South Welsh princes, whereas the 'earlier edition', as we may regard the Jesus pedigrees, recognises both Rhodri's paternal ancestry back to the great lines of the 'Men of the North', through Llywarch Hen to Coel Hen; and his maternal ancestry through the royal line of Powys to the great Vortigern, who—so Concenn, i.e. Cyngen, claimed, on the pillar-cross which he set up to his grandfather Eliseg—had married a daughter of 'King Maximus, who killed the king of the Romans'.[1] The claims represented by Concenn and the Jesus pedigrees might almost seem to suggest a proud boast of Roman sanction and tradition for the dynasty of Rhodri.

It remains to consider briefly another and quite a different type of tradition relating to North Britain. Hitherto we have concentrated on those which have been collected in written form in an

---

[1] For the cross-shaft and its inscription, together with an English translation and pictures, see V. E. Nash-Williams, *The Early Christian Monuments of Wales* (Cardiff, 1950), 123 f. See also A. W. Wade-Evans, *Nennius's History of the Britons*, 32 f.

antiquarian milieu and which have come down to us in MS. Harleian 3859 and allied collections. There is, however, a body of oral traditional poetry relating to the *Gwyr y Gogledd* and attributed to their court bards which is of the utmost importance in relation to the history of Gwynedd. A brief glance at this poetry will at once make this clear.

In the *Historia Brittonum* (c. 62), following immediately after the notice of Ida[1] as prince of Bernicia, and of Dutigern's[2] strenuous warfare against the Angles, we are told that 'At that time (*tunc*) Talhaern *Tataguen* was a renowned poet, and Neirin (*Aneirin*) and Taliesin and Bluchbard and Cian who is called *Gueinth Guaut*, were all at the same time renowned for British poetry (*simul uno tempore in poemate britannico claruerunt*).'

It is not impossible that the passage is a gloss which has crept into the text; but if so the insertion may have been made at an early date in the MS. tradition, for it is included in that part of the text which is believed to antedate the additions of Nennius.[3]

We have extant extensive collections of early poems which claim to be the work of Aneirin and Taliesin. The great corpus of early poems contained in the *Book of Aneirin*, of which the main part is the *Gododdin*, has reference to the heroes of Manau Guotodin, the territory lying apparently in south-eastern Scotland and to the east of Rheged. The work claims to be the composition of Aneirin. Immediately following the title are the words: 'This is the *Gododin*. Aneirin sang it.' The internal evidence of our poems suggests that Aneirin and Taliesin were the official bards of the North British courts in the sixth century, Aneirin of Manau Guotodin, Taliesin of the court of Urien and of his hardly less famous son Owen. We need not accept the authenticity of all the poems included in the corpus ascribed to Taliesin, but the validity of the tradition remains. We have no record of where the traditional poems of these northern princes were first committed to writing; but the evidence of the language points to somewhere in Wales in the ninth century. We do not even know the precise provenance of the manuscripts which contain the collections; but again it is almost certainly in Wales or Cumbria.

---

[1] According to Bede, Ida began to reign in Bernicia in 547.

[2] For *Dutigern* read *Outigern* (later *Eudeyrn*). Cf. p. 69, n. 5 above.

[3] See the form of this text as published by F. Lot, *Nennius et l'Historia Brittonum*, pp. 219 ff.; see especially p. 224.

From our study of the texts in Harleian 3859 it would seem that the poems in question must have been especially familiar to literary circles in Gwynedd. In these circumstances it is natural to associate the collection—the recording of the poems—with the same circle as that which has recorded the traditions and the pedigrees and annals of the princes whose exploits form the subject of the poems. This circle would seem to have flourished in the ninth century in North Wales. We have seen that there is much corroborative evidence in the poems for that material recorded in the principal documents in Harleian 3859 which is not known to us from any other source. There can be little doubt, therefore, that oral traditions relating to the north were cultivated in Gwynedd alongside the more serious Latin learning which made the records possible. Gwynedd must in fact have been a centre of culture and study whose interest was divided between native and Latin learning, with a keen concentration on native British, especially North British, material. The courts, first of Merfyn and later of Rhodri, in Gwynedd would seem to have supplied the resources and prestige for both, and here more than anywhere else the motive is apparent for exalting the northern ancestry and giving it permanent form in written record.

We are now in a better position to understand how it comes about that the Welsh genealogies in their oldest form converge on Rhodri the Great in the late ninth century, and with them perhaps the association of the *Annales Cambriae*, with their Irish elements and their inclusion of northern annals. In origin all these documents doubtless go back to originals older than either Rhodri or Merfyn. They go back to oral sources; and the annals and the *Historia Brittonum*, perhaps even the genealogies, originally had a separate existence at an earlier date. But at some period the association of the main body of the *Annales Cambriae* took place in close connection with the genealogies and the *Historia Brittonum*, to be recorded ultimately in the collection represented by Harleian 3859. I suggest that this may have been in Gwynedd, and that the interests of Merfyn and of Rhodri Mawr and his court put their intellectual weight on whatever traditions they could lay their hands on—monastic writings and heroic poems—which would serve as family archives and redound to the credit of their dynasty and, perhaps even more important, would keep before the minds of their subjects the close kinship of the Welsh people with the

'Men of the North'. They would naturally place an especial value on traditions and poems relating to the North—the home of their reputed dynastic ancestor, Llywarch Hen. The early history of their dynasty is far from clear, but our indications suggest that their ancestral home was somewhere in the North outside Wales. It will be worth while, therefore, to look more closely into the early history of this interesting family, and into its later political situation in Wales in the ninth century.

6. THE DYNASTY OF MERFYN VRYCH
AND RHODRI MAWR

In 825 or possibly even as early as 816,[1] it would seem that there had been a change of dynasty in Gwynedd. The male line, which had claimed to trace its ancestry back to Cunedag, had come to an end. According to the pedigrees recorded in Jesus MS. xx, no. 17, and in the opening of the *Hanes Gruffydd ap Cynan*,[2] the new king, Merfyn Vrych, traced his ancestry back to Llywarch Hen through Llywarch's son Dwc, and carried it back through Llywarch's father Elidyr[3] Lydanwyn, son of Meirchiawn, son of Gwrgust, grandson of Coel Hen. Harl. Pedigree 8 represents Urbgen (Urien) as a grandson of Llywarch Hen's grandfather Gwrgust, which would make Urbgen and Llywarch Hen first cousins. This is perhaps why the magnificent elegy or keen on Urien (cf. p. 88 below) is traditionally composed and uttered by Llywarch Hen himself. Urbgen, as we know on the testimony of Nennius, was the most warlike and aggressive of the North British princes, and highest in prestige. Merfyn's paternal ancestor Llywarch Hen is thus represented as closely allied to the most important of all the northern lines.

According to this pedigree the name of Merfyn's father was Guriat. It is tempting to identify this Guriat with the Guriat whose name occurs in a well-known inscription on a Manx cross, *Crux Guriat*;[4] but beyond the mere correspondence of the names

---

[1] On the date of Merfyn's accession, see Lloyd, *History of Wales*, i, 231. Cf. also *ibid.* 224, n. 145.

[2] Edited and translated by Arthur Jones, *The History of Gruffydd ap Cynan* (Manchester, 1910).   [3] Cf. pp. 75, 120 below.

[4] See the two articles by P. M. C. Kermode and Sir John Rhys in the *Zeitschrift für celtische Philologie*, i, 39 ff. Cf. also Kermode, *Manx Crosses* (London, 1907), 22, and plate xv.

we have no evidence. The claim to descent from Llywarch Hen points to southern Scotland;[1] but this would not be incompatible with rule in the Isle of Man. Either would satisfy the bardic tradition[2] that the dynasty came from *Manau*. There is, on the other hand, some further evidence, in addition to the pedigrees, for believing that this new dynasty in Gwynedd is directly descended from the *Gwyr y Gogledd*, the 'Men of the North'. While the Jesus pedigrees 17 and 19, and the pedigree at the opening of the *Hanes Gruffydd ap Cynan*, represent Gwriat, the father of Merfyn and grandfather of Rhodri Mawr, as a son of *Elidyr* or *Elidir*, a triad in the *Black Book of Carmarthen* and the *Red Book of Hergest* speak of:

Three kings who were of foreign origin.[3] Gwryat the son of Gwryan in the north (*yn y Gogled*), Chadavel the son of Kynuedw in Gwynedd, and Hyveid, the son of Bleidic in Deheubarth.[4]

The occurrence of the name *Gwrat ap Gwryan* in the triad, and its distinctive association with the 'North', together with the recurrence of the name in Rhodri's own family[5] and its rarity elsewhere in Wales, would seem to favour a northern provenance. The *Annals of Ulster* record the death of one *Guret*, king of Dumbarton, *s.a.* 657 (for 658).

Moreover the names *Gwryat* and *Gwryen* occur also in the *Gododdin*,[6] 1, 348, where their juxtaposition is striking, and though

[1] Lloyd, *History of Wales*, 1, 323.

[2] See *ibid.* 323, n. 13. See further H. M. Chadwick, *Early Scotland*, 146.

[3] Or perhaps 'of servile origin'; but the latter meaning is probably secondary. This, at least, would seem to be suggested by the etymology of the word. F. Lot translates (cf. the following note) 'fils de vilains', i.e. *vilani*, or non-tribe men, an early legal term.

[4] See the text in the *Red Book of Hergest*, edited by Sir John Rhys and J. G. Evans (Oxford, 1887), p. 308; and cf. the French translation by F. Lot, *Les Mabinogion*, II (Paris, 1913), 274. The *Chadavel* here mentioned is thought to be probably identical with the *Catgabail* mentioned in the *Historia Brittonum*, c. 65 (cf. F. Lot, *Historia Brittonum*, p. 76, n. 7). *Hyveid ap Bleidic* is doubtless identical with *Hyfaidd ap Bleddri* of the *Brut y Tywysogyon*, and the *Himeyd* (MS. A; *Hiveid*, C; om. B) of the *Annales Cambriae* who seems to have died *c.* 892.

[5] The *Annales Cambriae* enter the death of Rhodri *and his son Gwriad s.a.* 877. The *Brut y Tywysogyon, s.a.* 878 here refers to Gwriad as the brother of Rhodri. Both the versions of this *Brut* contained in MSS. Peniarth (National Library of Wales) and RBH. (Jesus College, Oxford, MS. CXI), have been edited by Thomas Jones (Cardiff, 1952 and 1955 respectively). In the same *Brut* both versions enter the death of one Gwgon ap Gwriad in 955–7, and MSS. BCD add after Gwriad the words *ap Rhodri*.

[6] See *Canu Aneirin*, edited by Sir Ifor Williams (Cardiff, 1938), 1, 1254, and cf. *ibid.* 348.

no relationship is expressed, the northern provenance of the name is again suggested. Further, the line in the *Gododdin*:

> a Gwryen a Gwynn a Gwryat

makes no sense alone, and must be read in connection with the preceding line:

> ys vyn tyst Ewein vab Eulat.

The sense seems to be:

> My witness is Owen son of Eulad
> and Gwryen and Gwynn and Gwryat.

Sir Ifor Williams gives no note on the passage, which should counsel caution; but though the exact relationship of Gwryan and Gwryat is not stated, their association, whatever its nature, is a constant one, for it occurs again in the poem on *The Graves* contained in the *Black Book of Carmarthen*:[1]

> The grave which the shower bedews—
> Men who would not succumb stealthily;
> Gwen and Gwrien and Gwriad.

We have seen that the house of Rhodri traces its ancestry to Llywarch Hen, and that a comparison of Harl. genealogy 8 with Jesus genealogy 17 suggests that according to tradition Llywarch and Urbgen (Urien) were first cousins. Genuine historical evidence dates Urbgen to the late sixth century, and Llywarch is treated in genealogy and poetry as his contemporary. Rhodri flourished *c.* 870. The genealogy places Rhodri nine generations after Llywarch, or, allowing thirty years to a generation, about 270 years later. If we regard Llywarch as flourishing about 600, the additional 270 years will bring us to Rhodri's period. The evidence on the whole, therefore, would seem to suggest that the genealogy is trustworthy; and in addition, as Sir Ifor Williams reminds us, a royal pedigree would be subjected to rigorous scrutiny. The presumption is that Rhodri's ancestors came south with the 'Men of the North' and obtained land for themselves ultimately in North Wales.

Whatever the origin of the family, Merfyn represents a new dynasty in Gwynedd, at least so far as the male line is concerned; but his father Gwriad seems to have allied himself to the old line

---

[1] Reproduced and edited by J. G. Evans (Pwllheli, 1906), 63. Translated by W. F. Skene, *Four Ancient Books of Wales*, I, 310.

by marrying Etthil,[1] a daughter of Cynan Tyndaethwy,[2] the last king of the old Anglesey line of Gwynedd, claiming descent from Enniaun Girt, one of the sons of Cunedag. Merfyn may thus be looked upon as having inherited Gwynedd through his mother. He himself married Nest, the sister of Cyngen, last king of the old line of Powys, who ruled from 808–54, at which date the *Annales Cambriae* record his death in Rome. By this marriage their son Rhodri Mawr succeeded not only to Gwynedd, his father's kingdom, but also to Powys through his mother. Finally by Rhodri's own marriage, soon after 872, to Angharad, sister of the drowned Prince Gwgon of Ceredigion, he found himself in possession of the large kingdom of Seisyllwg, which included Ceredigion and Ystrad Tywi, thus cutting off the little kingdom of Dyfed, or Pembroke, from the rest of Wales. He was now master of all Wales except Dyfed, Brycheiniog, and the south-eastern kingdoms of Morgannwg and Gwent.

The history of the dynasty is indeed a remarkable one. By a series of diplomatic marriages with Welsh princesses of the old native kingdoms, and apparently without striking a blow, within three generations[3] they had made themselves masters of more than half Wales. It is in no way surprising that Rhodri should feel it necessary to draw together genealogical documents establishing his own and his wife's claim as native Welsh royalty, and to expand them by notes in the form of annals and narratives. The interests of the dynasty on the male side would naturally be focused on the north, and on the genealogies of the *Gwyr y Gogledd*, the 'Men of the North', and on such information as could be produced to supplement their testimony. The traditions and genealogies of the north were no less relevant to Rhodri's prestige than were those of Wales. Of these genealogies the one which concerned him most closely was that of Llywarch Hen. This may possibly help to throw light on the strange fact that among the poems of the northern bards which were still prominent in tradition and memory in the ninth century, a large corpus should claim to be the work of Llywarch Hen himself.

[1] Pedigree 1 in MS. Harl. 3859.
[2] His death is entered in the *Annales Cambriae*, s.a. 816.
[3] That the line of Rhodri may have inherited still further back through marriages with royal princesses is suggested by pedigree 19 of Jesus xx, in which the name of Rhodri's great-great-grandmother Celenion figures as the daughter of Tutagual, whose ancestry is identical with that in Harl. no. 4.

By the middle of the ninth century Rhodri was the greatest man in Wales, and the founder of a great family. For this we have the independent testimony of Asser. We possess no 'Life' of Rhodri, no chronicle or commemorative saga, like the *Hanes* of his descendant, Gruffydd ap Cynan; but his importance is reflected in the fact that he is mentioned three times in the *Annals of Ulster*, while the Jesus pedigrees[1] invariably refer to him as *Rhodri Mawr*, an epithet also applied to him in a triad in the *Black Book of Carmarthen*.[2] It is noteworthy that the epithet is nowhere applied to him in the Harleian genealogies;[3] but the epithet is probably not fortuitous. His strenuous activities against the enemies of Wales, the Danes to the west and the Saxons to the east, are no less remarkable than his policy of British consolidation at home. The *Annals of Ulster* record *s.a.* 855 the death of 'Horm' (*Gorm*), leader of the Danes, at the hands of *Ruadhri*, son of *Mermin* 'king of Britain' (*rig mBretan*), and it is not impossible that the fame of this victory may have reached the Continent, where the court of Charles the Bald was apprehensively hearkening to the depredations of the Vikings on their own coasts, and where about this time we shall find Sedulius Scottus referring to a victory over the Danes in a panegyric on a certain *Roricus* (cf. p. 103 below).

But in 876 (for 877) the *Annals of Ulster* record how '*Ruaidhri*, son of *Muirmenn*, king of the Britons, came to Ireland, fleeing before the Black foreigners', and in the following year the *Annales Cambriae* record the death of *Rotri* and his son at the hands of the Saxons. His death is the consummation of a long struggle for power, not only between Powys and Mercia, but also between Gwynedd and Wessex. Under Merfyn and Rhodri the greater part of Wales had passed from a series of small and independent kingdoms to a consolidated realm, and when Asser applies the grandiose title *Britannia* to Wales he is thinking primarily of Rhodri's possessions. The constructive nationalist policy of the dynasty lies behind Asser's statements that after Rhodri's death his sons worked together in unison against the other southern dynasties; and that the rulers of Dyfed and of Brycheiniog,

---

[1] Nos. 17, 18, 19, 24, 26, 42.

[2] No. 153 in the French translation by F. Lot, *Les Mabinogion*, II (Paris, 1913), 324.

[3] Mr Huws points out to me that epithets are few in Harl. as compared with later texts of the genealogies, such as Jesus xx.

compelled by the force of the sons of Rhodri, made their submission to King Alfred and sought his protection.

By Merfyn's marriage to Nest and the consequent acquisition of
Powys, their son Rhodri had inherited not only the richest part of
Wales, but also the ancient Border feud which lies behind the
entry *s.a.* 822 when the *Annales Cambriae* record that the Saxons
destroyed Deganwy and 'took the region of Powys into their own
power'; the feud which still continued when *c.* 830 we find
Ecgbriht, the West Saxon king and eighth Bretwalda, conquering
Mercia and reducing the Welsh, thus bringing Wessex into direct
conflict with the North Welsh for the first time. A generation later
in 853 the *Anglo-Saxon Chronicle* tells of the Mercians under their
king Burgred obtaining the help of Æthelwulf, father of Alfred
the Great, and making a victorious expedition into Wales. It is
to this period of the subjugation of Powys by Burgred of Mercia
that we must probably attribute the tragic poems on the devastation of Powys, 'the Paradise of Wales', which purport to be
the compositions of Llywarch Hen. Perhaps also this is the occasion on which Cyngen, before his pilgrimage to Rome in 854, set
up the pillar in the vale of Llangollen to his grandfather Eliseg
in commemoration of his having formerly annexed the inheritance
of Powys from the English. In any case the pillar represents the
situation in Powys before the combined Mercian and Saxon attack.

There is an underlying unity in the ideals and the achievement
of Rhodri Mawr and Alfred the Great, and it is not impossible that
it was the untimely death of Rhodri which made possible the
constructive nationalism of Alfred and the important Welsh
elements in the ultimate union of South Wales under Hywel Dda
with England under Æthelstan. As a result of pressure from the
Viking onslaught Britons and Saxons alike had developed in the
ninth century from a group of relatively small units, whose
stability depended on immunity from outside pressure, into two
relatively powerful nations, each struggling for an existence which
was threatened alike from enemies without and racial animosity
within. Under Rhodri and his sons a selfconscious nationalism
developed in North Wales and Deheubarth which revived the hope
of an ultimate British victory and the extirpation of the hated
Saxon. It would seem likely that the terms *Deheubarth* and *y
Gogledd* arose at this period, and as a result of nationalist propaganda. The former term is used, not to denote all South Wales,

but that part to which the sons of Rhodri laid claim; the latter term implies the existence of the former, and bears a close relationship to it. Under Alfred an equally self-conscious realisation of the essential racial unity of the Anglo-Saxon peoples in Britain is manifest, and his advanced diplomatic policy among those South Welsh kingdoms which were still independent of Gwynedd resulted in the development of Wessex, the ultimate union with Wales, and the creation of the English nation.

There can be no doubt that throughout the latter part of the ninth century the tacit struggle for supremacy between Briton and Saxon was as fierce as between either nation and the Danes. When Alfred obtained the services of Asser and the homage of the South Welsh kingdoms the battle was virtually won, and the annexation of Powys by Hywel Dda, and his ultimate union with the English under Æthelstan were only the final stages. One cannot help wondering what the course of events would have been had Rhodri's death not cut short his activities and delivered Powys into the hands of Hywel and the power of Wessex. Was it as a refugee that Asser, an ecclesiastic of St David's, found himself at Alfred's court? For Hyfaidd Hen, the ruler of Dyfed, was persecuting both Asser and his uncle Nobis, the bishop of St David's; but Hyfaidd Hen was himself under fire from Rhodri and his sons who, by the annexation of Seisyllwg, held Dyfed and its ruler Hyfaidd in the hollow of their hands. We must not forget that even Hywel Dda never laid claim to Gwynedd, and when Anarawd, Rhodri's son and heir in Gwynedd, finally made his submission to Alfred, it was as an independent ruler, and as the result of his failure to negotiate an independent alliance with the Northumbrians.

There can be no doubt that Rhodri and his sons were aiming at a united British people and an ultimate Saxon conquest, and it is perhaps in the light of these ideals, even more than in a need of dynastic aggrandisement, that we must view the prominence given to the traditions and the poetry of Cumbria and the northern Britons in the Gwynedd of the ninth century. The common bond was racial unity, the common aim was the downfall of the Saxon, victory for the Britons. All the memories of the heroic past were called in to serve this great end, and after Rhodri's death, and even after Anarawd's submission, the indomitable British spirit sent its fiery cross throughout all Celtic lands, especially Cumbria, and all the Britons within our islands, calling upon them to rise and beat back the Saxons. A clarion call to arms is voiced in the greatest of all the Welsh patriotic poems, the *Armes Prydein*,[1] the 'Inspired Utterance', or perhaps more correctly the 'Story of the Affliction of Britain', believed to have been composed in the early years of the tenth century. The appeal throughout is made to the racial unity of the British as a whole. The Welsh are referred to as *Cymry* (*Combrogi*, 'fellow-countrymen'), and the appeal is to the men of Cumbria and Strathclyde no less than to the Welsh of Wales. Even the racial kinship of the men of Brittany is remembered, and the outer fringe of the Celtic peoples—the Irish, the Dublin Norse-men[2] and the Picts—are urged to unite and drive back to their ships the descendants of Hengest and Horsa, who had come as exiles to this island in the time of Vortigern, poverty-stricken and landless, to impose their taxes and conquer the land from the Britons.

The appeal is based throughout on memories of the great British Heroic Age. The Cymry will be led, not by the great men of the present or the recent past, but by the heroes of old, by Cynan and Cadwaladr. The speaker is not a Welsh patriot of the ninth or tenth century, but in turn the *Awen* (ll. 1, 107), the traditional spirit of inspiration familiar to all who knew the ancient poetry of the North; or again Myrddin or Merlin, the great British prophet of the ancient North (l. 17); or again the druids (l. 171), the most ancient spiritual leaders of the ancient Celtic world. The druids foretell that the Britons shall rule once more from Mynau to Brittany, from Dyfed to Thanet. But beyond that the poet has no concern with the future and no hint of policy. His appeal is based on the great past of his countrymen, and directed to enflame their resistance to the Saxons. He is familiar with names of their leaders, Hengest and Horsa, and he twice points his finger in scorn and hatred at Vortigern. His politics are those of the *Historia Brittonum* and the form of the pedigrees as recorded in Harl. 3859.

Reference has been made to the prominence of Llywarch Hen, both as the traditional northern ancestor of the royal line of

---

[1] The best edition is that of Sir Ifor Williams, *Armes Prydein o Lyfr Taliesin* (Cardiff, 1955), with forty-seven pages of introduction and sixty pages of notes. This edition is entirely in Welsh. An English translation, now requiring revision in many points, was published by W. F. Skene, *Four Ancient Books of Wales*, I (Edinburgh, 1868), 436 ff.

[2] Dublin was captured by the Norwegian Vikings in 837 or 838 and lasted as a Norse kingdom till the battle of Clontarf in 1014. The people of Dublin are regularly distinguished from the Irish throughout the period.

Gwynedd, and as a northern hero who claims to be the composer of a considerable body of early Welsh poetry.[1] Now Sir Ifor Williams has called attention to the fact that the name of Llywarch Hen is not included in the list of poets contained in the *Historia Brittonum* (c. 62). He has shown moreover that while the traditions depicted in these poems may enshrine some earlier memories, perhaps of Llywarch's own time, the more immediate background is that of the period in which the poems were composed, and that, in fact, they represent the disturbed conditions on the Mercian and Powys borders in the ninth century and the period preceding it. The question at once arises, therefore: Does the exclusion of Llywarch's name from the list of poets in the *Historia* imply that he was not, in fact, a poet? Or had his name already become associated with the Welsh border at the time when the list was drawn up?

Sir Ifor Williams has shown further that poetry which claims to be spoken by Llywarch Hen cannot date from the sixth century and is not the work of Llywarch Hen himself, but of a poet who lived on the Welsh border in the ninth century, and composed songs, *c.* 850, reminiscent of Llywarch and, presumably, expressive of the emotions and utterances believed to be appropriate to him.[2] They are, in fact, believed to be poems 'in character', and Sir Ifor Williams regards them as having been composed against the background of a saga about Llywarch, exactly like such later poetical compositions as we find in sagas in Ireland and Iceland, where, besides a few early traditional poems, we find many of later date, the latter poems being generally in the form of speeches. No prose narrative of Llywarch Hen has been preserved, but from the nature of poems which purport to be spoken by him he was evidently handed down in tradition as an old warrior who had lost all his sons in battle. His last and youngest son Gwen is killed in defensive warfare against the English;[3] but as Llywarch is depicted as present and as himself carrying on a dialogue with Gwen before the battle, the period is tacitly assumed to be the sixth century, but on the Welsh border; and Sir Ifor Williams has pointed out that the

---

[1] The poems attributed to him have been published by Sir Ifor Williams, *Canu Llywarch Hen* (Cardiff, 1953).

[2] For an important discussion of this subject, see Sir Ifor Williams, 'The Poems of Llywarch Hen,' *Proceedings of the British Academy* XVIII (1932); *Lectures on Early Welsh Poetry* (Dublin, 1944), 34 ff.; and more recently his Introduction to *The Saga of Llywarch the Old* by Glyn Jones and T. G. Morgan (London, 1955).

[3] See *Canu Llywarch Hen*, nos. I (strophes 11, 23, 39); XI (strophe 3).

conditions implied in the poem do not fit into our knowledge of sixth-century conditions in this area, but are applicable rather to the political situation as it existed in the eighth and ninth centuries, possibly even earlier, and, in fact, to what we have just seen to be the political situation in the time preceding and including that of Rhodri Mawr.

Moreover, other important poems, apparently in the language of the same period, and believed to be composed by the same poet,[1] the *Cynddylan* poems and the *Englynion y Beddau*, depict conditions which seem to reflect, not the sixth, but at earliest the seventh century, and again in Powys on the English border. Here a ninth-century poet may well have found good enough oral tradition, even in the form of a saga or developed prose narrative, as a background to his poems. But what motive can have compelled him to compose these sad songs as the expression of a stricken man and a stricken people,[2] and to have expressed at least the first group as if they were spoken by Llywarch Hen in the sixth century? And why are the *Cynddylan* and the *Englynion y Beddau* poems also in the collection of poetry ascribed to him? Why has he been transferred from North Britain to Powys?

Now there are other poems ascribed to Llywarch Hen in which the English border background is not always implicit. On the contrary the setting would seem to be North Britain, and Llywarch and his sons are seen in direct connection with the *Gwyr y Gogledd*, the 'Men of the North'. Here, then, Llywarch Hen is seen in his own period and among his fellows. He is the privileged poet of his cousin and lord, Urien of Rheged, whose head he removes from the dead body when Urien has been killed in battle against his enemies, and whose death he laments in a superb elegy.

Sir Ifor Williams has rightly observed that we have no evidence that Llywarch Hen was a poet,[3] and that the elegy, as its language suggests, has been composed in the ninth century and attributed to him. But the attribution is of itself important. Traditionally it places him very near his lord, according to all Celtic literary convention. Moreover the elegy shows familiarity with Urien's milieu and with the personnel of his enemies. It offers a tradition of the death of Urien different from that of Nennius. Finally it has

---

[1] Sir Ifor Williams, *Lectures on Early Welsh Poetry*, 45.
[2] Cf. Sir Ifor Williams, *loc. cit.*; and 'The Poems of Llywarch Hen', 23.
[3] *The Saga of Llywarch the Old*, 8.

all the characteristics of our earlier British elegiac poetry as these are seen in other survivals. The traditions of Urien and the *Gwyr y Gogledd* implied in this poem must have been remarkably well preserved. If it is a work of a ninth-century poet he must have had access to early and well-preserved North British traditions and traditional forms of elegiac poetry, and he must have composed in a milieu in which these were both valued for their own sake, and sedulously and strictly cultivated.

We have, then, two totally different pictures of Llywarch—that in his own period, his own setting in the North and among his contemporaries; and that in which he is in Powys under alien conditions and among unfamiliar companions. The first picture, marvellously true to tradition in its general features, has preserved for us the Llywarch of Merfyn's ancestry, before the descendants of Llywarch came to the throne of Gwynedd. The second is that of the struggle in the Border country, when, after Merfyn's marriage to Cyngen's sister, and the close of the Powys dynasty, the responsibility for the struggle on the border devolved upon Rhodri Mawr. This dynasty would naturally be responsible for the cultivation and circulation in Wales of the traditions and the poetry of the land from which they believed themselves to have come, and especially for the high prestige in ninth-century tradition of the name of their traditional ancestor, Llywarch Hen. But the tradition of the sixth-century northern Llywarch, Rhodri's ancestor, is that of an elegiac poet, no less than the Llywarch of Powys. His *Marwnad* (Elegy) on Urien of Rheged has set its seal on his tradition. It would seem a natural thing that when, after the long struggle on the Welsh border, Rhodri and his son finally themselves perished in battle against the English, the bards of Powys should pour forth their laments in the name of Rhodri's ancestor, who was still remembered as having chanted over the dead Urien what is perhaps the greatest elegiac poem or keen in early British tradition.

But even then the Llywarch tradition is not easy to explain. All the poems attributed to him, whether their background is in the North or in Powys, are expressive of disaster or defeat. Against a sixth-century background he mourns the death of Urien, the greatest of the northern princes, and the end, we may believe, of the great Cumbrian kingdom. In Powys, which he calls 'the Paradise of Wales', he presents himself to us as an old and decrepit man, a pitiful figure, not even exempt from the contempt of his own son. It is difficult to avoid a suspicion that the epithet *hen*, 'old', has been exploited with malicious intent. Could these Llywarch poems have been really composed under the patronage of either Rhodri or Concenn? Is not the Llywarch Hen of the poems an unsympathetic picture of the aged Cyngen himself?

We have seen reason to suspect that in the Harleian version of the pedigrees Rhodri's genealogies have been tampered with, including that of his mother, who belonged to the royal line of Powys. Is it beyond suspicion that the traditions of Rhodri's ancestor Llywarch have been subjected to a similar hostile influence? The contest in policy which throughout the ninth century was dividing North and South Wales, the fierce British nationalism of Rhodri's family in the north, and the ever tightening liaison between the South Welsh princes and Wessex in the south, would hardly fail to make itself heard in the literature of the ninth century, before the great clarion call of the *Armes Prydein* early in the tenth.

It is in the light of this struggle between the two opposing policies on 'ideals' in Wales that we can best hope to explain the controversy which was evidently raging round the name of the great Vortigern at this time. At the moment when Concenn was setting up his elaborate stone inscription tracing his royal pedigree of Powys back to Vortigern and the Roman emperor, Maxen Wledig, the *Historia Brittonum* was going out of its way to swear that the royal line of Powys was not descended from Vortigern, but on the contrary from a man of low rank, and at the same time representing Vortigern as the subject of a graceless scandal, hounded from the face of Wales by St Germanus. The same hostility to Vortigern is echoed in the *Armes Prydein*; and in both the poem and the *Historia*, and also indeed in the Harleian genealogies, the reason for the hostility is abundantly clear: he had brought in the hated Saxons. The spirit of British nationalism would have none of him, and by the close of the ninth century was driving him out of bounds. The Chartres text of the *Historia*, with its prime concentration on the story, gives us a date *c*. 900 for the height of the polemics. It remains to inquire what is the source of the Latin antiquarianism which has inspired the genealogies of Gwynedd and of Powys to claim a Roman origin, side by side with an origin in the native northern aristocracy; and moreover boldly to claim a connection between this early Roman origin and that of their native prince Vortigern. Where would the Latin documents be most readily to hand, and the men of Latin education qualified to make use of them?

There can be no doubt that both the Chartres text and that of the *Historia* as recorded in Harl. 3859 and also the *Armes Prydein* represent a single point of view, and one very hostile to Vortigern. A century earlier this was not so. The pillar of Concenn (†854) and the original pedigrees of Rhodri as represented by Jesus MS. xx, revered him and emphasised his proud connection with the Roman era.[1] This pride of the courts of Powys and Gwynedd in the Roman past must have been fostered by learned antiquarian influence. It is an element quite distinct from the pride in the past of the *Gwyr y Gogledd* and their traditions. It is fully in accord, however, with the early chapters of the *Historia Brittonum* itself, and with the antiquarian speculations embodied in the stories of Brutus, of the invasions, and of the story of Cunedag and his sons to which reference was made at the beginning of this paper.

One's thoughts naturally turn to Bishop Elfoddw of Bangor, who is credited in the *Annales Cambriae* (*s.a.* 768) with the greatest intellectual change in the history of the early British Church, that of bringing about its union with the Anglo-Roman Church and its entry into the *unitas catholica* (cf. p. 44 above). This Elfoddw is generally regarded as the Elfoddw of whom Nennius expresses himself a disciple in the preface to the Cambridge group of manuscripts of the *Historia Brittonum*. If Elfoddw is in fact identical in each of these references we may assume that he was a man of considerable intellectual activity. His part in the Easter controversy would imply no less, and the preface of Nennius his *discipulus* suggests that the writer had access to a considerable library of patristic literature. It is indeed not impossible that Elfoddw may himself have been in a position to put Nennius in touch with North British traditions, since Elfoddw would appear to have claimed to have some knowledge of Urien's family.[2] In view of the respect accorded him in this preface, and of his leading place in the early British Church, it would seem not impossible that the native British traditions were interrelated with those of Roman Britain in Bangor itself, whether Bangor in Arfon or Bangor Iscoed. It is safe to say that both sets of traditions would

[1] Cf. also his pedigree in the *Historia Brittonum*, c. 49, where Vortigern's grandfather is the eponym of the Roman city of Gloucester.

[2] See Sir Ifor Williams, *Lectures on Early Welsh Poetry*, 51.

be subjected to scrutiny before the British Church would be willing to abandon 'the customs of our forefathers', and adopt those imposed from Rome.[1]

It is clear from the contents of the *Historia Brittonum* that the writer had access to a number of ancient authors whom he could not at this time have found outside a monastic library. The preface to the Cambridge group claims that the compiler, who here calls himself Nennius, had made use of the 'annals of the Romans', and the 'Chronicles of the Sacred Fathers', such as Jerome, Eusebius, Isidore and Prosper. He also claims to have had access to the annals of the Irish and of the Saxons. He knew the works of Bede. A warning is necessary at this point. In considering this preface and this list we have always to bear in mind the possibility that the list has itself been deduced and compiled by a later scholar from the actual contents of the *Historia*, and that the list and the learning which it implies, indeed the entire preface, may be the work of a later writer who has attributed it to Nennius as the greatest British scholar and patriot of the ninth century, and as one who, moreover, was familiar alike with the Saxon and Latin learning of his day. This, however, is a question into which we cannot enter here. I shall have something further to say of Nennius as a scholar later. Meantime the existence of the preface and its association with Elfoddw attests at least a tradition that the centre of learning at which the *Historia* was compiled was associated with Gwynedd and Bangor, probably Bangor Fawr in Arfon. With the examples of the Irish monasteries before us we need have no hesitation in accepting an important ecclesiastical institution as the repository of ancient secular traditions. The proximity of the court of Gwynedd to Bangor would provide the necessary patronage for the cultivation of such traditions, and the financial help necessary to build up a library.

We have now made some study of the Latin documents relating to North Wales, and we have seen reason to believe that they were assembled in Gwynedd in the ninth century, probably under the auspices of the court of Merfyn and his son Rhodri Mawr. We have also made a brief inquiry into the probable channels by which the genealogies and traditions, and the materials incorporated in both the written annals and the traditional oral poems, may have reached Gwynedd; and we have seen that the ancestral line of the house of

---

[1] We may refer to the passage in which Bede relates the story of the conference of the British bishops with St Augustine. *H.E.* II, ii.

Rhodri claimed to be derived from the 'Men of the North'. Some of these northern traditions had somewhere found their way into annals which have been incorporated into the *Historia Brittonum* possibly compiled in the last instance by one Nennius, who lays claim in certain versions to be a disciple of Bishop Elfoddw who flourished *c.* 800. The poetry relating to these northern heroes, ancestors of the rulers of Gwynedd, was carried on orally, apparently down to about the ninth century, when it was written down in Wales in some area as yet unidentified, though on the whole, in view of the traditional ascription of the great majority of this poetry to famous poets of the 'Men of the North', Gwynedd would seem to have a strong claim. If we are correct in our conclusions Gwynedd must have had an active cultural life of her own during the ninth century, and both native and Latin learning must have been keenly pursued. The internal evidence of the *Historia Brittonum* and the *Annales Cambriae* makes it clear that she was in touch with the Latin education of Ireland. It remains to inquire whether we have any external evidence for this intellectual activity, and more especially for the cultivation of Latin education in Gwynedd at this period. It would be especially helpful if we could know whether Gwynedd had any contact with the intellectual life of the continent.

7. GWYNEDD AND THE CONTINENT

In regard to Latin and the influence of Continental culture in Gwynedd we have evidence from at least as early as the seventh century.[1] The memorial stone in the Church of Llangadwaladr near Aberffraw, the ancient capital of the island branch of 'Cunedag's dynasty' in Anglesey, commemorates Maelgwn's great-great-grandson[2] King Cadfan (fl. *c.* 625) in grandiloquent terms which demonstrate the high pretensions of the family, and which the late Dr Nash-Williams regarded as echoing the phraseology of the Byzantine court. The inscription runs:

Catamanus rex sapientis(s)imus, opinatis(s)imus omnium regum.[3]
(Here lies) King Cadfan, wisest and most renowned of all kings.

The memorial tablet now forms the lintel inside the north door of the church which bears the name of Cadfan's grandson Cad-

[1] See K. Jackson, *Language and History in Early Britain* (Edinburgh, 1953), p. 160. [2] See pedigree 1 in Harleian MS. 3859.
[3] V. E. Nash-Williams, *The Early Christian Monuments of Wales* (Cardiff, 1950), 55, and plate VII and figure 21.

waladr, and of which he was probably the founder,[1] and it is probable that Cadwaladr himself set up the stone in memory of a distinguished ancestor, as Concenn set up the pillar or cross near Llangollen to commemorate his own ancestor Eliseg. It is noteworthy that the inscription to King Cadfan is in almost pure manuscript half-uncials, and represents the latest fashion in Continental book-script.[2] It must not be supposed, therefore, that in the late seventh century this little western kingdom was a backwater, out of touch with Continental culture.

From Continental sources we have some evidence, not only of a certain measure of literacy and education at the courts of Merfyn and perhaps of Rhodri, but also apparently of contacts with the most learned elements in both Ireland and the Merovingian court. Indeed the court of Gwynedd at this time seems to have been on a through route from Ireland to the Continent, and to have formed a halting place on the way, perhaps a hostel for scholars. An Irish colony in Wales is implied by the name of that part of Gwynedd in or near which the court was almost certainly held, *Lleyn* (from *Laigin*, 'Leinstermen'), with its chief landing place *Porth Dinllaen* ('the harbour by the fortress, *din*, of the Leinstermen) (cf. p. 122, n. 1 below). This was the period when the movements of Irish scholars to the Continent are thought to have been greatly stimulated as a result of the Viking raids on Ireland; and we know that special facilities were accorded to them, and special hostels or colonies assigned to them at the great Continental centres of learning, such as Liége.[3] We have some reason for believing that the court of Gwynedd may well have been such a centre.

In a manuscript from Bamberg[4] believed to be derived from a

---

[1] See Lloyd, *History of Wales*, I, 182; cf. K. Jackson, *Language and History in Early Britain*, p. 161.   [2] Jackson, *loc. cit.* and the references there cited.

[3] See L. Gougaud, *Christianity in Celtic Lands*, revision and English translation by Maud Joynt (London, 1932), 177ff.

[4] MS. Class 6=H.J. IV, 11. See Derolez, 'Dubthach's Cryptogram', *L'Antiquité Classique*, XXI (1952), no. 2, 359ff. (Derolez [1], cf. p. 46 above): also *idem*, *Runica Manuscripta* (Bruges, 1954; Derolez [2]), 97ff. Some earlier references to the cryptogram were made by L. Gougaud, *Christianity in Celtic Lands*, 252ff.; cf. Whitley Stokes, 'On a Medieval Cryptogram', *The Academy*, XLII (1892), 71f.; J. Loth, 'Un nouveau Cryptogramme', *Annales de Bretagne*, VIII (1892), 289ff.; *idem*, *Revue celtique*, XIV (1893), 91. For a recent note on the subject see Kenney, *op. cit.* 556, where a translation is given of the cryptogram and the letter which accompanies it. I am indebted to Professor Kenneth Jackson for originally calling my attention to the cryptogram in a different connection.

ninth-century prototype, we have a cryptogram incorporated in a letter which purports to have been sent from four Irish scholars on the Continent to their teacher Colgu. In another MS., from Brussels (which I shall refer to as Br.),[1] the same cryptogram is again found, and also a key to its interpretation by the substitution of Greek letters for Latin in accordance with a fixed table. A reference to this key is also made in the letter contained in the Bamberg text. I shall refer to the two studies by Derolez as Derolez [1] and Derolez [2] respectively (cf. p. 46 above). The solution in both texts reads as follows:

> Mermin rex Conchen salutem,[2]
> Mermin (Merfyn), the king, greets Conchenn;

and the Brussels text adds:

> Suadbar scripsit,[3]
> Suadbar wrote [i.e. the letter].

The letter to Colgu contained in the Bamberg text (which I shall refer to as Ba.) explains why the cryptogram is being sent, claiming that it has been posed 'to the learned Irishmen at the citadel (*arx*) of Mermin, king of the Britons', by a certain Dubthach, apparently an Irishman to judge from his name, in order to test their intellectual acquirements, 'because', adds the writer of the letter, 'Dubthach thought himself so superior to all the Irish and the Britons that he believed no Irish scholar, far less a British one, would be able to read the cryptogram'. But Dubthach evidently overshot himself, for the writer assures the 'wise and estimable Colgu, our very learned teacher',[4] that to himself and his companions the cryptogram was perfectly clear. The writer addresses a scathing remark to Dubthach, pointing out that he has erred in his rendering of the form *Conchen*. The note shows that the writer was familiar with British ninth-century phonology.[5]

The cryptogram would seem to constitute the opening words of a letter, from Merfyn, king of Gwynedd (†844) to Concenn, the ruler of Powys, whose sister Nest Merfyn married. Concenn, as already stated (p. 82 above), was the last king of the old line of

---

[1] Brussels, Bibliothèque Royale, MS. 9565–6. For the Brussels text see Derolez, *Runica Manuscripta*, pp. 95 ff.

[2] There are one or two slight but significant divergences in spelling, which have given rise to a contemporary note on the lower margin of the Brussels text. See Derolez [2], 97.   [3] See Derolez [2], 95 f.

[4] 'Prudentię, optime Colgu nosterque doctissime magister.'

[5] See Derolez [1], 368 f.; Derolez [2], 98 f.

Powys who was reigning from 808, and who died in Rome in 854.[1] The letter was apparently transcribed by one Suadbar. Our MS. Br. is believed to be in a St Gall hand of this period (cf. p. 97 below) and St Gall, the famous halting place of pilgrims to Rome, is precisely the place where we should expect to find such a cryptogram.

The writer of the letter explains to Colgu that he is not sending the explanation of the cryptogram from any doubt that Colgu will understand it, but so that he may give this information to any of their unfortunate and less accomplished brethren who may wish to cross the British sea, and in order that they may be spared from blushes in the presence of Mermin, renowned (*gloriosus*) king of the Britons, by not being able to decipher the document.[2] In other words he asks Colgu to make sure that his countrymen may memorise the crib before visiting Mermin's court, where it will be put to them as an intelligence test. What a delightful bit of patriotic cheating!

From the writing of the Brussels MS. it is inferred that the portion containing the cryptogram and colophon cannot have been compiled much later than the text of the *Martianus Capella*, which forms a part of the same codex, and of which the glosses are believed to date from the ninth century (cf. Derolez[(2)], 95 f.). The key to the cryptogram, as we have seen, involved some elementary knowledge of Greek. It is interesting to note that another cryptogram,[3] interpreted by this same key, is contained in another ninth-century MS., generally known as the Cambridge *Juvencus*, written in a British hand, or perhaps, as the colophon would seem to imply, by an Irishman in a British scriptorium.[4] The point of interest in both cryptograms lies in their use of the two alphabets, Latin and Greek, and it is evident that knowledge of the Greek alphabet constituted the core of the intelligence test to which Dubthach subjected the four Irish scholars. We have already noted the curious story of the alphabet which, it was claimed, was invented extempore

---

[1] Apparently one of the earliest royal pilgrimages to Rome from a Celtic country. Cf. Rev. Aubrey Gwynn, *Irish Historical Studies*, VIII (1953), 197.

[2] See Derolez[(1)], *loc. cit.*

[3] For a transcription and note, see Whitley Stokes, *The Academy*, XLII (1892), 215.

[4] The cryptogram in question is on the upper margin of page 67 of the MS. in the Cambridge University Library Ff. 4. 42. See Derolez[(1)], 367 f.; cf. K. Jackson, *Language and History in Early Britain*, 49 ff. The colophon contains the words *araut di Nuadu*, which is interpreted 'a prayer for Nuadu', i.e. a request by the scribe to the reader for a prayer on his behalf. A fresh examination of the cryptogram by an expert palaeographer would be welcome.

by Nennius to parry an accusation made by a Saxon that the British possessed no alphabet of their own. The story, as already stated, is contained in another early ninth-century MS. (cf. p. 45 above). It would seem that in scholarly circles in Britain a special interest attached to alphabets in the ninth century, an interest which may possibly be connected with the development of Celtic scriptoria and book production, and of the writing of manuscripts, which at this period amounted almost to a national profession.

It should be noted that Dubthach held himself superior to the Britons as well as to the Irish. The emphasis here laid on the scholarship and ingenuity of the Britons as inferior only to that of the Irish is arresting: Dubthach believed that 'no Irish scholar, far less a British one, would be able to read the cryptogram'. Since the test on the occasion in question was specifically put to the 'four learned Irishmen', the allusion to the Britons would seem to require explanation. It might almost seem to imply that, contrary to expectation, a Briton had, in fact, succeeded in deciphering the cryptogram. But unless Colgu were himself a Briton such an interpretation would not be easy to fit into the context. Except Nemnivus himself we have no evidence of any distinguished Briton of the period who was a master of cryptic alphabets, and his associations are not with the Greek, but with the runic. One important point the passage seems to make clear, however. In the ninth century British scholars were in a position to claim comparison with Irish on the Continent in learning and ingenuity, not excluding some superficial acquaintance with elementary Greek.

The cryptograms in Ba. and Br., as Derolez has demonstrated, are derived from a common source and are mutually dependent. Both are derived from a ninth-century original. Br. is itself thought on high authority (see p. 96 above) to be written probably in a ninth-century St Gall hand. At some period the codex was the property of the chapter library of the abbey of St Laurent in Liége; and though its absence from the twelfth- and thirteenth-century catalogues of that abbey would seem to suggest that it was acquired later, it may, as Derolez observes, have been in the neighbourhood of Liége at an earlier date. Contacts between St Gall and Liége are known to have been numerous in the ninth century.[1] Manuscripts are also known to have reached Bamberg from Liége, and probably our cryptogram among them.[2] At this period Liége was a highly

[1] Derolez [2], 95.   [2] Derolez [1], 361, 373.

cultivated intellectual centre, of the circle of Charles the Bald. In view of the internal evidence of the cryptogram pointing to its close association with the court of Merfyn in Gwynedd, it may be worth while to pause for a moment to consider the manuscript context of this ninth-century cryptogram in order to see with what kind of documents it is associated.

In addition to the cryptogram our Brussels manuscript contains a runic alphabet of Anglo-Saxon type, known by its native name as a *futhorc*; and also a text on runic cryptography. We shall follow Derolez, the most recent editor of these texts, in referring to this *futhorc* itself and the accompanying text as the *isruna* tract, from the name used in the tract itself to describe the particular form of the native arrangements of the runes followed in this particular *futhorc*. The text occurs also in four other manuscripts. One of these, now at St Gall[1] but thought to be in an insular hand, and to date from about the middle of the ninth century,[2] is believed to be derived from the same original as Br.,[3] and can therefore hardly be later than the early ninth century. Br., as we have seen (p. 95 above), also shows familiarity with contemporary British phonology in the marginal note addressed to Dubthach. Now we have seen that the cryptographic material of Latin and Greek contained in Ba. and Br. is believed to be derived from a common original, dating from before the middle of the ninth century, and that the *isruna* text Br. and St Gall is derived from a common original text of the early ninth century. We have also traced insular influence, whether palaeographical, phonological, alphabetical (runic) or of contemporary allusion, in all three. Further, it has been mentioned that we possess in the Cambridge *Juvencus* MS. another cryptogram based on the same key as Ba. and Br., and this also is believed to be in an insular hand of the ninth century. It is difficult therefore to avoid a suspicion that all this cryptographic material is inspired from an insular centre. The archetype of the *isruna* tract is believed to have been drawn up on the Continent, possibly at St Gall; but the form of the runes, and indeed their arrangement, the *futhorc* itself as represented in our Continental MSS., are ultimately of Anglo-Saxon origin, probably developed on

[1] St Gall Stiftsbibliothek, MS. 270. The MS. does not appear in the St Gall catalogue before 1461.

[2] So apparently Bischoff. See Derolez[2], 91. Insular influence is traced in the contractions $I\mathbf{p} = autem$; $\mathbf{\mathfrak{o}} = con$; $\div = est$.

[3] Derolez[2], 89 ff.

the model of the Old Celtic *ogam* alphabet. Derolez himself is clearly of the opinion that the runic cryptographic material in question reached the Continent via Wales, and he concludes his account of the *isruna* tract with the significant words: 'There is perhaps one further argument in favour of connecting our *futhorc* with Wales: its *g*-rune is also found in Nemnivus's alphabet.'[1]

All this would seem to suggest that our Continental *isruna* tract with its *futhorc* of Anglo-Saxon origin may have derived its material from some British centre. In view of the derivation of Nennius's alphabet from the Anglo-Saxon *futhorc* it is tempting to suspect that such a centre was one with which Nennius was also associated or at any rate familiar. The association of this tract in the Brussels MS. with the so-called 'Bamberg cryptogram' would suggest, though of course it would not prove, that this centre was in Gwynedd. The cryptogram is concerned, of course, not with runic material, but with the Greek alphabet. It is perhaps not without significance, however, that in four of our Continental MSS. the runic material is found in the neighbourhood of Greek material. In the St Gall MS. 270 (cf. p. 98 above) it is followed by a paradigm of the Greek verb γράφω 'I write', and by Greek rhetorical terminology borrowed from Cassiodorus. In Br. it occurs at the end of the extracts from Cassiodorus containing many Greek words, and not far from a cryptogram based on the Greek numerical system. In yet another MS. (Vatican MS. Urbin. lat. 290) it is found on a page chiefly occupied by Greek alphabets and numerals.[2] The Continental manuscript tradition makes it clear that in the early ninth century British scribal tradition was active on the Continent in more than one centre, especially in Liége and St Gall;[3] and, moreover, that this tradition was especially pre-occupied with pedagogic material,[4] including some elementary knowledge of Greek. The milieu of the Bamberg cryptogram would seem to suggest that the court of Merfyn Vrych, and perhaps a related religious centre, may have been the British quarter in

[1] Derolez[(2)], 156, 161.

[2] Derolez[(2)], 160.

[3] It may have begun earlier. Hessels (*The Leiden Latin–Anglo-Saxon Glossary*, Cambridge, 1906, p. xiii) ascribes the famous *Leiden Glossary* to the late eighth century, and to St Gall, perhaps derived from an earlier glossary there.

[4] It may be mentioned here that the Eutychius section at the beginning of the ninth century MS. *Oxoniensis Prior* (cf. p. 45 above) begins with a treatise *de conjugationibus verborum*. See Bradshaw, *Collected Papers* (Cambridge, 1889), 457.

which this Latin–Greek cryptographic material was especially cultivated. Whether the British runic and Nennian cryptographic material are to be associated with the same centre depends largely on how far we accept the preface to the *Historia Brittonum*, with its reference to Nennius and Elfoddw, as a genuine production of Gwynedd and of the ninth century.

We have no clue as to where Dubthach was at the time when his cryptogram was posed to the 'four learned Irishmen' mentioned in the letter. These were evidently staying at the court of Merfyn in Gwynedd in North Wales when Dubthach's test was put to them. Their names are given as Caunchobrach, Fergus, Dominnach and Suadbar, and, without pressing individual identifications too closely, they seem to be connected with those Irish scholars working in various educated and literary circles on the Continent at this period. *Suadbar* has been identified conjecturally with the Irish bishop whose name appears as *Suathar* in a list of signatories to a deed of Beatus, abbot of Honau, an *ecclesia* or monastery of the Irish on an island in the Rhine near Colmar.[1] The deed, preserved only in a late copy, would seem to have been copied from an original probably written in 810.[2] It is of interest to note that the names of some of the other signatories of the same charter have been identified—again conjecturally, but again with considerable probability—as those of men closely associated with some of the leading Continental Irish scholars of the ninth century. One of these is *Congan episcopus*, probably the *Congan* who is known to have been one of the learned friends of Sedulius Scottus, and associated also with John Scottus Eriugena, and known to have been at one of the Irish centres on the Continent, perhaps Laon or Liége.[3] Another of the signatories, *Maucumgib* is perhaps the Irish monk *Maelchomber* known to have been at St Gall possibly in the second half of the ninth century.

Other names occurring in the Bamberg text may be identified conjecturally as those of Celtic scholars known chiefly but not exclusively from the marginalia of various manuscripts written on the Continent in the ninth century, where they formed an important element in the cultural, especially the monastic, life of the

[1] See Derolez[(1)], 372, n. 1.

[2] So J. M. Clark, *The Abbey of St Gall* (Cambridge, 1926), 40. For a suggested earlier possible date, see Derolez[(1)], *loc. cit.*

[3] Derolez[(1)] suggests that he may perhaps be the *Comgan* mentioned in the *Codex Boernerianus* and Berne MS. 363.

period. This aspect of Irish intellectual activity has been brilliantly reconstructed as the result of the labours of Nigra, of Traube and, in our own day, of Gougaud, J. M. Clark, Derolez and others. It is possible that the Dubthach who is held responsible for posing the cryptogram may be the scribe who wrote a manuscript now at Leiden (MS. Voss. Lat. 67) and who is also known from the *Codex Boernerianus* (Dresden MS. A. 145*b*), from St Gall (MS. 48), and from Berne (MS. 363), where *dub* (? for Dubthach) occurs three times.[1] He may also be identical with the scholar whose death is recorded in the *Annals of Ulster*, *s.a.* 868 (for 869): 'Dubthach mac Máel-Tuile, doctissimus Latinorum totius Europae, in Christo dormivit.'[2] We must not assume that Irish scholars who visited the court of Gwynedd in the ninth century were necessarily there on transit from Ireland. Some of them may have been visitors from their seats of professional activity, whether temporary or permanent, on the Continent.

Colgu, the *doctissimus magister* of the four scholars, is also probably referred to in the Berne MS. (363) referred to above. The text of the letter, as Derolez[1] points out, seems to indicate that Colgu was staying on the Continent (*trans Britannicum mare* = across the Channel). The common supposition that he was living in Ireland is based on the identification, believed to be erroneous,[3] of Colgu with Colcu of Clonmacnoise. The name, which is Irish, is a common one. It is chronologically improbable, though not impossible, that he is identical with the famous Colcu, the magister and teacher in Britain, doubtless at York, to whom Alcuin writes in 790: 'I thy son, and Joseph thy fellow-countryman', etc. The Joseph in question was also an Irishman.[4]

Of Dominnach, one of the two remaining Irishmen mentioned in the letter to Colgu, nothing appears to be known; but Fergus may possibly be identified with a Fergus who belonged to the learned circle of the scholar and poet Sedulius Scottus. The name is, of course, a very common one; but here we are not wholly without clues. In 848 Maelsechlainn, the high-king of Ireland, sent a mission to Charles the Bald, announcing a victory over the Northmen, and requesting a free passage for a pilgrimage to Rome.[5]

---

[1] Derolez[1], 371. See however V. H. Friedel, *Zeitschrift für celt. Philol.* III (1901), p. 122, n. 2.   [2] Kenney, *op. cit.* 557.
[3] See Kenney, *op. cit.* 534, n. 104.   [4] Kenney, *op. cit.* 534.
[5] *S. Prudentii Annales, sive Annalium Bertinianorum pars secunda*, Migne, *P.L.* cxv, col. 1401; *Les Annales de Saint-Bertin*, edited by C. Dehaisnes (Paris,

Sedulius arrived at Liége about the same time, possibly as a member of this mission;[1] and we know that he was well received by Bishop Hartgar and the bishops of the neighbouring sees; but he was also something of a courtier and a poet, and addressed pane-gyric poems to members of the royal families and the nobility.[2] Among the poems attributed to him[3] is one (*Carmen* XXXIV) in which Sedulius speaks of a certain Fergus and three of his com-panions (Marcus, Blandus, and Beuchell) as 'the four-wheeled chariot of the Lord, the glory of the Irish race', and Fergus himself is also credited with having composed a poem in honour of Charles the Bald (*Carmen* XXXV). Sedulius and the poet Fergus, then, both belonged to a learned and cultivated society, associated with Liége, and in close touch with Charles the Bald, who, till his death in 877, was the most zealous patron of learning in the West.

Have we any reason to suppose that Fergus, the poet and friend of Sedulius, was identical with the Fergus of the letter to Colgu, Fergus the Irishman who had sojourned at Merfyn's court? I think we have. It does not amount to proof; but cumulatively it is not inconsiderable. In the first place, Sedulius himself was one of the most learned men of his time, with a substantial, though doubtless limited, knowledge of Greek—not necessarily acquired in Ireland.[4] Fergus the poet, his friend, must himself also have been a learned man, to judge from the evidence of the poems cited above; and the suggestion that he may have been the learned Irishman of the letters to Colgu gains support from the fact that there is known to have been intercourse between Liége and Bam-

1871), part II by Prudentius, bishop of Troyes, p. 68: 'Scotti super Nortmannos irruentes, auxilio Domini nostri Jesu Christi victores, eos a suis finibus pro-pellunt; unde rex Scottorum ad Karolum pacis et amicitiae gratia legatos cum muneribus mittit, viam sibi petendi Romam concedi deposcens.'

[1] So L. Traube, 'O Roma Nobilis': *Philologische Untersuchungen aus dem Mittelalter, Abhandlungen der Philosophisch-Philologischen Classe der königlich-Bayerischen Akademie der Wissenschaften*, XIX, 1892 (VII. *Sedulius Scottus*), 342. Kenney (*op. cit.* 555) regards this suggestion as 'pure supposition' and considers that the mention of *Roricus* by Sedulius suggests that the latter may have spent some time in Wales on his way to the Continent. The two suggestions, however, are by no means mutually exclusive.

[2] *Sedulii Scotti Carmina. Monumenta Germaniae Historica: Poetae Latini Aevi Carolini*, III edited by L. Traube (Berlin, 1896), 151 ff.

[3] On the question of attribution, see Traube, 'O Roma Nobilis', 358.

[4] On the question of knowledge of Greek among the Irish, see Traube, 'O Roma Nobilis', 353 ff.; and more recently B. Bischoff, 'Das Griechische Element in der abendländischen Bildung des Mittelalters', *Byzantinische Zeitschrift*, XLIV (Münich, 1951), 27 ff.

berg at this time.[1] Above all there are some grounds for associating Sedulius himself with the court of Gwynedd in the middle of the ninth century, about the time when the Fergus of the letter to Colgu must have been there. The evidence is as follows.

Among the poems attributed to Sedulius three[2] have a special interest for us. At least one of these is a panegyric addressed to a certain King *Roricus* who has apparently set up a Christian 'altar' to contain the relics of the saints.[3] The Roricus in question has been thought by Nigra, Traube and most subsequent scholars to be identical with Rhodri Mawr, son of Merfyn Vrych, and ruler of Gwynedd.[4] This poem and two others by Sedulius, perhaps addressed to the same Rhodri, may have been written before Sedulius reached the Continent, for the first of the three (Carmen XLV) celebrates a victory over the Northmen, and the poet's apparent association with Rhodri Mawr suggests that it may have reference to the Welsh victory by Rhodri in 856,[5] when he killed the leader of the Danes who had previously ravaged Anglesey.[6]

The evidence suggests that Sedulius Scottus and his friend Fergus belonged to the same circle of learned and gifted Irish scholars as that of Colgu's four Irish pupils, and that all had been in residence, however temporarily, at the court of Gwynedd, first under Merfyn, then under his son Rhodri; and that they belonged to the colonies of Irish scholars which had grown up in various Continental circles from the seventh century onwards. It may be added that the wording of the letter to Colgu seems to make it clear that this sojourn of Irish scholars at the Gwynedd court was no isolated incident, but a regular practice for which careful intellectual preparation was to be made if the Irish scholars were not to be put to the blush. A high intellectual level, according to the standards of the time, was evidently exacted. The conclusion that the court of Gwynedd in the middle of the ninth century was in touch with the most educated elements in Ireland on the one hand, and with the colonies of the most learned and cultivated Irish scholars in western Europe on the other, is inescapable.

[1] See Derolez[(1)], 373 and the reference.
[2] *Ed. cit.*; the poems in question are *Carmina* XLV–XLVII, pp. 208, 209.
[3] *Carmen* XLVII.
[4] See Traube, 'O Roma Nobilis' (VII. *Sedulius Scottus*), 342; cf. however Traube, *Sedulii Scotti Carmina. Poetae Latini Aevi Carolini*, III, 342 f.
[5] The event was famous and is noted in the Irish Annals, e.g. the *Annals of Ulster*.　　　　　[6] Cf. the *Cambrian Annals*, s.a. 853.

Before leaving this subject I should like to call attention to another link in the chain which with reasonable probability may be forged between Ireland and the Continent through Gwynedd at this time, and more especially between Gwynedd and the circle of Sedulius and his friend Fergus. This is a certain Marcus of whom we have a number of scattered notices, and who seems to stand out as a clearer figure than any of those whom we have yet considered, perhaps not even excepting Sedulius himself. A brief study of these notices of Marcus and his milieu will be illuminating therefore as giving us some further insight into the type of scholars who passed between Gwynedd and the Irish colonies of the Continent, the level of their scholarship, and the kind of work in which they were engaged. This, after all, is a more important matter than the actual identification of the individuals.

First of all we learn from Ekkehard[1] that at the time of Abbot Grimald of St Gall (842–72), the abbey was visited by 'a certain Marcus, a bishop of the Scots' (i.e. the Irish) on his return from Rome. He was accompanied by his nephew Moengal, later called Marcellus by the brethren, after his uncle Marcus, who was, we are told, very learned 'in both human and divine matters'. Both remained in the monastery by the invitation of the brethren, and Marcellus and the famous Notker, later known as Notker Balbulus, were placed in the inner school. Notker later speaks of himself as the pupil of Marcellus (*magistro meo Marcello*).[2] It is clear from what is said that Marcus, the 'bishop of the Irish', had a store of books with him which he valued no less than his gold and his pallium. We must suppose that he had been to Rome to receive the pallium, as became a good bishop of the reformed Church of Ireland; and that, like Benedict Biscop, he had taken the opportunity to purchase a library for his own use, since he would hardly have taken a load of books from Ireland to Rome only to carry them back. It was evidently in the interests of scholarship that the monks of St Gall were anxious to retain the two travellers.

Now this is just about the time, soon after 848, that we find Sedulius composing the poem of welcome referred to above to his friends, the 'four-wheeled chariot of the Irish race', Fergus,

---

[1] Ekkehard, *Casus S. Galli*, edited by von Arx, in *Mon. Germ. Hist. Script.* II, 78, The passage is translated by Kenney, *op. cit.* 104.

[2] *Liber Sequentiarum, Praefatio*, Migne, *P.L.* CXXXI, col. 1004.

Marcus, Blandus and Beuchell, who have evidently just joined the Irish colony at Liége. As Clark points out,[1] Fergus and Blandus are addressed by Sedulius as men of his own age, while Beuchell appears to be younger. Blandus and Beuchell seem to have gone on to Milan. It becomes reasonably likely that Marcus went on, first to Rome, then to St Gall. In the Dresden *Codex Epistolarum Pauli Boernerianus*, which contains the Epistles of St Paul in Latin and Greek, we find on fo. 111 *b* a fragment of *De Lege Spirituali* by one 'Marcus monachus'. Traube regarded it as almost certain that this manuscript was written by Sedulius, who seems to have spent some time in Italy.[2] The learned Fergus,[3] associated with Marcus by Sedulius, and in all probability identical with Fergus, the friend of Sedulius, may well be the Fergus whose name occurs in several Continental manuscripts,[4] notably those of Leiden and Berne, and who has been thought to be probably the transcriber of the manuscript of the Greek and Latin Gospels contained in St Gall MS. 48, where his name appears on the margin.

Without vouching for the certainty of these identifications we cannot doubt that many of the most important manuscripts known to have been written at the centres of Irish learning on the Continent contain Irish names which are those of monks recognised as having belonged to the circle of Sedulius, viz. Fergus, Donngus, Dubthach, Cathasach, Congan, Johannes,[5] Marcus monachus, Dermoth, Blandus and Beuchell.[6] I think it is at least extremely probable that Marcus monachus is the 'bishop of the Irish' who joined the monks of St Gall.

[1] *Op. cit.* 35.

[2] 'O Roma Nobilis', 348. For a contrary view see Zimmer, 'Über die Bedeutung des irischen Elements für die mittelalterliche Cultur', in *Preussische Jahrbücher*, LIX (1887), 27 ff.

[3] Clark (*op. cit.* 37) suggests the possible identity of Fergus with Marcus's nephew Marcellus or Moengal. His evidence, though attractive, is inconclusive. Zimmer, on the other hand, suggested the identification of Moengal with Maonghal Alithir ('the pilgrim') referred to in the *Annals of the Four Masters s.a.* 840 as the author of a poem on the death of the high king Níall; and in the *Annals of Ulster, s.a.* 870, where reference is made to the death of Moengal Ailithir, abbot of Bangor (see *Keltische Beiträge*, III, *Zeitschrift für deutsches Altertum*, XXXV (1891), 113, n. 1). Traube ('O Roma Nobilis', 361) and Clark (*op. cit.* 37) both reject this identification on different grounds. See further Clark, *loc. cit.*, n. 1.

[4] See Nigra, *Reliquie Celtiche* (Turin, 1872), 12, 19.

[5] I.e. Johannes Eriugena, 'John of Ériu', i.e. of Ireland.

[6] See Clark, *op. cit.* 36, and the references there cited. Cf. also Nigra, *op. cit.* 11.

We have also important contemporary information of a British bishop Marcus who was living at Soissons *c.* 873. Our informant is Heiric of Auxerre, who became sub-deacon in the monastery of St Germain in Auxerre in 859,[1] and who composed a *Vita* of St Germanus in Latin hexameters in six books,[2] to which he later added two books in prose on the saint's *Miracula*.[3] It is particularly interesting to note that Heiric undertook this work at the request of Abbot Lothair of St Germain (864-5), son of Charles the Bald. All our evidence goes to show the keen interest of this family in the Celtic countries—an interest which extended not only to Irish and British pilgrims and residents in their domains but, it would seem, also to their traditions, at least in so far as these could be linked with those of the church of Auxerre. The two interests are indeed closely connected, for Celtic pilgrims must have been profitable guests, and I have shown elsewhere[4] that the cult of St Germanus was an all-important element in the cultivation of the prestige of his shrine and the see of Auxerre, in which Charles's son Lothair was the abbot of the monastery of St Germain.

Among the miracles of the saint which Heiric relates he cites one in particular which he claims to have on the authority of 'a holy old man Marcus, a bishop of that race', i.e. of the British nation among whom Germanus performed the miracle in question. And Heiric continues that this old man,

being by race a Briton educated in Ireland, and having for a long time filled the holy office of a bishop in Britain, elected to become a pilgrim. Accordingly, having come to France, enjoying the munificence of the most pious King Charles, he follows the life of an anchorite in the monastery of SS. Médard and Sebastian and in my own day is out-standing for his singular piety.[5]

---

[1] See Traube, 'O Roma Nobilis', 370. For a somewhat fuller account of Heiric and his work I may refer to my book on *Poetry and Letters in Early Christian Gaul* (Cambridge, 1955), 267.

[2] Edited by Traube, *Poetae Latini Aevi Carolini*, III, 421 ff. See also Migne, *P.L.* CXXIV, col. 1131 ff.

[3] *De Miraculis S. Germani*, Migne, *P.L.* CXXIV, col. 1207 ff.

[4] *Poetry and Letters in Early Christian Gaul*, 267 ff.

[5] 'Fertur unum famosum inter caetera, cujus ad nos notitia per sanctum senem Marcum, ejusdem gentis episcopum decucurrit. Qui natione quidem Brito, educatus vero in Hibernia, post longa pontificalis sanctitatis exercitia, ultroneam sibi peregrinationem indixit. Sic traductus in Franciam, piissimique regis Caroli munificentia illectus, apud beatorum Medardi et Sebastianique coenobium anachoreticam exercet vitam, singularis nostro tempore unicae philosophus sanctitatis' (*De Miraculis S. Germani*, Book I, c. VIII, 80).

And at the close of the account of the miracle he adds: 'These things the bishop affirmed by oath to be contained in Britain in Catholic writings'.[1]

Clark notes that the approximate date of the arrival of Marcus at St Gall is about 850; that Heiric wrote in 873, when the Marcus of Soissons was still living as an old man; that Heiric twice refers to him as a bishop; and that Marcus at St Gall was referred to as *Marcus episcopus*.[2] We must not overlook the fact that Marcus of Soissons came from Britain and enjoyed the munificence of Charles the Bald, and that it was under Charles's auspices also that Sedulius, and his friends Fergus, Marcus and their companions, lived and wrote in the neighbourhood of Liége. Equally significant is the coincidence of the association of Sedulius the Irishman with the court of Gwynedd under King Rhodri;[3] and so also is the British bishop who bore the same name as Sedulius's friend Marcus and who is cited as an authority on Welsh traditions about St Germanus—traditions known to us elsewhere only from the work of Nennius's *Historia Brittonum*, and recorded at latest about this time. We have already noted the close association of the 'Marcus monachus' of St Gall with Sedulius, and the occurrence of the name and epithet in a MS. believed by Traube to have been written by Sedulius himself. On the whole, there seem to be good reasons for thinking it probable that the Welsh anchorite of Soissons, with his Irish education and his Welsh episcopal title, and with his experience and his knowledge of Welsh tradition, and his subsequent 'pilgrimage' (*peregrinatio*), is no other than the friend of Sedulius and Fergus. It would seem probable also that he is the same 'Marcus monachus' who, with his nephew Marcellus, had undertaken a journey to Rome at an earlier date, and lived for a time in the monastery of St Gall.[4]

Perhaps we can trace him one stage further. We saw earlier in this article that the Vatican recension of the *Historia Brittonum* claims to be the work of a certain 'Marcus anachoreta eiusdem

---

[1] 'Haec ita apud Britanniam catholicis litteris contineri, praedictus mihi episcopus, jusjurandi interpositione firmabat' (*ibid.* 82).

[2] *Op. cit.* 34; cf. 31.

[3] Nigra long ago pointed to the connection here implied between Sedulius and Wales (*Reliquie Celtiche*, 12, 13). Cf. also Traube (p. 103 above).

[4] Clark has given careful consideration (*op. cit.* 33) to the fact that Marcus's name occurs in the St Gall *necrologium* but shows that this is no proof that he actually died in St Gall.

gentis [i.e. the British] sanctus episcopus'. Here I would call attention to the similarity of the actual wording of this description of Marcus to that used by Heiric (†876) of the British bishop Marcus to whom he expresses himself indebted for information about St Germanus—'sanctus senex Marcus ejusdem gentis [i.e. the British] episcopus...anchoreticam exercet vitam' (p. 106, note 5 above). The verbal correspondence may be of course fortuitous; but associated as the two passages are with a man of the name Marcus who was evidently an authority on St Germanus, the more natural explanation is to suppose that Marcus *anachoreta* and *episcopus* of the Vatican recension of the *Historia* is the Marcus the anchorite and *episcopus* of Soissons, perhaps also the Marcus *monachus* who evidently visited Rome and St Gall about the same time. The date of the Vatican text is, of course, too late to be itself the work of Heiric's friend; but the exemplar from which it was copied may have been his work;[1] and this may also be the source of the British glosses on the sites of Arthur's battles (cf. p. 40 above). In any case a belief was evidently current in some quarters that one Mark 'the anchorite' had been responsible for editing one of the recensions of the *Historia Brittonum*. We have already noted Thurneysen's view that the Vatican recension is based on the Harleian and the Chartres versions. But as the latter itself claims to be derived from a Life of St Germanus, is it not possible that this Chartres text, like the Vatican recension, represents an edition of a text of the *Historia* made after the *Liber Britannicus* had been combined with a *Liber Sancti Germani*,[2] the latter possibly supplied by Mark himself? It would seem that he was the principal authority on St Germanus in French intellectual circles in the ninth century.

A final word about Marcus. We have seen that the cryptogram represented by the Bamberg and Brussels texts contains a note of greeting by Mermen, ruler of Gwynedd in North Wales, to Concenn, ruler of Powys, who died at Rome in 854. We have also seen that the Brussels text of this cryptogram is thought to be probably in a ninth-century hand typical of St Gall; and we have noted that St Gall is exactly where we should expect to find it, since Concenn, if he travelled overland to Rome, would inevitably pause at St Gall

---

[1] Kenney (*op. cit.* 154, 593) recognises this possibility, while he also envisages the possibility that the compiler is merely referring to Heiric's indebtedness to Marcus.

[2] See Van Hamel, *Lebor Bretnach*, xxx.

on his journey. Moreover, this same Brussels codex contains the *isruna* tract with its runic alphabet of Anglo-Saxon type, its associations with Nennius, and its probable Welsh provenance. Again, we have seen that a St Gall codex of the early ninth century in an insular hand contained a closely related version of the *isruna* tract and other related material. Finally we have seen that Marcus, 'a bishop of the Scots...most learned in divine and human matters', together with his nephew Moengal, later known as Marcellus, made a stay of some length in St Gall *c.* 850 on their way north from Rome, and that Marcellus remained there permanently in charge of the cloister school, which included among other boys who had entered monastic life the famous Notker, afterwards called Balbulus, who referred to Marcellus later as his teacher (*magister meus*). The chronicler Ekkehard, to whom we are indebted for these notices, adds significantly: 'It is pleasing to remember how much the monastery of St Gall began to grow under these auspices.'[1] It would seem natural to suggest[2] that in addition to the matter relating to St Germanus, our cryptographic and pedagogic material formed a part of the stock-in-trade which gained Marcus his reputation for great learning, and which made him and his nephew, the teacher of the 'inner school', welcome inmates and promoters of education in the great school of learning at St Gall.[3] We know that Marcus carried with him a store of books. If, in fancy, we like to speculate still further on the travels of our cryptogram and runes, we may accompany them in a final journey to Liége, where later a St Gall monk Notker became bishop (972–1007).[4]

To sum up: the evidence discussed above suggests—it can be no more than a suggestion—that precisely at the time of Maelsechlainn's mission to Charles the Bald, three of the most important of the Celtic scholars whose subsequent careers were on the Continent, partly in Liége, partly in St Gall, were associated with Rhodri's court in North Wales, possibly as native Britons, in the

---

[1] Ekkehard, Casus S. Galli (*ed. cit.*), *Mon. Germ. Hist.: Script.* ii, 79. See J. M. Clark, *The Abbey of St Gall* (Cambridge, 1926), 32f.; Kenney, *op. cit.* 596.

[2] The suggestion has already been made by Derolez[(2)], p. 154, in regard to the cryptogram. In addition cf. p. 99, n. 2 above.

[3] A facsimile of a great plan of the complex of buildings associated (whether actually or merely as an ideal or project) with the monastery of St Gall in the time of Abbot Gosbert (*c.* 816–37) has been published, together with a commentary, by Hans Reinhardt, *Der St. Galler Klosterplan* (St Gall, 1952).

[4] *Ibid.* 95.

case of Marcus, or as temporary visitors in the case of Sedulius. The evidence of the cryptogram shows the court to have been a centre of learning and culture. Despite the tentative nature of much of the evidence, and the tenuous identifications of the names, we can hardly doubt that in the middle of the ninth century the court of Gwynedd was a halting place on a route for Irish scholars and *peregrini*, 'travellers' and 'pilgrims' journeying to the Continent; and that, like Liége and other centres, it offered special facilities for travellers (*peregrini*) and hospitality for learned and cultured scholars.

8. THE CULT OF ST GERMANUS

One is tempted to ask what motives, apart from the intellectual activity for which this dynasty is famous, may have stimulated Charles the Bald and his son Abbot Lothair to forward Celtic interests with so much vigour. Apparently the immediate purpose actuating both was the encouragement of Celtic pilgrims to the shrines of the Continental Roman saints. This would be doubly profitable, both as giving them the papal support which had already crowned Charlemagne emperor, and which was to crown Charles himself emperor in 875; and also as giving them the money which the Celtic *peregrini* would pay to the famous religious centres at which they would receive hospitality. Among these centres two of the most important were Tours, devoted to the cult of St Martin, and Auxerre, of which the patron saint was St Germanus. Auxerre was under the special charge of Abbot Lothair himself, and both the abbot and his royal father may therefore be presumed to have had a special interest in promoting the cult of its patron saint.

Now there seems to have been serious rivalry towards the close of the fifth century between the growing cult of St Martin and that of St Germanus, and I have shown grounds elsewhere[1] for thinking it probable that the *Life of St Germanus*, composed by Constantius about this time, may have been written with a view to superseding the *Life of St Martin* by Sulpicius Severus. We have good reason to believe that the cult of St Martin was introduced into Canterbury shortly before 588 by Liudhard, the Frankish chaplain of the Frankish princess Bertha who became the wife of King Æthelberht of Kent about this time. Apart from a few

[1] *Poetry and Letters in Early Christian Gaul*, 272f.

dedications in Kent the cult of St Martin seems to have made little headway in Britain till later times, when it was probably reintroduced into our islands from Ireland.[1] On the other hand in France, about the time of the introduction of St Martin into Kent by Bertha, the cult was reaching the height of its popularity.

It is probably not without significance for this struggle between the rival cults of St Martin and St Germanus that we find Bishop Aunachar of Auxerre,[2] whose activity fell between the years 575 and 589, writing a letter to the presbyter Stephen requesting him to write the life of St Germanus in verse, and that of St Amator, his predecessor in the see of Auxerre, in prose. The letter is still extant, and believed to be genuine; but if this verse *Life* was written it has not survived. We have seen, however, that Abbot Lothair, who seems to have found Aunachar's letter some three centuries later, induced Heiric to write a new *Life* of Germanus, to which a separate work on the *Miracula* was added by the same author. It would seem not improbable that this new stimulus was given by the presence of the British bishop who had settled at Soissons, and to whom Heiric claims to have been indebted for some information about the saint (cf. pp. 105 f. above). He tells us, moreover, that the British bishop had been induced to settle in the *coenobium* of SS. Médard and Sebastian at Soissons in response to the generosity of Charles the Bald. May we suspect that the British bishop's knowledge of the British traditions relating to St Germanus had been the reason why Charles had induced him to take up his residence among them? This, at least, would be in accordance with the use which Heiric made of the bishop's specialised British local knowledge, and with the keen interest taken by Charles's son Lothair, the bishop of Auxerre, in the cult of Germanus.

If I am right in suggesting that a special interest was felt by the family of Charles the Bald in the cult of St Germanus we must conclude that Gwynedd and Powys would be the Celtic area with which Charles's court would naturally encourage the most lively

[1] This is suggested by the distribution of dedications as well as by literary evidence.

[2] For Bishop Aunachar see Duchesne, *Fastes Épiscopaux*, ii, 431. His activities cover the years 573–89 or longer (*ibid.* 439 f.; cf. 427). W. Levison, 'Bischof Germanus von Auxerre, und die Quellen zu seiner Geschichte', *Neues Archiv der Gesellschaft für ältere deutsche Geschichtskunde*, xxix (1904), 158 f. Aunachar's letter to Stephen and Stephen's reply are published in *Mon. Germ. Hist.: Epist.* iii, 447.

communication. For this was the area where late tradition, as recorded in the *Historia Brittonum*, has located the saint's main activities; and Powys, down to its absorption in Gwynedd by Merfyn's marriage to Nest, the sister of Concenn, was ruled by a dynasty which the *Historia Brittonum* (c. 32) claims to have been created by the instrumentality of Germanus himself. For this and other information relating to the saint, the *Historia* claims (c. 47) to be recording information contained in a *Book of St Germanus* which, from the nature of its contents, was clearly totally distinct from the only extant *Life* of the saint, composed by the presbyter Constantius at the request of Bishop Patiens of Lyons towards the close of the fifth century. The *Historia* is believed to have been compiled in its present form at latest early in the ninth century. The reference to the *Book of St Germanus* can hardly be dissociated from Heiric's reference to the account of the saint's miracles which he had received from the British bishop, who had assured him that they were still preserved in Britain in written form. Can this be a reference to the *Historia Brittonum* itself, or to the *Book of St Germanus* on which the *Historia* claims to have drawn?[1]

We have other important witnesses to the concentration of French interest on St Germanus about this time. These are the Vatican codex, which, as we have seen, claims to be the work of Mark the Anchorite; and the Chartres MS. of the *Historia Brittonum*, our earliest known copy of the work, which, as already said (p. 39 above), is believed to date from c. 900, possibly a little earlier.[2] The text is poor and fragmentary, but highly selective, concerning itself especially with the activities of St Germanus. The deliberate character of this selection is indicated by the heading which occurs in this MS. alone, and which, despite its obscurity, seems to claim that what follow are passages (?'excerpts') made by a son of Urbgen, which he had found in a *Book of St Germanus*. This *Urbgen* is tentatively identified with *Urien* the lord of Rheged, to whom reference has been made above, and the son here referred to with the *Rum* (? for *Run*) *map Urbgen*, who is mentioned in c. 63 of the *Historia* as having baptised Edwin the Northumbrian king, known to have been converted in 627. From three ninth-century sources, therefore, we learn that a book about St Germanus,

[1] *Historia Brittonum*, c. 47.
[2] F. Lot seems to incline to a later date, perhaps tenth century (*Nennius et l'Historia Brittonum*, 30 f.).

and more especially his miracles, was believed to be current in Britain at that time. The Chartres text seems to associate it more particularly with the family of Urien, lord of Rheged, the most illustrious member of the family which, as we have seen, is traditionally claimed to have given to Gwynedd both its ruling dynasty under Merfyn and Rhodri, and in addition the patron saint of its principal monastery.[1]

There is at least a strong probability that the *Book of St Germanus* referred to by the author of the *Historia*, and partly incorporated in it, is the book referred to by Heiric's friend the British bishop. In both the *miracula* are evidently a prominent, if not the principal, element. To judge from the nature of the four passages in the *Historia* devoted to the activities of the saint, they are derived ultimately from oral tradition, or saga, rather than from a source composed by an educated monkish author.[2] In the Chartres text the claim made by the heading possibly suggests that Rhun, son of Urien of Rheged, had made use of the same written source. If so this written source would presumably have been composed in either south-western Scotland or North Wales, at some period not later than the seventh century, the period at which, as I have shown elsewhere,[3] the supporters of the Anglo-Roman party in the Celtic Church were beginning to write the *Vitae* of important saints. The use by Marcus of Soissons and by Nennius of this early *Life* suggests a possible origin in North or East Wales, and this, as we have already observed, is the region where the traditions of the saint seem to have been deliberately fostered, whereas written record, tradition and dedications are alike silent about Germanus in north-western England and southern Scotland.

At this point we may pause for a moment to consider briefly the various phases through which the Germanus tradition can be

---

[1] The death of St Deiniol of the 'Bangors' is recorded in the *Annales Cambriae, s.a.* 584; a comparison of genealogies 8, 11, 12, and 19 in MS. Harl. 3859 with that contained in the *Bonedd y Saint*, indicates that he was traditionally regarded as the son of a certain Dunaut Fawr, son of Pappo Post Priten, who was the brother of the father of Gwrgi and Peredur, themselves first cousins of Cinmarc, the father of Urien of Rheged.

[2] Sir Ifor Williams would derive them from a saga of Vortigern; but an ecclesiastical saga devoted to St Germanus himself is perhaps more probable. Perhaps these two suggestions are not mutually exclusive. I have discussed this subject more fully in *Studies in Early British History* (Cambridge, 1954), 39 ff.

[3] 'St Ninian: A Preliminary Study of Sources', *Transactions of the Dumfriesshire and Galloway Natural History and Antiquarian Society*, XXVII (1950).

traced. From Prosper early in the fifth century we gather that he was primarily an emissary to Britain against the Pelagian heresy. For Constantius, towards the close of the century, his mission to Britain was largely of a military character, and directed against the Celtic troublers of Roman Britain and their Saxon allies. In the traditions of the saint incorporated in the *Historia* the issue is represented as a local and a moral one; but the underlying political bias is manifest. Germanus's enemy is Vortigern, the traditional ruler of Powys; and the object of the saint's principal activities is his utter annihilation, even from his ancient and well-established position on the pedigree of the royal line. There can be no doubt that the incorporation in the *Historia* of these traditions, claiming derivation from a British *Book of St Germanus*, are inspired by strong and even bitter hostility to the royal line of Powys and perhaps also of Gwynedd. The most natural quarter from which such hostility might be supposed to come in the ninth century would probably be from the supporters of Hywel Dda. It would seem likely on the whole, therefore, that Marcus, whether deliberately or unwittingly, was bearing witness in the circle of Charles the Bald and the ecclesiastical circles in France to a tradition highly favourable to the political prestige of Powys and of Gwynedd, of Concenn, the pilgrim to Rome, and of Merfyn and Rhodri.

I have called attention elsewhere to the fact that Constantius nowhere mentions Vortigern in his *Life of St Germanus*. Presumably therefore the tradition of the contest of the saint with the British king is not so old as the fifth century. If we could trust the heading of the Chartres text, and believe that the account of the saint therein contained was derived by a son of Urien, probably Run, from a British source, we should presumably date these extracts to the seventh century; in fact to a period of about the time of the conversion of Edwin of Northumbria, recorded in the *Annales Cambriae* in 626. The conversion is attributed by Bede to Paulinus, bishop of York; but according to Nennius (c. 63) and to the *Annales Cambriae, s.a.* 626, it was Run the son of Urien who brought it about. We are not, of course, suggesting at this point that the testimony of Nennius should be accepted as against that of Bede; but the statement of Nennius is important not only as being derived from early (perhaps written) tradition, but as attesting, or perhaps attempting to establish, a tradition that a son of Urien was an important ecclesiastic of the early seventh century, presumably the one to whom the Chartres text attributed the responsibility for the Germanus legends incorporated in the *Historia Brittonum*. Since we know that Mark, the British bishop and anchorite, handed on to Heiric in the ninth century Germanus legends which he had obtained in Britain, as he alleged, in written form, one is tempted to think it likely that they may have been handed on from Run map Urien. It has been suggested that the written British source cited by Mark and Heiric as their authority for stories of St Germanus may, in fact, have been a version of the *Historia Brittonum* itself, perhaps closely related to the Chartres text. Is it possible to see in these two traditions of the conversion of Edwin the rivalry of the Celtic and the Roman Churches for the credit of the conversion of the Bernician king?[1]

This brief review of the growth and spread of the Germanus tradition in France and Britain may help to throw some light on the policy of Charles the Bald and his son Abbot Lothair. As a part of the deliberate encouragement of pilgrims to Rome and to their own great religious centres, notably Auxerre, they seem to have realised the importance of appealing to the popular imagination by developing the traditions of local saints.[2] For this purpose the important expedition of St Germanus to Britain, vouched for by Prosper of Aquitaine, and the local Welsh *additamenta* to the traditions related by Constantius, were eagerly exploited in France. Heiric even claims St Patrick as a disciple of Germanus,[3] which shows clearly the relatively high prestige which he attributed to the saint of Auxerre. But whatever the motive which inspired this concentrated literary activity in regard to St Germanus, there can be no doubt that its chief centre in the ninth century was not in Britain but in France.

Meanwhile Heiric was fully aware of the importance of Irish pilgrims, and it is thought possible that one of his own teachers may have been an Irishman, a certain Elian, afterwards bishop of

---

[1] It is tempting to call attention to the controversial tone employed by Nennius in his statement about the conversion of the Northumbrians by Run: 'If anyone wishes to know who baptised them, Rum map Urbgen baptised them.' But the phrase is used elsewhere by Nennius (e.g. c.c. 10, 15) and others, and it would be unwise to press the controversial nuance.

[2] Similarly St Paulinus already at the beginning of the fifth century had encouraged pilgrimages to the shrine of the local saint, Felix, at Nola by recording in fresco and in verse the stories of his miracles.

[3] See Kenney, *op. cit.* 593. The claim is, of course, made in a number of Irish sources, and is historically worthless.

Angoulême.[1] At the opening of the *Miracula* he attributes to Germanus an Irish disciple Michomeri,[2] and in the dedicatory Epistle to his *Vita Germani* he speaks of Irishmen coming to the country of Charles the Bald in such numbers that Greece herself is envious, adding that the whole of Ireland with her learned men is eager to brave the dangers of the sea and embrace the life of an exile to satisfy the wishes of the king of the Franks.[3] We know that they took their books with them. It is just about the time that Heiric was writing that the famous manuscript of the *Antiphonary of Bangor* found its way to Bobbio in Italy.[4] The plundering of the monasteries by the Vikings made a safe asylum for scholars and their libraries very necessary at this time, and the amenities offered them by Charles would be of mutual benefit from many points of view, whether the pilgrims remained with him permanently, or went on to other monastic centres of learning. We have already seen reason to regard Gwynedd as an intermediate centre offering similar amenities to Irishmen travelling to the Continent.

It is perhaps in the light of these considerations that we may interpret a note on the upper margin of the St Gall MS. of Priscian's Latin Grammar:[5] *Ruadri adest*.[6] The MS. is believed to have been in the hands of the circle of Sedulius, though not necessarily written by one of them. The script is Irish minuscule; the abbreviations and orthography are Irish; and the scribes all bear Irish names,[7] the master of the scriptorium being apparently a certain Máel-brigte. The MS. has been assigned to the middle or first half[8] of the ninth century. Nigra[9] favoured the date 845 or 856 suggested by Güterbock,[10] but this close dating depends on the

---

[1] See Kenney, *op. cit.* 593; cf. *ibid.* 592. In a sacramentary of the church of Angoulême a note has been added to the margin in an eleventh-century hand to the effect that 'Helias Scotigena acted according to this rule, and bishop Ugo according to the Roman order.' Hugues I was bishop of Angoulême *c.* 988.

[2] Migne, *P.L.* cxxiv, col. 1211. An alternative form *Michomeres* is also given. Kuno Meyer suggests that this should perhaps be *Michomairle* (*Learning in Ireland in the Fifth Century* (Dublin, 1913), 23 f.).

[3] Migne, *P.L.* cxxiv, col. 1133.

[4] F. E. Warren, *Antiphonary of Bangor* (London, 1893, 1895), xiiff.

[5] For a general description of this MS. see Whitley Stokes and John Strachan, *Thesaurus Palaeohibernicus*, ii (Cambridge, 1903), xix.

[6] Nigra, *Reliquie Celtiche* (Turin, 1872), 20; cf. Stokes and Strachan, *op. cit.* ii, p. xx.

[7] These are listed by Nigra, *op. cit.* 11. Among them we find *Fergus*.

[8] Traube, *op. cit.* 347. Cf. also Stokes and Strachan, *op. cit.* ii, p. xix, n. 5.

[9] Nigra, *op. cit.* 13.

[10] *Zeitschrift für Vergleichende Sprachforschung*, xxxiii (1895), 92, n.

identification of the *Ruadri* of the margin with Rhodri Mawr, whose reign probably began in 844, and who, as we have seen, killed a certain Horm (i.e. *Gorm*), the leader of the Danes, in 856.[1] Both the approximate dating and the Irish milieu[2] of the manuscript are supported by the gloss in the same manuscript, in which Dermot, a member of the folk of the unity of Tallaght in Leinster, is invoked as a saint. Dermot is known to have been a disciple of Máelrúain, and a prominent scribe and anchorite, whose obit is recorded in the *Annals* in 825, and who is there described as a religious teacher of all Ireland. To him is attributed the origin of Dísert Díarmada, the *desertum* or 'anchorite's cell of Dermot', an important centre of culture in south-eastern Leinster, of which the name survives today in *Castledermot*. Here we find still standing two of the finest examples of the Irish sculptured high crosses of the ninth century;[3] and the importance of the place at this period can be inferred from the fact that according to the *Annals of the Four Masters, s.a.* 885, Cormac of Cashel, the greatest Irish scholar of this period, was educated here. The occurrence of the name of the founder of this monastery, together with the name *Ruadri*[4] on the margin of this manuscript, in addition to the other considerations already mentioned, make it probable that the late Dr Flower was right in saying that it could be shown that the *St Gall Priscian* was 'written by scholars from Leinster passing through Wales on their way to the Continent, in the years 845-6'.[5]

I have suggested above that the original lost Irish annals were inspired by a cultural movement in south-east Leinster rather than in south-east Ulster, and that it was ultimately from some Leinster centre, and not from Bangor in Co. Down, that the inspiration, and even the original nucleus of Irish annals, came to the compiler of the *Cambrian Annals*. Two important factors must be stressed here. The first is that in the period of which we are speaking, the

---

[1] *Annals of Ulster, s.a.* 855.

[2] Not necessarily the Irish provenance, though this has been thought likely. See Traube, *loc. cit.*; cf. also Kenney, *op. cit.* 557, 675.

[3] See R. Flower, 'Irish High Crosses', *Journal of the Warburg and Courtauld Institutes*, XVII (1954).

[4] On the form and occurrence of the name, see Nigra, *op. cit.* 12. Professor K. Jackson reminds me that the name *Ruaidri* does not appear to be rare in Irish, though *Rhodri* is not common in Welsh. *Ruaidri* (Irish) and *Rhodri* (Welsh) are not etymologically the same name, though they fortuitously resemble one another. The Irish naturally rendered *Rodri* by their own form *Ruaidri*.

[5] 'Irish High Crosses', 93.

ninth century, and, indeed, for many centuries before, the Irish Sea was a unifying rather than a dividing factor, and the ease of maritime communication as compared with that overland made the Irish Sea the common cultural centre of the Celtic world. The second point of importance is one which we are only gradually coming to appreciate. This is the extent of the Irish population in western Wales. When we reflect that the population of both Pembroke and Gwynedd must have been to some extent bilingual in earlier centuries it is not at all difficult to understand how the Irish scholars, passing with their books from Leinster to the Continent, would stimulate centres of culture in the areas of Gwynedd and Dyfed. At the same time we must not overlook the fact that it was a two-way traffic, and that Irish and British scholars, returning from the Continent, would have much new intellectual experience, in addition to portable libraries, to bring back to Britain from their pilgrimages to Rome, and other great monastic and courtly centres.

9. SUMMARY AND CONCLUSION

The result of our survey may be summed up as follows. Round about the beginning of the ninth century, possibly as a result of the relaxation of the Viking pressure, there seems to have been a heightened intellectual activity and a keen sense of nationalism throughout all the Celtic countries, one important manifestation of which was a keen interest in the past, resulting in widespread gathering and recording of early traditions, and antiquarian speculation and inference. One aspect of this antiquarian speculative activity was the growth of various kinds of 'origin' stories, especially stories of the origin and development of the various Celtic kingdoms and dynasties after the close of the Roman period. In Wales the most interesting of these speculative antiquarian traditions is the account of the invasion of Cunedag and his sons, and the establishment of a number of Welsh kingdoms, each of which is declared to have had a ruling family directly descended from one of his sons.

The evidence suggests that in Wales this school of antiquarian activity flourished in Gwynedd about the beginning of the ninth century, and was fostered throughout that century at the courts of Merfyn Vrych and Rhodri Mawr. The former was the founder of a new dynasty. The latter, as the most powerful ruler in Wales, would naturally follow the lead of all princes in such a position, and support his claim and his prestige by a sedulous cultivation of his own early pedigrees and those of the families with which he inter-married and had political contacts; and by the recording of the early traditions of the North, whence the dynasty claims to have come. For such work it would seem that the ground had been well prepared. The evidence of stone inscriptions, scanty though it is, suggests that even in the sixth and seventh centuries North Wales was no isolated backwater. In the reigns of Merfyn and his son Rhodri the court was evidently a centre of some culture, and a place where learned Irish scholars and poets stopped on their way to and fro between Ireland and the Continent. The court itself was probably literate at this time.

The Church here, as in Ireland, is doubtless to be directly associated with the intellectual, including the secular intellectual, activities of Gwynedd. In the preface to certain texts of the *Historia Brittonum* Nennius claims intellectual indebtedness to Elfoddw, whom we have good reason for regarding as bishop of Bangor, and a man versed in Latin learning and Continental thought. It may well be he who was responsible for the library of Latin writings to which Nennius acknowledges indebtedness. And Elfoddw, as bishop of Bangor, may well have had access to the traditions of the North Britons which would be cultivated by the court of Gwynedd and the *clas* of Bangor, whose founder St Deiniol[1] claimed to be a member of the greatest of the families of the 'Men of the North'.

Be that as it may, there can have been no lack of oral traditional materials current in North Wales on which antiquarian writings could draw. We have seen that Nennius or a predecessor has recorded the names of five famous poets, of whom two are known to us as the composers of panegyric elegiac poetry on the grand scale. The heroic names and allusions in the works attributed to Taliesin and Aneirin would supply material for a comprehensive *Who's Who* of the North British Heroic Age. We know that these

[1] The *Martyrology of Tallaght* (c. 800) has on Sept. 11: *Daniel ep. Bennchair*, 'Daniel, bishop of Bangor'. See the edition by R. I. Best and H. J. Lawlor (Henry Bradshaw Society Publications, LXVIII), 70. The editors have indexed this entry, like others relating to *Bennchair*, under Bangor, Co. Down. See S. M. Harris, *Journal of the Historical Society of the Church in Wales*, V (1955), 6, 21, n. 8.

poems and genealogies of the North were transmitted orally by highly trained bards who enjoyed a proud status at the courts, and that ultimately they found their way into four early Welsh manuscripts. The task of writing down these ancient traditions would almost certainly be carried out in Wales, as we know it was in Ireland, by men trained in the monasteries. The court of Gwynedd was proud of these northern traditions, and fostered them as propaganda to stimulate the people of Cumbria and North Wales to a sense of British nationalism and opposition to the hated Saxons. It may be believed that in Gwynedd also in the ninth century there flourished, under the auspices of the court and the Church, a school in close touch with Irish and Continental culture.

ADDENDA

Note to p. 73 (*Carlisle in post-Roman times*).

Symeon of Durham (*Hist. de Sancto Cuthberto*, c. 5) states that King Ecgfrith had granted Carlisle to St Cuthbert, apparently on the occasion of his ordination. The source for this statement does not appear, but it is borne out by the passage in the Anonymous Life cited on p. 73; and William of Malmesbury (*Gesta Pontificum*, Prologus to Book III) states that even in his day fine Roman structures still survived in Carlisle.

Note to p. 79 (*Rhodri's Genealogy*).

The evidence of Rhodri's genealogy suggests that Gwriad and Elidyr were family names. The oldest version of the Venedotian Code of the Welsh Laws contained in the *Black Book of Chirk* relates the slaying in Arfon of Elidyr Muhenvaur, the grandson of Dyfnwal Hen from the North; the coming of his kinsfolk of the 'Men of the North' to Arfon to avenge him; and the counter-attack in the north by the men of Gwynedd, led by Run, son of Maelgwn. Is this a tradition of the early struggle between the old dynasty and the new one from the north?

ACKNOWLEDGEMENT

I wish to offer grateful acknowledgement to Professor Thomas Jones for help on a number of points in this chapter and in the one which follows.

II

Intellectual Life in West Wales in the Last Days of the Celtic Church

BY NORA K. CHADWICK

The importance of St David's as a seat of early culture needs no plea. The present city stands in the ancient kingdom of Dyfed, which originally included considerably more than the modern Pembrokeshire, and which shares with southern Ireland a wealth of inscriptions in the early Celtic alphabet known as *ogam*. The surviving inscriptions are almost exclusively funerary in character, and are believed to date from the fourth, or at least the fifth to the sixth, or possibly the early seventh centuries.[1] These *ogam* inscriptions are particularly rich in Dyfed,[2] and their linguistic evidence has led to the important conclusion that the population of Dyfed was at this early period bilingual, and that both Irish and Welsh were spoken and understood freely.[3]

These considerations preclude any possibility of the early culture of Dyfed and its close intercourse with Ireland being overlooked. But the bearing of this early culture on the history of St David and his sanctuary needs to be carefully scrutinised. Despite the wealth of *ogam* inscriptions in Dyfed generally, none is recorded from the actual vicinity of St David's.[4] In fact no immediate and intimate connection between the later Christian church of St David's and the culture represented by the *ogam* inscriptions has so far been traced. We must proceed with caution.

The evidence for intercourse between early Ireland and western Britain is by no means confined to inscriptions, whether in Latin or in *ogam* script, nor to the geographical area of Dyfed. The sagas

---

[1] For the origin and dating of the *ogam* inscriptions, see K. H. Jackson, *Language and History in Early Britain* (Edinburgh, 1953), 151 ff.; and earlier *idem*, 'Notes on the Ogam Inscriptions of Southern Britain', in *The Early Cultures of North-Western Europe*, ed. Sir C. Fox and B. Dickins (Cambridge, 1950), 197 ff.

[2] Of the forty *ogam* inscriptions in Wales, the great concentration is in Dyfed (Jackson, *Language and History in Early Britain*, 154).   [3] *Ibid.* 170 ff.

[4] It should, however, be borne in mind that the great building developments at St David's in the Norman period and later would inevitably cause the destruction of many such monuments.

and annals have many references to traditions of Irish occupation of and intercourse with our western seaboard[1] and to Irish septs settled in Wales. The Irish saga of the Déssi, which contains a genealogy of the royal line of Dyfed, and traces the origin of the family to an immigrant prince of the tribe of the Déssi from Leinster, supposedly in the third century, has an interesting parallel tradition in the Welsh form of the genealogy preserved among the pedigrees in the British Museum MS. Harl. 3859,[2] and Jesus College, Oxford, MS. xx. We need not accept the early date ascribed to this migration in the Irish story, but the family whose pedigree is preserved in both the Irish and Welsh versions continued to rule in Dyfed down to the tenth century, and perhaps kept in touch with their own people in Ireland at least until the eighth century.[3] They had come from the kingdom of the Déssi in Co. Waterford.

Again we may refer to the entry in the Old Irish *Glossary* attributed to Cormac, the king and probably bishop of Cashel, who died in 908, where it is stated that in the past the Irish had had rule over parts of Britain, their dominion in Britain being not less than in Ireland. The author instances two of their centres, one at *Dind Tradui*, ruled by 'Crimthann mac Fidaig, king of Ireland and Britain as far as the English Channel',[4] in reality a Munster king; the other '*Dind Map Letháin* in the land of the Cornish Britons'.

Dind Tradui is thought to be identical with the *Din Draithou* in Cornwall[5] referred to in the *Life* of the Welsh saint Carantoc, or Carannog; and probably also with the *Cair Draithou*, mentioned in Nennius's list of the cities of the Britons. *Dind map Letháin* is probably a reference to the stronghold of the *Uí Liatháin*, a sept of the Érainn, an important people living in the east of Munster, near

[1] The name for the Caernarvonshire peninsula *Lleyn*, for example, seems to represent the Irish plural *Laigin*, 'Leinstermen'; and *Porth Dinllaen*, the genitive plural *Laigen*, 'Harbour of the Leinstermen'. See W. J. Gruffydd, *Math fab Mathonwy* (Cardiff, 1928), 343. Cf. also *Mynydd Mallaen* (Carms).

[2] See the article and text (with English translation) of the saga and genealogy by Kuno Meyer, *Y Cymmrodor*, XIII (1900). This double tradition is commonly regarded as independent evidence for its validity; but the relationship of the two pedigrees is almost certainly a literary one.

[3] See K. Meyer, *op. cit.* 57 ff.; Cecile O'Rahilly, *Ireland and Wales* (London, 1924), 62.   [4] Lit. the Ictian Sea.

[5] *Din Draithou* has been identified with great probability as the district round Carhampton on the coast of Somerset between Minehead and Watchet. See G. Doble, *St Carantoc* (Shipston-on-Stour, 1932), 14 ff., and the references there cited.

to the Déssi. They may well, as Professor Jackson observes,[1] have been part of the same eastward movement which brought the Déssi to Wales. It is stated in the *Historia Brittonum* (c. 14) that the sons of Liatháin 'settled' (*obtinuerunt*) in the region of Dyfed, and in Gower and Kidwelly till they were expelled by Cunedag and his sons. It seems clear that the Irish were credited, at the time when such traditions were recorded, with having rule over the coasts of western Britain from the northern shore of the Dumnonian peninsula to St David's.

But it was a two-way traffic. The relatively greater wealth of our information about early Ireland tends to make us underrate the corresponding Welsh culture of the period, for which indeed we have all too little positive evidence. Yet the most recent investigator of the *ogam* inscriptions tends to the opinion that they originated in western—probably in south-western—Wales, and passed thence to Ireland, perhaps in the fourth century.[2] The Irish tradition related above from *Cormac's Glossary* is derived from a British tradition. The names are given in a British form, and the compiler of the *Glossary* feels himself under the necessity of translating them into Irish for his Irish audience. In the same *Glossary* we find other traditions which are also known in Wales, and it has been noted that the earliest example of the 'Invasions Story', known in Ireland as the *Lebor Gabála*, is recorded earliest by Nennius in Wales at a date which cannot be later than the close of the eighth century. From linguistic and literary evidence alike it would seem that the peoples of western and southern Wales and south-eastern Ireland shared a common culture in the pre-Norman period.

The ecclesiastical importance of St David's in later times, and of St David himself as the patron saint of Wales, has tended to induce us to overlook the claims of other areas of the Welsh seaboard to our consideration as cultural centres. The fact that our earliest *Life of St David* was the work of Rhigyfarch, a son of Sulien, a famous and learned bishop of St David's, has naturally added to the traditional prestige of St David's as a centre of literature and learning. This *Life* is probably the earliest of the extant Welsh

---

[1] *Language and History in Early Britain*, 156.
[2] K. H. Jackson gives it as his belief that the *ogam* alphabet was probably the invention of a man educated in the Roman schools in Britain and living in one of the Irish colonies settled on the west coast of Britain towards the close of the Roman occupation during the fourth century (*Language and History in Early Britain*, 151f., 156).

saints' *Lives*, and has undoubtedly had a marked influence on the *Lives* written later. Finally, and perhaps most important of all, the association of St David's with the great Asser, scholar and adviser to Alfred the Great, has added to the little cathedral city on the most westerly promontory of Wales a lustre which has far outshone the gleam of any other ancient seat of British learning and culture.

We must, however, be on our guard against allowing our knowledge of the culture of Dyfed in earlier times to colour our interpretation of Asser's text with preconceived ideas. Without entering upon the question of the genuineness of Asser, I would point out that Asser nowhere states that he had received his education at St David's. The text attributed to him informs us that, when asked by King Alfred to remain at his court, Asser replies that he cannot agree to this out of hand, 'because it did not seem right to me to leave those sacred places (or, very possibly, monasteries—*illa tam sancta loca*) in which I had been bred, educated, and tonsured, and finally ordained, for the sake of worldly promotion'.[1] There is no reference here to St David's, or indeed to any other specific locality, though western Wales is clearly implied. It is only later in the narrative that Asser refers to King Hemeid and his depredations on the monastery and 'parish' (*paruchia*)[2] of St Degui, and his expulsion of its prelates, including Asser's own relative Bishop Nobis, and Asser himself.[3] The passages in Asser are not contiguous; and they are, moreover, perfectly compatible with his having been educated elsewhere, such as, for example, at Llanbadarn Fawr, and as having a later interest in St David's, just as Bishop Sulien is known to have received his education at Llanbadarn Fawr and elsewhere, and to have come to St David's only later (cf. pp. 164f. below).

The evidence for Irish colonists in early Wales is of course by no means confined to the period of the *ogam* or the early Latin funerary inscriptions or to the genealogical and the hagiographical material. The close association of the Welsh and Irish elements in

---

[1] Asser, *Vita Alfredi*, c. 79 (W. H. Stevenson, *Asser's Life of King Alfred*, Oxford, 1904, 64).

[2] Asser seems to use the word *paruchia* almost in the sense of diocese as, for example, when it is said that Alfred gave to Asser the 'whole parish' (*omnis paruchia*) of Exeter. The *paruchia* of St David's covered a wide area, and included Llanbadarn Fawr on Cardigan Bay, close to Aberystwyth.

[3] Asser, *ed. cit.* 65.

the Celtic Church is well known, and the close association between the Welsh and Irish monks in the Welsh monasteries from the ninth to the eleventh centuries[1] is seen in the fact that the copy of *Juvencus's Poetical Version of the Gospels* preserved in the Cambridge University Library[2] seems to have been written by an Irishman Nuadu in a Welsh monastery, probably in the ninth century. Nuadu glossed his text in both Irish and Welsh, and the MS. bears the Old Welsh colophon *araut di Nuadu*, 'a prayer for Nuadu'. Other Welsh and Irish glosses in the same MS. are perhaps the work of two or even three Welsh-speaking Irishmen, writing in some monastery in Wales at dates apparently varying from the ninth to the eleventh century. As Professor Jackson observes, this 'must have taken place in some monastery in Wales where Irish influence existed over a long period'.

In addition to *Juvencus* we have a number of other manuscripts containing glosses, notes and scraps of poetry ascribed to the Old Welsh period, and believed to be of Welsh provenance. Of these the earliest, ascribed to the eighth century, are the notes to be found in the *Book of St Chad*, preserved at Lichfield.[3] The glosses in the MS. of the *Martianus Capella* preserved in the library of Corpus Christi College, Cambridge, are believed to date from the ninth century or even earlier; those of a MS. known as *Oxoniensis Prior* from the same century, about the year 820;[4] the entire MS. known as *Oxoniensis Posterior* seems to be Welsh of the tenth century. Other examples of Old Welsh glosses could be added,[5] some of them believed to have been written in Continental scriptoria, others in Wales and perhaps in Cornwall. Something has already been said about these manuscripts in the preceding chapter. What then, we may ask, is the provenance more precisely of the Old Welsh glosses?

[1] The evidence for date is largely but not exclusively palaeographical. See Jackson, *Language and History in Early Britain*, 49 ff.

[2] MS. Ff. 4. 42.

[3] They are in a mixture of Latin and Old Welsh, and are printed together with facsimiles by J. G. Evans in the Preface to his edition of *The Text of the Book of Llan Dâv* (Oxford, 1893), xliii ff.

[4] For some interesting notes on this MS. and some of its contents, see Sir Ifor Williams, 'Notes on Nennius', *Bulletin of the Board of Celtic Studies*, VII (1935), 380 ff. Cf. also p. 127, n. 1 below.

[5] See the list in the Appendix to Henry Bradshaw's *Collected Papers* (Cambridge, 1889). Cf. the more recent works of W. M. Lindsay, *Early Welsh Script* (Oxford, 1912); K. Jackson, *op. cit.* 53 ff.

Jackson, in his study of these glosses, has been primarily concerned with the linguistic evidence and its bearing on the history of the Old Welsh language. Naturally, therefore, he does not enter into detailed discussion of scriptoria. Bradshaw, however, had no hesitation in emphasising the importance of what he regarded as the work of the school of Bishop Sulien at St David's in these glosses, and in the Welsh palaeographical tradition to which they are assigned.[1] In this he is followed by W. M. Lindsay.[2] And again it is significant that in Lindsay's broad division of the scripts into two types, he describes them as: (1) the 'round' type 'seen obscurely' in the entries made by Sulgen Scholasticus in the *Book of St Chad*, etc., and (2) the 'flat-topped' type seen in the hand of one of the scribes of the *Martianus Capella*[3]—a book which he cites M. R. James as connecting with St David's on the ground that Bishop Davies of St David's was interested in the antiquities of his diocese and corresponded with Archbishop Parker about MSS.[4] And Lindsay goes on to add that this flat-topped type was 'the type adopted by the eleventh-century calligraphy of St David's'. The two examples which he cites to illustrate this last point are on plates XVI and XVII: the first from the MS. of St Augustine's *De Trinitate*, preserved in the library of Corpus Christi College, Cambridge, the second from the *Ricemarch Psalter* preserved in the library of Trinity College, Dublin.[5] Both these manuscripts are believed to be the work of sons of Bishop Sulien of St David's.

That these manuscripts are of Welsh provenance and the work of Sulien's sons is indeed beyond doubt; and the close affinities with contemporary Irish scripts is not open to question. When however we come to closer provenance it is difficult to accept the views of these learned palaeographers. A careful search through all their arguments fails to discover any positive evidence which points to St David's as the scriptorium from which any of them originated, even the two last mentioned. Indeed a scriptorium of

---

[1] See his paper 'The Oldest Written Remains of Welsh' (*passim*), in *Collected Papers* (Cambridge, 1889).

[2] *Op. cit.* 32.   [3] *Op. cit.* 40; cf. 19.

[4] *Op. cit.* 19; but does this mean more than that Davies perhaps collected the book from West Wales? Unfortunately the letter from Bishop Davies to Archbishop Parker cited by James appears to have been lost, and we do not know its precise contents. See further M. R. James, *Descriptive Catalogue of the MSS. in Corpus Christi College, Cambridge*, no. 153.

[5] Edited by H. J. Lawlor, *The Psalter and Martyrology of Ricemarch* (London, 1914).

St David's at the period in question, i.e. before the eleventh century, is an assumption hardly warranted by any evidence. St David's was certainly not the only centre in western Wales where Latin learning was highly cultivated at this period under Irish influence. On the contrary, centres farther north, notably Llanbadarn Fawr near Aberystwyth, played an important part in the education and culture of the period only a little later than that to which the Old Welsh glosses are ascribed. Two of our earliest manuscripts containing Welsh glosses come from Glastonbury,[1] and the *Book of St Chad* in the last instance from Llandaff.[2]

We have constantly to remind ourselves that what has survived of Welsh culture from the early period is only a negligible fragment of her intellectual heritage, both oral and written. A glance at the references to lost stories and poems in the late eleventh-century text of *Kulhwch ag Olwen* and in the Welsh *Triads* gives one some small idea of the amount of secular literature that has been lost. Such inevitable loss of early traditions and records is true of Wales in an even greater degree than of Ireland, for Ireland had already by the eighth and ninth centuries developed a number of important scriptoria for the writing and copying of texts, which has ensured their preservation. These scriptoria, which must have served the combined purpose of studies, libraries, and publishing centres in Ireland, have been discussed elsewhere (pp. 243 ff.) and I need not enter into details here. It must, however, be emphasised that they were inevitably dependent on financial support, and could not exist except in flourishing monastic centres under the patronage of a wealthy king or chief. These numerous important Irish scriptoria, and in addition the wealth of calf-skins offering a plentiful supply of good vellum, aided the development of the production of manuscripts in Ireland almost on commercial lines, and it may be that the actual Irish export trade in early manuscripts was more important than has been fully realised. It may be questioned whether the number of manuscripts of Irish provenance which found their way into Continental libraries at this period is not due even more to this output on commercial lines than to the 'Viking terror'.

[1] I refer to the *Liber Commonei* contained in *Oxoniensis Prior* (Bodl. Auct. F. 4. 32); Ovid, *De Arte Amandi* (contained in the same MS.). Two MSS. containing Breton glosses are also with good reason ascribed to Glastonbury. See Bradshaw, *Collected Papers*, 455 ff., 483 ff.

[2] Cf., however, p. 226 below.

In Wales the position was very different. The country was much poorer than Ireland, and the mountain mass of central Wales retarded economic development. The early scriptoria were less numerous, and probably in the eighth and ninth centuries less fully developed. When we have information about them at a later period they are integrally connected with the clerics, the members of the *clas*, the early type of Welsh monastic body, organised on somewhat different lines from the great Irish monasteries of this period and the later monasteries of Wales.[1] A fuller knowledge of the organisation of the Welsh *clas* is greatly to be desired, for it is to them that we must look for information not only about the Welsh scriptoria, but also about early Welsh-Latin culture generally. A number of *clasau* are known to have existed,[2] and the institution lasted late, with the fortunate result that we have a considerable amount of information about some of them, notably Llancarfan and Llanbadarn Fawr. The author of the *Life of St David* was a member of the latter, and a closer study of both his family and of the *clas* generally will help to throw light on the circumstances in which our knowledge of St David has been transmitted, and on the intellectual pre-eminence of Llanbadarn Fawr in the preceding period.

Before proceeding to a study of the *Life of St David* and of its author we may pause for a moment to reflect on the somewhat remarkable fact that our earliest written narrative traditions of Scottish and Welsh Christianity relate to saints of the remote western peninsulas. Both were in Irish-speaking areas. Both were in areas which became bishoprics. Our earliest records of the former, written not long before 700, claim St Ninian of Whithorn in Galloway as having been trained in Rome '*regulariter*'—a claim which, while not a practical impossibility, is a patent historical anachronism. Our earliest written information about St David, written some 500 years after his traditional lifetime, claims a total defeat for St Patrick and the triumph of St David, an outstanding saint of the Celtic Church in Pembroke. Yet in Scotland as a whole the Celtic Church prevailed, in Wales the Roman. These and other

[1] For a brief account of the Welsh *clas* churches and organisation, see Lloyd, *History of Wales*, I, 205 ff.

[2] A useful map of the distribution of the *clas* churches will be found on plate 27 of *An Historical Atlas of Wales* by William Rees (Cardiff, 1951); cf. also *ibid.* 24.

considerations will lead us to the conclusion that these early written sources are to be interpreted, not as historical records to be accepted uncritically, but as genuine and valuable traditions echoing a religious controversy of the period in which they were actually recorded. The genuine historical content of the works must necessarily be comparatively slight in relation to the periods with which they deal. Their greatest historical value and significance relate rather to the period in which they were composed. Before we can hope to ascertain the historical value of any document of the early Middle Ages we must first seek to ascertain when it was written, under what circumstance, and above all for what purpose. What is its tenor and its bias?

In the case of Whithorn we are fortunate in possessing first-hand records of the controversy in a comparatively early stage. About 700, when Bede and Bishop Pecthelm of Whithorn were in correspondence, northern Ireland had recently entered the Roman unity, largely through the efforts of Ecgberht of York. In the contemporary writings we are, as it were, privileged to stand behind the chairs of those seated at the conference table. In the case of Wales the initial sessions of the conference have taken place nearly three centuries before we are admitted, and only sparse minutes, Irish in provenance, have reached us from this early phase. But when in the eleventh and following centuries we are again privileged to hear the controversy at first hand the old struggle between the Celtic and the Roman Church has been revived in a new form; the old issues are being fought afresh. At Whithorn about 700 we were in the heat of the crisis in the struggle between the Celtic and the Roman Church; between the old order and the new; between what the British bishops had defined to St Augustine as 'their ancient customs' (*prisci mores*)[1] and innovations from Canterbury. In Wales in the Norman period we are living through the final struggle, and the voices are raised for the last time in defence of the liberty and autonomy of the Church of their forefathers. The issue is symbolised in the brilliant vignette by Giraldus Cambrensis, referred to above (p. 11), in which he relates the speech of an old Welshman at Pencadair to Henry II declaring his belief in the eternity of Wales and the Welsh language.

In both these phases of the struggle between the Celtic and the Roman Church we have to bear in mind that from the point of view

[1] Bede, *H.E.* ii, ii.

of the protagonists neither of our western peninsulas is in reality the remote terminus of a lengthy British route. It is on the contrary an important ecclesiastical centre, chosen for its influential position and easy accessibility, its advantageous site for rapid communication with eastern Ireland, the heart and centre of early Celtic ecclesiastical and intellectual life. It can never be too strongly emphasised that the early Celtic Church was a Church of seafarers, and that communication by sea was easier and quicker than by land, waves were easier to negotiate than mountains and bogs. The centre of influence and activity of the Irish Church in the age of the saints was the Irish Sea. We have seen that the author of the *Glossary* attributed to Cormac, king and perhaps bishop of Cashel, states that in the past,

When great was the might of the Gael over Britain, they divided Albion among them into territories, and each of them knew the house of his friend, and not less did the Gael reside to the east of the sea than in Ireland, and their homes and their royal strongholds were built there.... Thus did every tribe divide on this side, for it had its equivalent there, on the east; and they abode in that might for a long time, even after Patrick's arrival.[1]

His statement may or may not be true as history; but it certainly represents a tradition which could pass current in the ninth century —the time of Asser and King Alfred, supported by a consistent body of traditional genealogies, inscriptions, references, dedications and place-names representing the west coast of Britain from Somerset to Argyll, as colonised from Ireland. The account in the *Anglo-Saxon Chronicle, s.a.* 891, of the three Irishmen who landed in a curragh in Cornwall and made for Alfred's court is significant. In any question relating to the struggle between the Celtic and the Roman Church in Britain, Ireland is at least as important a factor as Britain itself.

This Irish factor is of particular importance in the early history of the see of Menevia, and of Dyfed. Its language, inscriptions, its royal dynasties and early colonisation, all point to a strong Irish influence. Yet St David, the patron saint of Wales, and founder of the monastery which bears his name, who is represented in his earliest biography as having exercised an important early influence

---

[1] *Cormac's Glossary*, MS. Laud 610, fol. 83*a*, translated by Whitley Stokes, *Tripartite Life of St Patrick*, II (London, 1887), 571; cf. also the Bodleian text, edited and translated by Stokes, *Three Irish Glossaries* (London, 1862), 29; English translation of the passage, *ibid.* xlviii.

on the Irish Church,[1] is not said in this biography to have been of Dyfed stock, but of the royal line of Cardigan. Moreover no early records of St David have been preserved independently from Dyfed. The earliest *Life of St David*, and the earliest literary source for much valuable information relating to the history of Dyfed, was written, not by a native of Dyfed, but a certain Rhigyfarch, a native of Llanbadarn Fawr on Cardigan Bay. If we view this *Life*, as I think we must, not as a historical document, but rather as our earliest and most authoritative surviving Welsh contribution to the last phase of the controversy about the independence of the Welsh Church, we shall see that it has more to tell us about the author Rhigyfarch, his milieu and background, above all his point of view and that of the *clas* at Llanbadarn, than about St David himself.

This literary relationship is neither surprising nor unusual. It is equally true of the *Life of St Germanus* composed by Constantius, and true in a very special sense of the *Life of St Martin* by Sulpicius Severus. The study of a saint in fact requires a special technique involving a double examination. It demands on the one hand an examination of the facts narrated in the *Vita* or biography and their relationship to supplementary evidence from other sources; and on the other hand an examination of the biographer himself—virtually two biographies inextricably interwoven. In accordance with this principle I shall attempt to give some account first of the tradition of St David as reported to us by Rhigyfarch and others; and then of his biographer Rhigyfarch and his milieu and background. This will not tell us all that we want to know of St David, for St David belongs to the sixth century,[2] the 'age of the saints', whereas his biographer Rhigyfarch lived during the Norman Conquest. But from Rhigyfarch's use of his materials, and from our knowledge of him from other sources, we may be able to reconstruct in some detail the religious outlook and the learning of an important intellectual and spiritual centre in western Wales in the later days of the Celtic Church.

Our earliest references[3] to St David come from Ireland. He is

---

[1] Cf. also the *Catalogus Sanctorum Hiberniae*, p. 132 below.

[2] See p. 49 above. An entry in the *Annales Cambriae* which, though the reading is far from clear, appears to relate to him, records his death *s.a.* 601. The reading of Harl. 3859 appears to be *David episcopus Moni Iudeorum*. J. Loth would read *Moniu Desorum = Mynyw*, for *Menevia*, 'Menevia of the Déssi'. See his edition of *Les Mabinogion*, II (Paris, 1913), 373; and cf. *Revue celtique* XXXVII, 315. See further A. W. Wade-Evans, *Life of St David* (London, 1923), 107, 114.

[3] See, however, p. 182 below.

mentioned in the *Catalogus Sanctorum Hiberniae* ('The Catalogue of the Saints of Ireland'), which has generally been believed to date from *c.* 730, but which Father Grosjean has shown[1] to have been composed more probably in the ninth or even the tenth century. In this document David is mentioned as one of the saints of the 'second order' along with SS. Gildas and Docus—his name occurring first of the three—as having given a *missa* to the Irish. This document is obscure both in origin and provenance. We next hear of the saint, however, in the *Félire* or *Martyrology of Oengus the Culdee*, commonly dated about 800, and thought to have probably been composed partly in the monastery of Tallaght,[2] a few miles south-west of Dublin, partly elsewhere but from Tallaght documents. He is also mentioned in the *Martyrology of Tallaght*, which was probably composed in the early ninth century, but possibly later.[3]

The associations with Óengus and Tallaght are significant, for Óengus 'the Culdee', Óengus mac Óengobann, was a monk of Leix who became a disciple of Maelrúain, abbot of Tallaght. In the *Félire*, or martyrology ascribed to Óengus, Máelrúain (†792) is the last saint commemorated, and the preface claims that the work was completed at Tallaght. The kings mentioned in the preface as dead would seem to be the high-king Dunnchad (†797), and Bran, king of Lagin (slain 795). It is interesting to find this early reference to David in close association with Leinster, and more particularly with Máelrúain and Tallaght—an association which testifies to his place in the esteem of those responsible for the monastic reform and the anchorite movement of the eighth and ninth centuries in Ireland. We shall see that the peculiar form of Menevian asceticism associated with St David and his followers by his earliest biographer Rhigyfarch has close affinities with this movement, and with Leinster.

In the ninth century we have our first reference to St David's sanctuary in Britain. It comes from Asser, who makes mention of both the *paruchia Degui*,[4] and more particularly of the church of

---

[1] In a recent article published in *Analecta Bollandiana*, LXXIII (1955), 197 ff.
[2] See Kenney, *op. cit.* 469, 479.
[3] See Kenney, *op. cit.* 410, n. 140; cf. 482. See further, however, the edition by H. J. Lawlor and R. J. Best, *The Martyrology of Tallaght* (London, 1931).
[4] One of the Old Welsh spellings of the Welsh form of the name, *Dewi*. His shrine is always referred to by Rhigyfarch as *Vallis Rosina*; but elsewhere (e.g. in the *Annals*) it is spoken of as *Menevia* or under some modified form of this word. Later it was known as *Tyddewi*, 'David's House', or St David's.

St David in Dyfed, of which Asser's *propinquus* Nobis had been bishop. He also refers to the *clas* or bishop's *familia* of St David's of which he himself was a member. It should be mentioned also that David is referred to as *David Aquaticus*[1] in the *Life of St Paul Aurelian*,[2] believed to have been composed towards the close of the ninth century by a Breton monk Wrmonoc. Again in the early Welsh poem known as the *Armes Prydein*, David is the saint who is prophesied to be the future leader of the Cymry against the Saxons. He is referred to four times in this poem, which Sir Ifor Williams would date *c.* 930.[3]

At Glastonbury there is evidence of a vigorous cult of the saint in early times, for already in the ninth century she claims to be in possession of his relics; and his name, under its Welsh form *Dewi*, was inserted in the so-called *Leofric Kalendar*, at some time between the date of its compilation at Glastonbury, *c.* 970, and a date *c.* 1050 when it was in use at Exeter. The commemoration of St David in another kalendar from Sherborne[4] dated *c.* 1061 has been ascribed to the influence of Asser, who had been bishop of Sherborne in 884;[5] and it is possibly to Asser's influence also that we may ascribe the presence of both St David and St Padarn among the confessor bishops in the litanies contained in a tenth-century manuscript of the *Salisbury Psalter*.[6] It is perhaps significant that in yet another Wessex kalendar of about the eleventh century the saint's name again appears in a form identical with that used by Asser. All this suggests that the cult had been introduced into Wessex in Asser's day, and had survived in West Saxon circles till a late date. We can hardly doubt that the earliest of these liturgical uses would be accompanied by a certain amount of other written material containing allusions to the saint's Life, in however brief a form. It should be added that the Rev. S. M. Harris believes that Rhigyfarch's *Life of St David* contains certain prayers which the compiler has incorporated from earlier liturgical sources, both at

[1] Probably with the meaning 'water-drinking'—a reference to the asceticism practised in his monastery. Rhigyfarch also refers to David's *aquatica vita* (c. 2).
[2] The Latin text was published by M. C. Cuissard, *Revue celtique*, v, 421 ff.; English translation by G. H. Doble, *Life of St Paul of Léon* (Cornish Saints Series, no. 46, printed at Lampeter, 1941).
[3] *Lectures on Early Welsh Poetry* (Dublin, 1944); and cf. his recent edition of the poem *Armes Prydein* (Cardiff, 1955), p. xvii. Cf. also p. 86 above.
[4] In the library of Corpus Christi College, Cambridge, MS. 422.
[5] S. M. Harris, *Saint David in the Liturgy* (Cardiff, 1940), 8 ff.
[6] Salisbury Cathedral Library, no. 180, fols. 170 ff. See also Harris, *op. cit.* 11.

St David's, and throughout the *paruchia Degui*—'the sphere of influence or "diocese" of Dewi in Wales and the West country'.[1]

At this point reference should be made to a document of uncertain date and doubtful authenticity[2] popularly known as the *Penitential of St David*. The actual title in the text is *Incipiunt Excerpta quaedam de Libro Davidis*.[3] This penitential is said to have close parallels with the *Collectio Hibernensis* and the Celtic penitentials generally, as well as with those of Theodore, of Bede, and St Gildas.[4] On the strength of the ascription above, and of these parallels, it has been suggested that the so-called *Penitential of David* represents a genuine work of the time of St David from which the later Celtic and Saxon penitentials referred to above have borrowed;[5] but this claim hardly seems to be supported by evidence from the texts in question. It is easy to see how such an ascription might arise, even at an early period, in view of the tradition of the part played by David in the synods of Brevi and Lucus Victoriae as related by Rhigyfarch (cf. p. 139 below). I hope to be able to show later, however, that this part of Rhigyfarch's narrative carries little or no conviction as a historical record.

The earliest *Life of St David* of which we have any knowledge is that of Rhigyfarch, son of Sulien (the latter twice bishop of St David's), which was written in the latter part of the eleventh century. The more precise date will be discussed later. The *Life* is extant in several manuscripts, representing various recensions of the work, but none of these would seem to be in Rhigyfarch's own hand. The fullest text is contained in MS. Vespasian A. xiv[6] in the Cottonian collection in the British Museum, a manuscript dating probably from about 1200; but this text is probably not an exact copy. There are, moreover, other anonymous recensions of

---

[1] *Op. cit.* 13 ff.   [2] Hugh Williams, *Gildas* (London, 1899), ii, 275.

[3] For the text and an account of the MS. collection in which it is found, see *ibid.* p. 286 f.

[4] See Wasserschleben, *Die Irische Kanonensammlung* (Leipzig, 1885), 101–2.

[5] T. P. Oakley, *English Penitential Discipline and Anglo-Saxon Law* (New York, 1923), p. 36.

[6] The MS. was edited and translated by W. J. Rees, *Lives of the Cambro-British Saints* (Llandovery, 1853); but this work fell far short of modern standards of scholarship, and it has again been edited and translated by A. W. Wade-Evans, *Vitae Sanctorum Britanniae*, etc. (Cardiff, 1944). In this edition the translation of the *Life of St David* is omitted because Mr Wade-Evans had already published it in 1913 in *Y Cymmrodor*, xxiv, 4–28; and again as a separate book (London, 1923). My references throughout are to the text by Wade-Evans, and his translation in the edition of 1923, except where otherwise stated.

the *Life*, some of even earlier date; but all are generally thought to represent more or less shortened versions of Rhigyfarch's work.[1] It is believed however—and this is important—that none of our extant texts represents an exact copy of what Rhigyfarch actually wrote. It may prove to be that the version which has come down to us is even in substance very different from his own version. Unfortunately this is a matter into which it would be unsafe to venture further till we are in a position to have before us the result of a collation of the various MS. versions of the Latin texts of Rhigyfarch's *Life*.[2]

It may be added here that at the end of the version of Rhigyfarch in Vesp. A. xiv three liturgical prayers are found—a collect with its accompanying secret and post-communion. These are interesting, not only as indicating some of the material on which Rhigyfarch had to draw, since this liturgical matter was probably in use at St David's long before Rhigyfarch's day; but also, as the Rev. Silas Harris points out, because 'they afford us almost the only glimpse of the actual prayers of the pre-Norman Welsh Church'. Still another liturgical fragment of this character is contained in the body of the *Life* at the close of c. 55, while the Cotton MS. Nero E. 1 contains what appears to be a part of the episcopal benediction at Menevia on St David's Day.[3]

A second *Life of St David*, written by Giraldus Cambrensis, probably about 1200, is based either directly on our *Life* by Rhigyfarch, or on some early recension of this work. It exists in two manuscript traditions, the older being Vitellius E. vii, dating from the early thirteenth century, but much damaged by fire, and now defective. This text formed the basis of Wharton's edition in the *Anglia Sacra*, ii, 628 ff. Brewer's text, published in the Rolls Series, is a reprint of Wharton with some slight changes. The other manuscript is also in the British Museum, Royal 13. C. i, fols. 171–80. It does not appear to be a copy of Vitellius E. vii, and contains an appendix of miracles of the saint not known elsewhere, as well as some *Lectiones de Sancta Nonnita*, St David's mother. These

[1] Wade-Evans, *Life of St David*, xi.

[2] It is greatly to be hoped that we may have such a study from (The Rev.) Chancellor J. W. James, in continuation of his invaluable study of the texts of the later Welsh *Life of St David* (cf. p. 147 below).

[3] For this and all other liturgical matter relating to the *Life of St David* I am indebted to the Rev. Silas Harris, *Saint David and the Liturgy* (Cardiff, 1940), 12 ff.

manuscripts have not been fully examined, and it is not at present possible to say which text Giraldus was following, or how far he is responsible for the identifications of persons and places which distinguish this version.

A Welsh *Life* (*Buched*) of St David has also come down to us in several MSS., but all are much later than the preceding. The earliest, now in Jesus College, Oxford, was written in 1346 by an anchorite of Llandewi Brevi, Cardiganshire, and was edited with introduction and textual and linguistic notes by Sir John Morris Jones and Sir John Rhŷs in the series *Anecdota Oxoniensia* in 1894, under the title *The Elucidarium and other Tracts on Welsh from Llyvyr Agkyr Llandewivrevi*, A.D. 1346 (Jesus College MS. 119); and again reprinted (text only) under the title *Buched Dewi*, 'The Life of Saint David', at the Clarendon Press, Oxford, 1912. It occurs also in the Llanstephan MSS. 4 and 27, both dating from about 1400; in the British Museum Cotton Titus D. XXII, written in 1429, and in the Peniarth MSS. 15 and 27, both of the fifteenth century. The text of Cotton Titus D. XXII was edited with a useful English translation by W. J. Rees in his *Lives of the Cambro-British Saints*. The Welsh version is usually regarded as an abridgment of the *Life* by Rhigyfarch,[1] though the Rev. Canon G. H. Doble held that the writer of the Welsh *Life* 'did not copy Rhigyfarch, but an older *Life* containing substantially the same matter; since every story he relates differs in detail from Rhigyfarch's account even where there could be no motive for altering it'.[2] These views will be discussed more fully below.

Before attempting any estimate of the relative importance of these versions, or any discussion of the value of their contents or of the milieu in which they were composed, it is necessary to give a brief outline of the *Life of St David* as this is related in our earliest biography, that of Rhigyfarch. David's father, we are told, was a son of a king of Ceredigion, who eventually gave up his kingdom to become a recluse. One night he was warned by an angel in a dream that a son would be born to him 'and to the monastery of Maucannus', which has not been certainly identified.[3] The writer then (c. 3) proceeds to tell us how St Patrick came to Wales from Ireland,

---

[1] See Wade-Evans, *op. cit.* xiii.
[2] *Saint Teilo* (Lampeter, 1924), 10.
[3] For a discussion of the name, see Wade-Evans, *Life of St David* (English translation, London, 1923), 57 f.

landing in Ceredigion (Cardiganshire), and passed thence to Vallis Rosina[1] in Dyfed where the cathedral of St David now stands, and where Patrick proposes to 'serve God faithfully'. He is, however, informed by the angel that Dyfed has been appointed by God himself, not for Patrick, but for St David, who will be born in thirty years' time; and Patrick accordingly withdraws to Ireland, not without great reluctance. Rhigyfarch evidently wishes to make it clear that St David is chosen by God as the saint of Dyfed in preference to St Patrick.

Thirty years later, we are told (c. 4), divine power (*virtus divina*) sent Sant, king of the country of *Ceredigion* (Cardiganshire) to a community (*misit ad plebem*)[2] in Dyfed where he violated a certain Nonnita, a nun, who afterwards became the mother of David. She claims to be of noble Breton stock, but no details of her family are given, and from the names of David's parents, 'Saint' and 'Nun', it would seem that Rhigyfarch knew no reliable Welsh genealogy. He seems indeed to locate the saint's birth in Dyfed somewhat uneasily, for he has already represented St Patrick as landing in the first place in Ceredigion, and he further claims that David's father, the king of Ceredigion, was on a temporary visit in Dyfed, far from his home, at the time of the saint's conception. David is stated (c. 7) to have been baptised by Bishop Aelvyw[3] (*Helve*) and then to have been educated at a place called *Vetus Rubus*[4] to which he again returns after his ordination to the priesthood and a period of further preparation in a retreat (*insula*) with Paulens (or Paulinus), a disciple of St Germanus, followed by the foundation of a series of churches. Here (c. 14) he informs his

[1] Rhigyfarch never refers to St David's as Menevia but always as *Vallis Rosina*. Moreover he never mentions *Mynyw*, or any other *Rubus* save *Rubus Vetus*. In c. 7 *Meneuiensium*, 'of the people of Mynyw', is thought to be due to a copyist c. 1200. Wade-Evans points out (*Life of St David*, 89) that neither *Mynyw* nor *Vallis Rosina* was a current or popular term in Rhigyfarch's day, for the latter explains 'Vallis Rosina which the Britons commonly call Hodnant'. Wade-Evans suggests that *Vallis Rosina* may contain the Old Irish name (*ibid.* 90). It is strange that Rhigyfarch here writes almost as if he were not himself a Briton.

[2] For a note on the word *plebem*, see Wade-Evans, 70.

[3] 'Aelvyw, bishop of the people of Mynyw [or of the people of Munster]', according to an old interlinear gloss. See Wade-Evans, *Life of St David*, 77.

[4] Evidently a different place from the modern *Vallis Rosina* in which the cathedral now stands, and which is today known as St David's (L. *Menevia*). For a discussion of these names and some suggested identifications, see Wade-Evans, 78 ff. and 83 ff.; also p. 155 below.

fratruelis, Bishop Guistilianus,[1] that he has had a message from an angel, and as a result of this he sets forth with three disciples, Aedán, Eiludd and Ysvael to the place which the angel has indicated, that is *Vallis Rosina*, 'which the Britons call Hodnant',[2] and the author assures us that the smoke from the hearth of this new foundation circled round the whole of this island and Ireland besides. Rhigyfarch never loses a chance of emphasising the wide influence exercised by his saint in Ireland.

We next hear (c. 16) of his successful encounter with a certain Baia, a hostile Irish chief of this district of Dyfed; and especially with Baia's wife. Then, after a brief reference to the building of a monastery in the place, some nine chapters of the *Life* (21–30) are devoted to an account of the ascetic practices, or 'Rule', observed by the inmates. Here we notice the emphasis on holy poverty and on manual labour, especially agriculture (*jugum in humeris ponunt*), so that the monastery should be self-supporting and the monks should live on the simplest fare, working hard and owning nothing. There follows a series of David's miracles, interrupted by a brief account of the holiness of his disciples Aedán and Modomnoc and of their departure for Ireland (c. 35–43), after which David is enjoined by the angel (c. 44) to make a pilgrimage to Jerusalem, together with St Teilo, who is said to have been formerly a monk in his monastery, and also with St Padarn, 'whose life and miracles are contained in his history'. During their visit we are told that the patriarch, having been previously so enjoined by an angel, consecrates all three to the episcopate. David, however, is promoted to the archiepiscopate, and is presented with four gifts, an altar, a bell, a crozier (L. *baculus*), and a precious tunic. It should be added that the visit of the three saints to Jerusalem is also related in the *Lives* of St Teilo and St Padarn, where, however, the four gifts are not presented to David only, but are distributed among the three saints, Padarn receiving a *baculus* and a tunic (see p. 158 below).

Immediately after this passage we are told in c. 49 ff. that the

---

[1] In MS. Vespasian A. xiv Guistilianus is celebrated in the Kalendar of the saints of Wales after St David and before St Nonnita, i.e. on March 2, and his name occurs in the Sarum Missal, which was evidently used by the clergy of Llanbadarn before 1538.

[2] Hodnant is mentioned elsewhere, e.g. in the *Life of St Illtud*, c. 15, 16. See Wade-Evans, 89. Cf. the occurrence of *Blaen Porth Hoddnant*, now simply *Blaen Porth*, in the *Brut y Tywysogyon*, *s.a.* 1116 (the true date). The river is called *Howni*, from earlier *Hoddni*, and *Hoddnant* is from *Hodd*+*nant*. Cf. J. E. Lloyd, *History of Wales*, II (London, 1912), 434, n. 116.

Pelagian heresy, after having been twice suppressed here by St Germanus, is again reviving. A synod is held at a place called Brevi to which David is summoned by SS. Daniel and Dubricius, whereupon the heresy is expelled by his preaching, and as a result David is made 'archbishop of the whole Britannic race, and his monastery (*civitas*) the metropolis of the Britons' (c. 53). After this Rhigyfarch adds that 'decrees of Catholic and ecclesiastical rule are confirmed'; and he continues: 'They are found in part in the oldest writings of the father, enjoined in his own sacred hand.'

Thus writes Rhigyfarch at the close of the eleventh century of the deeds and writings which he gravely ascribes to David in the sixth, along with an archbishopric and a metropolitan power which we now know never existed. When in the following chapter we learn of a second synod called that of *Lucus Victoriae*,[1] apparently with the same or a similar object to that of the preceding, we may well suspect that Rhigyfarch is echoing the two anti-Pelagian campaigns ascribed to St Germanus, to whom he has referred immediately before. We need not therefore take very seriously the writer's statement that the bishop (i.e. David) committed to writing with his own sacred hand the decrees which he himself had enunciated verbally; nor the tradition that the penitentials which passed current under the titles[2] of these synods are texts which actually originated at such synods. We must insist that our only authority for such synods is the late eleventh-century work of Rhigyfarch, which here reads suspiciously like an echo of Constantius's *Life of St Germanus*, a work by which Rhigyfarch would seem to be directly influenced. Before bringing his work to a close with the death of David, Rhigyfarch claims emphatically (c. 57) that the primacy of David and his right of sanctuary were recognised by all the bishops, and are to be enforced on pain of incurring the anathema of the Church.

Before concluding this brief summary of Rhigyfarch's *Life* I should like to return for a moment to a curious incident which he relates (c. 49–52) in connection with the synod of Brevi, and to which I shall have occasion to return later. So great a multitude have assembled—118 bishops, and an innumerable multitude of

[1] Cf. also the word *Victoriae* (*lucus*) with the Hallelujah victory attributed to Germanus by Constantius.
[2] For the texts, see Haddan and Stubbs, *Councils*, I, 116ff.; Hugh Williams, *Gildas*, II, 286ff. Cf. also p. 134 above.

presbyters, abbots and other orders, kings, princes, laics—that it is found impossible for a preacher's voice to reach them all. It is arranged therefore that a lofty pile of garments shall be erected on high ground, and that he whose voice shall reach to the most distant of his listeners shall be made by universal consent metropolitan archbishop; but all to no purpose. Then Bishop Paulinus, St David's former teacher, suggests that they shall send for 'one made bishop by the patriarch...who has an angel as comrade'. Twice messengers are sent, and twice the saint refuses to come; but at last when St Daniel and Dubricius come and press him he sets out in their company.

What follows is curious. In the course of the journey to Brevi the saint raises from the dead a boy called Magnus, whose mother forthwith dedicates the youth to the saint and to God, and David, placing on his shoulders the copy of the Gospel which he always carried on his own breast, takes him to the synod. The saint, on arrival, refuses to mount the pile of garments, but orders the boy newly risen from the dead to spread his *sudarium*, and standing upon this David preaches in a voice which all can hear. As he does so the ground beneath him rises into a high hill.[1] On the top a church is situated.[2] Heresy is expelled; the faith is confirmed. Then, 'with the consent of all the bishops, kings, princes, nobles, and all grades of the whole Britannic race', he is 'made archbishop, and his monastery too is declared the metropolis of the whole country, so that whoever ruled it should be accounted archbishop'. Thus concludes the strange story of the synod of Brevi. It is not impossible that a fuller knowledge of the variant manuscript traditions may help to throw light on some of the obscure details, as I hope to show; but as it stands it is not easy to interpret.

In the meantime we may consider briefly the bias and other outstanding features of the *Life* in its present form. In the first place it is clear that the author is writing in the tradition of certain Irish literary conventions. Particularly striking is the conventional theme of the guardian angel which had already been developed by Muirchú in his *Life of St Patrick*, where we see Victor as an angel guiding and directing St Patrick throughout life, just as we

[1] Reference may here be made to a similar incident recorded in the *Life of St Kentigern* (cf. p. 318 below).

[2] This element in the story is manifestly closely connected with the site of the present beautiful church of Llandewi Brevi, dating from the late Norman period or slightly later and situated on a lofty eminence overhanging the river Teifi.

see the angel in Rhigyfarch's account guiding St David, and controlling every incident in his career. Thus we see Paulinus, one of the bishops present among the assembly at Brevi, recommending him to the synod (c. 49) as 'one who has an angel as his companion'.[1] By the same literary convention the angel is said to warn the patriarch of Jerusalem of the coming of David and his companions.

The Irish elements in the *Life* are an integral part of the story in its present form, and the pronounced Irish element which we know from other evidence to have been present in the population of Dyfed would seem to be implicit throughout the narrative. Thus when St Patrick is preparing to depart from Porth Mawr to Ireland he raises from the dead a man named Criumther[2] (c. 3), who has lain buried for twelve years by the shore, and takes him with him to Ireland, afterwards making him a bishop. David himself is probably baptised by St Ailbe of Munster (c. 9) though the text has the names in the form of *Aelvyw* of *Mynyw*. In c. 16 we are told how, as David and his three disciples are approaching 'Vallis Rosina, which the Britons commonly call Hodnant' (cf. p. 138 above), they meet with hostility and persecution from a certain 'chieftain and magician' (*satrapa magusque*) of the neighbourhood, an Irishman called Baia (*Baia vocatus, Scottus*) who evidently rules the land from his royal citadel (*arcis menibus residens*), for he and his wife are in a position to present to David 'the whole of Vallis Rosina for a perpetual possession'.[3] In neither case, however, does Rhigyfarch display any consciousness that the presence of an Irish chief in possession of land in Vallis Rosina calls for explanation.

The author associates David closely with Ireland through his disciples and the intercourse of Irish saints, though he is never said to visit Ireland, and indeed, apart from his visit to Jerusalem, he never appears to leave Dyfed, and our picture is that of a purely local saint. The Irish element in the *Life* is nevertheless very

---

[1] *Cui angelus comes est.* We may compare Adamnán, *Life of St Columba*, III, v, in which St Finnian sees St Columba approaching, 'qui sui commeatus meruit habere socium angelum cœlicolam'. A similar convention is made use of in the *Cáin Adamnáin*, a very composite document, in which it is claimed (c. 33) that an angel gave instructions to Adamnán as to the enactment of the 'Law of Adamnán'. The convention was in use in Brittany as late as the twelfth century, as we see in the *Life of St Gurthiern* contained in the cartulary of Quimperlé.

[2] The word is apparently Irish. Wade-Evans suggests (p. 70) that it is a mistake for *cruimther*, an Irish word meaning 'priest'.

[3] 'Terra', inquiunt, 'in qua es, tua in sempiternum fiat.'

extensive and varied in character. The Irish orientation is indeed made very clear at the outset by the introduction of St Patrick and the bold claim made by the author of the *Life* (c. 3) that David's advent is prophesied by an angel of God, and that St Patrick's purpose of establishing a sanctuary in Dyfed is frustrated in his favour.

After this we are hardly surprised to learn (c. 42; cf. 15) that about one-quarter or one-third of Ireland is subject to St David *Aquaticus*. This is David's claim to south Leinster, of which the chief saint was Aedán of Ferns, the disciple who had been with St David from the beginning of his mission (cf. c. 35, 36; cf. p. 138 above). It is in accord with such ambitious claims for David's influence in Ireland that we read of constant intercourse between his monastery and Ireland, e.g. the journey of St Aedán to Ferns (c. 36); that of Scutinus from Ferns to Dyfed (c. 37); and again that of Modomnoc to Ireland (c. 43). In view of the large Irish population in Dyfed, and also of the fact that the peninsula on which St David's now stands is a natural point of departure for Ireland, it is not surprising that we find St Barre, the famous saint of Cork, calling at St David's on his return voyage from his pilgrimage to Rome. Many of the incidents related of these saints in the *Life of St David* are probably derived by Rhigyfarch from Irish sources.[1]

Other features in the *Life of St David* show a certain relationship to Irish and other hagiological and secular themes. Thus the story (c. 7) of the monk born without nostrils or eyes, who receives normal eyes and features by the touch of the water with which St David has been baptised, recalls the story of Morann,[2] born with a caul obscuring his features, and ultimately receiving his normal features when washed by a wave. Perhaps a symbolical theme of rebirth or regeneration by the rite of the baptism of water lies behind such stories. Again the engaging story of St Barre riding a horse from Dyfed to Ireland[3] and meeting St Brendan at sea on a marine animal must have its origin in some secular Irish story such as that of the *Voyage of Bran*. It is noteworthy that the story of St Barre's ride over the sea to Ireland is

[1] On this point, see Lawlor, *Psalter and Martyrology of Ricemarch*, xvi.

[2] Text and translation by Whitley Stokes and E. Windisch, *Irische Texte*, 3rd series (Leipzig, 1891), 188 ff. (English translation, 206 ff.).

[3] Cf. the similar anecdote of St Barre in the Bodleian MS. (485) of the Latin text of the *Life of St Barre*, Plummer, *Vitae Sanct. Hib.* 1, 69, n. 8.

related in one version of the *Life* of that saint, while an incident virtually identical is related of St Aedán of Ferns (c. 32).[1]

It is perhaps more important to note certain apparently Irish elements in what appears to be a paraphrase or synopsis of a 'Rule' embodied in c. 21–31. This passage and its contents are conformable to the practices associated with the Anchorite Reform at Tallaght, as we infer from the text of the curious little document embodying notes on the customs of Tallaght[2] and other relevant documents. I have shown elsewhere[3] that we have reason to believe that the early Irish story of *Suibhne Geilt* and similar tales such as the references to Nyniaw and Peibiaw in the early medieval Welsh story of *Kulhwch ag Olwen* reflect satire at the expense of these vegetarian monks who cultivated holy poverty and the ascetic life. The close relationship between the ascetic practices ascribed to the early community of St David's and those ascribed to the little community of St Déclán of Ardmore to the east of Cork, find expression in c. 15 of the *Life of St Déclán*,[4] which relates his visit to St David, and the 'brotherhood' which the two saints are there represented as confirming between themselves and their followers.

There are a number of obscurities and inconsistencies in the *Life* which are possibly to be explained on the supposition that the author is following variant traditions which he makes no very successful attempt to reconcile. These are particularly striking in the opening chapters, in the references to the place of the saint's upbringing and early activities. To some of these, more especially in regard to the place-names, I have already referred, and it is possible that these and others will be resolved when we are in fuller possession of the manuscript tradition. In the meantime some of the more important discrepancies are worth noting.

As one example we observe that the traditions of St David's promotion to the see are both strange and varied, and Rhigyfarch's account is inconsistent. In c. 46 he tells us that the patriarch of Jerusalem promoted him to the archiepiscopate ('ad archiepisco-

---

[1] *Vitae Sanct. Hib.* II, 304. Here the animal which carries Aedán to Ireland is described as *animal magnum in similitudinem equi magni.*

[2] For references to the text and translation, and some comments on the contents, see Kenney, *op. cit.* 471. The matter is closely related to that of the prose *Rule of the Céli Dé* or 'Culdees'.

[3] 'Geilt', *Scottish Gaelic Studies*, V (1942), 106 ff.

[4] Edited and translated by Patrick Power for the Irish Texts Society (London, 1914).

patum David agium provehit'). Yet in c. 49 Bishop Paulinus, David's former preceptor, informs the synod of Brevi that David had been made 'bishop' by the patriarch ('quidam qui a patriarcha episcopus factus'). The two statements are not necessarily contradictory; but they are strange as they stand, and suggest a discrepancy somewhere.

Again in c. 53 we are told that David is made archbishop at the synod of Brevi, apparently by popular acclamation, 'And his monastery is dedicated the metropolis, so that whoever ruled it should be accounted archbishops'. This synod consisted of 'bishops, kings, princes, nobles, and all ranks of the whole Britannic race'. In c. 55 we are again told that after a number of seasons this decision was ratified at the synod of Victory by what appears to be a more ecclesiastical body, consisting of 'an assembly (*turba*) of bishops, priests, and abbots'; and Rhigyfarch adds that from these two synods 'All the churches of our country take their standard and rule from Roman authority'. Is Rhigyfarch following variant traditions, or is he merely seeking to emphasise the claim of David to be a metropolitan by insisting that his election at home had had the authority, or at least the approval, of the patriarch of Jerusalem? And what is the force of his 'Roman authority' in c. 55? Is he there seeking to establish that David's consecration was of the 'correct' Roman Order, and not merely a Celtic consecration?

Rhigyfarch's account is certainly a muddled one as it stands, and it is not easy to see what the sources of his information may be. One further detail of the narrative may be mentioned here. It is a curious fact that the messenger chosen to accompany Dubricius to summon David to Brevi should be St Daniel. Why is Daniel introduced in this context? It is true that he is traditionally stated to have been a disciple of Dubricius; but he is not mentioned anywhere else in the *Life of St David*, and his fame rests in general on his prestige as the patron saint of Bangor, later the episcopal see of Gwynedd in North Wales. It has however been demonstrated recently by the Rev. Silas Harris[1] that in a manuscript text[2] of nine lections and a collect for St Deiniol's feast the saint is

---

[1] 'Liturgical Commemorations of Welsh Saints', *Journal of the Historical Society of the Church in Wales*, v (1955), 5 ff.

[2] MS. Peniarth 225 in the National Library of Wales. The text in question has been edited and translated by Harris, *loc. cit.*

associated in early life with Pembroke, where he is said to have had a hermitage on a high hill (*mons*) outside the town, and where 'a large and beautiful church' was afterwards erected.[1] Has Rhigyfarch introduced St Deiniol summoning David to this synod because he wished to represent David as superseding Deiniol?

Rhigyfarch's account of David's election as archbishop of St David's was of course known at Llanbadarn Fawr and also at Llandaff, as the *Life of St Teilo*, written in the twelfth century, makes clear,[2] for, as we have seen, the latter work draws about a third of its material from the *Life of St David*, and accepts Rhigyfarch's version of the journey to Jerusalem of David, along with Teilo and Padarn, which the Welsh *Life* omits altogether. Indeed Rhigyfarch's is the oldest extant version of this story, which reappears in the *Lives* of both St Padarn and St Teilo (see below); so that though these two later *Lives* each seek to exalt their own saint above St David, they must needs accept the original story in its broad outline as it was already accredited.

It is, therefore, a very curious fact that when the chapter of St David's put up their claim to be a metropolitan see in 1124–30[3] they make no reference to Rhigyfarch, or to his implication that at the synod of Brevi it was decided by acclamation that the ruler of the monastery of St David's from the time of St David himself should always be accounted archbishop. On the contrary the chapter claims that the church of St David's had been a metropolitan see from the time of the first introduction of Christianity into Britain. And they claim further that David was elevated to the position of archbishop by the whole kingdom of western Britain, and consecrated archbishop by St Dubricius, his predecessor, whose sphere of activity is traditionally stated to have been in Gwent, i.e. in south-eastern Wales and western Herefordshire. Finally they claim that the conversion of Ireland by St Patrick took place from their see, and that the disciples of St David had taken part with him in the consecration of her bishops and in the prosperity of the Irish Church; and for all these reasons they claim that their 'prosperous dignity in its most ancient right' should be restored to them. It should, however, be

[1] An important church, dedicated to St Deiniol, still stood on an eminence less than a mile from the town in 1603. See Harris, *op. cit.* 17.

[2] See Canon G. H. Doble, *St Teilo* (Lampeter, 1942), 10f., 16.

[3] See *Episcopal Acts relating to Welsh Dioceses 1066–1272* (ed. James Conway Davies for the Historical Society of the Church in Wales), I (1946), 249.

pointed out that in making this last claim the chapter were urging their instrumentality, not as forwarding the interests of the Celtic Church in Ireland, but that of the Roman Order as represented by the see of Armagh. Already at the synod of Birr in 697 Flann Feblae, abbot and bishop of Armagh, had accepted the Roman Order, the *Unitas Catholica*, on behalf of the see of Patrick (cf. p. 54 above). Moreover diocesan episcopacy had already been established throughout Ireland before the Anglo-Norman invasion, and Armagh held the primacy. The bishops and clergy of each diocese now derived their commissions, through their archbishop, from the Pope.

The chapter's later claim of 1145–7[1] ascribes David's promotion to the synod of Brevi, as did Rhigyfarch himself. Again, however, no reference is made to Rhigyfarch by name in their letter, and the chapter adds certain information not found in Rhigyfarch, to the effect that the privilege granted to St David by acclamation of the whole province at the synod of Brevi was confirmed by the Pope of Rome by the gift of the pallium, David himself being present with his two suffragans, Thelia (Teilo) and Padarn. It is possible that a common tradition lies behind these specific details in the letter of the chapter and the account of the synod of Victoria referred to by Rhigyfarch in c. 55 of the *Life*, where he seems to imply that the assembly consisted exclusively of ecclesiastics (bishops, priests and abbots), and that the proceedings were of a more official character than those of Brevi; and where, moreover, the 'Roman authority' of the two synods is insisted on. Nevertheless it cannot be said that the chapter make any direct reference to Rhigyfarch, at least by name. This curious omission is, it seems to me, capable of only two possible explanations. Either the chapter were unaware of Rhigyfarch's work, or at least of his authorship; or they deliberately ignored it with a view to minimising the Celtic element in the claim of the church of St David. We shall see that the latter reason offers the more likely explanation.

Turning now to the text of the Welsh *Buched* ('Life'), it will be noticed that this is very closely related to the *Life* by Rhigyfarch. Indeed the two texts correspond so closely as to be virtually verbally identical in a very large proportion of the narratives. Hugh Williams regarded the Welsh *Life* as 'only a condensed reproduction of the Latin *Vita*', but with striking omissions,

---

[1] *Episcopal Acts*, etc. (*ed. cit.*), I, 262 f.

changes, and additions, made with a view to modifying it to suit a popular sermon for the saint's day.[1] Wade-Evans also regarded this Welsh *Life* as 'an abridgment of the work of Rhigyfarch', but he adds 'whether translated directly from the original or from some recension of it is yet to be discovered'.[2] More recently the late Canon G. H. Doble expressed the view that the Welsh *Life* was based, not on Rhigyfarch, but on his sources.[3] I shall discuss these views in more detail after enumerating the principal features in which the *Buched* differs from Rhigyfarch's narrative.

A study of the manuscripts of the *Buched* by the Rev. J. W. James has given us a basis for examining the relationship of this text to that of Rhigyfarch. These manuscripts are ten in number, but their differences are unimportant as regards subject-matter, and MS. 119, written by the anchorite of Llanddewi Brevi in 1346, and now preserved in Jesus College, Oxford, seems to be the oldest and would appear to supply a basic text virtually homogeneous with the later ones. In view of the close relationship of the Welsh *Life* to that of Rhigyfarch, the question arises as to which particular Latin text the *Buched* is based on. From a close study of the texts James demonstrates that the Welsh version is derived from texts related to two Latin MSS. of Rhigyfarch—one contained in Vespasian A. xiv and another, closely related to it, in Lincoln Cathedral Library, MS. 149. He concludes his study significantly enough with the words: 'The precise relation of the various Latin texts of Rhigyfarch's *Life of St David* requires another and a much more complicated study.'[4]

We are, however, in a position to estimate the significance of the principal points in which the Welsh *Life* differs from that of Rhigyfarch, and which consist chiefly of omissions.

(1) The Welsh *Life* omits the long and specific list of ascetic practices of David's monastery which, as enumerated by Rhigyfarch, almost amounts to a monastic 'Rule'.

(2) Immediately after this passage Rhigyfarch relates two miracles (c. 35) associated with David's disciple St Aedán, by which the oxen which he has taken to fetch timber are miraculously saved from death after being hurled from a precipice into the sea

---

[1] *Christianity in Early Britain*, 381f.　　[2] *Life of St David*, xiiif.

[3] G. H. Doble, *St Teilo* (Lampeter, 1942), 10f.

[4] (The Rev.) Chancellor J. W. James, 'Rhigyfarch's Life of St David', *National Library of Wales Journal*, ix (1955), p. 21.

with their load; while a book which he has left open when he sets out is found unwetted by a deluge of rain. These two miracles are omitted by the Welsh *Life*, which records only Rhigyfarch's story of the angel's warning to Aedán, after his departure to Ireland, of poisoned bread prepared for David by the treachery of his disciples, and of David's immunity through his faith.

(3) The Welsh *Life* then passes directly to the synod of Brevi, but makes no reference to the second synod, of Lucus Victoriae.

(4) Rhigyfarch's *Life*, on the other hand, introduces between these narratives about Aedán, and before the two synods, a series of fantastic stories, clearly characteristic of the Irish secular stories of *Immrama* or 'voyages', such as (c. 39) the journey of St Barre over the sea on David's horse and his encounter with St Brendan 'who was leading a wondrous life on a marine animal'. Still further stories follow of David's Irish disciples (c. 41, 43), Maedoc and Modomnoc, the latter followed to Ireland by the bees he had been wont to tend; but again the Welsh *Life* contains no hint of these.

(5) Immediately after these Irish stories Rhigyfarch introduces the journey of David to Jerusalem in company of St Teilo and St Padarn. The Welsh *Life* makes no reference to such a journey, which, however, occurs in a number of other saints' *Vitae*.[1] The Welsh version merely states by the mouth of Paulinus that David was 'ordained to be archbishop in Rome', while Rhigyfarch tells us that he had intended to visit Rome, but was satisfied with the account of the holy pilgrimage which he had received from an Irish abbot, Barri. Curiously enough Rhigyfarch omits to tell us how David was consecrated bishop of Mynyw.

It was, as I have said, suggested by Hugh Williams (cf. p. 146 above) that the Welsh *Life* omits these incidents with a view to making the *Life* more suitable for a sermon. But there can be no doubt that Rhigyfarch shared this homiletic purpose, as the closing words of c. 65 make clear. Moreover it is a remarkable fact that the sections omitted by the Welsh *Life* are consistently those which would seem to link the saint with Ireland, more especially the ascetic practices; the fantastic and humorous stories of a specially Irish kind; the disciples with Irish names and direct associations with Irish monastic life. These omissions in the *Buched*, taken together with the pointed substitution of Rome for Jerusalem as the

---

[1] SS. Cadoc, Cyngar, Cybi (Wales); Budoc and Tudwal (Brittany); Petroc (Cornwall).

148

objective of the journey of David, Teilo and Padarn, seem to indicate a deliberate breaking away from the traditions of the early Celtic, and more particularly the early Irish, Church, and an attempt to emphasise Dewi's Roman tradition, as the chapter of St David's had done earlier. They hardly afford serious ground for suggesting that the Welsh *Life* is based, not on Rhigyfarch, but on his source. On the other hand the strong pro-Irish bias of Rhigyfarch's *Life* is in itself extremely interesting and calls for explanation. I shall return to this subject again later.

I have already referred to the view held by the late Canon Doble[1] that the *Life of St Teilo*,[2] written some forty years after Rhigyfarch's lifetime, offers evidence for a *Life of St David* which was used independently by both Rhigyfarch and the Welsh *Life*. Doble points out that the *Life of St Teilo* borrows about a third of its material from the *Life of St David*; but that while the material remains substantially the same as Rhigyfarch's and the Welsh versions, every story differs in detail from Rhigyfarch's account, even where there could be no motive for altering it. A detailed comparison such as Doble offers would be out of place here; but it may be said that neither his comparison nor a careful reading of the *Life of St Teilo* shows convincing evidence for his conclusion. Such differences of detail as the *Life of St Teilo* show from Rhigyfarch can all be easily accounted for by the freedom with which its author uses all his materials, and the object which he has in view—that of increasing the prestige of the church of Llandaff at the expense of St David's.

It remains to speak of the *Life of St David* by Giraldus Cambrensis.[3] We do not know the date at which Gerald wrote this *Life*. He himself seems to have lived from *c.* 1147 to *c.* 1223. The general outline of the work follows that of Rhigyfarch very closely, and though Giraldus nowhere mentions Rhigyfarch by name, his dependence is beyond doubt. He tells us in his proem that he has undertaken to write the *Life* in elegant style in response to insistent pressure from the brethren and canons of St David's, and his words seem to imply that he is performing his task somewhat perfunctorily, owing to the many calls on his time. He only

---

[1] *St Teilo* (Lampeter, 1942), 10 ff.
[2] In the *Liber Landavensis*, ed. and trans. by W. J. Rees (Llandovery, 1840), Latin text, 92; English translation, 332; also ed. by J. G. Evans, (Oxford, 1893), 97.
[3] For details of the edition, cf. p. 155, n. 3.

vaguely claims to have supplied some of the deficiencies and pruned some of the superfluities ('et superflua rescindi et defectiva suppleri') of the 'old lesson' ('lectionis antiquae'). The only important new matter which he adds, and which does not appear in any other extant version, is the story told in *lectio* 6 of how the Gospel of St John, which David was engaged in copying, was completed by an angel in letters of gold. His plan is clearly liturgical, because his narrative is arranged in ten *lectiones*, doubtless to be read at matins on the saint's feast. His close adherence to Rhigyfarch's version of the story, however, and his reference to the *lectio antiqua* of his source seem to suggest the possibility that he is following a recension of Rhigyfarch which is already cast in the form of *lectiones*. Again at the end he adds some liturgical prayers, an antiphon and a collect. We have already seen that Rhigyfarch also concludes his *Life* with liturgical matter.

In his brief account of the saint contained in his *Itinerary through Wales*[1] (Book II, 4) Giraldus again makes brief reference to the story of St David's promotion to the archbishopric, and here he may be trying to reconcile variant traditions. Again he does not refer to Rhigyfarch by name. He speaks of all the bishops, abbots, and clergy as electing David by acclamation to the archbishopric at the synod of Brevi, whereas we have seen that according to Rhigyfarch his concourse would seem to have consisted mainly of laity, from the kings and nobility downwards, while it was the synod of Victory which consisted of bishops, abbots, and clergy. Giraldus here makes no reference to this second synod, though he makes a brief mention of it in the *Life*. In both texts also he notes the fact that the ground rose under David's feet at Brevi, so that he was standing on the summit of a hill (cf. p. 140 above), though he omits the curious tradition of the *sudarium*. It appears, however, that he was possibly aware of a variant tradition of David's election to the archbishopric,[2] for he refers to it in the *Life* (*lectio* 8), and more fully here he adds:

Dubricius had a short time before resigned to him this honour in due form at Caerleon, from which city the metropolitan see was transferred to St David's.

---

[1] Giraldus accompanied Archbishop Baldwin through Wales in 1188. His *Itinerary* was probably written shortly afterwards.

[2] This passage in Giraldus may, however, reflect the influence of Geoffrey of Monmouth.

One cannot help wondering if some of the obscurities in the *Life* of Rhigyfarch, and also in that of later versions, would not disappear could we have Rhigyfarch's text before us in its original form. A case in point is the eminence formed of the clothing of the multitude at Brevi, from which David refuses to preach, whereas he readily mounts the hill which miraculously rises under the *sudarium* or shroud of the boy whom he has just raised from the dead. Rhigyfarch has described how, immediately on the boy's coming to life, the saint placed on his shoulders a copy of the Gospel 'which he himself always carried on his breast' and, taking him with him to the synod, took 'the shroud' (*sudarium*) from him and stood thereon to preach the Gospel. There can, I think, be little doubt that the miraculous hill which then arose under him is due to the contact of the shroud with the Gospel, whether we suppose the Gospel to have been wrapped in it or not. Again one wonders if this can have been the Golden Gospel of which Giraldus alone tells us. It is curious that Rhigyfarch's story of St Aedán, whose Gospel remained dry through torrential rain; Giraldus's story of the Golden Gospel; and the story told by both of the saint's Gospel placed on the boy's shoulder, with Rhigyfarch's further account of the miraculous result at the synod of Brevi—only vaguely narrated by Giraldus—are all in close sequence. Have some connecting links dropped out?

On the whole I am inclined to suspect that the divergences which have been noted above between these three versions of the *Life of St David* are due to a difference of emphasis and of policy rather than to variations in the original tradition as this has been handed down at St David's. It does not appear probable that the chapter were unacquainted with Rhigyfarch's work, though they do not mention his name. Their letter of 1124–30 makes reference to the synods by which David was promoted, and that of 1145–7 refers specifically to the synod of Brevi. The claim of the chapter that David was consecrated archbishop by Dubricius was probably a traditional one, though possibly an invention. Rhigyfarch ignores such a tradition; but that he was aware of it may probably be inferred from the fact that he represents Dubricius, along with Daniel, as summoning David to Brevi, while at the same time he omits to mention who precisely it was who consecrated David. The reference of the chapter to David's receiving the pallium from Rome is quite in accordance with the practice and ideals of the twelfth century; but that the chapter were aware of, and deliberately 'improving on', Rhigyfarch's account of the journey to Jerusalem may be inferred from their reference to SS. Teilo and Padarn as having been present as David's suffragans at his receipt of the pallium from the Pope of Rome. Further it may be urged that the reference of the chapter in the letter of 1124–30 to the 'histories' which claim that it was from their see that St Patrick was first sent to convert the Irish must surely be a direct reference to Rhigyfarch.

The chief difference implied in the letter of 1124–30 from facts as related by Rhigyfarch lies in the chapter's claim that Menevia was an episcopal see from the time of the conversion. This is a vague claim which Rhigyfarch, had he known it, might have regarded as outside his scope as the biographer of a particular saint. But, as we have seen, the chapter strengthen their claim by emphasising the unbroken history of their church as a metropolitan see from a time long before St David was born, and in fact from the introduction of Christianity into Wales. As Professor Brooke points out (pp. 211 f. below), the chapter, in their 1124–30 letter, by pressing the foundation of their see back to Roman days, put themselves into the full current of eleventh- and twelfth-century metropolitan claims. It was persistently urged in France—and in essence probably truly—that archbishops and primacies were based ultimately on Roman organisation and it is doubtless for this reason that the chapter stress their claim back to second-century history. In this, as in so much else in the writings under consideration, the issue stated is determined by a *parti pris* rather than by actual tradition.

I am inclined to regard the matters in which the *Buched Dewi*, the Welsh version of the *Life*, differs from Rhigyfarch as likewise due to a difference of emphasis and of policy. The trend of the Welsh version throughout, as of the letters of the chapter, is to stress the Roman and the Catholic elements in the history of the church of St David's, and in the career of the saint himself. In accordance with this object the *Buched* not only omits the stories of David's intercourse with Ireland through his disciples, and all reference to the journey to Jerusalem and the patriarch; but in the speech in which Paulinus urges that David be invited to Brevi, and in which the saint's virtues are enumerated, it is noteworthy that the *Buched*, while following Rhigyfarch's text closely, indeed almost verbatim, nevertheless entirely omits all reference to the qualification which Rhigyfarch places at the head of his list, namely that David had been made bishop by the patriarch. It would seem to be in conformity with this same 'Romanising' and 'anti-Celtic' tendency that the *Buched* omits the ascetic practices of David and his monks, as well as the general 'Irish' communications and affinities of the monastery, which form so large an element of Rhigyfarch's story.

On the whole it does not appear that the evidence before us warrants the view that any *Vita* of St David other than that of Rhigyfarch was known at St David's and utilised by the author of the *Buched*. There may of course have been written materials of a different kind, now no longer extant, relating to David, and accessible to all—not only to Rhigyfarch, but also to the author of the *Buched* and the chapter. Rhigyfarch himself refers to 'sparse materials' (*pauca*) scattered in very ancient writings of the country, especially the monastery itself, written in antiquated style, and eaten away along the inner and outer margins. It would be unsafe to rely too credulously on such a statement. Such phrases were the commonplaces of late Latin and early medieval writers. There is, however, some ground for crediting Rhigyfarch's statement, for, as we have already seen (pp. 131 f. above), St David was so widely known in liturgical literature before Rhigyfarch's day that it is difficult to doubt the existence of some such documents, which may have been in actual use at St David's when he was writing, while in Ireland David was apparently known already in the eighth century.

Again it may be surmised that some of the outstanding incidents of the life of the saint may have survived till the eleventh century in the form of a *passio*, a short sermon devoted in the early Church to a saint on the day of his commemoration. In such *passiones* the account of the death of a saint formed sometimes the chief element. A number of such commemorative sermons have survived, one of the earliest and best known being that of St Hilary of Arles in commemoration of St Honoratus, the founder of the island monastery of Lérins.[1] It is a striking fact that the closing portions of both Rhigyfarch's *Life* and the *Buched*, the portions, be it noted, where scholars have remarked the greatest differences between these two versions,[2] bear a close resemblance to such a *passio*. It

[1] Migne, *P.L.* L, col. 1257. A more recent edition is that of S. Cavallin, *Vitae Sanctorum Honorati et Hilarii* (Lund, 1952).

[2] See, e.g., Hugh Williams, *Christianity in Early Britain*, 382.

has, indeed, been remarked that the entire *Lives*, Latin and Welsh alike, appear to have been composed as sermons. This we need not assume from the texts before us. It seems more probable that the authors' closing addresses to their readers are taken directly from some *passio* still extant in the church of St David's. It is not impossible that the chapter had certain *acta* preserved in liturgical references, and that a *passio* of the saint was still in existence in the eleventh and twelfth centuries, which may have been utilised by Rhigyfarch and the composer of the *Buched*.

How then are we to account for the most prominent feature in Rhigyfarch's *Life*, the Celtic element, ignored by the chapter and deliberately eschewed by the *Buched* save in connection with the villainous Irish tyrant Baia and his followers who oppose David at the outset? It will have become apparent from the preceding pages that the evidence has been carefully selected by all the writers in question, that all have a *parti pris*. We are, in fact, dealing not so much with variant traditions as with a vigorous religious controversy. In this controversy Rhigyfarch proclaims his sympathies with the conservative party, with the supporters of the Celtic Church in general. And to this end he emphasises the importance of the Irish Church and its relations with Britain. The authors of the Welsh *Life* and the chapter, on the other hand, are at pains to obliterate anything which will identify the interests of St David's with the Celtic Church and the old Order, and to this end they— and apparently Giraldus also—feel it judicious to omit any reference to Rhigyfarch by name. While the object of both parties is to promote the interests of St David's in the hope of its acquiring the primacy of all Wales, the methods which they employ are directly opposed to one another. Rhigyfarch, as we shall see, is a keen patriot and traditionalist. The authors of the *Buched* and the chapter, writing at a later date, have come to realise that their best means of obtaining their end is to identify their see and its traditions in every possible way with the interests of the Roman Church, the Church of their Norman rulers. Giraldus, later still, though a patriot like Rhigyfarch before him, has now no thought of giving loyalty to any tradition save Rome. While claiming independence for a Welsh Church, founded, as he insists, by a Welshman, he omits Rhigyfarch's characteristically Celtic elements, more especially the asceticism, and feels it prudent to make no reference to his name.

At this point it is necessary to emphasise once more the obscurity and apparently conflicting nature of some of the traditions relating to the saint's early life, and Rhigyfarch's evident uneasiness in the handling of them. This obscurity and apparent inconsistency in the early tradition is particularly evident in regard to the locality of the saint's birth and education. In c. 8 of Rhigyfarch's *Life* the saint is said to have been educated at a place called *Vetus Rubus*, which, as Wade-Evans has pointed out,[1] is clearly a different place from *Vallis Rosina* in Hodnant in which the cathedral now stands, and which is today known as St David's (L. *Menevia*). The Welsh version of the *Life* translated *Vetus Rubus* quite directly as *Hen Llwyn*, 'Old Grove', evidently not recognising *Vetus Rubus* as a translation of *Hen Fynyw* ('Old Mynyw').[2] Actually *Hen Fynyw* is the same place as that called both *Vetus Rubus* and *Hen Llwyn*. Giraldus Cambrensis thus explains[3] (III, 384) *Vetus Rubus*: 'In Welsh *Hen Meneu*, in Latin *Vetus Menevia*, "Old Mynyw".' Clearly 'Old Mynyw', like *Vetus Rubus*, is a different place from St David's. It would seem therefore that the name *Mynyw* was transferred to *Vallis Rosina* in Dyfed from an original *Mynyw*, which later came to be called *Hen Fynyw*. No place of this name is known in the neighbourhood of St David's today, but it is undoubtedly to be identified with the place of this name on the coast of Cardigan Bay (cf. p. 156 below). Such a transference would surely imply that the original *Mynyw* was one of considerable importance. It would seem moreover that *Old Menevia* was not only a place of learning and education, but also the seat of a bishop, since David's *fratruelis*, Guistilianus, is so described (cf. p. 138 above).[4]

This chapter (14) is crucial. Rhigyfarch continues: as David and Guistilianus comforted one another with religious talk St David said:

'An angel of the Lord hath spoken to me saying, "From the place where thou dost propose to serve, scarcely one in a hundred will be able to escape to the kingdom of God". And He hath shown me a place whence few shall go to Hell, for everyone who shall have been buried in the cemetery of that place in sound faith shall obtain mercy.'

It would appear probable, though not certain, that Rhigyfarch means us to understand that David's intention had been to serve

---

[1] *Life of St David*, 78, cf. also p. 137, n. 1 above, and the references there cited.
[2] With *Mynyw* cf. Old Irish *muine*, 'bush', 'brake'.
[3] *De Vita S. Davidis*, c. III. Edited by Wharton, II, 632. This is the text reproduced by J. S. Brewer in his edition in the Rolls Series, *Giraldi Cambrensis Opera*, III, 386.   [4] See Wade-Evans, *op. cit.* 83 ff.

God in *Vetus Rubus* or Old Menevia, the place of his education; and this is evidently how the Welsh *Life* understood it, for in the following passage the Welsh *Life* has substituted 'from this place' (i.e. *Vetus Rubus*) for the phrase 'from the place where thou dost propose to serve'.

Immediately after this David sets forth with his three disciples, 'And with one mind they go together to the place which the angel had mentioned beforehand, i.e. *Vallis Rosina*, which the Britons call Hodnant'. This chapter seems to make it clear:

(1) that *Vetus Rubus*, where David had been educated, and where he evidently spent his early life, was not the same as *Vallis Rosina*, the modern St David's;

(2) that Rhigyfarch is at pains to disparage *Vetus Rubus* as a future sanctuary, whatever it might have been in the past;

(3) that he had also strong reasons for wishing to substitute *Vallis Rosina* for it;

(4) that Rhigyfarch advertises *Vallis Rosina* with the strongest argument he possesses, namely a promise of eternal life for those who are buried there.[1]

It would appear that Rhigyfarch is writing with a definite end in view, his aim being to supersede some earlier sanctuary in favour of a new one at Vallis Rosina in Hodnant. This earlier sanctuary would seem to have been in all probability *Hen Fynyw*, a place in Cardiganshire immediately to the south of Aberayron (cf. above). The name clearly implies that it was superseded by a later Mynyw. Rhigyfarch is at pains to tell us that St David was educated here, though he has made it clear to us that he was born elsewhere; and the parish church is still dedicated to St David; but, as Wade-Evans has pointed out,[2] the fact that this was the place where he received his early training from his *fratruelis*, Bishop Guistilianus, would suggest that it was already known as a sanctuary at an earlier date.

When, and for what purpose, did the sanctuary of Mynyw supersede that at Hen Fynyw? On our evidence the transference was closely connected with the growing importance of the cult of St David and its association with Dyfed. It is not, indeed, our only evidence of the transference of the saint's prestige to Dyfed

---

[1] Plummer has a valuable note in which he enumerates many instances from the *Lives* of the Irish saints to show how salvation was regarded as obtainable by burial in a certain cemetery. See *Vitae Sanct. Hib.* I, xciii, n. 3.

[2] *Life of St David*, 84.

from farther north. We have seen that Rhigyfarch represents his father as a king of Cardigan, and the saint's conception as having taken place during his father's temporary visit to Dyfed. St Patrick also, somewhat inexplicably as it seems to us, lands in Cardigan when his intention is to establish his cult in Dyfed.[1] We have seen that the atmosphere of religious controversy which permeates the *Life* is particularly noticeable in these earlier chapters. What is Rhigyfarch's interest in it, and why does he emphasise the saint's birth in Dyfed while he would seem to know traditions of his earlier cult farther north in Ceredigion or Cardiganshire?

Ultimately the question seems to resolve itself into one of prestige. Rhigyfarch, for whatever reason, is concerned to exalt the present St David's as a great sanctuary, one which has apparently superseded another farther north. Moreover he is concerned to exalt St David above all the other saints in Wales, and more specifically above other Cardigan saints, St Carantoc and St Padarn. Yet we know St Padarn to have been the saint of Llanbadarn Fawr, Rhigyfarch's own home. Why does Rhigyfarch thus transfer his loyalty? Before we can answer this question we must first glance very briefly at the *Lives* of the two Cardigan saints just mentioned, and finally at the family to which Rhigyfarch himself belonged, and at the part which it played in the history of the two great sanctuaries of Dyfed and Cardigan, St David's and Llanbadarn, at the time when the *Life* of St David's was written.

The *Lives* of St Carantoc and St Padarn are two *Lives* of saints belonging to what we may perhaps call the Cardigan group,[2] with which that of David is closely associated. The activities of both these saints belong essentially to the shores of Cardigan Bay, and the *Lives* of both are contained in MS. Vespasian A. XIV.[3] Of St Carantoc we have two *Lives*, the longer of which was written not long after that of St David, while the shorter version is a little later. These *Lives*, all of them comparatively late, probably owe their origin to a common stimulus, for there are indications that the longer *Life of St Carantoc* is not independent of that of St David,

---

[1] This may be due to an early but erroneous identification of the *Coroticus* to whom St Patrick addresses his famous *Letter*, with *Ceredig*, the eponymous king of *Ceredigion*.

[2] For some account of this group see E. G. Bowen, *The Settlements of the Celtic Saints in Wales* (Cardiff, 1954), pp. 50ff.

[3] Text and translation by A. W. Wade-Evans in *Vitae Sanctorum Britanniae et Genealogiae* (Cardiff, 1944).

and that it aims at superseding it. We are specifically told in both *Lives* of Carantoc that the saint was a son of Ceredig, the eponymous king of Cardigan and the chosen heir to his kingdom, though he abandoned it for the life of a religious recluse. It is further claimed that he had been well received in Ireland thirty years before the birth of St David. Indeed the close reference which the author makes to the *Life of St David* is clear down to the minutest details.

The writer goes on to tell us that St Carantoc and St Patrick decided to divide Ireland between them, St Patrick taking the north, and St Carantoc Leinster—a proud claim, surely not wholly independent of the claim made by Rhigyfarch that St David was preferred by the angel of the Lord to St Patrick when Patrick attempted to establish his sanctuary in Dyfed. Both these claims aim at limiting the sphere of Patrick's influence (and that of the see of Armagh) in the interests of Cardigan saints, as representing the conservative Celtic interests. It may be added that, despite the Irish bias of the *Life*, the author is well acquainted with the locality of Cardigan in which the saint's principal activities took place. It is therefore perhaps not surprising that he is concerned to exalt the local Cardigan saint above the saint of Dyfed; but perhaps more significant still are the claims made for his prestige in Ireland.

The most interesting, and for us the most important, of the saints of the Cardigan group is St Padarn, the traditional founder of the great Celtic (pre-Norman) monastic site of Llanbadarn Fawr on Cardigan Bay near Aberystwyth, hardly inferior in renown to St David himself.[1] Here again, as in the *Lives* of St David and of St Carantoc, the close connection with Ireland is stressed. We are told that the saint was born in Armorica of noble stock; but after the conception of Padarn, his father retires to Ireland to devote himself to a life of chastity. Padarn himself settles in Britain at an early age, and after visiting his father in Ireland and his brethren (*fratres*) in Brittany, he establishes monasteries, doubtless of Irish type, and churches (*monasteria et ecclesias*) throughout the kingdom of Cardigan. Subsequently he makes a pilgrimage to Jerusalem together with St David and St Teliau (*Teilo*), where gifts are bestowed on them all by the patriarch, those of St Padarn being a *baculus* (a staff), and a precious tunic (cf. p. 138 above). It is claimed in the *Life of St Padarn* as we now have it that he passed the latter part of his life in Vannes; but it is generally believed that

---

[1] For the early importance of the site, cf. p. 164 below.

the *Lives* of more than one saint of the same name have been combined, and that one of these was a Breton.

While the saint is in Ireland on the visit to his father referred to above, the country is devastated by the wars of two of the kings of the provinces of Ireland, and it is told to the bishop of the two royal cities that peace can only be restored by St Padarn. This the saint effects, apparently by some 'sign' (*signum pacis*), for the people then cry:

'May it be to thee for ever as a sign of peace, by which thy name may be famous in the earth while thou livest, and after thy death; which is fulfilled in the gift of *Cirguen*. For so great is the service (*utilitas*) of that *baculus* that if any two are at discord, they are made to agree by swearing together on it.'

The passage is obscure as it stands, but in the margin is written: *nomen baculi pacificatur*. This gloss doubtless refers to *Cirguen*, which the glossator evidently regards as the *baculus*, the crozier by which the saint effected the peace; and the implication is that the saint through his staff is a powerful instrument of peace, both during his lifetime and after his death. The incident takes place in the story before the pilgrimage to Jerusalem referred to above, and the gift of the *baculus* to Padarn; but this is nevertheless in all probability a reference to the *baculus Cirguen*, and either the incident in Ireland or the visit to Jerusalem is probably misplaced. At least the scribe associates the two incidents and knows the power of the *baculus*, and we shall see reason to regard the peace-giving functions of the sanctuary of Padarn at Llanbadarn Fawr, his chief monastery, as its most important and constant features. It is interesting to find him exercising it in inter-tribal affairs in Ireland.

The *Life of St Padarn*, as we have it in Vesp. A. xiv, is believed to have been composed at Llanbadarn Fawr,[1] perhaps *c.* 1120, or even later. But a *Life of St Padarn* was evidently already current in some form and known to Rhigyfarch before he wrote his *Life of St David*, because in reference to the joint journey to Jerusalem which the *Lives* of SS. David, Padarn, and Teilo all ascribe to these three saints (cf. p. 138 above), he makes mention of St Padarn as

---

[1] The internal evidence is strong. Cf., e.g., the use of the word 'here' in speaking of Padarn's farewell to his brethren at Llanbadarn on his departure to Letavia (cf. the *Life*, c. 23; cf. also Doble, *Saint Patern*, 16).

one whose life and miracles are contained in his 'history' (*historia*),[1] i.e. presumably his *acta*.

The most interesting references to St Padarn occur in a Latin poem, the *Carmen de Vita et Familia Sulgeni, Episcopi Menevensis*,[2] composed by Ieuan (John), a brother of Rhigyfarch. The poem is our chief source of information about the *clas* at Llanbadarn and the family to which Rhigyfarch belonged. Ieuan was himself an ecclesiastic of Llanbadarn Fawr,[3] and it is therefore not surprising that both Rhigyfarch and Ieuan should make reverent reference to St Padarn, from whom this ancient sanctuary takes its name. The poem in question, written *c.* 1100 by Ieuan chiefly about his father, Sulien the 'Wise',[4] twice bishop of St David's, will be discussed more fully below. Here it will be enough to mention that it contains an invocation to St Paternus (*Padarn*), and in the section headed *De Patria*, Ieuan, after describing the situation of Llanbadarn Fawr, makes reference to the number of years spent by Paternus at Llanbadarn—a number corresponding with that mentioned in the *Life*—and makes clear the strength of affectionate loyalty felt by the members of Llanbadarn for their founder.[5] St Padarn was indeed the saint to whom the loyalty of the family was strongly bound, and in choosing St David and not St Padarn as the hero of his narrative Rhigyfarch must have been actuated by some very strong motive.

From our brief survey of the three chief Cardigan saints, it is clear that the most important external contacts emphasised by their biographers are with Ireland.[6] Brittany is not wholly out of the picture; but except for vague family origins we hear little of

[1] Père Grosjean reminds me that the word *storia* is already used as the technical term for the written acts of a saint in the eighth century. See the *Leiden Glossary* (edited by Hessels, Cambridge, 1906, where it forms the title of section III), 7.

[2] A facsimile of a part of the poem is given facing p. 3 of an article by J. E. Lloyd, 'Bishop Sulien and his Family', *The National Library of Wales Journal*, II (1941), 1 ff. The text is printed by Haddan and Stubbs, *Councils*, etc., I (Oxford, 1869), appendix D, 663 f.

[3] *Brut y Tywysogyon*, *s.a.* 1136: 'In that year died Ieuan, archpriest (*archoffeiriad*) of Llanbadarn.' Sulien's name is not mentioned here, but there can be hardly any doubt as to the relationship.

[4] The word *sapiens* means a clerk or scholar, a person in the Latin tradition, later *magister*. It has no meaning of specially outstanding wisdom.

[5] H. J. Lawlor (*Psalter and Martyrology of Ricemarch*, I (London, 1914), xiv, n. 3) calls attention to the long eulogy of St Padarn in the poem, ll. 69–85. Cf. also Bradshaw, *Collected Papers*, 457.

[6] In regard to the Irish elements in Rhigyfarch's *Life*, see Lawlor, *op. cit.* xvff.

Brittany save in the case of St Carantoc, where it is believed that more than one saint's *Life* has been used in the composition as we now possess it, and one of these may have reference to a purely Breton saint, distinct from the Cardigan Carantoc. St David himself appears to be a purely local saint, and except for his mythical journey to Jerusalem he never appears to have left south-west Wales. It is noteworthy that none of our group has any close relations with south-western Scotland or with South Wales. The saints of Cardigan and Dyfed look westwards to Ireland.

It has been noted above that along with the prevalence of Irish elements and Irish influence throughout the *Lives* of these Cardigan saints we also find everywhere a strong emphasis on asceticism. We recall not only the austerities of the monastic life attributed to David and his disciples, the *Aquatici*, 'water drinkers', and how they 'drew the plough like oxen'. We recall also how St Carantoc renounced his claim to the kingdom of Ceredigion in favour of an anchorite life; and St Padarn's long preliminary retreat from the world, and the permanent renunciation and retreat of his father, also king of Ceredigion. It is important to bear in mind, however, that David's 'Rule', as we see it in c. 21–30 of the *Life*, while austere, is in no sense penitential. It aims at simplicity of life, but not at actual mortification of the flesh. Its affinities lie with the contemplative Orders of a later age rather than with the active Orders on the one hand, or with the extreme asceticism of the saints of the Eastern Church on the other. Even the *Penitential* traditionally, though erroneously, ascribed to him is in no way remarkable for extreme asceticism. But above all there is nowhere any emphasis on book learning.

This asceticism, or, better, austerity, is characteristic, not only of the saints whom we have chiefly under consideration here, but also of others of West Wales, notably St Brynach of Nevern in Cardiganshire; St Cybi of Caer Gybi on Holyhead; and St Seiriol of Penmon, also in Anglesey. On the other hand it is not necessarily a characteristic of the Welsh saints as a whole. It is not, for example, so strongly emphasised in the school of Llantwit Major, in records relating to St Illtud and St Gildas, where the emphasis is rather on the intellectual than the ascetic discipline, and where the Church may have retained something of its earlier Roman tradition; and though David and Gildas are mentioned together in the *Catalogus* as influential in Ireland among the 'sacred order of saints', as in fact, giving them a *missa*, the later biographies constantly stress the rivalry between the followers of these two great saints. In fact in later times the saints of Cardigan and those of South Wales represent two distinct ideals. The more intellectual saints of South Wales have their early traditional contacts chiefly with North Brittany; the more austere and spiritual saints of West Wales with Ireland; but in the Norman period the apparent opposition of these two schools has been deliberately exploited by the supporters of their rival claims for the archiepiscopacy, the rivalry between St David's and Llandaff. The asceticism of St David's and the intellectual qualities of Illtud, Samson and Gildas are stressed as rival weapons of propaganda in this great historic struggle. There can be no doubt that the ascetic practices prominent in the West Welsh *Lives* have been developed, in a large measure, by the advocates of an independent Church in West Wales which should carry on the inherited Celtic ideals independent of control from Canterbury.

The atmosphere of the *Lives* of these Cardigan saints is thus an atmosphere of religious controversy, and reflects the struggle which had raged in Ireland from the period of the Viking age till the creation of the episcopal sees, the adoption of territorial episcopacy at the beginning of the Norman régime, and the final establishment of the primacy of Armagh under St Malachy. In the Cardigan *Lives* the prerogatives of St Patrick are ruthlessly forced within closely prescribed limits, the claims of the traditional Celtic Church insistently emphasised. In particular the close liaison of St David with southern Ireland, with the saints of Munster and Leinster, is insisted on; and while the supremacy of Patrick in Ireland is tacitly denied, supremacy is boldly claimed for David in Wales. We are, in fact, following page by page the literature of ecclesiastical propaganda during the eleventh and early twelfth centuries, integrated as a series of hagiographical narratives. The ancient traditions of the Age of the Saints, and the traditional Celtic Church, with all its individuality and administrative independence, are making their last stand against the *Unitas Catholica*.

Throughout the preceding pages reference has frequently been made to the early Celtic monastery of Llanbadarn Fawr, and its claim to be regarded as a seat of learning and culture, probably at least as important as, possibly even more important than, St David's in early times. We have seen that this was the home of the author of the earliest *Life of St David*, and that it was also the traditional home of at least two important Cardigan saints. A word or two on the position and early history of Llanbadarn will therefore be in place before we discuss the monastery itself, and the milieu to which the author of the *Life of St David* belonged. The history of the place is a long and interesting one, topographically, ecclesiastically, and politically, but space will not allow of more than a few brief introductory notes in this place.

The village of Llanbadarn Fawr is in Cardiganshire, situated on the north bank of the river Rheidol some three to four miles east of Aberystwyth, of which today it is becoming a rapidly growing suburb. The early importance of the site is incontestable. The place itself precedes Aberystwyth as a market town, and the earliest charter of Aberystwyth is said to make mention several times of Llanbadarn, but never of Aberystwyth.[1] The present town of Aberystwyth is first known as *Llanbadarn gaerog*, 'fortified Llanbadarn', doubtless with reference to the Edwardian castle, of which the ruins are still standing. Meyrick is probably correct in his statement that the Roman road, known today as Sarn Helen, in its course northward from the Roman station of Bremia (the modern Llanio) to the Roman fortress at Cefn Caer near Pennal on the Dovey, passes through a farm in the parish of Llanbadarn Fawr called Llwyn Rhingyll.[2] Although the most recent edition of the Ordnance Survey fails to link the stretches of this road during its passage over the Ystwyth and the Rheidol, it is difficult to believe that it would pass from Carmarthen to Pennal without ever approaching the shores of Cardigan Bay, and it is not impossible that the site of *Maes Heli*, by which name Llanbadarn Fawr is said to have been first known,[3] owes its initial importance to the crossing of the Rheidol by Sarn Helen at this point.

In the poem already referred to which Ieuan ap Sulien composed in honour of his father *c.* 1090 he thus describes his home at Llanbadarn Fawr:

A lofty mountain arises on the east, profitable for the breeding of cattle; a great river washes the southern slopes; on the western front is the flowing tide of a broad sea; the northern parts are shut off by another great stream.[4]

[1] S. R. Meyrick, *History and Antiquities of Cardigan* (London, 1808), 488.
[2] *History and Antiquities of Cardigan*, 376.
[3] J. E. Lloyd, *The Story of Ceredigion* (Cardiff, 1937), 5.
[4] I quote the translation by J. E. Lloyd, *Story of Ceredigion*, 1.

He tells us moreover that the land of Ceredig was formerly very wealthy, dreaded by its enemies, but famous throughout Wales for its hospitality, and specially gracious to pilgrims.

Little is known of the early ecclesiastical history of Llanbadarn, but there is no doubt that it was a *clas* or Celtic monastery of high prestige, traditionally founded by St Padarn, to whom is dedicated the present parish church. It was ruled by an abbot, and according to early medieval tradition it had formerly been the seat of a bishop,[1] like many other important *clas* churches; for although a bishop was of higher ecclesiastical rank than an abbot, the office in the early Celtic Church carried with it no territorial diocese, and the ruler of the mother churches or *clas* foundations often seems to have combined the double office of bishop and abbot.[2] The foundation at Llanbadarn was still ruled by an abbot in the twelfth century, and the church was served by a body of clergy with an *archoffeiriad* or 'archpresbyter' at their head. The remains of two stone crosses of pre-Norman date, formerly in the churchyard, but now in the south aisle of the church, bear witness to an earlier skill and technique in stone carving. They are carved in low relief, and the style is crude; but one of the crosses is a slender shaft over eight feet high, with designs on all four sides.[3]

The *clas* or monastic foundation of Llanbadarn was a wealthy body and owned extensive lands. In the time of Edward I it was the mother church of the whole of northern Cardiganshire as far as the Ystwyth, and probably in earlier times of a much wider region.[4] Its income was correspondingly large, exceeding that of any other parish church in the diocese of St David's.

To this wealthy and important *clas* at Llanbadarn Fawr belonged the author of the earliest *Life of St David*. He was a son of Bishop Sulien, who was twice bishop of St David's, and he probably wrote the *Life of St David* at Sulien's request. On the other hand there is no reason to accept the view commonly held that this *Life* was composed at St David's, and in fact this is on the whole improbable, as I hope to show.

---

[1] See Lloyd, *History of Wales*, I, 208, and note 67, and the references there cited.   [2] Lloyd, *loc. cit.*

[3] For an account of these crosses, and pictures, see V. E. Nash-Williams, *The Early Christian Monuments of Wales* (Cardiff, 1950), nos. 111, 112; and figure 89 and plates XLIV, XLVIII. Lloyd published a good photograph of the smaller cross in *The Story of Ceredigion*, facing p. 7.

[4] Lloyd, *Story of Ceredigion*, 7.

The family of Sulien is one of outstanding interest, and its history has been already traced by both Lloyd[1] and Conway Davies.[2] Nevertheless the relevance of the history of the various members to the circumstances in which the *Life of St David* was written, to the nature of the community of Llanbadarn Fawr, and to the culture of West Wales at this period must be my excuse for again tracing briefly this important family history. I do so, though not without diffidence, as my own conclusions are not wholly in agreement with those of the learned historians just referred to.[3]

The first member of the family of whom we have definite knowledge was Sulien (Old Welsh *Sulgen*), who was the last but one of the independent bishops of St David's before the see became merged in that of Canterbury, the last independent bishop being Wilfred, who seems, despite his name, to have been a Welshman.[4] According to the *Brut y Tywysogyon*, the 'Chronicle of the [Welsh] Princes', Sulien was appointed bishop of St David's for the first time *c.* 1073,[5] or a year or two later, but resigned *c.* 1078. Again, *s.a.* 1078 we read that Menevia was pillaged and Abraham its bishop died, 'And Sulien was induced *against his will*[6] to assume the bishopric a second time'. These were troubled years (cf. p. 175 below) and Sulien's reluctance to assume the bishopric a second time was probably something more than a conventional *nolo episcopari*. In 1085 he again resigned it, and was succeeded by Wilfred (1085–1115). In 1089 (*recte* 1091) the *Brut* records Sulien's death:

> Sulien, bishop of Menevia, the most learned and most pious of the bishops of the Britons, and the most praiseworthy for the instruction of his disciples and his parishes, died in the eightieth year of his age and the nineteenth of his episcopate....

As Lloyd observes,[7] this obituary notice of Sulien in the *Brut* was probably written by an admiring relative in Llanbadarn.

---

[1] *History of Wales*, I, 459 ff.; *idem, The Story of Ceredigion* (Cardiff, 1937); largely reprinted as a separate article in the *National Library of Wales Journal*, II (1941), 1 ff.

[2] *Episcopal Acts...relating to Welsh Dioceses, 1066–1272*, II (nos. 3 and 4, Historical Society of the Church in Wales, 1948), 493 ff.

[3] See however p. 172 below, where I have called attention to the fact that Lloyd in his later work seems to favour Llanbadarn Fawr as an important centre of learning.

[4] See Lloyd, *History of Wales*, II, 451, n. 207.

[5] The date is that given by Conway Davies.   [6] The italics are mine.

[7] *Story of Ceredigion*, 31.

Sulien was not a man of Dyfed, and we have reason to think that of his long life not more than twelve years—the period of his episcopate—were spent in Dyfed. From the Latin poem[1] composed by his son Ieuan to which I have already referred, we gather that he was a native of Llanbadarn Fawr, sprung apparently from a family of clerics (*sapientium...parentum*), and that he was eager and apt to learn from his early years, having 'recited (*edidit*) the psalter while still young (*tener infans*)'. After studying in the Welsh schools he sailed for Ireland, hoping to continue his studies there, and stimulated by the example of his forebears (*exemplo patrum commotus*), from which it is clear that he was not the first learned man in his family, or the first of them to receive his education in Ireland. Adverse weather, we are told, drove him to Britain, perhaps to Scotland (*Albania*); but after five years spent in hard study he proceeded to Ireland (*Scotorum arva*), where he remained for perhaps thirteen years.[2] He then returned to his native Cardigan (*ad patriam remeans*), where he became famous as a teacher. Four sons were born to him, for whose education he made himself responsible. It was not till late in life that he was made bishop of St David's (*Vallis Rosina*). At his consecration in 1073 he must have been at least sixty-one years of age.

Ieuan's poem clearly implies that Sulien's lifetime up to this point had been spent at Llanbadarn Fawr, except for his years in Scotland and Ireland; and moreover that it was in Llanbadarn that he had received his education, and that he imparted his knowledge as a teacher to others. His education during the years when he was out of Wales—whether in Scotland or Ireland—must have been wholly Irish in character. He must have been twenty-eight years of age when Gruffydd ap Llewelyn ravaged Llanbadarn Fawr in the year 1039. As Lloyd points out,[3] the mention of this in the *Brut* suggests that the clerks in Llanbadarn had already begun to keep a chronicle of local events of importance. Was Sulien himself, with his Irish education, responsible for this?

In view of the fact that Sulien was sixty-one when he went to St David's as bishop, the educational work for which he is famous, and more especially the education of his sons, would probably be

[1] For the text of the poem see p. 160, n. 2 above.
[2] So Lawlor; but the number is not quite certain.
[3] *Story of Ceredigion*, 25.

completed before he left Llanbadarn Fawr. As Rhigyfarch died eight years after his father at the age of forty-two, he must have been already fourteen years old when his father departed from Llanbadarn for St David's. Nor does it appear that Sulien ever settled permanently in St David's. The roots of the family were deep in Cardiganshire, with the school of learning which seems to have formed their only permanent milieu. Let us look at some of the other members of the family.

His sons continued the family tradition of learning. The poem referred to above was written by Ieuan ap Sulien a few years before Sulien's death. Sulien has resigned the see of St David's for the second time and is still alive (cf. ll. 136, 139). Ieuan's poem is written on the fly-leaves of a copy of the *De Trinitate* of St Augustine, which he was copying between 1085 and 1091[1] at Sulien's request (*complere genitoris vota*). It is now in the library of Corpus Christi College, Cambridge (MS. 199).[2] The manuscript is written in Irish minuscules in a beautiful round hand of the eleventh century, and many of the books and chapters begin with fine Celtic initials.[3] These are also probably the work of Ieuan, for we know that he painted the initial letters in the psalter of his brother Rhigyfarch, which was written by one Ithael between 1064 and 1082, and is now in the library of Trinity College, Dublin (no. 50 in Abbot's catalogue). The initial letters by Ieuan in the *De Trinitate* are fine examples of the characteristic Celtic style in a restricted colour scheme, employing only yellow, red and black.

In addition to the long poem to his father already mentioned, Ieuan has also included a number of shorter poems of his own composition, e.g. 'Verses of Jo [for Johannes, i.e. Ieuan], son of Sulien', on folio 1 b,[4] and another set at the conclusion of the prologue on the same page. He habitually prefixes a distich at the beginning of

---

[1] Lloyd, *Story of Ceredigion*, 31.

[2] For an account of the MS. and of the Latin poems and distichs of Ieuan which this MS. contains, see M. R. James, *Descriptive Catalogue of the MSS. in the Library of Corpus Christi College, Cambridge* (Cambridge, 1912). See also W. M. Lindsay, *Early Welsh Script* (Oxford, 1912), 32 f. See further the article by J. E. Lloyd, 'Bishop Sulien and his Family', in the *National Library of Wales Journal*, II (1941), 1 ff.

[3] Photographs of two pages of Ieuan's MS. are given by Lloyd in the article cited above.

[4] A facsimile of this page of the MS. will be found in the article by Lloyd cited above.

each book. He has adopted the habit of the Irish scribes[1] of beginning his writing each day with a prayer entered in the top margin. Thus fol. 9ᵛ has the prayer:

> Conditor humane sobolis pariterque redemptor
> Nunc mihi praesidium scribenti ferre memento.

Many of these prayers in the top margins are preceded by his own monogram *Io*. It is noteworthy that one of these poems is addressed to St David, another to St Paternus (Padarn), fo. 10*b*. From this Bradshaw[2] concluded that the MS. was written at Llanbadarn Fawr, and this conclusion seems to be supported by the long eulogy on St Padarn (ll. 69–85).[3]

At the top of fo. 10*b* Ieuan ap Sulien invokes his patron saint: 'Auxilium...tuum fer sancte Paterne.' Then on the next page (fo. 11*a*) he writes a Welsh quatrain in his honour.[4] This may be a verse of his own composition; or it may be a quotation from a poem in honour of St Padarn by an old Welsh bard. The second alternative is perhaps on the whole the more probable. The verse seems to contain a panegyric on *Cyrwen*, Padarn's pastoral staff or *baculus* (cf. p. 159), and Sir Ifor Williams tentatively suggests the following translation:

> Much accomplishing, much loved, it gives protection,
> Its holy power reaching the limits of the three continents.
> No other relic can be compared with Cyrwen—
> A wonderful gift—Padarn's staff.

From the poem and the story it seems clear that the staff of St Padarn was a famous peacemaker called *Cirwen*. The point is not without significance for later history. We shall see that peacemaking in disputes, skill in diplomacy, and equity in legal matters are attributes of Bishop Sulien's family to the third, perhaps even

---

[1] See W. M. Lindsay, *Early Welsh Script* (Oxford, 1912), p. 32.

[2] *Collected Papers* (Cambridge, 1889), 457.

[3] M. R. James (*loc. cit.*) gave it as his opinion that the MS. was sent to Archbishop Parker by Bishop Davies from St David's, and refers to two letters, now lost, mentioned by Stanley in his catalogue of the Corpus Christi library as having been sent by the Bishop of St David's to Parker, and adding: '*Quae extant ad finem huius libri.*' See further p. 126 and n. 4, above.

[4] The text is contained in *Archaeologia Cambrensis* (series 4, vol. v, 1874) p. 340; cf. also the *Collected Papers of Henry Bradshaw*, 465. For a recent account of the text and interpretation of this Welsh quatrain, together with a facsimile, see Sir Ifor Williams, 'An Old Welsh Verse', *The National Library of Wales Journal*, II (1941–2), 69 ff.

the fourth, generation, and it would seem from the passage in the *Life*, and from Ieuan's poem, that the same qualities were a special feature and tradition, even a profession, of the school of Llanbadarn Fawr. Ieuan belonged to a patriotic Welsh *clas* and is here praising its special merit in peacemaking. It would be interesting to know when and how this quality of peacemaker was first associated with this sanctuary. What is its connection with the part played by Bishop Sulien when the banished princes of North and South Wales, Gruffydd ap Cynan and Rhys ap Tewdwr of Aber Teifi, landed near St David's under his auspices in the same year as that in which William the Conqueror made his pilgrimage to the same shrine? I will try to answer this question later.

We will now examine the more personal history of Sulien's family. Ieuan himself tells us in the longest of his poems—the one on his family discussed above—that he himself belonged to Cardigan.

> Quod mihi Ceretica tellus sit patria certe,
> Confiteor cunctis coram.

In the *Brut y Tywysogyon*, *s.a.* 1136 (for 1137) we read: 'In that year died Ieuan, archpresbyter (*archoffeiriad*) of Llanbadarn, the most learned of the learned, having led a pious life without mortal sin till his death'—a notice which can refer to no other than Ieuan ap Sulien.

His brothers were no less distinguished than himself. In the poem of Ieuan on his family discussed above we have a reference to Rhigyfarch (*Ricemarch Sapiens*), 'Rhigyfarch the Clerk', the author of the *Life of St David*, and the most famous of Sulien's sons. Rhigyfarch is frequently, though erroneously, stated to have succeeded Sulien as bishop of St David's;[1] but there is no reason to believe that he was ever a bishop.[2] We have, however, several personal references to him. We have seen that the *Life of St David* claims to be his work. Further, at the close of the MS. of the *Psalter and Martyrology* of *Ricemarch* already referred to (pp. 126, 160, n. 5 above), preserved in the library of Trinity College, Dublin,[3] commonly referred to as the *Psalter of Ricemarch*, written *c.* 1079[4]

---

[1] See, for example, *Collected Papers of Henry Bradshaw*, 464.

[2] For the occasion of the error, see Lloyd, *History of Wales*, II, 452, n. 208.

[3] Edited with a number of facsimile plates by H. J. Lawlor, *Psalter and Martyrology of Ricemarch* (2 vols., London, 1914).

[4] Cf. Lawlor, *op. cit.* xxi f.

and illuminated by Ieuan (see above), we have a Latin poem (fo. 158ᵛ) composed and possibly transcribed by Rhigyfarch himself, in which it is stated that he himself was the son of *Sulgen* (i.e. Sulien) and the brother of John (Ieuan); that one Ithael[1] had written the book, and that John had illuminated it.[2] The close connection of the *Psalter and Martyrology* with Llanbadarn Fawr is emphasised by the absence of any mention of St David in the book, while St Padarn is commemorated on April 15.[3]

The script of the *Psalter and Martyrology* is again written in minuscule of Irish style, and the decoration is also of the later type of Irish illumination. It is probable that the *Psalter* is a copy of an Irish exemplar. Lawlor would account in this way for the inclusion in the *Martyrology* of some names of Irish saints, and for some further coincidences with Irish martyrologies, as well as for the division of the *Psalter* into three parts, each containing fifty psalms.[4] The beauty of the script and the quality of the illuminations show that these are the works of a scriptorium with an advanced tradition. The references also in Rhigyfarch's verses preserved in the *Psalter* show evidence of a knowledge of St Jerome, St Augustine, and other patristic writers, and Ieuan's copy of St Augustine's *De Trinitate* in Cambridge gives further evidence of patristic studies by the School. Rhigyfarch was a good enough scholar to appreciate a psalter translated direct from the Hebrew, as his verses testify.[5]

Rhigyfarch died in 1099. The entry in the *Brut, s.a.* 1097 (for 1099), is as follows:

In that year died Rhygyfarch the scholar (*sapiens*), son of Bishop Sulien, greatly honoured by all, for he was the most learned of all the race of the Britons, and there had not been before him his equal, nor after him his like, nor in his lifetime his peer, without his having received instruction from anyone save from his own father. And he died in the forty-third year of his age.

---

[1] It is again commonly stated, though without any evidence, that Ithael was another son of Sulien. Nothing is known of him save this reference.

[2] See Bradshaw, *Collected Papers*, 477; Lindsay, *Early Welsh Script*, 33. The text of the poem is given by Haddan and Stubbs, I, 189–90.

[3] Lawlor, *op. cit.* xiv. See, however, a different explanation suggested by S. M. Harris, *St David in the Liturgy* (Cardiff, 1940), 5. Harris suggests that the omission of St David may be due to the fact that the MS. is a more or less exact copy of the current Continental *Martyrology* of the Pseudo-Jerome.

[4] Lawlor, *op. cit.* xvf., and notes.

[5] See Lawlor, *op. cit.* xv.

It would seem from this that he did not go to Ireland for his education, and that he owed his epithet *sapiens*, the distinctive epithet of a man of learning, entirely to his local training at Llanbadarn.

It may be this local Llanbadarn training which inspired him with his deep love of his native country. A manuscript in the British Museum (Cotton Faustina C. i), composed *c.* 1094, contains a poem[1] (fo. 66*a*) known as the *Lament of Rhigyfarch*. The poem is composed in an unusual metre, and contains the line:

Haec ego Ricemarch defleo mestus.[2]

The subject is the sufferings of the author's compatriots and the terrors of the Norman attack in 1093, and the poet chides them for their feeble resistance. A notable feature of all the poems and distichs of these sons of Sulien is the excellence of their Latin verse.[3] We have already seen that the illumination and handwriting of Ieuan are of a quality and refinement which speak highly for the taste and scholarship of Bishop Sulien and his Irish training, and for the school of Llanbadarn Fawr. We have also noted the high standard of its scholarship. It may be added that in all probability we owe our entries in the Welsh chronicles from the end of the eleventh to the middle of the twelfth century to this same family, and that at this period there was a local record of events kept up at Llanbadarn, later transferred to Strata Florida.[4]

At Rhigyfarch's early death at the age of forty-two he left a son whom he called Sulien after his grandfather the bishop, and it is clear that the family nucleus was still at Llanbadarn and not at St David's, for in the entry of the death of the later Sulien in the *Brut*, *s.a.* 1145 (for 1146), we are told that he had first been a 'foster-son',[5] and later a teacher in the church of Llanbadarn. He was a worthy member of this intellectual family, for he is described as 'mature in accomplishments, a speaker and a pleader for his people, and a mediator for various kingdoms, peaceful towards men

---

[1] There is a facsimile of the complete poem in the article by Lloyd already cited (*National Library of Wales Journal*, ii, 1941), facing p. 6. The text is given in full by Lawlor, *op. cit.* 121 f. It is translated into English in part by Wade-Evans in his translation of the *Life of St David*, xvii.

[2] Lindsay, *Early Welsh Script*, 33. [3] Lindsay, *op. cit.* xv.

[4] See Sir John Lloyd, *The Welsh Chronicles* (Sir John Rhys Memorial Lecture to the British Academy, 1928), 16 ff.

[5] Mab maeth eglwys llan Padarn, *Brut y Saes.*, *s.a.* 1145.

of the church, and an ornament of secular judgments'. From this we may gather that he was learned and expert in legal pleading, a diplomat and respected judge, and a peacemaker between nations. Could the functions of the peace-making *Cyrwen*, the crozier of St Padarn, have come into a better family?

In Ieuan's long poem on his family he mentions two other sons of Sulien, Arthgen and Daniel. The latter became archdeacon of Powys, between which province and Cardigan there was a close connection. He died in 1127, having played a distinguished role as an intermediary between Powys and Gwynedd, or North Wales, as the obituary notice in the *Brut* makes clear.[1] He was, in fact, clearly an accomplished diplomat and jurist; and, as Conway Davies points out,[2] the close relationship between Powys and Llanbadarn during this period is emphasised by the Powys tendencies of that clerk of Llanbadarn who kept the chronicle which was later embodied in the *Brut*. Daniel's son Cydifor died as archdeacon of Cardigan in 1163. The family was evidently still rooted in Cardigan, and still maintained its lofty standards of intellectual vigour. We have no information about Sulien's son Arthgen, but in the same annal as that which records the death of Cydifor ap Daniel we read of the death of Henri ap Arthgen, who was no doubt the Arthgen son of Sulien, and who is described as 'an eminent teacher supreme among clerics'.[3]

I see no reason for associating any of the literary works of Sulien's family with St David's,[4] and having come independently to this conclusion I have been happy to find that in his latest pronouncement on the subject Sir J. E. Lloyd himself seems to have arrived at the same view.[5] 'It has', he writes, 'been customary to associate this school of learning with St David's.... But, on close examination, it does not seem necessary to seek for it any other home than Llanbadarn, where the family had its roots and where it was influential until far on in the twelfth century.'[6] The belief that the

[1] See Lloyd, *History of Wales*, II, 461. On the subject of the jurisdiction in Powys of an archdeacon appointed by a bishop of St David's, and belonging to the Llanbadarn family, see J. Conway Davies, *Episcopal Acts*, II, 503.

[2] *Loc. cit.*

[3] For further members of this family whose identification is less certain, see J. Conway Davies, *op. cit.* 504.

[4] Even Stevenson has assumed this; cf. his edition of Asser, *Life of Alfred the Great*, lxi.

[5] Despite Haddan and Stubbs, I, 205, 297, 298.

[6] *The Story of Ceredigion*, 32 f. See also Lawlor, *op. cit.* xiii.

literary centre of the family was at St David's is partly due to the fact that the *Life of St David* was written by the son of its bishop. The belief is, however, undoubtedly due in the main, as we have seen, to the inference that Asser was educated at St David's—an inference which I have tried to show is not justified by Asser's own narrative, and which would not, in any case, prove that no other school of learning existed in the period preceding the Norman Conquest in West Wales. It may, of course, be argued that we lack early evidence.

At this point our thoughts naturally go back to the Old Welsh glosses in the *Juvencus* and other manuscripts mentioned above. These glosses, as we have seen, and some of the manuscripts which contain them, are believed to have been written in Wales, and in a milieu where Irish influence was strong. They were probably not all written in one place; but a certain amount of uniformity is believed to be traceable in one or two groups (see above) which has led scholars to the conclusion that these at least are the works of a single school. Where was it? Previous scholars have assumed that it was St David's, but without direct evidence, or even, as it seems to me, any indirect evidence that is valid. On the other hand, the first specifically documented localised handwriting that we possess from western Wales is known to be from a family sprung from Bishop Sulien, and settled for many generations in Llanbadarn Fawr. As Sulien claimed that his own forebears had been highly educated people, the local Llanbadarn learning which he represented must have been flourishing here already in the ninth century, the period of Asser, and the period to which most of the Old Welsh glosses are ascribed.

We have seen ample evidence for the close association of this great family of learned ecclesiastics with Llanbadarn Fawr, which, with its deeply rooted Cardigan connections, had remained the nucleus of the family for at least three, probably four, generations, bringing up and educating the young, spreading learning and culture, exercising ecclesiastical, diplomatic, and juridical functions in Ceredigion, Dyfed, Powys and even Gwynedd, i.e. in West, South-West, East and North Wales. We have seen the loyalty with which the members of the family dwell on Llanbadarn as their native place, and the co-operation between the sons of Sulien in their literary and artistic work, their educational and fostering care of the younger members of the family, notably the orphan son of

Rhigyfarch. We have seen the reluctance with which Sulien occupied his see at St David's. We look in vain for any hint that his sons or grandsons transferred their sphere to Dyfed, even temporarily. Yet as the quality of their learning proves, the family is in no way parochial or local in the narrower sense. They are like a local ecclesiastical dynasty of scribes and clerics, the finest type of the old Welsh *clas*, and a lasting monument to the Celtic Church in Wales, handing on their intellectual gifts and professional specialisation from generation to generation. It is perhaps only in Ireland that we could look to find a similar family scribal tradition. In Ireland it would be quite natural;[1] but we have to remember that our surviving records of Wales are relatively few.[2]

The *Life of David* by Rhigyfarch is, as we have seen, the earliest existing *Life* of the saint, upon which all subsequent *Lives* are based. We may say with Conway Davies: 'It is no exaggeration to say that Rhygyfarch's *Vita* is responsible in no small measure for the popularity of the medieval cult of St David.'[3] Yet from this narrative we really learn more about Rhigyfarch himself and the milieu in which it was composed than about St David. Why, then, since his milieu was in fact that of the community of St Padarn, did Rhigyfarch write the *Life of St David*?

It is generally thought that the work was probably composed towards the end of the author's life, that is to say, before his death in 1099. But by *c.* 1095, when he wrote the long patriotic poem already referred to, in which he deplores the devastation of his native land by the Normans, and seeks to stimulate his countrymen to resistance, it is clear that he already saw the end of Welsh independence at hand. The *Life of St David*, on the contrary, shows no sign of doubt or despair. It would seem rather to be a part of an earlier constructive policy, offering to the homage of the Welsh people a saint who would commend himself to future generations as the most important saint of Wales, safeguarding the Welsh Church against encroachments from Canterbury, and perhaps commending himself to the Norman conquerors as located at the

[1] Cf. Charles Plummer, 'On the Colophons and Marginalia of Irish Scribes' (*Proceedings of the British Academy*, 1926), 5, 7, 9; Robin Flower, 'Ireland and Medieval Europe' (*Proceedings of the British Academy*, 1927), 276.

[2] A very interesting study of the family of Bishop Herewald and the old monastic foundation of Llancarfan through a lengthy period has been made recently by James Conway Davies, *op. cit.* 106 ff. There may well be others still awaiting investigation.   [3] *Op. cit.* 499.

furthest point from the Marches. That he did in fact commend himself to the Conqueror we know on the best possible evidence, for in 1081 William the Conqueror himself visited his shrine. It was the year after Sulien had returned to St David's as bishop for the second time—'against his will'.

Let us glance for a moment more closely at this strange 'pilgrimage' of the Conqueror to the most westerly point of Wales. The political situation in Wales had reached a crisis. In 1081, shortly after the recall of Bishop Sulien to the episcopacy of St David's, we learn from the *Brut* that Rhys ap Tewdwr, prince of Cardigan, hard pressed by the efforts of Caradog ap Gruffydd to conquer Deheubarth, or south-west Wales, was forced to take refuge in the church of St David's. Here he was joined by the great Gruffydd ap Cynan—prince of Gwynedd, or North Wales, who had been in exile in Ireland. These two princes, one from North Wales, one from South, together with their Irish allies, landed at Porth Clais near St David's. Here they were received by Bishop Sulien—armed, we may guess, with the peace-bestowing *Cyrwen*, St Padarn's staff. The occasion is shortly before the Battle of Mynydd Carn, which established Rhys ap Tewdwr as ruler of South Wales.

The same year we learn from the *Brut* that William I made a 'pilgrimage' (*causa orationis*) to St David's. Here the hand of the ecclesiastical chronicler is clear, for the *Anglo-Saxon Chronicle* (MS. E., *s.a.* 1081) tells us that the expedition was made at the head of an armed force, and it resulted in the 'freeing' of many hundred men—doubtless, as Lloyd observes, bands of Normans shut up in isolated castles. It is probable that William actually met Rhys, for from this time there was peace between them throughout the lifetime of Rhys, and in the Domesday survey of 1086 we learn that Rhys paid that king an annual rent of £40, the same sum as that paid by Robert of Rhuddlan as lord of Gwynedd,[1] and evidently a fixed and recognised rent. The argument must have been an official and technical one. I think we can hazard a guess that it was Sulien or one of his family who was responsible for the negotiations between the two Welsh princes and the Conqueror at St David's. Sulien resigned his see for the second time in 1085 and died in 1091.

[1] Lloyd, *History of Wales*, II, 394; cf. more recently Prof. J. G. Edwards, 'The Normans and the Welsh March', *Proceedings of the British Academy*, XLII (1956), 161.

In 1093 Rhys was killed while fighting against the Normans in Brecon. It was doubtless during the consequent confusion in South Wales that Rhigyfarch composed his famous *Lament*.

There can in my opinion be no doubt that the meeting between the two Welsh princes, simultaneously with the arrival of William the Conqueror at this remote spot, was negotiated by Sulien himself with pacific intent. Its effect seems to have been to reinstate the princes in their former domains, while the king was able to settle affairs in South Wales and obtain the nominal loyalty of Rhys and Deheubarth in exchange for his support. At the same time he had an obvious opportunity of examining the amenities of Porth Clais near St David's and the Dyfed coast as a *point d'appui* against Ireland when opportunity should arise. The practical effect of the compact seems to have been that during the lifetime of Rhys, Dyfed and Seisyllwg (Ystrad Tywi and Ceredigion) remained free from further Norman aggression.

In this meeting of the three royal powers at St David's the co-operation of Sulien must surely have played an important part. We have seen that the functions of diplomatists and welders of peaceful compacts were a constant feature of the family from generation to generation, and that these functions were traditionally regarded as appertaining to the *clas* of St Padarn and the tenure of his *baculus*. In such compacts as that discussed above certain formalities, possibly of a technical kind, would doubtless be called for, and we may suspect that it was for his proficiency in negotiations and forms of diplomacy that Sulien had been summoned and reinstalled at St David's. It would seem natural to suppose that the *Life of St David* would be composed on this occasion, both in support of Sulien's policy, and in celebration of the visit of the Conqueror to St David's. We may perhaps regard the *Life* as one factor in the *rapprochement* between the native princes of West Wales and their powerful Norman enemy, an appeal by the native Welsh Church to the Conqueror for his protection against encroachment from Canterbury. The Conqueror had won a bloodless victory in Dyfed. The shrine of St David which he had 'honoured' must be duly 'celebrated'. It is probably as a factor in the implementation of this great compact at St David's in 1081 that we must regard the composition of the *Life* of the saint, and it is to this period that we must look for the spectacular rise of his sanctuary to prominence.

In conclusion a word may be added on the fate of Llanbadarn under the Normans. Reference has already been made to the patriotic poem in which Rhigyfarch lamented the end of all his hopes that his countrymen would shake off the foreign yoke, and his despair that 'the acres of the fathers will not pass to the sons', that 'the songs of the bards fall upon deaf ears';[1] and though Welsh rule was restored in the year of Rhigyfarch's death, it lasted only a few years. In 1110 Henry I bestowed the province as a marcher lordship on Gilbert Fitz Richard of Tonbridge, and *c.* 1115 the *clas* of Llanbadarn was broken up, and the endowments of the church bestowed on the Benedictine abbey of St Peter's, Gloucester, some of whose monks were sent to Llanbadarn to form a priory or cell.[2] The Welsh clergy were probably not all ejected, for the contemporary chronicle, which appears to have been kept at this time at Llanbadarn (cf. pp. 179 f. below), shows an intimate knowledge of the country and its chief personalities, which continues unbroken for some ten years after the change of status. Indeed it would be unlikely in any case that the Norman incomers would readily dispense with the local knowledge and skill of the hereditary members of the *clas*.

The monastery's vicissitudes were by no means over. In 1117, on the death of Gilbert Fitz Richard, his son Richard succeeded to Ceredigion, and is said to have confirmed the grant of his father which bestowed Llanbadarn and its ancient possessions on St Peter's, Gloucester.[3] Some years later, however, after the death of Henry I in 1135, the Normans lost hold of Ceredigion, and Giraldus Cambrensis tells us how, as a result, the Benedictines were expelled from Llanbadarn, and the *clas* recovered its possessions. He himself visited Llanbadarn in 1188, and has left us a lively picture—both from personal observation and report—of the restored *clas*, still in undisputed possession, with a lay abbot in office. Nevertheless we learn from a late fourteenth-century document that over 250 years later St Peter's still laid claim to the land between the Clarach and the Rheidol (cf. p. 179 below).

[1] Lloyd, *Story of Ceredigion*, 38.
[2] The foundation charter of Gilbert, the confirmation of Henry I, and the concurrence of the bishop of St David's in this foundation are still preserved in the cartulary of St Peter's, Gloucester. See the *History and Cartulary of Gloucester*, edited by W. H. Hart (*Historia et Cartularium Monasterii Sancti Petri Gloucestriae* (London, 1863), I, 106; II, 73–9). Cf. Giraldus Cambrensis, *Itinerary through Wales*, Book II, c. 4.   [3] Lloyd, *Ceredigion*, 50.

Meanwhile a few miles away near Tregaron at the foot of the Plinlymon range, on the banks of the little River Fflur in the valley of the upper Teifi, a Cistercian monastery had been founded in 1164 from Whitland in Carmarthenshire.[1] The foundations can still be traced at the farm known as Hen Fynachlog ('the old monastery'), where also some of the fine golden-coloured Bath stone from the original buildings can be seen in the walls of the buildings of the present farmstead.[2]

Sometime before 1184 the Lord Rhys had taken the monastery under his patronage, and confirmed the early privileges and increased the endowments,[3] and c. 1180 the monastery was moved to a new site about two miles to the north-east, close to the bank of the River Teifi.[4] The monks carried the name of their earlier home to the new site which now bore the name *Ystrad Fflur* (L. *Strata Florida*), 'the Bank of the Flur', while the little River Fflur now flowed past only a dismantled ruin.

The *Brut y Tywysogyon*, *s.a.* 1201, states that 'In this year the community of Strata Florida went to the new church on the eve of Whitsunday, after it had been newly and handsomely built'. It was inevitable that the prestige of this new abbey under the highest Welsh patronage, and in the new Continental monastic tradition, should gradually supersede the more conservative school of learning at Llanbadarn; and some time between the visit of Giraldus and the middle of the thirteenth century the Welsh *clas*

[1] For some account of this early foundation of Strata Florida, see Lloyd, *History of Wales*, II, 597 f.; and somewhat fuller, J. F. O'Sullivan, *Cistercian Settlements in Wales and Monmouthshire* (Fordham University Studies, History Series, No. 2, New York, 1947), 11 ff.

[2] The farm stands on the eastern side of the road from Lampeter to Tregaron. Within the memory of the present occupants of the farm and their immediate forebears much more of the ruin was still above ground, and the present farmhouse also incorporates a part of the original building. The foundation of the church stands on a slight eminence in the field immediately across the little River Fflur, and within a few yards of the farmhouse. A large field across the road is traditionally believed to have been the site of the cemetery.

[3] The charter of the Lord Rhys, confirming the grants and privileges of the original founder, and enumerating the original endowments and the later ones made by Rhys himself, is preserved in the Calendar of Patent Rolls (1317–21), 528. See O'Sullivan, *loc. cit.*

[4] For details of the excavation and architecture of this great abbey, see S. W. Williams, *The Cistercian Abbey of Strata Florida* (London, 1889). For a valuable account of its history and economy see Prof. T. Jones Pierce, 'Strata Florida Abbey', *Ceredigion*, I (1950), 1 ff.

of Llanbadarn is generally thought to have disappeared. The rights of St Peter's, Gloucester, seem also to have lapsed, and the patronage was seized by Henry III in 1245, and with it the income. In 1359–60 the church was appropriated to the Cistercian monastery of the Vale Royal, Cheshire, Edward III confirming, and the bishop of St David's concurring in the appropriation in 1361.

As an ecclesiastical centre the church still retained importance, perhaps even a heightened prestige. About 1200 or shortly afterwards the splendid large church of Llanbadarn was built which still stands today, possibly, as some have thought, the gift of the Lord Rhys himself. He had close family connections with Llanbadarn about this period, and his daughter-in-law died there, with the last offices of its church, as we learn from the *Brut, s.a.* 1209–10.

It was probably the wealth of Llanbadarn, possibly also its position and its easy access from Ireland, which had enabled it to develop as a great school of learning and monastic life. It was the mother church of all Penweddig, the northernmost of the four cantrefs of Cardiganshire. It claimed as Church property all the territory between the Rheidol, and the Clarach and in the Taxation of 1291 it appears as by far the richest church in the diocese of St David's.[1] As a centre of learning it is almost certainly responsible for initiating the most important historical document of Norman Wales, the *Brut y Tywysogyon*, 'The Chronicle of Princes'. The three most important and distinctive variant versions of this work are believed to represent three independent translations of a single Latin original, itself compiled at Strata Florida towards the close of the thirteenth century.[2] But the compiler refers to 'Annals of the monastery of Strata Florida' which he has before him while writing, and Lloyd is undoubtedly right in his conclusion that from about 1100–75 the *Brut* was a Llanbadarn document.[3] In his latest work Lloyd frankly assumes the Llanbadarn home of the chronicle for at least the first three-quarters of the twelfth century, and simply refers to the author of the annals of this period as 'the Llanbadarn chronicler'.[4]

[1] J. E. Lloyd, 'Aberystwyth', *Archaeologia Cambrensis*, LXXXVI (1931), 201 ff.; cf. Lloyd, *History of Wales*, II, 432, n. 11; cf. also F. R. Lewis, *Short History of Llanbadarn Fawr* (Aberystwyth, 1937).
[2] See Thomas Jones, *Brut y Tywysogyon*, Peniarth MS. 20 (Cardiff, 1952), p. xxxix.
[3] Lloyd, *Ceredigion*, 77; cf. Thomas Jones, *op. cit.* xli.
[4] *Op. cit.* 37, 40, 48, 50.

Strata Florida undoubtedly owed much of its high prestige to the fact that it became for a time the royal cemetery of South Wales, most of the descendants of the Lord Rhys being buried there, as the obits in the *Brut* make clear.[1] Yet the territory in which Llanbadarn lay still continued in the possession of the descendants of Gruffydd, son of the Lord Rhys; and his wife[2] in 1210, and their grandson Maredudd ab Owen in 1265, both died at Llanbadarn, and the nature of Maredudd's obit in the *Brut*— 'the protector of all Deheubarth and the counsellor of all Wales'— sounds like a far-off echo of the pacific and diplomatic nature of the ancient *clas*. There can in any case be no doubt that Llanbadarn continued as a cultural centre after the time at which the monastery is generally thought to have disappeared, and that this branch of the family of the Lord Rhys were cultivated people. The Maredudd ab Owen whose death took place here was a member of a literary family. He was celebrated in *englynion* and *marwnadau* by the South Welsh court bard, Y Prydydd Bychan ('The Little Poet'),[3] and a number of these have been preserved, including his elegy. It was at the request of his son Gruffudd that Madog ap Selyf made a Welsh translation of the Latin legendary *Chronicle of Turpin*,[4] and it was for his daughter Efa that Brother Gruffudd Bola translated into Welsh the Athanasian Creed,[5] and to whom the poet Cynddelw addressed a graceful love-poem.[6] Of Madog ap Selyf and Brother Gruffudd Bola little or nothing else appears to be known. Thomas Parry suggests that both were monks of Strata Florida;[7] but for Madog, Llanbadarn Fawr, the special sanctuary of the family of Maredudd ab Owen, to whom the territory of

---

[1] The Lord Rhys himself, however, is buried in the cathedral of St David's, where his tomb is still shown.

[2] She was the daughter of William de Braose.

[3] For this poet see the *Welsh Dictionary of National Biography*, 756 f.; Thomas Parry, *History of Welsh Literature*, translated by H. Idris Bell (Oxford, 1955), 46, 66. See also the fully annotated edition and (French) translation of his poems by J. Vendryes in *Études celtiques*, III (1938), 274 ff., and more particularly the *marwnad* and *englynion* addressed to Maredudd, 299 ff. They were also edited earlier in the *Myvyrian Archaeology of Wales*, I (Denbigh, 1870), 259 ff. A large proportion of his poems are addressed to the descendants of the Lord Rhys.

[4] *Ystorya de Carolo Magno*, ed. S. J. Williams (Cardiff, 1930), 41. See Lloyd, *Ceredigion*, 103. See also *Bulletin of the Board of Celtic Studies*, V (1931), 203.

[5] See J. E. Lloyd, *Ceredigion*, loc. cit.

[6] See Thomas Parry, *op. cit.* 58, 108.　　　　[7] Parry, *op. cit.* 90, 94.

Llanbadarn belonged, seems not impossible.[1] In any case the local monastic connection with the ruling Llanbadarn princely family is obviously very close and intellectually stimulating. One cannot help wondering whether the monastic foundation of Llanbadarn, the *clas* and school of Latin learning and native culture, did in fact cease automatically with the withdrawal of its privileges and its wealth.

As one glances through the entries in the *Brut*, especially the obits, one gets an impression that some kind of a tie, perhaps only of good will, or even mutual obligation, existed between Llanbadarn and Strata Florida. Anyone who studies the terrain today must recognise that such a *rapprochement* would be wholly to the advantage of the latter monastery, which, for all its hollow sheltering among the hills, is situated in a bleak upland spot contrasting harshly with the snug position of Llanbadarn. Llanbadarn, too, had all the advantages of situation for communications, north and south along Sarn Helen, west over Cardigan Bay with Ireland, or with Lleyn and Dyfed, yet duly protected from the west winds. It is possibly by some such conditions that we may seek to explain the fact that the abbey of Strata Florida seems to have supported the opposition made in Ceredigion to the activities of the agents of the Vale Royal, and that in 1435 the abbot of Strata Florida had to swear to keep the peace and offer no hindrance to the abbot of Vale Royal in collecting his revenues from the church of Llanbadarn Fawr.[2]

A further and later occurrence testifies both to the continuation of the *clas* or *familia* of Llanbadarn, and to the strength of its opposition to the claims of the Vale Royal. In 1429 we hear of a certain Dafydd ap Maredudd Glais, together with John Robury and Gruffydd Proth or Prwth, as giving bail for Thomas Kirkham, abbot of the Vale Royal, for a fine. The three men are described as clerics, and doubtless belonged to the church of Llanbadarn, which, as we have seen, had been under the Vale Royal since 1360. In 1442 Dafydd was found guilty of the murder of Gruffydd Proth, but as he was in orders he was not put to death. A list of the

---

[1] This would seem to be suggested by the form of his name, with its Welsh patronymic, as opposed to that of *Brother* Gruffudd Bola. He was, however, evidently a 'clerk'.

[2] See the account quoted by Dr Frank R. Lewis in his *Short History of the Church of Llanbadarn Fawr* (Aberystwyth, 1937), 10; and for references and bibliography, *ibid.* 19.

noblemen who went bail for his fine is found in the accounts of the officials of the shire. In 1444 he wrote MS. Peniarth 22, which contains a copy of Geoffrey's *Brut* and his own translation of the *Brut y Saeson* from Latin into Welsh, and his name is on record as provost of Aberystwyth from 1459 to 1462 and from 1467 to 1468.[1] The clerics of Llanbadarn seem to have retained their vitality and intellectual activity down to the fifteenth century.

[1] See the *Welsh Dictionary of National Biography* (*Y Bywgraffiadur Cymreig*, 1940), *s.v.* Dafydd ap Maredudd Glais, by E. D. Jones, to whom I am indebted for this reference.

ADDENDUM

Note to p. 131 above.

At the close of the seventeenth century Edward Lhuyd claimed to read the name of St David on a stone inscription built into the fabric of the early medieval church of Llandewibrev in Cardiganshire. The inscription as a whole has been assigned to the close of the sixth or the first half of the seventh century; but the portion on which Lhuyd claimed to have read the name of the saint is now lost, and the reading awaits confirmation (see Geraint Gruffydd and Huw Parri Owen, 'The Earliest Mention of St David', *Bulletin of the Board of Celtic Studies*, XVII (1957), 185 ff.). I am indebted to Mrs Rachel Bromwich for calling my attention to this notice.

III

British Museum MS. Cotton Vespasian A. XIV ('Vitae Sanctorum Wallensium'): its purpose and provenance

BY KATHLEEN HUGHES

The first manuscript bound up in Cotton Vesp. A. XIV is a collection consisting of *Lives* of Celtic saints and extracts from monastic cartularies, preceded by a document described as a kalendar, a glossary, a short tract *De Situ Brecheniauc* and a list of contents. The manuscript has been described by Robin Flower as written in a number of Anglo-Norman hands of about 1200 'all of the same general type and period, but of varying accomplishment'.[1] Its importance for a study of the Celtic Church has long been recognised. Just over a century ago the Rev. W. J. Rees printed some of the *Lives* for the Welsh MSS. Society. This is an execrable though amusing edition. There are hundreds of mistakes in the transcription of proper names. Rees occasionally creates exciting new names —out of the MS. reading *uoce in audientia* he produces *nomine Snaudrentia*—or raises the hopes of his readers with words such as *antiqui* for the more prosaic MS. *antequam*. Kuno Meyer in 1900[2] gave twenty pages of *corrigenda*, but never completed his arduous task. Charles Plummer used the Vespasian manuscript for his excellent critical edition of the *Life of Maedoc* published in 1910;[3] and the Rev. A. W. Wade-Evans re-edited most of the Vespasian *Lives* for the University of Wales Press in 1944.[4] The peculiarities of the *Vita Cadoci* have recently been noted by H. D. Emanuel.[5] Though most of the texts are well known, there is no satisfactory study of the problems raised by the manuscript as a whole. The Rev. Silas Harris has cleared much of the ground with an enlightening and provocative study of the kalendar.[6] He provides an introductory discussion of the kalendar, notes on individual entries and an edition of the text, and reaches three

[1] Description in *Vitae Sanctorum Britanniae et Genealogiae*, ed. A. W. Wade-Evans (Cardiff, 1944), viii–xi.
[2] *Y Cymmrodor*, XIII (1900), 76–96.
[3] *Vitae Sanctorum Hiberniae* (Oxford, 1910), II, 295–311.   [4] *Op. cit.*
[5] *National Library of Wales Journal*, VII (1951–2), 217–27.
[6] *Journal of the Historical Society of the Church in Wales*, III (1953), 3–53.

conclusions which have not before been publicly stated. He claims an eighth-century origin for the 'basic framework' of the kalendar, argues that kalendar and *Lives* from the first belonged together and that the whole compilation was put together by the monks of Monmouth. We shall return later to these theories.

In the century before Vesp. A. XIV was written the Anglo-Normans had pushed their conquest across South and Central Wales. The Church in Wales assumed a new look; the old *clas* system was disintegrating, ecclesiastical lands were redistributed and new religious communities were set up. Where Anglo-Norman and Celtic influences met, there was sometimes inquiry into the historical or pseudo-historical past. It was both profitable and interesting for the monks to know of the origin and development of the traditions into which they had entered. So they pursued their studies and speculations, and wrote up the results, or employed someone to do it for them. Outside Wales at Glastonbury, another part of the 'Celtic fringe', William of Malmesbury was invited to write *Concerning the Antiquity of Glastonbury*. Caradoc of Llancarfan and other hagiographers were busy compiling or composing the *Lives* of Celtic saints. The clerics of the newly created see of Llandaff forged the brief for their claims to diocesan boundaries, rewriting charters and including *Lives* of saints. Geoffrey of Monmouth, concentrating on secular rather than ecclesiastical romance, created a *History of the Kings of Britain*. It is against this background of pseudo-historical research and literary activity that Vesp. A. XIV must be considered.

The question of its provenance immediately arises. Robin Flower, in his excellent description cited above, suggested that it was written at Brecon, about twenty miles north-west of Monmouth. The contents to some considerable extent show a Brecknock interest. A tract *De Situ Brecheniauc* precedes the *Vitae* which form the bulk of the MS. Brecon was in the diocese of St David's, and the collection contains a number of saints from West and south-west Wales. In the sixteenth century the manuscript belonged to Sir John Price, in whose hand it is annotated, and Sir John held a lease of Brecon priory. Flower had therefore strong grounds of general probability for suggesting Brecon as its original home. But the arguments are not decisive. Sir John Price was one of the visitors to the monasteries at the time of the dissolution and could have picked up the manuscript at some house other than Brecon, and the Brecknock association of the contents can find another explanation.

The contents of the manuscript suggest three great influences on its compilation—the peculiar connections of Monmouth, the wide authority of Gloucester and the interests of the hagiographical school of Llandaff. Mr Harris argues that certain independent clues point to the monks of Monmouth as the compilers of the manuscript. The kalendar contains the feast of a very rare saint, Dochelinus, the patron of Allonnes and Varrains, two villages near Saumur. Both these places were connected with the great Benedictine house of Saint-Florent de Saumur. Allonnes was one of the ancient priories of Saint-Florent. The church at Varrains was built after the destruction of the chapel in the château of Saumur—a chapel which had housed the relics of St Dochelinus and had been used by the monks of Saint-Florent before their new church was built after the fire of 1025. The cult of St Dochelinus comes from the neighbourhood of Saumur, and the monks of Saint-Florent would have retained an interest in it after their new church was built in the eleventh century. But the Vespasian kalendar is clearly the production of a Welsh scriptorium. It requires special circumstances to account for the familiarity of a Welsh house with Dochelinus, so Mr Harris looks for a Welsh house connected with Saumur. He finds it in Monmouth, the one Welsh priory of Saint-Florent. Monmouth was founded about 1080 by the Breton Gwethenoc, who became a monk of Saint-Florent and gave lands in the neighbourhood of Monmouth to found a dependent priory of twelve monks and a prior.

The presence of St Dochelinus is obviously of vital importance in any discussion of the provenance of the Vesp. kalendar. Mr Harris finds support for a Monmouth origin in two other entries. One of these is the obit of *Hathulfus de Aura*. Nothing is known of Hathulfus, but the church and manor of Awre belonged to Monmouth. Cuthman of Steyning is a rather surprising entry, but may be explained by the position of Steyning, a mile from St Peter of Sele, a sister house of Monmouth and a cell of Saint-Florent.

There are a number of very odd features in the kalendar which this explanation leaves unaccounted for. Dochelinus is the only Saint-Florent saint here; Florentinus himself is absent and his day is a blank. Nevertheless there are so many peculiar gaps in this kalendar that it is very dangerous indeed to base an argument on omissions. Dochelinus is here, extremely rare and unusual, and must be accounted for. Of the other four rather unexpected Continental saints, Bar[ba]cianus January 2, Ludger March 26, Sigismund May 1, Teuderius October 29, three at least were known at this date in south-west England, the area from which the Old Cornish glossary in Vesp. presumably comes.[1] Ludger and Sigismund are in the twelfth-century manuscript of the Exeter Martyrology, and although the period containing the dates January 2 and October 29 is lost from this Exeter MS., Barbacian is in an inferior fourteenth-century copy.[2] Dochelinus, on the other hand, shows knowledge which in Wales could only come via Monmouth, and forms a very strong argument for Vespasian's Monmouth origin.

To argue the provenance of the kalendar along orthodox lines of liturgical criticism, seeking in its omissions as much as in its entries evidence of the type of community, religious or secular, to which it was attached, or trying to find in its local feasts the liturgical interests of one particular house, implies a fundamental misconception about the nature and purpose of the kalendar. For it is not a liturgical document. Mr Harris accepts without question the liturgical purpose of the kalendar and of the *Lives* which follow.[3] So also, in his brief introduction, does Robin Flower, who suggests that the manuscript was intended as a 'supplementary legendary of Welsh saints for use in one of the new Benedictine monasteries of the Anglo-Norman foundation, in addition to the ordinary legendaries'.[4] Some of the *Lives* are homiletic in type,[5] but the document which precedes them does not appear to have any liturgical intention. There is no colour or grading which would point definitely to a liturgical purpose. The Roman element is unusually thin, and Mr Harris explains this by saying that the original framework of the kalendar goes

[1] The Old Cornish glossary was a version made at the beginning of the twelfth century from a Latin–Anglo-Saxon glossary drawn up by a monk of Cerne. K. H. Jackson, *Language and History in Early Britain* (Edinburgh, 1953), 60–1.

[2] Edited from the later MS. by J. N. Dalton, for the Henry Bradshaw Society, XXXVIII (London, 1909), with variants from the earlier by G. H. Doble for the H.B.S. LXXIX (1940).

[3] *Op. cit.* 20.   [4] See above, p. 183, n. 1.

[5] E.g. the *Lives* of Padarn, Brynach, Cybi, Carantoc; Tatheus has a homiletic conclusion, the Passion of St Cadoc could be used for lections (it is divided up for this purpose in the Titus D. XXII copy) and other *Lives* could be adapted.

back to a type antedating the Carolingian reforms. But the complete absence of octaves, some of which go back to the ninth century or earlier, and of other important Roman feasts gives the document, as a liturgical kalendar, an impossibly peculiar look.

What then is the purpose of this document, which it is convenient to call a kalendar? It can hardly be regarded as a supplementary martyrology. Such an explanation would account for the absence of St Florentinus, who would already be in the monastery's main martyrology; but it does not fit all the facts, for the Roman feasts and one or two of the Welsh saints, such as Cadoc and Dubricius, would already be well known to the monks of Monmouth. Nor is the kalendar merely an index of the *Lives* which follow, since it contains a number of saints of whom the *Lives* make no mention, and it omits other saints who occur in the *Lives*. It looks as if the kalendar was intended as a means of identification and record. Someone entered the major Roman feasts to act as a framework and added a number of rather haphazardly selected saints, whose particulars happened to be accessible. Its purpose is historical, not liturgical, and the manuscript should probably be regarded as an example of that activity in pseudo-historical research which has already been mentioned. Mr Harris's theory of a pre-Carolingian kalendar from Saint-Florent as the basic framework of the Vespasian document is too ingenious. The kalendar which the monks of Monmouth presumably brought from Saint-Florent when they settled in Wales in the late eleventh century must have been one embodying their contemporary practices. To imagine them using an eighth-century original for their twelfth-century compilation is strained and unnatural, and leaves far too many peculiarities unnoticed.

It is essential to consider whose interests the compilation represents, and for this purpose the kalendar must be considered with the *Lives*, for kalendar and *Lives* are, as Mr Harris shows, complementary texts. He argues that the Welsh entries in the kalendar were made by referring to the *capitula* (or list of contents on f. 12^v), and not directly to the *Vitae*. There are certain cases where the entries of kalendar and *capitula* agree together, and differ from the corresponding entry in the *Lives*. For Cybi and Carantoc dates are correctly given in the *Lives*, incorrectly in the *capitula* and kalendar. In six cases the titles of saints in *Vitae* and *capitula* are slightly different, and in all these the kalendar agrees with the *capitula*.[1] The palaeography of the manuscript supports Mr Harris's view. Kalendar and *capitula* are a part of two irregular gatherings at the beginning of the manuscript. The manuscript is written in a number of different hands, but the scribe who transcribed the last section of the *Vitae* (from Carantoc onwards) also wrote the first two gatherings. It is probable that he finished transcribing the available *Lives*, and then turned to drawing up the *capitula* and kalendar. The *Lives* are faithful copies; the kalendar is an original production.

Vesp. A. xiv is a peculiar collection both for what it brings in and for what it leaves out. The Welsh ingredients raise interesting problems. There are a number of saints from south-east Wales in kalendar and *Lives*, as might be expected in a manuscript put together in this area. But how did saints, in some cases extremely obscure saints, from the far west of Wales and from Ireland enter the compilation? St David's own cult was of course widespread, so he may be excluded from the discussion. Padarn was also, at any rate in the Celtic period, a most important saint. His great foundation at Llanbadarn Fawr (on the west coast near Aberystwyth) was claimed to be one of the three greatest ecclesiastical centres in pre-Conquest Wales.[2] But there seems to be no reason why Brynach, whose chief church was at Nevern, a few miles south of Cardigan,[3] should occur twice in the kalendar. He is the only Welsh saint for whom a feast of translation is given, and the date of his translation, which is not in his *Vita*, is recorded in no other source. Brynach, Carantoc and Cybi are all saints of West Wales. Carantoc's churches are to the north and west of Cardigan, at Llangrannog and St Dogmael's.[4] His festival is correctly given in his *Vita* at May 16 and his *Life* identifies him with the Irish Cairnech of Dulane. Cybi also seems to belong to this group of West Welsh saints. He has dedications in south-east Cardiganshire, Anglesey and Monmouthshire. The two *Lives* of Cybi in Vesp. A. xiv have a very strong Irish element, and are more likely

[1] Harris, *op. cit.* 18–19.

[2] E. G. Bowen, *Settlements of the Celtic Saints* (Cardiff, 1954), 53–5 shows that Padarn's dedications are ranged along the north–south routes in West Wales and in Radnorshire, where the road ran from Brecon northwards.

[3] For distribution of his cult see Bowen, *Settlements*, 28–9.

[4] He also has a dedication in the parish of Llandudoch, Pemb., and another near Newquay. Bowen, *Settlements*, 89.

to come originally from a West Welsh foundation than from Monmouthshire: if the *Life* came from Llangibby in southern Monmouthshire some mention of Llandaff might perhaps be expected. Another Irish *Life* is given in the collection—that of Maedoc of Ferns. This is no place to discuss whether the Irish Maedoc and the Welsh Madoc are historically identical:[1] they were certainly identified in Welsh tradition, where Maedoc of Ferns is represented as the disciple of St David at Cill Muine,[2] and the Irish *Life* was used for Welsh circulation. Madoc has dedications in Gower and in Brecon, besides two churches on St Bride's Bay. There are other saints appearing in the Vespasian kalendar who have festivals localised in the diocese of St David's. A kalendar of the St David's diocese may be partially reconstructed from two sources—from the sixteenth-century Llanbadarn Fawr kalendar edited by Mr Harris[3] and from the sixteenth-century additions to an unpublished kalendar in B.M. Add. 22,720. The reconstruction is not very satisfactory because it does not provide a complete kalendar, and the entries are very late. But it does appear that David, Gistlian, Nonnita, Kieran and Caradoc of St David's were commemorated in the diocese. On the evidence of dedications, three other saints may be added to the local festivals: Ishmael, who has a cult with one exception confined to Pembrokeshire and who is attested in no other calendar than Vespasian, Decuman with his chief foundation at Rhoscrowther in southern Pembroke, and Justinian, with dedications only in southern Pembroke. These saints (twelve in number if we exclude St David) have cults whose native source is in West Wales. Monmouth may have become acquainted with one or two of them through churches within her own geographical orbit—this applies to Cybi with a dedication in Monmouthshire and to Madoc, patron of Llanvadog in Brecknock. But others of them, notably Gistlian, Nonnita, Kieran, Caradoc, Ishmael and Justinian have no dedications in the east and their cults are confined to the south-west of Wales. The compilers of Vesp. must have had access to a Llanbadarn or St David's kalendar. What was their most likely source of information?

---

[1] In Irish Calendars Maedoc of Ferns is commemorated at January 31, in Vesp. at February 28. This apparent disparity of dates may be a slip on the part of a scribe. It would be easy to confuse *Prid.kl.feb.* with *Prid.kl.mart.*

[2] Wade-Evans, *Vitae*, 159–60; Plummer, *op. cit.* II, 297–300.

[3] *Ceredigion* (1952), II, 18–26.

The influence of Gloucester constantly intrudes on the composition of Vesp. A. XIV. The Benedictine house of St Peter's, Gloucester, had profited by the Anglo-Norman advance to secure extensive grants of properties in Central, South and West Wales, as her cartulary records. Llanbadarn Fawr was granted to Gloucester with its properties and appurtenances probably soon after 1115, and was clearly regarded as an important acquisition.[1] Padarn entered the Gloucester calendar,[2] and the monks probably had a short *Vita* for use at his festival. The Vesp. *Vita Sancti Paterni* seems to be a twelfth-century production and may have been compiled soon after Gloucester obtained the church.[3] Through Llanbadarn, Gloucester could have had access to some West Welsh legendary containing *Lives* of Padarn, his neighbour Brynach, Carantoc and Cybi (whose *Lives* have Irish elements), and the Irish *Lives* of Maedoc and Brendan. None of these shows any Llandaff influence. The *Lives* of Maedoc and Brendan were certainly known to a West Welsh hagiographer about 1090.[4] Rhigyfarch, a member of the hereditary ecclesiastical house of Llanbadarn Fawr, used them in writing his *Life of St David*, and it is not without significance that these two Irish *Lives* appear at the end of Vesp., a manuscript with an undeniable Ceredigion element. Apart from Gloucester's direct connection with Llanbadarn Fawr, her abbots were on friendly terms with the bishops of St David's. Bishop Wilfred of St David's returns the pastoral staff which William of St Peter's has lent him, thanking him warmly for his support.[5] Bishop Bernard witnesses the charter granting St Padarn's to Gloucester.[6] St Peter's, Gloucester, held properties elsewhere in the diocese of St David's. She was in a most favourable position for providing information on the saints of West Wales.

It is probable also that Gloucester influence may account for

[1] Cf. p. 177 above, J. E. Lloyd, *Hist. of Wales* (1939), II, 432–3, points out that though the *Cart. of St Peter's* dates the foundation 1111, the foundation charter is witnessed by Bishop Bernard, and cannot therefore be earlier than September 1115.

[2] Ed. F. Wormald, *English Benedictine Kalendars after 1100* (London, 1939–46), II, 47, 41.

[3] It ends with an interesting *possessio agrorum sancti Paterni*, which must be derived from a much longer and more explicit source. In so far as the boundaries are defined they may be compared with the more particular account in *The Gloucester Cartulary*, ed. W. H. Hart (3 vols., Rolls Series, London, 1863–7), II, 76.

[4] J. C. Davies, *Episcopal Acts relating to Welsh Dioceses, 1066–1272*, II, 500–1.

[5] *Ibid.* I, 236.　　　　　　　　　　[6] *Episcopal Acts*, I, 249.

some of the eastern saints in the kalendar and *Lives*. Ailwin almost certainly entered the Vesp. kalendar via Gloucester, which owned Coln Saint Aldwyn. His festival is attested only in Vespasian and in the kalendar of St Peter's, Gloucester, compiled before 1170. The presence of so rare a saint forcibly suggests Gloucester influence. Keneder is another obscure saint who appears in the Vespasian kalendar and whose main foundation at Glasbury was owned by Gloucester. St Peter's acquired Glasbury in 1088 during the time of Serlo. Bernard of Neufmarché, lord of Brecon, was the donor, and he granted St Keneder's church at Glasbury to Gloucester with certain rights in Brecknock:

Be it known both to those present and future, that I, Bernard of Neufmarché, have given to God and St Peter, and to Abbot Serlo and the monks of Gloucester: Glasbury, with all things pertaining to it, free and quit of all secular service and custom, for perpetual alms; and the church of St Keneder in the same village, with all things pertaining to it. I also grant to them, and confirm by my charter, an entire tenth of my whole lordship through all the land of Brecknock in woodland and meadow wherever my lordship is acknowledged, that is to say, in grain, herds, cheeses, venery and honey and in all other things of which tithes ought to be granted....[1]

It is possible, though the point cannot be pressed, that Gloucester's interest in Brecknock may account for the presence in Vesp. of the tract *De Situ Brecheniauc*. The note on Egwin in the kalendar is clearly inserted in order to connect him with Keneder and Cadoc; it identifies the three saints as sons of Gwynllyw.

Cadoc himself is clearly the most important saint in the collection. His *acta* are followed by a detailed account of the property of the canons of Llancarfan and by a group of charters, the whole of which section is from a different source. Where would these charters be kept? Llancarfan was granted to Gloucester with fifteen hides of land some time between 1093 and 1104 during the abbacy of Serlo.[2] Gloucester leased it for some years to archdeacons of Llandaff, but her ownership was carefully safeguarded, and when Archdeacon William overstepped his rights, Gloucester successfully resumed seisin (1175–80).[3] It seems probable that the final section on Llancarfan properties was added with the co-operation of Gloucester.

[1] *Glouc. Cart.* I, 314. Confirmed, I, 222.
[2] *Glouc. Cart.* I, 93. Confirmations, I, 222, 349.
[3] *Glouc. Cart.* II, 12–14. *Episcopal Acts*, II, 660–1, 664–5.

Gloucester also owned the chief church of Cadoc's father, Gwynllyw, whose *Life* is the first in the Vesp. collection. She was granted his foundation at Newport between 1094 and 1104.[1] In the middle years of the twelfth century Theobald of Canterbury granted indulgences of fifteen days to those who visited and assisted the church.[2] Gwynllyw's *Life*, as we have it, was rewritten some time after 1120.[3] Gloucester would have been closely concerned in attempts to increase the revenues of Newport.

A connection with Gloucester is explicitly attested in one of the two *Lives* of Dubricius which appears in Vesp. The author introduces himself, 'ego Benedictus habitu cenobii apostoli Petri Claudiocestrie monachus'. This explicit reference to Gloucester is particularly valuable, since otherwise Dubricius's presence in Vesp. would be attributed solely to the influence of either Monmouth or Llandaff. Monmouth would have been specially interested in both Cadoc and Dubricius. The monks had used the church of St Cadoc for nearly twenty years before their new church dedicated to St Mary was built; they owned Dubricius's foundation at Whitchurch, were interested in his chief church at Hentland, and were living in a part of the country where his dedications were thickly clustered.[4] And Llandaff's claim to Dubricius as one of her three great patrons is too well known to need further comment here.

Gloucester influence on the Vesp. collection seems undeniable, though the manner in which it was exercised must be a matter of dispute. But it cannot be accidental that two very rare saints, Ailwin and Keneder, are connected with Gloucester and also appear in the Vesp. kalendar. Gwynllyw was patron of an important church owned by Gloucester, the second *Life of Dubricius* was indubitably composed by a St Peter's monk, and the Vesp. compilers could most readily have copied their Llancarfan charters with the co-operation of Gloucester. Gloucester's ownership of Llanbadarn Fawr accounts not only for the *Life of Padarn*, but for the definition of his boundaries with which it concludes. Gloucester

[1] *Glouc. Cart.* II, 51. Davies dates the grant, *Ep. Acts*, II, 612.
[2] *Glouc. Cart.* II, 62. *Ep. Acts*, II, 636, 651.
[3] The *Life* implies recognition that Newport came within the diocese and under the jurisdiction of Llandaff and her bishop Dubricius. These conditions were not fulfilled before 1120. The title *episcopus Landavensis* is not found before 1119, and Dubricius's body arrived at Llandaff in 1120.
[4] Bowen, *Settlements*, 35–9.

interests provide the essential link between the eastern and western elements in the Vesp. collection.

It seems therefore almost certain that, some time before Vesp. A. xiv was compiled, the acts of certain Welsh saints had been collected at Gloucester. It may be possible to venture a more precise statement on the date at which this material was accumulated. Llanbadarn Fawr was acquired by Gloucester soon after 1115, and became independent again after the Welsh rebellion of 1136. Gloucester would have had access to Llanbadarn and West Welsh sources most readily between these dates. Of the two *Lives* of Dubricius in our manuscript, one, post-dating the death of Bishop Urban in 1134, is the same as the version now found in the *Book of Llandaff*, a collection for which Christopher Brooke elsewhere suggests a date in the 1130's.[1] The other, by Benedict of Gloucester, uses the Llandaff *Life* and Geoffrey of Monmouth's *History*, first published in 1138.[2] Geoffrey dedicated his work to Robert, earl of Gloucester, who was in charge of the temporalities of Llandaff during the vacancy of 1134–40,[3] and Robert's charge may have created considerable opportunities for exchange between Llandaff and Gloucester. It would appear that in the 1130's Gloucester, whose influence on Vesp. A. xiv is evident, had particularly good opportunities for obtaining hagiographical material.

The peculiar selection of saints present in the Vesp. MS. is thus accounted for partly by the connections of Monmouth, partly by the interests of Gloucester. It is clear that the compilers also drew on Llandaff material, though in a version which seems in some respects to be earlier than that of the *Liber Landavensis* itself. The *Life of Teilo* is certainly in the pre-*LL* version, though the rubric suggests that it may be a product of the Llandaff school.[4] The Vesp. *Life* of Clydog corresponds to the material in the *LL Life*, but it is differently arranged, with the one long formal witnessed charter, obviously a Llandaff forgery, at the end of the collection and following the *Life* and miracles. This would appear to be a

---

[1] See pp. 201, 204, n. 3, 205, n. 1, below.
[2] J. S. P. Tatlock, *The Legendary History of Britain* (Berkeley, Cal., 1950), 434. Griscom, *Historia Regum* (London, New York, 1929), 42, suggests 1136 as the date. See p. 231, n. 2, below.
[3] Davies, *Episcopal Acts*, II, 634.
[4] *Incipit vita Teliavi episcopi a magistro Galfrido* [glossed *id est Stephano*] *fratre Urbani Landavensis ecclesie episcopi dictata.*

more logical order than that of *LL*.[1] In Vesp. the *De Primo Statu Landavensis*, the first *Life of Dubricius* and account of his translation are, with minor variations, identical with the version in the *Book of Llandaff*.[2] Oudoceus, the third patron of Llandaff, does not appear in the Vesp. kalendar and his *Life* is not given.

This presentation of Llandaff material raises some problems, but it helps to solve others. Most important, it shows that it is very unlikely that the manuscript was compiled at Llandaff. Monmouth, Gloucester and Llandaff had the greatest influence on the contents of our manuscript, and if the theory of a Monmouth origin is rejected, Gloucester and Llandaff are the most obvious alternatives. But surely no Llandaff scribe writing after the composition of the *Book of Llandaff* would spend his energies copying the *Life of Teilo* in a version which omits the Llandaff claims? A few comparisons will show the kind of propaganda which the *LL Teilo* includes and Vesp. omits:

St Teilo received the pastoral care of the church of Llandaff to which he was consecrated with the whole *paruchia* adjacent to it which had belonged to his predecessor Dubricius. (*LL* 107.)

Both *LL* and Vesp. begin their accounts of his end: 'Now on the night of his death a great dispute arose between the three clergies of his three churches, with each claiming his own authority and privileges for possessing the body.' *LL only then enumerates the three churches, in particular pressing the claims of Llandaff, the see of Dubricius.* Both versions then describe how, after a night of prayer, three bodies appeared, of equal splendour, and each cleric took one home for burial in his own church. *LL then alone continues*: '*It was known to all the people both by the great number of miracles and the records of former persons in authority (monimentis antiquorum seniorum) that it was indubitably taken to Llandaff.*' (*LL.* 116–17.)

LL. and Vesp. give a final account of his miracles: 'Wherefore celebrate the feast of so great a man with all zeal of mind'—*and LL continues*: '*frequent his church, and each of you according to your ability bestow your substance on the poor*'. (*LL* 117.)

The older *Life of Teilo*, as we have it preserved in Vesp., has been emended with considerable skill in the version contained in the *Book of Llandaff*. It is unreasonable to suppose that the Vesp. *Life* would have been copied by a Llandaff scribe writing in a centre where the Llandaff text was available.

---

[1] J. G. Evans's edition of *LL* (Oxford, 1893) gives the Vesp. variants of Clydog on p. 362.
[2] The Vesp. variants by Evans, *LL*, 358–60.

Llandaff had some knowledge of the Llancarfan charters, and used them in forging her own title-deeds,[1] as we may see from the one charter in the *Life of Clydog*. Here two of the witnesses, Bishop Berthguin and Saturn of the church of Docquinn, are identical with witnesses in a charter of Llancarfan, in which Goidnerth makes a grant of Llan Catgualader to Cadoc.[2] Elsewhere in the *Book of Llandaff*, in a long forgery, the same man is made to grant the same church to Llandaff.[3] The contents of the Llancarfan charters are not in fact consistent with the Llandaff claims, and betray the sources of the Llandaff forgeries. After the publication of *LL* they would be best forgotten. Moreover, the *Life*, miracles and charters of Cadoc, whose *Life* is the most important one in the Vesp. collection, have not been edited in the Llandaff interest and give no hint of a Llandaff interpretation, as they would surely have done had they come from a scriptorium which had earlier in the century produced the *Book of Llandaff*.[4]

It is mainly the date of Vesp. A. xiv in relation to the *Liber Landavensis* which makes Llandaff so unlikely a centre for its compilation. But Vesp. is certainly the *kind* of source-book which lies behind the *Book of Llandaff*. If we had any evidence that, at the end of the twelfth century, the authorities of Llandaff were planning a claim to metropolitan status and primacy in Wales, then Vesp. A. xiv is just the kind of collection of sources which they would have needed. Geoffrey of Monmouth and the *Book of Llandaff* had made an archbishop of Dubricius, but the papacy had not believed them. During the century metropolitan pretensions were being hotly debated for St David's. We know that St David's first put forward a claim to metropolitan status in the 1120's,[5] and that Bishop Bernard raised the case again *c.* 1144.[6] The controversy was reopened by Gerald of Wales, and pursued with skill and energy between 1199 and 1203. In the first half of the century Urban of Llandaff and his *familia* had provided, in the *Book of Llandaff*, a formidable counter-claim to the St David's propaganda. They failed to establish against St David's the boundaries which they asserted, but it was not for want of trying. Did they make any

---

[1] Davies, *Episcopal Acts*, I, 163, 171.
[2] Wade-Evans, *Vitae*, 134. [3] *LL*, 180–2.
[4] Far from supporting the Llandaff brief, the *Life of Cadoc* provides material which St David's was quoting to support her opposing claims. Cf. Wade-Evans, *Vitae*, 54, 60, and Davies, *Episcopal Acts*, I, 262. Cf. below, p. 221.
[5] *Episcopal Acts*, I, 249–50. [6] *Ibid.* I, 260.

counter-moves *c.* 1200? It is tempting to speculate, but unless any evidence is forthcoming the arguments must be weighted against Llandaff provenance.

There is a hint, no more, in Vesp. that the compilers borrowed a copy of some Llandaff material for transcription. The Vesp. *Life of Teilo* concludes, quite irrelevantly, with the word *valete.* The text or texts may have been received with a polite message and salutation; in copying, the scribe correctly omitted the opening greeting but inadvertently copied the concluding farewell. This is too slender a piece of evidence to bear much weight, but, if it does indicate that a copy of Llandaff material was borrowed, it might explain why Vesp., compiled after the *Book of Llandaff*, contains pre-*LL* matter. Llandaff would not be likely to let so precious an authority as the *Book of Llandaff* out of her keeping, but she might be persuaded to lend other copies of the *Lives* of her saints.

The Llandaff material in Vesp. also throws a little more light on the Gloucester connection. Benedict, a Gloucester monk, was sufficiently interested in Dubricius to write his *Life*, using the Llandaff text which is in Vesp. and Geoffrey of Monmouth's *History*. Teilo, the second Llandaff patron, is entered as a later addition in the twelfth-century Gloucester kalendar;[1] so Gloucester may have possessed his *Life*.[2] Of all the Llandaff texts in the Vesp. manuscript, the *Life of Clydog* is the most difficult to account for in a book not of Llandaff provenance, since Clydog is not a popular saint. His cult is confined to Merthyr Clydog in Ewias, three or four miles west of Ewias Harold. But Gloucester was interested in Ewias Harold. Harold of Ewias had granted certain churches and tithes to St Peter's. After a specification of certain properties his charter continues:

> I also grant and confirm to the aforesaid monks of Gloucester all my churches of my whole honour, and the lands which belong to them, with all tithes which my men shall grant to that church, freely and quit of all secular service and exaction, to have as alms for ever.[3]

Gloucester made no claim to the church of Clydog, but she had rights in neighbouring property, and this may have aroused her

---

[1] Ed. Wormald, *op. cit.* II, 45.

[2] Did she borrow the pre-*LL* Teilo, ending *valete*, when she obtained the Llandaff *Life of Dubricius* which Benedict of Gloucester needed for his *Vita S. Dubricii*?

[3] *Glouc. Cart.* I, 285–6.

interest in Clydog and the boundaries which Llandaff claimed for him.

It is possible that the material in Vesp. which must come originally from Llandaff did not do so directly, but entered the compilation via Gloucester. There were plenty of opportunities for exchange between the churches. Conway Davies shows that the Benedictine Nicholas ap Gwrgant, bishop of Llandaff 1148–83, had previously been a monk of Gloucester;[1] and the litigation in which Gloucester was not infrequently involved brought her into contact with the bishop and his *familia*.

Our examination of the evidence suggests that, in the 1130's or later, material from the hagiographical schools of Llanbadarn Fawr in West Wales, and possibly from Llandaff, was gathered together at Gloucester.[2] These texts were copied about 1200 into the Vespasian manuscript. The final compilers belonged to a scriptorium which had several competent scribes, one of whom glossed many of the Welsh names. After the *Lives* had been transcribed, the 'kalendar' was drawn up, by someone familiar with the feast of Dochelinus. Monmouth was a border monastery, in an anglicised area accessible to Welsh influences; her monks were the only people in Wales likely to know the date of Dochelinus's festival. Until further evidence is produced it seems likely that Mr Harris is right in claiming the Monmouth monks as the actual compilers of the manuscript.

Wherever the compilation was made it has odd omissions. Its purpose was to identify and record Welsh saints. Monmouth monks might therefore be expected to enter the native patrons of the churches which formed part of their own properties.[3] Cadoc and Dubricius are here, for Monmouth owned two churches of St Cadoc and St Dubricius's foundation at Whitchurch. But

---

[1] *Episcopal Acts*, II, 655.

[2] Christopher Brooke has suggested to me that some of the diverse interests represented in the compilation may reflect the work of one or more professional hagiographers: Caradoc of Llancarfan was working at this time, and someone of his type might account for elements as diverse as the Old Cornish glossary (above, p. 186, n. 1) and the variety of the *Vitae*. This suggestion, though it is hypothetical, may explain some of the details discussed above. It does not affect my argument that, at a preliminary stage, materials were assembled at Gloucester.

[3] Cf. F. Wormald, on the custom of the canons of the Augustinian priory of Launceston of entering 'the patron saints of the churches appropriated to them, or over which they exercised some jurisdiction'. *Journal of Theological Studies*, XXXIX (1938), 4–5.

native patrons of other properties are absent. Gwénolé,[1] Tudy,[2] Constantine,[3] comparatively well-known saints with local cults, all had churches in the immediate neighbourhood of Monmouth, and yet they are omitted. The absence of octaves, of the feast of the dedication of St Mary's, Monmouth,[4] of the feast of St Florentinus, need cause no surprise if it is accepted that the purpose of the kalendar is not liturgical but historical. But the absence of Oudoceus from the Llandaff material is illogical, for the legend of the three patrons was by this time fully developed. The collection of material is indeed so haphazard as to require comment. The palaeography of the manuscript provides some explanation of the way in which the monks went to work.

The gatherings of the manuscripts are normally in eights, though there are four exceptions: the kalendar, glossary and Brecknock tract at the beginning of the manuscript are on two gatherings of ten and four, and of the twelve gatherings on which the *Lives* are transcribed one is of five and one of seven. The last gathering of the MS. is lost. The standard of execution throughout the manuscript varies considerably. The beginning is carefully produced, but as the MS. proceeds it acquires a less finished appearance. The first three *Lives* in the collection—Gwynllyw, Cadoc and Illtud—have coloured capitals, paragraphs, and chapter headings which were filled in afterwards. The next four have coloured capitals and paragraphs, but the spaces left for rubrics have not been filled in. The remainder, with the exception of Aed and Tatheus, have no coloured capitals, no paragraphs and no chapter headings. After the first few gatherings little care is taken to secure uniformity—the hands vary in size and the ink and colours change. The amount of care taken over the appearance of the manuscript has declined. This is, in itself, a common enough

[1] Marchegay, *Chartes anciennes du prieuré de Monmouth* (Les Roches-Baritaud, 1879), 15, for *ecclesia sancti Wingaloei*. For his church at Wonnastow, near Monmouth, see Wade-Evans, *Y Cymmrodor*, XXII (1910), 74. Some of his relics were at Glastonbury and at Exeter; he is in the Leofric Missal and in the litany from Salisbury MS. 160. His *Life* must have been known to the Breton founder of Monmouth.

[2] Marchegay, 18. Patron of Dixton, *Y Cymmrodor*, XXII, 111. In the Exeter Mart. at May 9.

[3] *Ecclesia S. Custenin de Bicenovria*, Welsh Bicknor near Ross, Marchegay, 15, 28.

[4] We know that this was being observed in 1398 from *Cal. of Papal Letters*, V, 257.

occurrence; it must, however, be considered together with the extent of revision in the manuscript. The first three *Lives* of Gwynllyw, Cadoc and Illtud have been intensively revised with marginal interpolations and interlinear glosses. In Cadoc's *Life* two leaves were inserted with five extra chapters to be interpolated at different points in the text. In the next four *Lives* there is a little revision—the interpolator's hand appears occasionally in the margin of the Gloucester *Life of Dubricius*, and in the other three of this group there are a few interlinear glosses. The Brecknock tract at the beginning of the manuscript has also received one or two interlinear glosses, and a few additions have been made to the kalendar. Practically no revision occurs in the remaining ten *Lives*. How is this palaeographical evidence to be interpreted, and what light does it throw on the selection and omissions in the contents?

The scribes set to work first on the *Vitae*. The *Life* of Gwynllyw, the first in the collection, starts at gathering three, and this begins a series of regular gatherings, with two exceptions in eights. The first three *Vitae* were carefully written, and coloured capitals and rubrics were filled in. The life, passion, miracles and genealogy of Cadoc, the second saint in the series, are followed by an account in a different hand of the possessions of Llancarfan and a series of its charters. The charters are on an irregular gathering and have not been revised; they were most probably obtained from some outside source. The manuscript was continued in various hands, and the scribe who copied the last group of *Lives* wrote the first two irregular gatherings, which contain the *capitula* and kalendar. After the first few *Lives* had been written, other texts came to light. Someone, call him the Master of the Scriptorium, started to go through the manuscript, making extensive additions in the margins and on odd inserted leaves, with notes at relevant points, 'Require signum scedulae', 'Require istud signum', which may have been made with an eye to retranscription. But the revision was very unevenly applied, and, for some reason to which the known evidence provides no clue, it was never completed. Only the first three *Lives* have been fully revised. The succeeding four have been partially revised, and the kalendar has likewise received a few additions, but more than three-quarters of the days in the year are still completely blank, and a number of saints whom one would expect to find are omitted.

The compilers of Vesp. wished to provide some record of the

Celtic saints of Wales. They seem to have observed no special order in copying the *Lives*, but to have transcribed them as they came to hand. Their 'kalendar' takes a Roman framework, adds the saints of the *Lives* which they had transcribed, and uses other native sources, which almost certainly included a kalendar derived from Gloucester. In the space between kalendar and *capitula* they copied out a glossary and a Brecknock tract for good measure. There is uneven and incomplete revision. The whole effect is extremely haphazard, as though the plan of the collection had only been worked out on the broadest lines. It contrasts sharply with the impression conveyed by the main body of the *Book of Llandaff* of a work uniformly executed and planned. Both the contents and palaeography suggest that Vesp. A. XIV may have been considered as a source-book for historical record. The interests it represents are varied and contradictory: it is in no sense a brief in support of a case like the *Book of Llandaff*. It may not even, as we have it, be complete. It is possible that the Vesp. manuscript may have been in progress for some time: the changes of hand and inks and the occasional spaces are of too common occurrence in manuscripts to act as evidence for such a suggestion, but they certainly do nothing to weaken the possibility. It looks as if the compilers must have intended to make other entries as opportunity offered. If they ever clearly formulated a detailed plan, the present manuscript can hardly be a complete expression of it; their kalendar gapes with omissions and their revision was abandoned half-way through.

The manuscript is another illustration of the interest which the Anglo-Norman settlers felt in the pseudo-historical traditions of the Celtic past. It lacks the polish of William of Malmesbury's work for Glastonbury, or the ingenuity of the *Book of Llandaff*, or the creative imagination of Geoffrey of Monmouth's *History*, but it is an industrious record of texts mainly written or rewritten in the twelfth century. It reflects the restless enterprise of this period of Norman-Welsh history—the splendid expansion of Gloucester, the rise of Llandaff, and the preservation, though abbreviated, enfeebled and but half-understood, of the traditions of the Celtic Church in the west.

IV

The Archbishops of St David's, Llandaff and Caerleon-on-Usk

BY CHRISTOPHER BROOKE

ABBREVIATIONS

Tatlock   J. S. P. Tatlock, *The Legendary History of Britain* (University of California, 1950).

EA   J. Conway Davies, *Episcopal Acts and Cognate Documents relating to Welsh Dioceses, 1066–1272*, vols. I and II (Historical Society of the Church in Wales, 1946–8).

HRB   Geoffrey of Monmouth, *Historia Regum Britanniae*, ed. A. Griscom (New York, 1929) (G), and ed. E. Faral, *La légende arthurienne*, I, iii (Paris, 1929) (F).

LL   *The Text of the Book of Llan Dâv*, ed. J. G. Evans and J. Rhys (Oxford, 1893).

VSB   *Vitae Sanctorum Britanniae et Genealogiae*, ed. A. W. Wade-Evans (Cardiff, 1944).

I

The one thing which all the prelates incorporated in my title had in common was that they never existed: in the sense in which we use the word, none of the cities named was the seat of an archbishop before the disestablishment of the Welsh Church in 1920. As an honorific title, the word may have been applied in early days to St David himself and to some other Welsh bishops;[1] it is possible that Bernard, bishop of St David's from 1115 to 1148, was in possession of a pallium sent from Rome for a short time in the last decade of his life. But St David's was never the centre of a metropolitan province; and the archbishoprics of Llandaff and Caerleon were figments without existence outside the two most considerable historical forgeries of medieval Britain, the *Liber Landavensis* and Geoffrey of Monmouth's *History of the Kings of Britain*—both completed, by a strange coincidence, in the 1130's. My purpose in this paper is to investigate the process by which

[1] Cf. L. Gougaud, *Christianity in Celtic Lands* (London, 1932), 219f.; C. N. L. Brooke, *Downside Review*, LXIX (1951), 228 n.

these shadowy archbishops were conjured from the mists of Wales in the late eleventh and early twelfth centuries.

Geoffrey of Monmouth was one of the world's great story-tellers. Whatever we may think of him, it is hard to deny this credit at least to the man who invented King Lear, and (more than any other single person) floated King Arthur on the world of the twelfth century and made him a respectable subject for courtly romance. The fact that almost none of his stories was historically true does not mean that he was ignorant of legend and history;[1] but it makes it exceedingly difficult to reconstruct his sources without definite and specific evidence by which to check them. Our first task is to see how he came to create the archbishopric of Caerleon-on-Usk.

For Caerleon, the City of Legions, 'situated in a passing pleasant position on the river Usk in Glamorgan, not far from the Severn sea', Geoffrey of Monmouth had a particular affection. Here he placed the climax of his *History*, the crown-wearing ceremony of King Arthur. The chief glories of Caerleon, he writes,

were the two churches, one built in honour of the martyr Julius, charmingly adorned by a choir of virgins dedicated to God's service, and the second dedicated to the blessed Aaron, his companion, served by a community of canons—and this was the cathedral of the third[2] metropolitan see of Britain. It had, in addition, a school of two hundred philosophers, skilled in astronomy and the other arts, who diligently observed the course of the stars, and accurately foretold the wonders that were shortly to befall King Arthur. Such was the city, famous for abundance of everything delightful, which was now preparing herself for the festival.

Geoffrey peoples Arthur's court with all the fish he could catch in his net, including the archbishops of the three metropolitan sees, 'of London and York, and Dubricius of Caerleon. Dubricius, primate of Britain (*Britannie primus*) and legate of the apostolic see, was of a devotion so eminent that he could by his prayers cure anyone afflicted by a disease.' Dubricius himself, since the ceremony took place in his diocese, placed the crown on Arthur's head; but when the majestic display was over, he resigned his see, 'yearning for a hermit's life...', and 'David, the king's uncle, was consecrated in his stead, whose life was an example of all goodness

---

[1] For Geoffrey's knowledge of Welsh legend, cf. especially Mrs R. Bromwich in *Studies in Early British History* (Cambridge, 1954), 125–8; for Geoffrey's sources in general, see Tatlock.

[2] Reading *tertiam* with Faral; Griscom's *tercia* is impossible in the context.

to those who came under his instruction'. And so we proceed to other promotions. 'In succession to Samson, archbishop of Dol, was appointed Teliaus (or Teilo), an illustrious priest of Llandaff, with the consent of Hoel, king of the Bretons....' Other promotions followed; but the proceedings were brought to a sudden and dramatic conclusion by the arrival of ambassadors from the Roman consul (or emperor) which precipitated Arthur into the greatest of his wars, that against Rome.[1]

It is beyond doubt that every detail of this splendid vision of Arthur's court is fiction, and that Geoffrey knew it for such. Its historical importance is none the less great. In the portions which I have selected from his account, Geoffrey glanced at the claim of Canterbury to primacy over Britain, and the claims of St David's and Llandaff to be (or to have been) metropolitan sees, and passed judgment on the conflicts which these claims inspired. He also sowed the seeds of future conflict. His narrative was employed by the chapter of St David's in their struggle for independence against Canterbury; and his references (here and elsewhere) to the archbishopric of London were one of the principal grounds for Gilbert Foliot's claim that he owed no allegiance to Thomas Becket.[2] Geoffrey put new ingredients into an extraordinary cauldron of troubles, very characteristic of the age in which he lived.

St Dubricius was undoubtedly a historical character, though his date and his career are exceedingly obscure.[3] He figures in the earliest surviving life of a Celtic saint, the *Vita Samsonis*, as the bishop who ordained Samson deacon. In the Welsh annals a bishop 'Dubric' (possibly a different man) is made to die in 612. His early cult seems to have centred in Archenfield, in the border country between England and Wales. But he owes his later fame to the activities of a group of forgers in their way no less audacious than Geoffrey himself—the men who founded (or refounded) the cathedral of Llandaff in the 1120's, and adopted Dubricius as its patron and original founder. They translated his relics to Llandaff

---

[1] *HRB*, IX, 12–15; G, 451 ff.; F, 242 ff. On Geoffrey and Caerleon, cf. Tatlock, 69–72.

[2] Cf. M. D. Knowles, *The Episcopal Colleagues of Archbishop Thomas Becket* (Cambridge, 1951), 160–2. There is evidence of an earlier attempt by a bishop of London to acquire a pallium in 1108 in the letters of Anselm (*Opera omnia*, ed. F. S. Schmitt, V (Edinburgh, 1951), 399, no. 451).

[3] G. H. Doble, *St Dubricius* (Guildford, 1943); E. G. Bowen, *Settlements of the Celtic saints in Wales* (Cardiff, 1954), 36 ff. (on which cf. W. O. Chadwick in *Studies in Early British History*, 175 ff.).

in 1120,[1] and in or shortly after 1134 wrote a life of him in which he appears as archbishop of Llandaff.[2]

This *Life* forms the nucleus of the celebrated *Liber Landavensis* (or *Book of Llandaff*), the main body of which consists of the *Lives* of three saints supposed to have been the first three archbishops of Llandaff, Dubricius, Teilo and Oudoceus; charters attributed to the lifetime of each of these saints, and charters and other records covering all the bishops of Llandaff from the age of the saints to the consecration of Bishop Urban in 1107. In addition it contains two other saints' *Lives* connected, or altered to have a connection, with Llandaff, and some other historical jottings; and the blank space at the end of the quire containing the Dubricius matter and an additional quire have a mass of documents from the later years of Bishop Urban's episcopate, 1119–32. The book is now bound up so that the miscellaneous matter comes before the straightforward historical sequence from Dubricius to Urban; with a copy of St Matthew's Gospel preceding and later additions following. The *Book of Llandaff* proper—both *miscellanea* and chronological sequence—is written in a variety of hands which could all belong (with one exception) to the second quarter of the twelfth century.[3] If we assume (as seems rational) that the book was all written more or less at one time, then the palaeographical evidence seems to establish fairly conclusively that it was composed not later than

[1] *LL*, 5, 84–6.

[2] Bishop Urban (d. 1134: *EA*, II, 633) is referred to as 'uir bone memorie' (*LL*, 85), which almost certainly means that he was dead; but this may not have been in the original *Life*—it may be an addition by the compiler of *LL*.

[3] J. G. Evans (*LL*, introduction) offered a variety of dates in the second and third quarters of the twelfth century for the original hands of *LL*; E. D. Jones ('The Book of Llandaff', *National Library of Wales Journal*, IV (1945–6), 152 ff.) preferred to date most of the hands in the third quarter of the twelfth century at earliest. I think a more general view would be that all except one (hand C in Evans's analysis; cf. Jones, *art. cit.* 152) are of approximately the second quarter of the century, but that a new analysis of the hands is needed. Allowing for the uncertainties of palaeographical evidence, it seems fairly clear that the bulk of the present contents of *LL* (i.e. col. 1–336, excepting 33–5) was written at about the same time; and probably between 1134 (the earliest possible date for the *Vita Dubricii* in its present form) and *c.* 1150. None of the experts whom I have consulted would quarrel with the date 1134–*c.* 1140 suggested in the text for the main hands of *LL* (as illustrated in Evans's edition). The writing of col. 33–5 (the agreement of Bishop Urban and the earl of Gloucester in 1126) has peculiarities which set it apart from the other hands; Mr N. R. Ker and Dr Dorothea Oschinsky would date it to the early thirteenth century (I have to thank Mr Ker, Dr Oschinsky, Mr T. A. M. Bishop and Dr C. R. Dodwell for kindly giving me their opinion on the hands of *LL*).

say 1160 and probably some years earlier; while the evidence of the contents shows that the *Life of Dubricius*, with which the chronological sequence opens, cannot be earlier than 1134. Some of the writing may be earlier, some a little later, but the bulk of the book must have been written *c.* 1135–50.

This approximate date is strongly confirmed by two pieces of evidence. Considering how richly provided the book is with material from every generation down to the time of Urban, and especially for the dozen years down to 1132, it would be very surprising that no later document should have strayed into the body of the book unless it was completed within a very few years of Bishop Urban's death.[1] And there can be no doubt—although

---

[1] Against this it could be argued that the book is unfinished and that we cannot tell what it would have contained if complete; and, secondly, that what we have is a fair copy, and may have been made some years after the original. The answer to the second point is that the documents of Urban's episcopate are entered in a haphazard manner, and not as part of the chronological sequence— so far as they are concerned, the book does not look like the fair copy of a completed whole; and in addition the palaeographical evidence is fully consistent with a date in the 1130's.

The book is unfinished in two ways: the Urban documents end in the middle of a bull of Innocent II; the chronological sequence concluding with Urban's consecration ends in the middle of a sentence—one leaf is lost at the end of the last quire, so far as one can tell. The first break is not serious, since it comes in the middle of a quire: apparently there was no more space; also the surviving documents are not in chronological order, and it is clear that the documents of 1130–2 in this quire were not copied down as they were received. For the chronological sequence we have some control, since there are two other sources containing some of the accounts of election and consecration which provide the framework for the later centuries—notes in Ralph de Diceto's *Abbreviatio chronicorum* and notes on the dorse of the Canterbury profession roll (on these see *EA*, I, 54 ff.). Comparison of the three makes it clear that Diceto and the roll (both probably written in the late twelfth century, the roll possibly a little later) are based on a common source, a version of the Llandaff professions kept—and tampered with—at Canterbury. The Canterbury list must be based on a Llandaff source, but not on the *Book of Llandaff* itself, since it contained some additional information (and also the complete entry for Urban's consecration in 1107). What it did not contain is any entry for the consecration of Urban's successor, Uhtred, in 1140; and I therefore consider it likely that the material collected for the composition of the *Book of Llandaff* contained nothing later than the episcopate of Urban. (Other evidence about the material used in *LL* is contained in MS. Cotton Vesp. A. XIV, cf. above, pp. 193 ff. This does not seem to affect the argument.)

It seems probable that the *Book* was originally intended to have a full account of Urban's doings, but was abandoned before this had been accomplished. This would explain why the Urban documents are added *pêle-mêle*, and not where they should be in the chronological sequence; and it would also suggest that the incomplete state of the *Book* has deprived us of very little that it might have contained.

it has often been denied—that there is some link between the *Book of Llandaff* and Geoffrey of Monmouth's *Historia*. In both St Dubricius is made an archbishop and given a status not accorded him in earlier documents; in both he retires to become a hermit. Even more remarkable is Geoffrey's reference to Teilo, 'an illustrious priest of Llandaff', as Samson's successor as archbishop of Dol. In the first *Life of Teilo* concocted at Llandaff there was no mention of the saint's visit to Brittany, and precious little of his relations with Llandaff. In the revised version in the *Book of Llandaff* more is made of his Welsh bishopric, and there is a long insertion (largely derived from a *Life of St Turiau*, an authentic bishop of Dol), which takes Teilo to Dol and makes him a bishop there.[1] Whether or not the motive for this exile was a counter to St David's claim to St Samson cannot be determined; but it can hardly be a coincidence that both Geoffrey of Monmouth and the *Book of Llandaff* associate Teilo both with Llandaff and with Dol. It is easier to imagine that the careers of Dubricius and Teilo were reconstructed at Llandaff than by Geoffrey; and if the authors of the *Book* knew Geoffrey's work, it is very strange that (unlike almost all later Welsh ecclesiastical historians) they made no effort to harmonise his story with theirs. The natural conclusion from these and other details[2] is that Geoffrey knew the *Book of Llandaff*, or at least the material from which it was composed.[3] Since

[1] For Dubricius, cf. Tatlock, 245, Doble, *op. cit.*; for Teilo, *idem, St Teilo* (Lampeter, 1942), esp. 23–5. Gerald of Wales makes Teilo archbishop of St David's (*Opera*, VI, ed. J. F. Dimock, 102).

[2] For unusual personal names used by Geoffrey and to be found in *LL*, cf. Tatlock, 76, 142, 154, 160; and for place-names in Geoffrey explicable by reference to *LL*, *ibid.* 75–6. But none of these coincidences is sufficiently striking by itself to establish a link, and the place-names may be due to Geoffrey's local knowledge. The same is true of his location of the churches of SS. Julius and Aaron in Caerleon, which may easily be based on Bede, local legend and the knowledge that there was a church dedicated to them in the neighbourhood. On the other hand, the passage from Bede is quoted in *LL* (26) with the place of their martyrdom specified as Caerleon; and the church is referred to on pp. 225–6. It is also possible that Geoffrey derived his knowledge of St Samson from the *Life* in *LL*. The suggestion that Geoffrey used the *LL* was also made by F. Lot (*Mélanges d'histoire bretonne* (Paris, 1907), 274 n.) but has since been ignored. Lot suggested that the prowess of 'Armorican' cavalry in *HRB*, VIII, 5 (G, 404; F, 208) was a reminiscence of *LL* 113.

There is undoubtedly a connection between the *LL* account of King Lucius and Geoffrey; but if the letter of the chapter of St David's (see below) is genuine, it was the intermediary between the two.

[3] It is impossible to decide whether it was the *LL* itself or the material for it which Geoffrey knew; but if the latter, it was at a late stage in its composition,

Geoffrey's *History* was certainly completed by *c.* January 1139,[1] we can probably date the later stages in the compilation of the *Book of Llandaff* 1134–8; but we must allow for the possibility that what Geoffrey used was not the final article.

From 1134 to 1140 the see of Llandaff was vacant. For the men who had assisted Bishop Urban in the great endeavours of his later years, this must have been an anxious time. They had already, while he lived, laid the foundations of the great collection of forgeries which is the monument of Urban's efforts. It is extremely likely that they completed their labours in the years immediately following his death, as a brief for the great causes when they should be resumed, and as a manual to instruct Urban's successor, when appointed, in the heritage into which he had stepped.

The Llandaff chapter had made no claim to independence from Canterbury; they merely asserted that their see was, by ancient tradition, the greatest in Wales, and had once been the seat of an archbishop. Their claim was intimately associated with an attempt in which they were engaged to extend the boundaries of the diocese at the expense of the bishop of Hereford, but more especially at the expense of St David's.[2]

The case of St David's was older and more far-reaching. In the decade before the writing of Geoffrey's *Historia* (between the years 1125 and 1130) the chapter of St Andrew and St David addressed an extraordinary letter to Pope Honorius II. Their church (so they asserted) had been metropolitan since the first beginnings of Christianity in Britain, since the days of Pope Eleutherius, who had sent to King Lucius the preachers Fagan and Duvian, and founded three archbishoprics and twenty-seven (or twenty-eight)[3]

since he evidently used the *Life of Dubricius* (*c.* 1134, unless it has been revised) and the revised version of the *Life of Teilo.*

[1] Cf. Tatlock, 433–4. I accept Tatlock's argument that the book was probably not finished before 1138 (see below, p. 231, n. 2), but this does not affect the argument here.

[2] Cf. *EA*, I, 147–90; for the obscure history of later disputes and compromises, see *EA*, I, 180–1; II, 519 ff.

[3] Twenty-seven in the only MS. of the chapter's letter; twenty-eight in Geoffrey of Monmouth (*HRB*, I, 2; G, 221–2; F, 73). Both are obviously derived from the twenty-eight British cities of Gildas, Bede and Nennius.

The legend of King Lucius was a very fertile one: in the second quarter of the twelfth century at least four new versions of it were composed in England and Wales, one in support of the pretensions of St David's, one in support of Llandaff, one in support of Glastonbury, and the fourth—Geoffrey of Monmouth's—for fiction's own sake. All owe something to Bede; but they all have bishoprics in the kingdom. In the course of time St David held the archbishopric—the third *in textu historiarum*, but in the list of provinces the first. He had been consecrated by his predecessor St Dubricius and by the synod (as the custom was), and from that day to the coming of the Normans (*nostre gentis*) the see had been an independent archbishopric. These claims are supported by various historical details, notably by reference to Bede, to St Samson (who had taken his pallium from St David's to Dol, and so founded a new archbishopric in Brittany) and St Patrick. The chapter demands that its ancient rights be restored.[1]

This letter survives only in the *De Invectionibus* of Gerald of Wales (*c.* 1203),[2] and until recently it has attracted remarkably little attention.[3] But there is good reason to regard it as genuine;[4] and if genuine, the letter or its substance was undoubtedly known to Geoffrey of Monmouth. It has provided him with the names of Eleutherius's emissaries; with the number of ancient bishoprics and archbishoprics in the island; with the fact that David was successor to Dubricius; and perhaps, too, with the notion that Samson held a British as well as a Breton see.

words and ideas in common apart from their debt to the master. I have laid out a skeleton text of the passages which any of them have in common with another in Appendix II. I am personally convinced that there is a verbal link between the St David's version and the Llandaff; and between the St David's and Geoffrey. Since the St David's version is from a letter addressed to Pope Honorius II (December 1124–February 1130), it must be earlier than Geoffrey whose work was probably published in 1138, certainly not earlier than 1135–6 (Tatlock, 433 ff.). Since Llandaff is very much closer to Bede than St David's, it is reasonable to suppose that the chronological order is Bede: Llandaff: St David's. William of Malmesbury's narrative in his treatise *De antiquitate Glastoniensis ecclesie* may possibly be the inspiration of the Llandaff tale—but to that problem we shall return anon (see below, p. 230, n. 4).

[1] The letter is preserved in Gerald's *De Invectionibus*, II, 10 (ed. W. S. Davies, *Y Cymmrodor*, xxx (1920), 143–6); cf. *EA*, I, 190–2. Its discernible sources are the *Notitia Dignitatum*, Bede, a *Life of Samson* (cf. *ibid.*), possibly Nennius (cf. above, p. 207, n. 3 and the reference to *Trinovantum*), Rhigyfarch's *Life of St David* (cf. especially the ref. to St Patrick) and the *De primo statu Landavensis ecclesie* (see above, p. 207, n. 3).

[2] The first book was written in 1203, the rest somewhat later, and the fifth and sixth were not finished before 1206 (*op. cit.* 5 ff., cf. 202); but a reference to Peter de Leia in bk. II (p. 133) seems to indicate that his successor had not then been consecrated (i.e. that it was written before 7 December 1203), or at least before Gerald had accepted the fact.

[3] E.g. it is ignored by Tatlock, 230, although referred to on p. 266. Needless to say, full use has been made of it by Dr Conway Davies, to whose book I owe a profound debt throughout this essay.

[4] See below, Additional Note 1, p. 233.

It is immediately clear that this letter was one of Geoffrey's chief sources for church organisation in early Britain;[1] and his use of it places in perspective his account of the early British Church. In part, he simply used material that was to hand for his own purposes, ignoring its original significance when it suited him to ignore it. But there is more to it than that. His account of Arthur's court was a glorified picture of the Anglo-Norman court of his day, attuned to tickle the fancy and yet to seem familiar and plausible to an Anglo-Norman audience. Similarly, his account of ecclesiastical organisation is exceedingly topical: he places his episcopal elections in the royal chapel (correctly, for Henry I's reign); he calls Dubricius—as William de Corbeil, archbishop of Canterbury, had called himself—primate of Britain and legate of the Holy See; and by introducing Dubricius, David and Samson he reflects some current controversies.

The monks of Canterbury had claimed that their see had had a primacy over all Britain (and especially over the archbishopric of York) since the days of St Augustine; and William de Corbeil had attempted to sustain his weakening grasp of this primacy by becoming papal legate.[2] The chapter of St David's had claimed that Dubricius was David's predecessor, and that he had consecrated David archbishop; that Samson was David's successor, and fleeing from the plague had carried his pallium to Brittany, and so founded the archbishopric of Dol. The chapter of Llandaff claimed that by ancient tradition they owed no allegiance to St David's, but rather to Canterbury. They wrote a *Life of St Teilo* to show that Llandaff ought by rights to have the allegiance of a considerable slice of the diocese of St David's; a *Life of St Samson* to show that he had never been an archbishop at all before he crossed the water; and a *Life of St Dubricius* to show that David's predecessor had been archbishop of Llandaff.[3]

We can now see more clearly what a hash Geoffrey of Monmouth has made of all these precious claims. There was in Arthur's day no

[1] Together with texts of canon law probably derived from Anselm of Lucca (S. Williams, *Speculum*, XXVII (1952), 184–90).

[2] H. Tillmann, *Die päpstlichen Legaten in England...* (Bonn, 1926), 30 ff.; the fullest accounts of the primacy dispute are in M. Dueball, *Die Suprematstreit zwischen den Erzdiözesen Canterbury und York, 1070–1126* (Berlin, 1926; cf. *English Hist. Rev.* XLV (1930), 148–9) and R. Foreville, *L'Église et la royauté en Angleterre...* (Paris, 1943), 48ff.

[3] Doble, *St Teilo*; R. Fawtier, *La vie de saint Samson* (Paris, 1912), 18–21; Doble, *St Dubricius*.

archbishop of Canterbury; the primate and legate of the time had his see in Wales; Samson was an archbishop, but archbishop of York, not of St David's; David was also an archbishop, but he too was not archbishop of St David's; Teilo came from Llandaff, but had not been a bishop there, only a priest. St David's indeed could claim the body of an archbishop; and in the *Prophecies of Merlin*[1] Menevia is clothed with the pallium of Caerleon—a passage obscurely echoed in Geoffrey's later *Life of Merlin*, which may indicate slightly increased respect for Menevia's pretensions. But in the *Historia* he describes David's death in such a way as to make it clear that he was still archbishop of Caerleon;[2] and throughout the *Historia* he gives nothing away to the claims of St David's or Llandaff. If Wales must have an archbishopric (and why not?) we will place it where our fancy takes us—at Caerleon, 'situated in a passing pleasant position on the river Usk'.

It was impossible that Geoffrey should describe the ecclesiastical organisation of Arthurian England without violating the sacred tradition of one or other of the warring factions of his day. In fact, he succeeded (with complete impartiality) in disposing of them all. It might, I suppose, be argued that impartiality was his aim; by cutting across every one of the existing claims he saved himself from being implicated in any of them. If so, he miscalculated; for critics and harmonisers circumvented his scheme to their own advantage,[3] and a claim hitherto scarcely adumbrated, that for

[1] *HRB*, VII, 3; G, 385; F, 191: 'Menevia pallio urbis legionum induetur et predicator Hybernie propter infantem in utero crescentem obmutescet.' The second half seems to be a conflation of the roles of Patrick and Gildas in Rhigyfarch's *Life* (*VSB*, 150–2–cf. esp. 152: 'Crescente...utero, mater... quandam ingreditur ecclesiam...Gildas obmutescens...tacuit'); both parts refer forward to Geoffrey's account of David's death and burial in *Menevia* (see next note); and cf. below, p. 216, n. 4. The passage in the *Vita Merlini* (ll. 622–6, ed. Faral, *op. cit.* 325; ed. J. J. Parry, *Illinois Studies in Language and Literature*, x, 1925, 66–9) is similar, but unintelligible. In both cases it may well be that Geoffrey was pointing the way for the reconciliation of his story with the pretensions of St David's; but if he had wished to support those pretensions, he would hardly have introduced Caerleon into the story in the first place.

[2] *HRB*, XI, 3; G, 502; F, 279. Geoffrey partly chose Caerleon, no doubt, because its Roman remains gave it a plausible claim to have been the seat of an ancient archbishopric (see below, pp. 212–13).

[3] Benedict of Gloucester (H. Wharton, *Anglia Sacra*, II, 661, cf. 658) makes Dubricius bishop of Llandaff as well as archbishop of Caerleon (and cf. below, p. 216, n. 4); Gerald of Wales takes advantage of the loophole offered by Geoffrey (see above, note 1) to make David translate the see from Caerleon to St David's, and specifically quotes the prophecies of Merlin as evidence (*Opera*,

London, arose from the dust which he had thrown. But in any case, Geoffrey's love of mockery and mystification was such that we need not doubt that mockery was his intention. He was making fun of the pretensions of his contemporaries, for this if for no other reason, that he found them absurd. Early in his history, Geoffrey solemnly assures us that Dunuallo Molmutius composed the Molmutine laws in the British tongue; that Gildas turned them into Latin and King Alfred into English; and that they are still held in honour.[1] A man who could do this most certainly had a taste for scoffing at the treasured institutions of his day.

II

So far I have treated the chapters of St David's and Llandaff as Geoffrey himself treated them, as figures of fun. But if we are to understand how their claims arose and why they came to be treated by Geoffrey in this way, we must take a more sympathetic look at the world in which they had arisen.

Among the host of problems which faced the monks of Christ Church, Canterbury—the cathedral of the southern province—in the years immediately following the Norman Conquest, none was more pressing than their need to convince their new masters and the world at large that the cathedral possessed by right its ancient properties and privileges. They furnished their new archbishop, Lanfranc, with the materials with which he fought two prolonged battles: the battle for the properties of the see against the encroachments of Norman landowners, and the battle for the primacy of the see over York, which is with us still.[2] In fighting for their properties Canterbury was doing what every English cathedral and abbey had to do in the century following the Norman

---

III, ed. J. S. Brewer, 171, 401, cf. VI, 56, 101–2, 120; *De Invectionibus*, ed. W. S. Davies, 131). William of Newburgh (ed. R. Howlett, *Chrons. of the reigns of Stephen...*, I, 16) scouts the idea of an archbishopric of Caerleon in his celebrated attack on Geoffrey.

[1] *HRB*, II, 17; III, 5; G, 275, 282; F, 108, 113.

[2] On Lanfranc's struggle for the properties of the see, cf. A. J. Macdonald, *Lanfranc* (Oxford, 1926), 126 ff.; D. C. Douglas in *Historical Essays in honour of James Tait* (Manchester, 1933), 47 ff.; J. Le Patourel in *Studies in Medieval History presented to F. M. Powicke* (Oxford, 1948), 15 ff. On the dispute with York, cf. above, p. 209, n. 2, and C. N. L. Brooke, *Downside Review*, LXVIII (1950), 462 ff.; LXIX (1951), 210 ff. [See *addendum* on p. 242.]

Conquest; and in fighting for her primacy, she entered an arena in which the archbishops of France had been engaged for over 200 years.[1]

In origin, the titles 'primas' and 'prima sedes' seem to have been little more than honorific alternatives for 'archiepiscopus' and 'metropolis', and to have indicated primacy only over suffragan bishops. If in the course of time an archbishop's primacy came to have wider significance, it was at first a mere primacy of honour; a pale reflection of the general primacy of the see of Rome. But from the ninth century at least the word came to be used more and more with a technical significance, of an actual supremacy of one archbishop over another; and in the forged decretals of Pseudo-Isidore it was laid down that the extent of these primacies was to be based on the organisation of provinces in the later Roman empire. This organisation was known from the *Notitia Dignitatum* (and similar documents), to which the name of Pope Anacletus came to be attached.[2] The *Notitia Galliarum* was freely glossed and rewritten to fit contemporary claims. Thus Narbonne was primate of the provinces of Narbonensis; Lyons of Lugdunensis; Trier, the *caput* of Belgica Prima, was primate over Rheims, of the province of Belgica Secunda—a plea which raised such a storm from the French at the council of Rheims in 1148 that it had to be abandoned.[3] By analogy, there ought to be a single head for all the provinces of Spain and Britain: hence the pretensions of Toledo and Canterbury. None of these primacies was won without a struggle; and the struggles occupied the energies of numberless men, honest and dishonest alike. Thus Pope Calixtus II, a former archbishop of Vienne, sincerely believed the claims of his see, and treated them

[1] For what follows, see P. Hinschius, *System des katholischen Kirchenrechts*, I (Berlin, 1869), 581–629; H. Fuhrmann, 'Studien zur Geschichte mittelalterlicher Patriarchate', *Zeitschrift der Savigny-Stiftung für Rechtsgeschichte, Kan. Abt.* XXXIX–XLI (1953–5), esp. XL, 14 ff. (on Pseudo-Isidore and the ninth century), XL, 61 ff., XLI, 95 ff. (on the French primacies).

[2] Pseudo-Isidore (ed. Hinschius, Leipzig, 1863, 82–3) was responsible for the notion that the *Notitia* was a work issued by Pope Anacletus (Pseudo-Isidore in fact merely makes Anacletus say 'Civitates...conscriptas in quodam thomo mittimus'), the second after St Peter, specifically to ensure that the Christian ecclesiastical organisation followed the lines of Roman provincial organisation (cf. Fuhrmann, *art. cit.* XL, 24 ff.). For revisions of the *Not. Galliarum*, cf. Mommsen's edition (*Mon. Germ. Hist., Auct. Antiquiss.* IX, 552 ff.).

[3] John of Salisbury, *Historia Pontificalis*, ed. R. L. Poole (Oxford, 1927), 6 (for other claims, cf. 5–6, 93–6), ed. M. Chibnall (Nelson's Medieval Texts, London, 1956), 5–6.

with the greatest sympathy when he was Pope.[1] All these disputes were at their height in the late eleventh and early twelfth centuries, especially in France and England. They are the context of the more obscure and local ambitions of the sees of South Wales. Above all, the connection between the eleventh- and twelfth-century primacies and Roman provincial organisation explains how crucial was the evidence of British history in the second and succeeding centuries; and how so balanced a man as Gilbert Foliot could come to take the absurdities of Geoffrey of Monmouth's ecclesiastical geography so seriously.

The difficulty in establishing a claim to primacy in the tenth and eleventh centuries was that, however sincerely one might believe in it, historical proof was lacking, and documents could not be produced to support it.[2] Similarly, however strong might be a church's claim to property in Norman England, documentary evidence might never have existed, or, if it had existed, time and chance and the Danish invaders might have destroyed it or rendered it illegible. This is one of the reasons why the century following the Norman Conquest saw such a renaissance of historical research, saw the unearthing of lost or forgotten charters and the traditions of saintly founders. Histories of abbeys and cathedrals were written here and there; but the chief types of record produced were charters, and (especially in Wales) *Lives* of the saints. The eleventh-century chartulary of Landévennec in Brittany contains a long *Life* of the saint who founded the house (St Winwaloe) and a rather small collection of charters.[3] This seems to have been the pattern followed in Wales, although only two early collections survive in the *Life* and letters (so to speak) of St Cadoc of Llancarfan,[4] and in the *Book of Llandaff*. From one point of view, the aim and achievement of William of Malmesbury, who wrote *Lives* of the saints of Glastonbury Abbey, and compiled a history of the

---

[1] Cf. R. L. Poole, *Studies in Chronology and History*, ed. A. L. Poole (Oxford, 1934), 127–8.

[2] The idea of primacy is ancient, but the technical significance of the word was no older than Pseudo-Isidore. Since his work was universally accepted as genuine, it was inevitable that deductions should be made from the *Notitiae*; but any other foundation for such claims could only consist (as at Canterbury) of skilful interpretation of earlier documents and downright forgeries.

[3] *Cartulaire de Landévennec*, ed. Le Men et É. Ernault, *Mélanges historiques*, v (Coll. de docts. inédits, Paris, 1886), 540.

[4] *VSB*, 24–141. Similar material is attached to other saints' *Lives*, e.g. St Padarn's, *VSB*, 266–9.

house from the traditions and the written evidence (especially of charters) with which the monks of Glastonbury supplied him, are little different from those of Guerno, author of the forged privileges on which the primacy of Canterbury was based, forger, too, to half a dozen other houses besides,[1] or of the authors of the *Book of Llandaff*. All were historical research students; all were concerned to boost the morale of a great institution. Morally and intellectually there was a world of difference between William, one of the greatest historians of the later Middle Ages, and a gang of ingenious crooks. But it was the same set of needs and interests which gave them their chance.

For centuries St David had been a great name among the saints of Wales and Ireland, and he had been honoured in calendars and martyrologies with the honorific title of 'archbishop'.[2] The first sign of an attempt to make specific use of the tradition of the saint comes in the *Life* by Rhigyfarch, son of Sulien of Llanbadarn Fawr, twice bishop of St David's in the late eleventh century. Mrs Chadwick has argued[3] that Rhigyfarch's *Life* was written in or about 1081, in an attempt to boost the greatness of St David's shrine, and defend the humble Welsh see from encroachments by Canterbury or Armagh. Hitherto, I take it, St David's had been too remote politically and ecclesiastically to attract the attention or the envy of its great neighbours—and certainly of Canterbury. In Rhigyfarch's *Life* David is specifically made archbishop by the patriarch of Jerusalem, and given suffragans, St Padarn and St Teilo.[4] Subsequently, by the consent of all the bishops, kings, princes, magnates and all the orders he is made 'archbishop of the whole British race' and his *civitas* 'the metropolis of the whole country'. These phrases have a sinister ring for anyone who has studied the Canterbury forgeries of the preceding decade.[5]

---

[1] On William's *De Antiquitate* (ed. T. Hearne, *Adami de Domerham Historia*, I (Oxford, 1727)), see the indispensable study of J. Armitage Robinson, *Somerset Historical Essays* (London, 1921), ch. 1 and 2; on Guerno, W. Levison, *England and the Continent in the Eighth Century* (Oxford, 1946), 206 ff.; C. N. L. Brooke, *Downside Review*, art. cit., esp. LXIX, 231.

[2] S. M. Harris, *St David in the Liturgy* (Cardiff, 1940).

[3] Above, pp. 174 ff.   [4] *VSB*, 163–4.

[5] *VSB*, 166–7; cf. H. Böhmer, *Die Fälschungen Erzbischof Lanfranks von Canterbury* (Leipzig, 1902), 145–61 (I refer to individual privileges as CC 1–10). *VSB*, 166: omnium ordinum tocius Britannie gentis archiepiscopus...civitas eius tocius patrie metropolis...(CC 2: metropolitanus totius Britannie, etc.; CC 9: in...civitate metropolim...; CC 3: primatum omnium ecclesiarum

In creating Padarn and Teilo David's suffragans (if I have interpreted his meaning correctly), Rhigyfarch appears to imply that the leading bishops of South Wales were the successors of these saints. The bishop of St Padarn must have sat at Llanbadarn Fawr; and there is other evidence that Llanbadarn had once been the seat of a bishopric.[1] It did not survive the Norman Conquest (by Norman Conquest I mean the Norman Conquest of *England*); and there is no reason to suppose that there was ever a diocese of Llanbadarn, nor indeed, that the pre-Conquest bishops of Wales had dioceses in the modern sense at all.[2] But the bishopric of St Teilo is a more difficult, and a more important problem, to which we shall return anon.

The tradition that St David's had once been or ought to be the seat of an archbishopric survived the death of Bishop Sulien in 1091 and the return of his family to their old home at Llanbadarn Fawr—if, indeed, they had ever really left it. Whatever claim Rhigyfarch's *Life* may have been intended to promote, the establishment of the diocese of St David's and the campaign of the 1120's was the work of the *entourage* of the first Norman bishop of St David's.

Sometime before 1093 Arnulf of Montgomery established the first Norman castle at Pembroke; and from that time forward Pembrokeshire was the most stable centre of English power in South Wales.[3] In 1102 Henry I destroyed the great house of Bellême-Montgomery, and took Pembroke into his own hands; his castellan was Gerald of Windsor, one of the grandfathers of Gerald of Wales, and one of the husbands of the Lady Nest. It was apparently with a view to making Dyfed the base of the ecclesiastical as well as the civil conquest of South Wales that Bernard, chaplain and chancellor to Queen Matilda, was made bishop (under royal influence) in 1115.

Britannie, etc.—and cf. a bull of Alexander II closely connected with the forgeries, Eadmer, *Historia Novorum*, ed. M. Rule, 20: metropolis totius Britannie; CC 7: totius Anglie regionis; CC 6: universosque ordinum gradus). *VSB*, 166: David...summus *speculator* (cf. CC 7),...summus *predicator* (cf. CC *passim*)...patrie capud; and *VSB*, 167: omnis Brittanice gentis capud (CC 2: caput totius gentis Anglorum; and cf. note to John of Salisbury, *Letters*, I, ed. W. J. Millor, H. E. Butler and C. N. L. Brooke (Nelson's Medieval Texts, London, 1955), no. 116, p. 191). These links are slight, but it seems highly likely that Rhigyfarch was acquainted with movements in Canterbury. [See now p. 242.]

[1] Cf. above, p. 164; Haddan and Stubbs, *Councils and Ecclesiastical Documents*, I, 145–6; J. E. Lloyd, *Hist. of Wales*, I³ (London, 1939), 208 and n.
[2] *EA*, I, 44ff., etc.   [3] For what follows, see *ibid*. I, 114ff.

Bernard was certainly the most considerable figure in the Norman Conquest of the Welsh Church in the twelfth century. His achievement has been summarised by Dr Conway Davies thus:

He laid the foundations of the bishopric of St David's as a large yet well-organised diocese. He divided his diocese into effective territorial archdeaconries, having due regard for the historical background of the ancient Welsh kingdoms of Dyfed, Deheubarth, Brecheiniog, and Ceredigion. He subdivided those archdeaconries into rural deaneries, having due regard for the historical background of the ancient Welsh divisions of cantrefs and commotes. He developed a parochial organisation. He converted the ancient *clas* of St David's into a medieval cathedral chapter. He reorganised the property of the bishopric and the *clas* on partly feudal lines, but had due regard in the major part of the territories for the ancient Welsh law and custom. On the disciplinary side, for clergy and laity, he provided the machinery of ecclesiastical courts and officers, without endeavouring to impose impossible[1] moral maxims or ecclesiastical canons on an unreceptive or unwilling people. He brought his diocese into line, in most essential respects, with the English dioceses. The foundations which he laid were sometimes adapted, but generally securely built upon by his successors throughout the medieval period.[2]

His success was so complete that we tend to forget how hard-fought it was. When he became bishop he was the only effective diocesan in Wales; and when he died it was still doubtful whether the bishops of Bangor and St Asaph would ever establish themselves. Shortly after Bernard's death the bishopric of St Asaph came as an ironical reward to Geoffrey of Monmouth: it was at this time an honour of even more dubious value than in the eighteenth century, and the see was almost as shadowy as the diocese of Caerleon. It is doubtful if he ever resided.[3]

It is a remarkable tribute to the ability of Bernard of St David's that he came nearer than any other man—Gerald of Wales himself not excluded—to raising his see to the status of an archbishopric. There is some evidence that he was, for a while, in possession of a pallium in the late 1130's or early 1140's; but the details of the story are very obscure.[4] Indeed, there were clearly two stories, quite

---

[1] Perhaps one should rather say 'alien'.   [2] *Ibid.* I, 144.

[3] J. E. Lloyd, *Eng. Hist. Rev.* LVII (1942), 465.

[4] Cf. Tatlock, 266 and nn. Henry of Huntingdon (*Historia Anglorum*, ed. T. Arnold, 7, 10) twice refers to Caerleon as the former seat of an archbishopric, on the second occasion saying 'Tempore autem nostro recepit episcopus S. David pallium a papa, quod scilicet fuerat olim apud Kairlegion; sed statim tamen amisit'. These passages were not in Henry's first edition (of 1129: cf.

separate and both of them most imperfectly known. There is the story of how Bernard, a Norman of the Normans, was captivated by the legend of an independent Welsh Church, and so came to dedicate his later years to pursuing this phantom; and of how, in his turn, he captured the Welsh princes, and at the height of the great rebellions of Stephen's early years was accepted as primate by Owen Gwynedd and his brother Cadwalladr.[1] It looks, in fact, as if there were some political advantage in Bernard's campaign, though I doubt if he had calculated much on it in the first instance. It looks too as if he played the role in the Welsh Church in his last years which Theobald was playing in the English: a centre of ecclesiastical unity above the political chaos of the anarchy. The story is woefully obscure, and Bernard's confused loyalties cannot be disentangled: but it is salutary to remember when studying this period of Welsh history that a Welshman is not always consistently a Welshman, and a Norman almost never consistently an Englishman. But in the last analysis, so Gerald of Wales informs us,[2] Bishop Bernard, like so many of his successors, longed for translation to an English see.

The other story is set in the papal court, to which the original claim of the chapter of St Andrew and St David had been sent in the 1120's. It seems likely that Bishop Bernard took advantage of the death of the archbishop of Canterbury and political chaos in Wales in 1136 to renew his claim; and he may have won an initial success.[3] But the new archbishop, Theobald, was eventually able

F. Liebermann in *Forschungen zur deutschen Geschichte*, XVIII (1878), 276, F. Haverfield and G. Macdonald, *Roman Occupation of Britain* (Oxford, 1924), 292, Tatlock, 69 and n., 264 and n.), and are undoubtedly due in part to the influence of the *HRB*. Henry was not above interpreting the reference in the prophecies (above, p. 210, n. 1) as of an actual pallium in his own day, but it seems more likely that he was writing from personal knowledge; and it is even possible that the prophecy was inspired by similar knowledge. Even so, we cannot be certain that the pallium existed: it is strange that there is no other evidence of it; and it would be an obvious gambit in a campaign to acquire a pallium to start a rumour that one had recently been sent. Whatever lies behind it, Henry's note is not correct evidence; but if correct, the pallium was presumably supplied by Innocent II or one of his immediate successors, and repudiated (at the latest) by Eugenius III, before whom Bernard's effort finally foundered. It would be interesting to know what relation there was between Geoffrey's Caerleon and Henry of Blois' plan to become 'archiepiscopus occidentalis Anglie' as bishop of Winchester (*Hist. Pontificalis*, ed. Poole, 80, ed. Chibnall, 78).

[1] *EA*, I, 259–60.   [2] *Opera*, III, 153.
[3] Cf. *EA*, I, 192ff.; cf. also above, p. 216, n. 4 and H. Tillmann, *Die päpstlichen Legaten*, 51.

to prove (by the testimony of nearly half the English bishops) that Bernard had made profession of obedience to Canterbury when he was consecrated; and to this the Pope held him until the whole issue of right had been fully threshed out. Perhaps by chance, perhaps by design, it was due to be discussed at the Rheims council of 1148, when so many of the primacies of western Europe were examined and disputed.[1] But Bernard never got to Rheims; when the council met he was apparently sick and within a month he was a suitor at a higher court.[2]

The only rival to Bernard's power as bishop of St David's and the leading diocesan of Wales was the bishop of Llandaff, whose achievement was in some ways the exact converse of Bernard's.[3] Both Bernard and Urban of Llandaff established dioceses on the Norman or Continental model—Urban, if anything, even more fully than Bernard. But whereas Bernard was a Norman working from a Norman base in territory mainly Welsh, Urban was a Welshman with a base originally Welsh, working in territory mainly Norman. The church of Llandaff was a chapel when he found it, and he left it a cathedral. The name Llandaff means 'the church near the River Taff';[4] unlike so many place-names in *Llan*, it does not reveal the saint to whom it was dedicated; and it is a measure of the success with which Urban and his associates blinded his contemporaries and still blind us that we do not know to whom the church of Llandaff had originally been dedicated or whether it had been the centre of a diocese at all before his accession. Urban's *familia* forged a book—the *Liber Landavensis*; they may also have forged a diocese.

The Gwysaney manuscript of the *Liber Landavensis* (now on deposit in the National Library of Wales) is the most remarkable

---

[1] Cf. above, p. 212, n. 3.

[2] Bernard died in 1148, probably on April 22 (for the year, *EA*, I, 268 ff., cf. Gilbert Foliot, *Epistolae*, ed. J. A. Giles, I, no. 75; for the day, the Hereford obituary in R. Rawlinson, *Hist. and Antiquities of...Hereford* (London, 1717), Appendix, (11): 'Obitus Domini Bernardi episcopi'—the only Bishop Bernard known to have been connected with the see of Hereford is Bernard of St David's, who had custody of it, as a royal clerk, in 1101–2 (J. H. Round, *Calendar of Docts. preserved in France* (London, 1899), no. 1138; and the date fits well with the evidence of Foliot's letter). There is no record that he ever went to the council, which met on March 21, and since he is not among the bishops suspended for non-appearance, and had, indeed, every reason to be there, we may presume that he was prevented by sickness.

[3] On Urban see *EA*, I, 148 ff.; II, 515 ff.

[4] Bowen, *op. cit.* I n.

product of a great literary family, and one of the most interesting monuments of medieval Wales.[1] It was completed soon after the death of Bishop Urban in 1134,[2] as a memorial of his struggles and successes; to ensure that his successor should know how great a legacy he had entered into; and to prepare a jumping-off ground for further adventures. For some reason, it was never finished; but most probably we have the bulk of what it was intended to contain. It originally opened with the *Lives* of three saints: the first three bishops of Llandaff, St Dubricius, St Teilo, and St Oudoceus. The *Lives* are interspersed with charters granted to these saints; and the remainder of the *Book* consists in the main of charters and other documents connected with the twenty-six bishops of Llandaff between Oudoceus and Herewald, Urban's predecessor. Towards the end the bleak recital of charters is relieved by elaborate accounts of the election and consecration of successive bishops; and the blank spaces in the manuscript have been filled with papal bulls and other authentic documents of the time of Bishop Urban. The *Life of St Teilo* is an older work, written about 1120 or earlier by Urban's brother Stephen.[3] The version in the *Liber Landavensis* is interpolated and in part rewritten. Excluding this one *Life*, some other hagiographical material and the contemporary documents, the whole of the book was undoubtedly composed by a single author. He used older material—a great deal of it—but he has so completely rewritten his material that his hand is visible in every line. The charters are a classic statement of the principles of fake diplomatic. Centuries pass; dynasties come and go. But the charters of the bishops of Llandaff never vary in their form, which is a curious amalgam of local custom and the practice of the chanceries of Europe in the late eleventh or early twelfth century. There is variety in the opening of the charters, which is sometimes a formal address, sometimes the tale of how a savage Welsh princeling was in need of repentance. The outcome in either event

[1] The fullest description of *LL* is in the *National Library of Wales Journal*, IV (1945–6), 123–57, by E. D. Jones; there are illustrations and facsimiles in Evans's edition and in Jones, *art. cit.*

[2] See above, pp. 204 ff.

[3] Or Geoffrey, as he is more commonly named. But the sole evidence is an entry in the text of the life in MS. Cotton Vesp. A. xiv, reading 'a magistro Galfrido', with the correction 'i(d est) Stephano' interlined. The corrector seems more likely to be right; but there is no other evidence about the man. The life seems to have been written after the translation to Llandaff was contemplated, but before the full development of its legendary basis.

is the same: a grant of land to God, St Peter, St Dubricius, St Teilo, St Oudoceus and the bishop of Llandaff, in perpetuity; 'pro salute anime sue' or 'pro anima sua', 'cum omni sua libertate sine ullo censu terreno, in campo et in aquis et in silva et in pascuis', with a list of boundaries in Welsh and a number of witnesses, concluded by a simple (but adequate) anathema. The words vary, but only like the variations on a musical theme; phrases from the charters creep into the *Lives* of the saints, and *vice versa*; even the annals of the later bishops have been affected by the process of assimilation, so that each bishop whose death is mentioned (like St Dubricius and St Teilo) 'migrated to the Lord', and all those (like St Oudoceus) whose consecration is described received lay investiture at the hands of an English king, and made profession to an English archbishop. A single mind presides over the whole enterprise, warped perhaps, but exceedingly ingenious.[1]

The materials from which the author worked have mostly disappeared; but sufficient survives for us to describe his tools with some precision. The *Life of Teilo* is an earlier work of the same circle, largely based on Rhigyfarch's *Life of St David*; apart from this *Life* the author of the *Liber Landavensis* knew the first *Life of St Samson*, the *Life of St Turiau*, bishop of Dol (whom he identifies with St Teilo), the first *Life of St Cadoc* (by Lifris of Llancarfan), the local legends of various parts of South Wales, and—for the *Lives* of the three saints—precious little else. The *Life of St Dubricius* is the *Vita Samsonis* and water; and the *Life of St Oudoceus* (who never existed) is even less substantial.[2] In all these works he showed himself a skilful exponent of the Welsh hagiographical tradition, but nothing more. His originality is revealed in the charters.

The *Life of St Cadoc* by Lifris of Llancarfan, son of Bishop Herewald, Urban's predecessor, has attached to it fourteen charters —a kind of diminutive chartulary of the old Welsh monastery of

---

[1] For an analysis of *LL* and its method of composition, see Appendix I.

[2] For the sources of the *Lives* of Dubricius, Teilo, Oudoceus and Samson in *LL*, see the works of Doble and Fawtier already cited (pp. 203, n. 3, 206, n. 1, 209, n. 3) and Doble, 'St Oudoceus', *Journal of Theological Studies*, XLIII (1942), 204 ff.; XLIV (1943), 59 ff. Doble (*Teilo*, 15) suggests that the *Life of David* used by Stephen was not Rhigyfarch's, but a common source; this I do not accept, but the point cannot be argued at length here. The *Life of Dubricius* also shows knowledge of local Monmouthshire and Herefordshire legends.

Llancarfan.[1] There is reason to doubt that they are genuine in their present form; but no reason to doubt that they are fairly closely based on the sort of informal entries in the margin of a Gospel Book which we know from the *Book of St Chad*[2] to have been one at least of the ways in which grants to Welsh churches were recorded in the ninth and tenth centuries. By great good fortune, these charters were used by the author of the *Liber Landavensis*.[3] A comparison of the two reveals two outstanding facts: that the charters are completely rewritten from beginning to end so that almost nothing remains of the original save the association in time of a bishop, a local prince and a gift of land; and secondly, that the gifts originally made to Llancarfan have been in each case transferred by the forger to Llandaff.

It has been shown by E. D. Jones[4] that if we arrange the kings of Morgannwg in the order suggested by the charters in the *Book of Llandaff* they coincide almost exactly with the relevant genealogy in the Harleian pedigrees. From this one might deduce one of two things: either the names of the kings are derived from genuine charters, or the forger had in front of him a copy of the genealogy. The truth, I am convinced, is a mingling of the two; and I believe that the forger worked something like this.[5] He had a mass of charters and at least three genealogies to work from—two for Morgannwg which we know from the Harleian and Jesus collections, and a genealogy (not otherwise known) of the kings of

---

[1] Ed. A. W. Wade-Evans, *VSB*, 124–37, with a commentary by the same writer in *Archaeologia Cambrensis*, LXXXVII (1932), 151–65. Cf. above, pp. 191, 195, 199.

They bear a sufficient resemblance to the ninth-century charters in the *Book of St Chad* (see next note)—especially in their anathemas—for it to be reasonably certain that they are based on earlier grants; and indeed there is no reason to doubt their substantial authenticity. But they seem to have been harmonised (and some of them perhaps translated) by an antiquary of the late eleventh or early twelfth century, possibly by Lifris himself. The same anathema occurs somewhat too often, and the phrase 'liberam et quietam ab omni terreno servitio' (*VSB*, 130, cf. 126, 132) suggests a late hand: it is the version of this ancient formula current in England in the late eleventh century and later. Furthermore, some of the charters have been moved back to the age of St Cadoc himself—a manœuvre made easy by the medieval practice of making grants to the patron saint of a church as to a living person (there is a striking example of this personification in the St Chad charters, to one of which St Teilo is witness, and to another God himself!). We seem to have here the first lesson in revising old charters, which was to end in the *LL*.

[2] *LL* xliii–xlvii. Cf. pp. 125 f. above.

[3] Doble, 'St Oudoceus', 210 ff.; E. D. Jones, *art. cit.* 147–8.

[4] *Art. cit.*   [5] For what follows, see Appendix I.

Archenfield. He also had some annals, local traditions and his own knowledge from which to reconstruct the more recent history. From the charters he deduced which bishop should be associated with which king in the genealogies, and so was able to group his bishops roughly in three blocks, corresponding (1) to the Archenfield genealogy, (2) to the Morgannwg genealogies, and (3) to the known facts of recent history. These three blocks he placed end to end in that order, and put a few other unidentifiable bishops in where he had space. Then he set to work to expand and assimilate the charters, and to compose elaborate witness lists out of the names he had before him. These witness lists were so skilfully and plausibly devised that it has proved possible for a modern scholar to reconstruct the chronology of the abbots of the three leading monasteries of Glamorgan from them.[1] But they are certainly faked, although in the absence of the vast majority of the originals off which the forger worked we cannot tell how completely they have been faked.

The technique I have described entitles the author to a high place among twelfth-century antiquaries as a student of historical method; but before we discuss his identity, we must consider the motive and achievement of the work. To whom was it addressed? To what extent were the rights claimed genuine rights? What part did it play in the making of the diocese of Llandaff?

There is a certain similarity between the endeavour lying behind the *Book of Llandaff* and the creation of the county of Flanders 200 years earlier by Count Baldwin II.[2] Viking invaders had cleared the old Carolingian hierarchy out of the counties which formerly comprised what we call Flanders, and left the country desolate. Baldwin II went round (like an American speculator buying up a defunct railway system) collecting the empty titles which no one wanted any more. He was soon count of the whole of Flanders, on paper; and it only remained for him to realise his assets, drive the Vikings into the sea, resurrect the old comital authority, and build a ring of forts against a renewal of the Viking onslaught, and Flanders was his. The Norman invaders of Glamorgan did not destroy the churches and monasteries of the land; they pocketed them. The conqueror of Glamorgan was

---

[1] A. Anscombe, in *Celtic Review*, VI and VII (1909–12).

[2] The best recent study is F.-L. Ganshof, *La Flandre sous les premiers comtes*[3] (Brussels, 1949).

Robert fitzHamon, who about the turn of the century presented a great part of the ecclesiastical property which he had acquired by conquest to two English abbeys. In particular, the ancient monastery of Llancarfan was handed over to Gloucester Abbey, and one of the other chief monasteries of the area, Llantwit, went to form part of the original endowment of fitzHamon's new foundation at Tewkesbury.[1] Llancarfan was only one of several ancient houses which Gloucester acquired at about this time; and the abbot of Gloucester was evidently looked on as the man to organise the resurrection of monastic life in the Welsh Church; so much so that in the days of the anarchy Gilbert Foliot as abbot of Gloucester seems to have acted as the archbishop of Canterbury's chief representative for treating with the princes and bishops of Wales, as well as providing a postal link with the English counties under the control of the empress.[2] It is reasonably clear that there was nothing in these monastic houses which the Normans (or anyone else) would have recognised as regular or monastic. The urge to make monastic properties serve genuinely monastic communities no doubt provided the religious excuse for their expropriation by Robert fitzHamon and his like; and a notion that they were his *Eigenkirchen* by right of conquest doubtless provided the legal excuse for the action—if indeed the Norman conquerors troubled themselves with legal excuses at all. The family from which Llandaff drew its leaders were hereditary leaders of the monastery of St Cadoc of Llancarfan, and so bound to take notice of these losses.[3] They had the intelligence to see that half measures were inadequate to deal with such a crisis; they fought physical violence with moral and legal violence of an extreme kind. Like Baldwin II accumulating the vacant countships of Flanders they claimed that the properties of all these three houses and several more belonged to the see of Llandaff: they claimed everything the

[1] Henry I's confirmation of Robert fitzHamon's grants to Tewkesbury (*EA*, II, 614; H. W. C. Davis, *Regesta Regum Anglo-Normannorum*, II, ed. C. Johnson and H. A. Cronne, no. 847) is spurious, but there seems no reason to doubt the reality of the grants, which were confirmed to Tewkesbury by the bishop of Llandaff in the middle of the century (*EA*, II, 659; cf. *ibid*. 636 for a settlement between the bishop of Llandaff and the abbey in 1146). Gloucester's possession of Llancarfan was the subject of a series of arrangements between the abbey and the old Llancarfan family (*ibid*. II, 517 ff.).

[2] This will be discussed in the introduction to the forthcoming edition of Gilbert Foliot's letters by A. Morey and C. N. L. Brooke.

[3] Cf. *EA*, II, 506 ff.

Normans had taken and a good bit more; and they took their claim straight to Rome.[1]

The bull of confirmation which Urban received from Pope Calixtus II in 1119 confirmed to Llandaff Cathedral several of the leading houses of the diocese and much other property; and at the same time Bishop Urban was pressing for newly defined diocesan boundaries. The principle on which the Llandaff chapter had defined its rights has an extraordinarily modern ring. They claimed jurisdiction over a large segment of the diocese of St David's and over Archenfield (now in the diocese of Hereford), on the ground that some bishops whom they imagined to have been bishops of Llandaff had once exercised jurisdiction in these areas. But however little we may think of the claim, it is clear that some arbitrary principle had to be called into play to define the area of the diocese, since hitherto there had been no defined boundaries at all. The case on the boundaries was fought out in the papal court and up and down England; Hereford won Archenfield very rapidly, and in the long run St David's preserved the whole of Ystrad Tywi. Of the properties she claimed, Llandaff successfully defended her right to a proportion. The basis of the claim to the properties was twofold: she first of all collected all the charters of the old communities and rewrote them in the manner I have described; and she then added to the properties thus acquired anything which belonged to her three saintly founders, St Dubricius, St Teilo and St Oudoceus, that is, virtually any churches dedicated to those saints in South Wales.[2] The cult of St Dubricius centred in Archenfield; and whether Llandaff claimed Archenfield because it was Dubricius's country or claimed Dubricius to shore up a claim to Archenfield is impossible to decide. Almost certainly, the truth (once again) is a mingling of the two. But it is remarkable that if one plots the cult of Dubricius and Teilo on the map, their great

[1] For what follows, cf. *ibid*. 1, 147 ff.

[2] This seems to be the only explanation of the principles on which Llandaff's substantial claims were selected. In the early Middle Ages a church was regarded as the property of the saint to whom it was dedicated; and the large number of churches dedicated to the saints—especially to Teilo—among the properties claimed by Llandaff makes it clear that possession of the saint and his properties was the basis of a number of the claims. The evidence cited above for the use of the Llancarfan charters also shows that an effort was made to absorb the property of the ancient monasteries. For example, the church of Llantwit was claimed, and by analogy we may suppose its properties too; but we have no early charters by which to check them.

centres lie in a wide arc round Glamorgan—they had few churches within the county—and they cover exactly the territory claimed for his diocese by Urban.[1]

In 1120 the inauguration of the new diocese was solemnised with the foundation of the cathedral and the translation of the relics of Dubricius from Bardsey Island.[2] It seems that they already possessed one of St Teilo's three surviving bodies. Quite apart from his Archenfield connection, it was a stroke of genius to claim St Dubricius, a man with a great place in the early traditions of the Welsh Church, but without any binding local association to any other part of Wales. Teilo raises a more difficult problem. Urban's predecessor, Herewald, had undoubtedly performed episcopal functions primarily in Glamorgan, although he had no fixed diocese, and (so far as we can tell) no fixed cathedral.[3] But it seems likely that if he had a centre to his diocese, it was dedicated to St Teilo; there is some faint but converging evidence to suggest that Teilo was associated with the bishopric of Glamorgan before Bishop Urban cleaned the slate.[4] The easiest solution would be

[1] For the cult of Dubricius and Teilo, cf. Doble, *St Dubricius* (with a map on p. 33), *St Teilo* (map on p. 40); Bowen, *op. cit.* figs. 8A, 15, pp. 36ff., 56ff.; W. Rees, *Hist. Atlas of Wales* (Cardiff, 1951), pl. 25a. Apart from a Holy Well near Llancarfan, Monmouth and St Maugham's are the places with known Dubricius dedications nearest to Llandaff, and Merthyr Mawr (Glam.) the nearest for Teilo. The age of most of the dedications is completely uncertain, but many were undoubtedly established by the early twelfth century.

[2] *LL*, 5, 84ff. There is no evidence that Urban was called, or called himself, bishop of Llandaff before 1119 (*LL* 87–8): the charter of Henry I of 1107 which he witnesses with that title is spurious (see above, p. 223, n. 1).

[3] In addition, the circumstantial account of Bishop Herewald's activities in Archenfield (*LL*, 277ff.) must be substantially genuine, but like most things in *LL*, one cannot be sure that it has not been appropriated from another bishop. *EA*, II, 632, no. L 78, shows us Bishop Urban treated as episcopal superior of Llanthony Priory (Mon., later dioc. St David's) in 1131, and when Robert de Bethune became prior well after 1108 but before *c.* 1123 (cf. J. C. Dickinson, *Origins of the Austin Canons* (London, 1950), 111; *Ancient Charters*, ed. J. H. Round (Pipe Roll Soc., 1888), no. 11).

[4] In the days of Gerald of Wales (i.e. the late twelfth century), the church of Llandaff seems to have been regarded as essentially Teilo's church (*Opera*, VI, 67, 170; cf. the *Vita S. Caradoci* in *Nova Legenda Angliae*, ed. C. Horstman, I (Oxford, 1901), 174—a work probably based on the lost *Life* by Gerald). Similarly, the *Life of Teilo* seems to be the earliest hagiographical element in *LL* (for its composition, cf. Doble, *St Teilo*, 5ff.), and the privilege of Teilo the first of the forged charters—it was referred to already in Bishop Urban's letter of 1119 (*LL*, 87–8) which was evidently the first step in the campaign at the papal curia. Part of the existing Teilo privilege (*LL*, 118ff.) is in the form of a papal bull, and is almost identical in wording with the Dubricius privilege (70f.) and very similar to genuine papal bulls of 1119 and 1128 (89ff., 30ff.). It is possible that

to say that Llandaff itself was an old community dedicated to Teilo, anciently associated with the bishop. We know that in the ninth century there had been a bishop of 'Teilo', and the see which produced the *Book of St Chad* may have been centred in Llandaff. This is still the simplest theory, and it cannot (I think) be disproved. Nevertheless, I find it hard to believe. There is not a scrap of evidence that Llandaff was a place of any significance, politically or ecclesiastically, before the Norman lords of Glamorgan built their chief castle at Cardiff a couple of miles away.[1] If Llandaff had been one of Teilo's chief churches, we should expect to find it in the centre of the area in which his cult flourished. In fact it lies twenty miles from the nearest Teilo church; and the Teilo area lies mainly outside Glamorgan altogether. If one had to guess where the seat of the ninth-century bishop of Teilo had lain, my vote would be for Llandeilo Fawr, in the north of Ystrad Tywi, lying from this time forward in the diocese of St David's; and this seems to be the commonest opinion among scholars today.[2] The only thing certain about the origin of Llandaff is that in great part it was an act of creation, of very daring creation, by Bishop Urban and his associates; the extent of their creative work is impossible to gauge. But we can be sure that their methods were violent, however much we may sympathise with the intolerable situation which they had inherited.

It may seem extraordinary that so daring a series of inventions should have imposed on anyone even in the ages of faith. But we must remember that the audience to which the Llandaff forgeries were mainly addressed was a distant audience; and that even if it

---

it is based on one of these; but it is perhaps more probable that it was forged by someone accustomed to the formulae of the papal chancery in or before 1119, and is the document referred to by Urban. Cf. also Rhigyfarch's reference to St Teilo (cited above, p. 214).

[1] It is fair to say that we have very little evidence for the history of this area earlier than the *LL*; and we are in danger of treating the *LL* either too credulously or altogether too sceptically. There must be an element of truth at least in its eleventh-century documents; but it cannot be too strongly emphasised that all the pre-Urban documents in the book, *in their present form*, are the work of wholly unscrupulous forgers, and in the absence of any control of their statements, they can very rarely be used as secure evidence.

[2] So, for example, Doble, *St Teilo*, 4. Llandeilo Fawr (Carm.) is given as one of the seven 'bishop's seats' in Dyfed in the list appended to the Welsh laws (Haddan and Stubbs, *Councils and Ecclesiastical Docts.* I, 280–1). Dr Conway Davies, *EA*, I, 184–5, suggests that Llandaff was a daughter house of Llandough: his argument is ingenious, but highly conjectural.

tried to ascertain the true facts, after the Norman usurpation and at a time when dioceses were being arbitrarily defined in a land formerly innocent of them, there were no true facts (in any simple sense of the term) to find. The ultimate decision (barring violence by the Welsh princes) lay with the English king, the English bishops and the Pope; and the *Book of Llandaff* was well calculated to appeal to these distant potentates. To the king it told of a line of bishops who submitted faithfully to lay investiture from England; to the archbishop it told of a line of Welsh bishops who had never doubted that they should be subject to Canterbury, in spite of being the successors of three saintly archbishops and of a greater than St David; to the Pope it revealed a structure of rights firmly founded on papal privileges, especially the so-called 'privilege of Teilo', which is based verbatim on some genuine privilege.[1] The enterprise was altogether too bold for complete success; but in point of fact the bishopric of Llandaff came out of the struggles which followed the floating of its claims firmly established within Glamorgan, and possessed of a good deal more property than it probably had any original right to.

The *Book of Llandaff* itself is the end, not the beginning, of these struggles; only a few of the documents in it were certainly used by Bishop Urban, though the material was in the making in his time; the rest were finally put together shortly after his death as *pièces justificatives*, as it were, of his career. I have said that the book itself has a single author; but he was not, of course, the author of the original claims. He was evidently closely associated with the circle of Bishop Urban; but it is to that circle as a whole, and especially to the bishop himself, that we must give credit for the creation of the diocese. At the centre of the bishop's *familia* lay the family of Llancarfan, the relatives of his predecessor Herewald. One member of the family had written the great *Life of St Cadoc*, another had written the original *Life of Teilo*.[2] It is natural to

---

[1] Cf. above, p. 225, n. 4.

[2] The ramifications of the family have been thoroughly examined in *EA*, II, 506–37. Some of the evidence for relationship is tenuous, and an exact family tree cannot be constructed; but even so the picture of a great ecclesiastical clan is very remarkable. The charters which show Lifris (author of the first *Life of St Cadoc*) as son of Bishop Herewald, archdeacon of Glamorgan and master of St Cadoc, are spurious (*LL*, 271–5); and although the facts of his career would be well known when the *LL* was composed, his archdeaconry at least is probably an anachronism—part of the campaign to give Llandaff the appearance of a normal diocese. Bishop Urban was certainly related to the Llancarfan family

suppose that it was a member of this family circle who completed the great work of the family by compiling the *Book of Llandaff*.

Natural, but not inevitably correct. Discussion of the authorship of the *Lives* of the Welsh saints has been bedevilled by the fallacy that the author must be personally interested in one of the communities in which the saint was specially honoured; just as scholars used at one time to talk as if the author of a forged charter must be a monk of the house in whose interest the forgery was perpetrated. I have already mentioned the case of Guerno, monk and (by his own confession) a professional forger. It is coming to be more generally realised that forgery was a profession;[1] and that even if the inspiration for forgery must come from within the house, and even if local men sometimes dabbled in it, it was normal and natural to call in a professional forger for the work itself. With *Lives* of the saints, we are dealing for the most part with more honest activities; but equally with specialised activities performed by recognised experts. No one would produce the fact that William of Malmesbury wrote on the history and the saints of Glastonbury as evidence that he was a monk of that house. Yet Professor Tatlock argued that Caradoc of Llancarfan, a more humble colleague of William's, was a monk of Glastonbury on the ground that he wrote a *Life of St Gildas* in the Glastonbury interest; and Canon Doble refused to allow that he was author of the *Life of Iltut* on the ground that he was not an inmate of Llantwit Major.[2] There is conclusive evidence that Caradoc wrote a *Life* of St Cadoc and St Gildas; and he probably also wrote *Lives* of St Cyngar (for the canons of Wells) and St Iltut, and possibly one or two more.[3] He was certainly connected with the ancient house of Llancarfan, from which he took his name; but it would be fantastic to say that he was also a member of Llantwit, a canon of

(although it is little more than assumption that everyone with the surname 'of Llancarfan' belonged to a single clan), and we know the names of two of his brothers (Esni the dean and Stephen, author of the *Life of St Teilo*, for whom see above, p. 219, n. 3). Similarly, the position of Bishop Uthred (if any) and Bishop Nicholas ap Gwrgant (1148–83) cannot be established; but we may probably accept the reading of two MSS. of the *Brut y Tywysogyon*, which make him 'vab Gwrgant *escob*', i.e. son of *Bishop* Urban (*Brut y Tywysogyon* . . . *Red Book of Hergest Version*, ed. T. Jones (Cardiff, 1955), 126–7 and nn.).

[1] Cf. Levison, *op. cit.* 210; C. N. L. Brooke, *art. cit.* (p. 211, n. 2), esp. LXIX, 230–1; Dorothy Whitelock, *English Historical Documents* (London, 1955), 339.

[2] Tatlock in *Speculum*, XIII (1938), 141; G. H. Doble, *St Iltut* (Cardiff, 1944), 29.

[3] See below, Additional Note II, pp. 233–4.

Wells and a monk of Glastonbury. It is virtually certain that he was none of these things: he was simply a professional hagiographer.

Caradoc was at least the third hagiographer which the Llancarfan circle had produced; and there may have been more. His hagiographical activities were not of the most honest; but he may have been more naïve than knavish, though that is to put a kindly interpretation on some of his activities.[1] But it is certain that the Llancarfan family could breed forgers as well as hagiographers: the genius or geniuses who devised the great plan I have been outlining had the stuff of great forgers in them; and one member of the clan of the next generation was strongly suspected of forging papal bulls in his own interest.[2] We may therefore conclude that, although there is nothing impossible in supposing that Bishop Urban called in an outsider to compile the *Liber Landavensis* itself, the hypothesis is redundant: there was plenty of native talent within his own *familia* for such a task.

Can we go further, and identify the author of the book? We can certainly make a guess, but I very much doubt if we can make more than a guess. There are four distinctive features of the work, its style, its subject-matter, the circle which inspired it, and the extraordinary historical (or quasi-historical) skill of its compiler; and, for what they are worth, each of them points in the same direction. Canon Doble observed some likeness in the style of the *Liber Landavensis* and the works of Caradoc of Llancarfan; but he hinted (I think correctly) that they were probably quite common at the time, or at best only proved the influence of a school, not a single hand.[3] We have already seen how closely the book is connected with the circle and the family of Bishop Urban. After Urban's death at the papal curia, the Pope wrote to the archbishop of Canterbury letters of protection for Urban's clerks (five of whom are named) and also his relations, of whom two are named, Caradoc priest and Gugan of Llancarfan.[4] The identification of

---

[1] Even if we confine our attention to the *Lives* certainly by Caradoc, the *Life of Cadoc* is an arbitrary revision of the *Life* by Lifris (see below, pp. 235–6), and the *Life of Gildas* is fiction eked out by stories from the *Lives* of Cadoc and David (cf. Lot, *op. cit.* 267 ff.; it has themes in common with other *Lives*, e.g. of Cyngar and Iltut, but we cannot usually tell which is the source, which the copy). The *Life of Cyngar*, if it is Caradoc's, seems to be pure invention from beginning to end.

[2] *The Letters of John of Salisbury*, i, ed. W. J. Millor, H. E. Butler, and C. N. L. Brooke (Nelson's Medieval Texts, London, 1955), no. 57—probably, though not certainly, a member of the clan.

[3] See below, Additional Note III, pp. 234–5.   [4] *EA*, II, 633–4.

Caradoc with Caradoc of Llancarfan is very probable,[1] and confirms the natural conjecture that he was a relative of Urban's, and so also related to Lifris of Llancarfan (whose *Life* of St Cadoc, *pace* Father Grosjean, Caradoc rewrote)[2] and Stephen, author of the *Vita Teilonis*. Caradoc was on any showing the most prolific hagiographer of the circle. Finally, the *Liber Landavensis* is a historical reconstruction (among other things) of a brilliant and original kind. The fundamental historical principle is to deduce a succession of bishops from a collection of charters, and to date the charters from the kings who granted them. This may seem normal to us; but it was extremely abnormal in the twelfth century. The only other example known to me from this country at about the same period is William of Malmesbury's *De antiquitate Glastoniensis ecclesie*, written between 1129 and 1139.[3] It would be much easier to understand the *Liber Landavensis* if we could suppose that the author had been to school with William of Malmesbury, had either read or, better still, had been present while the author was writing the *De antiquitate*. We therefore inquire if any member of the Llandaff *familia* had a connection with Glastonbury or Malmesbury at about this time; and the answer is that Caradoc himself wrote a *Life of Gildas* for the monks of Glastonbury; that it was written in the 1120's or the 1130's (more probably the latter); and that it bears some relation, not easy to define, to the *De antiquitate*.[4]

---

[1] It has been suggested by Dr Conway Davies, *EA*, II, 517 n. Tatlock's attempt (*Speculum*, XIII (1938), 145–9) to identify Caradoc of Llancarfan with the Master Caratocus of the *Life of Elgar* (*LL*, 2) has thrown the chronology of Caradoc's life and writings into some confusion. It is really impossible to identify a man who was a distinguished teacher *c.* 1088 with a man who was described by Geoffrey of Monmouth as his own contemporary fifty years later, and it is much more probable that Master Caratocus was St Caradoc, the last of the Welsh saints, who had been at the court of Rhys ap Tewdr (1081–93) as a young man, and died in 1124 (on him see S. Baring-Gould and J. Fisher, *Lives of the British Saints*, II (London, 1908), 75 ff.—they suggest this identification on 76 n.—and above, p. 225, n. 4).   [2] See below, Additional Note IV, pp. 235–6.
[3] Armitage Robinson, *Somerset Historical Essays*, 4.
[4] If we took the text of the *De antiquitate* as it stands in Hearne's edition, there would be close verbal links (cf. F. Lot, *Romania*, XXVII (1898), 564–7); but the only relevant passage certainly authentic is William's account of Gildas as given in later editions of the *Gesta Regum* (ed. W. Stubbs, I, 24), from which it is clear that William was not acquainted with Caradoc's version of the legend. Doubtless this passage, or the legend it enshrines, was Caradoc's starting point.
  There is a verbal connection between the account of King Lucius in the *De antiquitate* and in *LL* (see Appendix II), but only a slight one. It is possible, even likely, that *LL* (or rather, the *De statu*) is a conflation of Bede and William, but the point cannot be established: it is not impossible, nor even seriously im-

This does not amount to proof; but I doubt if a better candidate for the authorship of the *Liber Landavensis* can be found than Caradoc and I am sure that he was the sort of man who wrote it.

Our investigation began with Geoffrey of Monmouth, and with Geoffrey it must end; for with him lies the last and most tantalising word on Caradoc of Llancarfan.

The kings who have ruled in Wales from that time [he writes in his epilogue] I leave as a theme for Caradoc of Llancarfan, my contemporary (*contemporaneo meo*), and those of the Saxons for William of Malmesbury and Henry of Huntingdon: but I forbid them to say anything of the kings of the Britons, since they have not that book written in Breton which Walter archdeacon of Oxford brought out of Brittany; which is a true account of their history; and which I have thus in these princes' honour taken pains to translate into Latin.[1]

Four of Geoffrey's contemporaries are named in this passage— Walter archdeacon of Oxford, evidently his accomplice; Henry, Walter's colleague and archdeacon of Huntingdon, evidently singled out to be one of the first and most considerable victims of the fraud;[2]

probable, that other versions of the Lucius legend were current at this time, from which the two might derive independently. The link is too slight to prove direct borrowing; but William's statement that the emissaries' names are lost is just the sort of thing to inspire a Llandaff forger to invent them. If borrowing there was, we are involved in a chronological difficulty. The sequence seems to be William of Malmesbury: Llandaff: St David's. Since William's tract cannot be earlier than November 1129 (see above) nor the St David's letter later than early 1130, we are forced to date them all very close together. On the other hand (*a*) it is likely enough that the two Welsh documents were stimulated by the crucial stage in the dispute between the two sees which arose in 1129 (*EA*, I, 176–7); (*b*) the argument in the text suggests that Caradoc may have seen William at work, i.e. have seen the *De antiquitate* before it was completed—in which case he may have written the *De statu* or provided its author with the passage from William a year or two before 1129; an alternative possibility (*c*) is that the St David's letter is a forgery (see below, Additional Note I).

[1] *HRB*, epilogue; G, 536; F, 303.

[2] Although an archdeacon in the diocese in which Geoffrey lived, and a colleague of Geoffrey's accomplice, Henry was left to 'happen on' the history in France in January 1139, as he tells us in one of his letters (Robert de Torigni, *Chronique*, ed. L. Delisle, I, 97 ff.). This can hardly have been more than a few months after the completion of the *HRB*, and so I accept Tatlock's date of 1138 for that event (*op. cit.* 433 ff.). In discussing the date of *HRB*, too much has sometimes been made of the political condition of England, and of the difficulty of supposing that Geoffrey's dedicatees were on opposite sides when he dedicated the book. But no one was to realise in 1138 that the rebellions of that year were the prelude to prolonged anarchy; the Church sometimes acted as if there were no dispute between the leading magnates; and in any case it was not a bad idea to have patrons in both camps.

William of Malmesbury, the greatest historian of the day, who had provided Geoffrey with much of his understanding of historical technique, and may also have been the first to give him the idea of celebrating King Arthur in 'a true history'.[1] William was somewhat older than the rest of these men; but there is no reason to doubt that Walter and Henry, who both died (like Geoffrey) in the 1150's, were approximately his contemporaries. Why, then, is Caradoc singled out as 'my contemporary'? It is possible that they were in fact contemporaries in some special sense; perhaps even born on the same day. But *contemporaneus* is an exceedingly rare word, and Geoffrey would hardly have used it without special reason. The word is known to the editors of the *Thesaurus Linguae Latinae* from only one passage, which appears to be an addition to the text of Aulus Gellius made by a medieval scribe.[2] It asserts that M. Varro and P. Nigidius *contemporaneos fuisse* of (or to) Caesar and Cicero. This simply means that they lived about the same time; but the implication of the passage is that you can identify the age of the two lesser prose authors by the great luminaries of the age. If Geoffrey had a similar idea in mind, he is saying (with characteristic bravado) that Caradoc was a lesser exponent of an art of which he (Geoffrey) was the supreme master of the age. Even if this is accepted, it still remains an open question whether they were contemporaries in writing Welsh history or in composing historical forgeries; and the analogy is hardly sufficient ground for an assured interpretation of Geoffrey's meaning. But whatever the explanation, I am inclined to think that the prominent place which Geoffrey gives to Caradoc in his epilogue is an insinuation that Caradoc was his colleague—'mon semblable, mon frère'—and I am sure, from his references to Dubricius, Teilo and Samson, that Geoffrey knew a good deal more than he ought to have known about what was afoot at St David's and Llandaff. I have given it as my opinion that the *Book of Llandaff*, whether written by Caradoc or another, was written by a member of the Llancarfan circle. But the point cannot be wholly proved: they may have hired an assassin from outside the walls. If it was not

---

[1] Cf. his *Gesta Regum* (ed. Stubbs), I, 11: 'Hic est Artur de quo Britonum nugae hodieque delirant; dignus plane quem non fallaces somniarent fabulae, sed *veraces* praedicarent *historiae*, quippe qui labantem patriam diu sustinuerit, infractasque civium mentes ad bellum acuerit ....'

[2] Gellius, XIX, 14 (in the Teubner ed., ed. C. Hosius (1903), II, 257 n.): 'contemporaneos fuisse Caesari et Ciceroni M. Varronem et P. Nigidium.'

written by Caradoc, then I should feel tempted to resuscitate the old and much abused theory that it was the work of Geoffrey of Monmouth himself.

ADDITIONAL NOTES

I. THE AUTHENTICITY OF *De Invectionibus*, II, 10
(*see above*, p. 208)

Gerald of Wales's use of early documents was impugned in his lifetime and has often been suspect since. But the view seems to be gaining ground that he was (according to his lights) an honest transcriber of earlier material; the other documents in Book II of the *De Invectionibus* all seem to be genuine; and Gerald himself had difficulty in reconciling this letter with other evidence. Apart from this, and the chronological difficulty discussed above (p. 230, n. 4), the only serious ground for doubting the authenticity of the letter is its remarkable resemblance to Geoffrey's *HRB*, its use of similar sources to Geoffrey, and its observation that St David's archbishopric was the third *in textu historiarum*—which is inexplicable in terms of surviving texts unless we take it as a reference to Geoffrey's account of the archbishoprics, in which Caerleon is named third. But in any case Geoffrey and the letter made independent use of the sources they had in common, and this explanation of *in textu historiarum* is as difficult as the difficulty—it is more likely that a legend of the chronological order of the sees lies behind the letter.

On three occasions (apart from the occasion of this letter) in the period 1080–1203 the pretensions of the see of St David's led to a statement of the legend of its origins, in Rhigyfarch's *Life* (*c.* 1081—see above, p. 176), in the 1140's (*EA*, I, 262–3) and in the time of Gerald of Wales. Each of these legends differs in some details from any other; and if the letter in question had been concocted in the 1140's or later, we should expect it to tell the same story as one or other of the later versions. In fact, it provides us with yet a fourth version; and this seems most easily explained if we suppose it to represent the state of the legend in fashion at St David's in the late 1120's, when the dispute with Llandaff caused the chapter of St David's to resurrect its ancient traditions and claims.

II. THE WORKS OF CARADOC OF LLANCARFAN
(*see above*, p. 228)

For Caradoc's authorship of the *Lives* of Cadoc and Gildas (which carry his signature) and Cyngar, see P. Grosjean, *Analecta Bollandiana*, LX (1942), 35 ff., Doble, *St Iltut*, 29; the *Life of Cadoc* has been edited by Father Grosjean, *loc. cit.*, the *Life of Gildas* (most recently) by T. Mommsen, *Mon. Germ. Hist.*, *Auctor. antiquiss.*, XX (1898), 107 ff., and by H. Williams, *Gildas* (Cymmrodorion Record Series, III, 1899), 394 ff., the *Life of Cyngar* by J. Armitage Robinson, *Journal of Theological*

Studies, xx (1918–19), 97 ff. That the *Life of Cyngar* was by the same author as the *Life of Gildas* is proved partly by the common occurrence of a stylistic trick (cf. below, Note III), partly by very close links in matter and words. Canon Doble noted the same stylistic trick in the *Vita Iltuti* (*VSB*, 194 ff.) and also some other links, but he did not note quite how close these links are. Thus the *Vita Gildae* (c. 3; cf. c. 12) and the *Vita Cungari* (c. 8, p. 102) have a very similar account of their heroes' ascetic life; but the account in the *Vita Iltuti* (c. 7, 18–19) is equally close, and has a verbal connection with both the other *Lives*. There are also two passages (c. 3, 11), clearly derived from a *Life of Cadoc*, which can be shown by verbal comparison to be Caradoc's (c. 12, 16) and not Lifris's—save that in c. 3 the *V. Iltuti* has preserved Lifris's *deglutivit*. These and other characteristic touches (e.g. the oratory of the Holy Trinity in c. 7) have convinced me that the *Life of Iltut* is the work either of Caradoc or of a disciple (and see further below, Note III). The same can probably be said of other *Lives* in *VSB* (from the same MS., Vesp. A. xiv, as the *Vita Iltuti*): e.g. the *V. Gundleii* (*VSB*, 172 ff.), which has a similar account of the ascetic life (c. 6), and a reference (c. 5) to Dubricius, 'bishop of Llandaff', with verbal links with the same passage in the *V. Iltuti*; it also contains a miracle story (c. 12) which F. Lot thought to be connected with a story in the *V. Gildae* (c. 10; Lot, *Mélanges d'histoire bretonne* (Paris, 1907), 269). The *Life* of St Tatheus (*VSB*, 270 ff.) has stylistic similarities, the little verses found in one or two of Caradoc's writings, a 'temple' in honour of the Trinity, a bishop of Llandaff, twelve canons (c. 6—as in the *V. Cungari* —cf. Armitage Robinson, *art. cit.* 106), and a passage about St Cadoc (c. 12) which seems verbally closer to Caradoc (c. 8; cf. esp. '*igne extincto*') than to Lifris (c. 7). Similar links are to be found in other *Lives*; but there is no space here for a full analysis of them, and much work remains to be done before the questions they raise can be finally solved.

III. Links between Caradoc and the *Book of Llandaff*
(*see above*, p. 229)

Cf. *St Iltut*, 30 and n. The stylistic trick (cf. *ibid*. 29) of repeating 'the same word, or the same root, in various formations' (Armitage Robinson, cited *ibid*.) occurs in the *Lives* listed above, Note I, in some others in the *VSB*, and in all three lives in *LL* (81, 97, 131). It is noticeably less common in *LL* than in Caradoc's *Lives* of Cyngar and Gildas; but these have it in an altogether exaggerated form, distinctly worse than in the *Life of Cadoc*. Its most striking occurrence in *LL* is in the *Life of Teilo* (97), and in that part of the *Life* written by Bishop Urban's brother Stephen. This establishes that it was the idiosyncrasy, not of an individual, but of a school, as one would expect. The Teilo passage has clear indications that it was intended to be declaimed in church—either as a sermon (so Doble, *St Teilo*, 6) or as lections; and this is the key to the stylistic trick. It is a rhetorical device, a kind of exaggerated alliteration, and it was evidently thought appropriate for rhetorical purposes. It was therefore more freely employed in works written for public performance rather than for private reading. The *Life of Gildas* was probably written to be recited as lections at Glastonbury (hence its brevity), and the *Life of Cyngar* was certainly used as lections at Wells. For later use of the stylistic trick, cf. below, p. 275, n. 2.

The following is a list (making no claim to completeness) of other links between *LL* and Caradoc's writings. Chapels dedicated to the Trinity (cf. Lifris's *Life of Cadoc*, *VSB*, 44) occur in the *Lives* of Gildas (c. 9, 12), Cyngar (c. 7), Iltut (c. 7, 18; also Tatheus, c. 6), and in the *LL* three times (80, 161-2); Gildas is referred to as 'historiographus' in his own *Life* (c. 6) and Iltut's (c. 19) and twice in *LL* (100, 138-9: 'historiographus Gildas...qui eo tempore conversabatur in insula Echni', which looks like a reminiscence of the *V. Gildae*); there are references to a bishop of Llandaff in Caradoc's *Life of Cadoc* (c. 14) and in the *Life of Iltut* (Dubricius, c. 7)—also in the *Life of Gwynllyw* (Dubricius, c. 5, 10, Herewald, c. 14); Caradoc and *LL* both made use of Lifris's *Life of Cadoc*.

IV. The Relation between Caradoc's and Lifris's *Lives* of St Cadoc
(*see above*, p. 230)

Father Grosjean (*loc. cit.* 38-42) expounded the difficulty that Caradoc makes vital alterations to the story, including the suppression of Cadoc's bishopric and martyrdom, and revises Lifris's story very extensively; he therefore suggests that both writers made free use of similar material. This solution softens, but does not abolish, the difficulty: there can be no question that they used very similar material, and even in the account of Cadoc's death and burial, a part of the narrative in which the two *Lives* diverge most completely, there is a verbal connection. To make them use a common source spreads the blame between the two authors, but only slightly diminishes it. The problem is not simplified by the unsatisfactory state of Lifris's text (cf. H. D. Emanuel, *Nat. Library of Wales Journal*, VII (1951-2), 217-27; cf. above, p. 199). Allowing for the fact that some of the chapters in the printed text of Lifris are inter-polations from Caradoc, it yet remains true that only five of Caradoc's twenty-seven chapters are without parallel in Lifris; that many of them contain verbal links; that some sections of Caradoc's *Life of Gildas* and possibly also of Cyngar are derived from Lifris (and cf. above, Note II); that Caradoc's verse colophon confessing his authorship is very similar in form to Lifris's. In addition, there is a passage in Caradoc with a succession of subjunctives running 'permaneat...minuatur, ut... valeant', where the scribe of the surviving MS. has written 'minuetur' in error (c. 15, p. 57, n. 7); it is a slight coincidence, but it is the fact that in the closely parallel passage in Lifris (*VSB*, 90) the word is, quite correctly, 'minuetur'. Finally, it is clear that Lifris's *Life* was very widely known in Welsh hagiographical circles in the twelfth century, and it would be an amazing coincidence if one of the few Welsh writers not to know the *Life of Cadoc* by Lifris of Llancarfan should have been the author of the second *Life of Cadoc*, Caradoc of Llancarfan. (True, if a common source existed for the two *Lives*, it and not Lifris may have been the work so widely known; but the postulation of imaginary sources in so small a world as that of Welsh hagiography requires stronger evidence than is forthcoming in this instance.)

Lifris's *Life* is long and diffuse—a welter of diverse materials. A motive for abbreviating it, for toning it down, for setting it in better frame, is not far to seek. And we know from the *Lives* of Cyngar and Gildas that Caradoc was not above the invention or the reorientation of a legend. We can only guess at Caradoc's exact motives, but they are not entirely beyond conjecture. Lifris's *Life* made Cadoc altogether too great a figure for the days when the Llancarfan family wished to treat their native abbey as subordinate to Llandaff. In Lifris Cadoc bursts his bonds, and becomes a martyred bishop of Benevento. Llancarfan in the twelfth century had great difficulty in maintaining its tradition as an ancient Welsh monastic house; it required a saint who was a great abbot and a great local figure—not a bishop, still less a substitute for Dubricius as St David's rival (cf. Lifris, c. 17). Along these lines we may glimpse the explanation of the divergences. In any case it seems to me to be reasonably certain that Caradoc worked on Lifris's *Life*, altered it in many ways, above all in suppressing Cadoc's bishopric and martyrdom —but showing sufficient respect for his predecessor (possibly his forebear) to take Cadoc to Benevento to die.

APPENDIX I

The Making of the 'Book of Llandaff'

This is not intended to be a full analysis of the *LL*, but merely to explain the views expressed in the text (above, pp. 219 ff.). I am not concerned with the scribes of *LL* (for whom, cf. above, p. 204, n. 3), nor with the Gospels with which the MS. now opens nor with the later additions at its close (for which see Mr Jones's article, cited *ibid.*, and Evans's edition), nor with the authentic twelfth-century documents (see pp. 204–5), nor with the *Lives* of Elgar and Samson, whose position in relation to the main body of *LL* is somewhat peripheral (on the *Life of Samson*, cf. p. 209, n. 3: a full and final analysis of *LL* would certainly have to take note of their evidence). The hard core of the *LL* consists of the *Lives* of Dubricius (the *De primo statu* and the *Life* proper), Teilo, Oudoceus and Clitauc and the 'chronological' sequence of charters and bishops down to 1107. The *Lives* (all except Clitauc's) have been thoroughly analysed by Canon Doble (above, pp. 203, n. 3, 206, n. 1, 220, n. 2), who shows that only in the case of the *Vita Teilonis* can we postulate a *Life* earlier than the *LL*, a *Life* known to us from Cotton MS. Vesp. A. XIV; it is possible that comparison of the *LL* accounts of Dubricius and Clitauc with Vesp. A. xiv might reveal more of their composition—but my present concern is almost exclusively with the charters.

Comparison of those charters in *LL* derived from charters in the *Vita Cadoci* with their exemplars (cf. above, p. 221) shows how ruthless the author of the *LL* was; and even without this control, the application of ordinary diplomatic tests to the body of charters leaves little doubt that they are all forged, and by a single hand. This is now, I believe, the normal view (it is expressed, in a rather more moderate form, by Mr Jones); that it has not been stated more clearly and emphatically long ago is, I think, due to the fact that the *LL* lives almost in a vacuum—that we have so few other Welsh charters with which to compare its contents (cf. above, p. 221, n. 1). The evidence for unity of authorship (which implies comprehensive forgery) is most clearly seen by an analysis of certain recurring formulae, and confirmed by an examination of the witness lists, which are very revealing about the author's methods.

(1) There are in all about 163 charters in *LL*, excluding documents like the ordinations in Archenfield (275 ff.), but including the privileges of Teilo and Dubricius, which for obvious reasons have a pattern of their own. There are many variations in these documents, but they have much in common; and of this the following figures will give some indication. In the dispositive clauses the phrase:

'cum omni (or 'tota') sua libertate' occurs 125 times;
'sine ullo censu terreno' (or 'magno uel modico ullo homini terreno' etc.), 75 times;
'cum tota communione' (or 'omni' or 'data communione' or the like), 100 times;
'in campo et in aquis et in silva et in pascuis' (in varying orders), 105 times.

A list of boundaries (in Welsh or Latin or both) opening 'finis' occurs in 80, following or preceding a witness list, which in 135 takes the form: 'De clericis testes sunt [sometimes 'testes sunt de clericis']...De laicis....' (These figures are the result of a rough count, and are given to the nearest five.)

The charters sometimes open 'Sciendum est' etc., or with some such formula; more often with a short narrative. The beneficiaries appear normally as 'Deo et sanctis Dubricio, Teliavo et Oudoceo' (there is variation among the early charters, but from Berthguinus's third charter, p. 176, Oudoceus is regularly present), the bishop and/or the church of Llandaff. The motive is 'pro anima sua' about a score of times, less often 'pro anima patris sui' etc., 'pro salute anime sue', 'pro redemptione anime sue' and so forth. The theme of the opening story is often the occasion for some act of penance ('iuncta sibi [*or* ei] penitentia' is the favourite formula), often following an elaborate ceremony of excommunication; other themes which recur are the king or prince taking part in a perambulation of the property, carrying a Gospel Book on his shoulders, or, more simply, swearing an oath on the Gospels and sometimes on relics as well. Other phrases familiar to students of medieval diplomatic are: 'libera [et quieta] ab omni regali servitio' etc., 'cum toto territorio', 'quietam clamavit'. Finally, the large majority of the charters have a sanction (usually anathema and blessing), which varies a great deal; but certain themes and clauses recur very frequently. This is far from being an exhaustive analysis of the recurring themes and phrases of the charters.

All the really common forms are fairly evenly spread over the charters from Dubricius to Herewald; and the effect is a curious mingling of formless narrative clauses and constant variety in the use of forms, with a literary unity and the use of constantly recurring formulae such as one would only find (in authentic documents) emanating from the papal chancery, or from the highly organised royal and episcopal writing offices of the twelfth and later centuries. There is in fact a unity about these documents of a very exceptional kind, even for large collections of forgeries.

The privileges of Teilo and Dubricius reveal a knowledge of papal diplomatic not found elsewhere; three documents ascribed to the late tenth and eleventh centuries (*LL*, 243, 265–6, 269–70) reveal a knowledge of the verbosity of late Anglo-Saxon diplomas, genuine or forged. Several of the formulae given above ('cum omni sua libertate', 'in campo et in aquis' etc.) are common in Anglo-Norman charters of the late eleventh and twelfth centuries (they are the current versions of ancient formulae). Most of the other formulae, the form of the witness lists and the anathemas could be derived from the Llancarfan charters; and no doubt there were a number of other Welsh charters, genuine and forged, in the forger's armoury. What still remains to be explained—and it is the most important question of all to the historian—is what other materials lie behind the *LL*, and to what extent they may be recovered. The author clearly had lists of churches and ordinations; some annals; much tradition; and a certain amount of local memory on which to work. But the analysis of these lost sources is beyond the limits of this appendix.

(2) The evidence of royal and episcopal names and of the witness lists takes on a new complexion in the eleventh century, when we may presume that the author of the *LL* (at least to some extent) had local knowledge and memory to guide him. For earlier centuries he may have had some annalistic evidence; but all that we can be certain of is that he used (*a*) associations suggested by charters, (*b*) chronology suggested by pedigrees, and (*c*) invention. (*a*) is illustrated by a charter in the Llancarfan collection (*VSB*, 132–5). Eudoce, bishop, whom Canon Doble showed to be one of the sources of St Oudoceus, is associated with a layman called Mouric; in four charters (*LL*, 140, 143, 144, 147) we duly find him associated with a King Mouric (probably quite a different person, but at least bearing the same name); three of these charters also have Jacob, abbot of Llandough, as witness, and possibly one or two other names derived from the Llancarfan document. (*b*) is illustrated by the tables on pp. 141–2 of Mr Jones's article, comparing the genealogies deducible from *LL* with the Harleian pedigree of the

Morgannwg dynasty,[1] and these in their turn with the list of bishops. It is clear that the author of *LL* controlled his lists of lay magnates by the pedigree, although it is far from clear that all the brothers and nephews whom he has added to it are historical characters; and the list of bishops bears some relation also to the order of the genealogy. That is to say, bishops 13 to 18 (Grecielis to Cerenhir) are all in their right order according to the kings in the pedigree, save that Grecielis looks as if he ought to be later than Berthguinus—a very minor error compared with some our author perpetrated. From the later tenth century onwards he was on firm ground, and the list of bishops is historical. To bridge the gap between the end of the Harl. pedigree and the days of Morcant Hen caused him some trouble, and very little can be made of the principles on which he accomplished it (he may possibly have had access to an extended version of the pedigree, similar to Jesus pedigree no. 9).

Before Grecielis we have the age of the saints and a group of bishops who deal mainly if not almost entirely in property in Archenfield (Herefordshire) and its environs. From these documents (and some attributed to Dubricius) a pedigree of the kings of Archenfield (Erging) can be deduced, which is otherwise unknown, but probably authentic— Morcant vab Gurcant vab Cinuin vab Peipiau vab Erb (cf. *LL*, 163–4, 162–3, 72 ff., 75). There is very little attempt at chronology among these bishops; they are all made much of a date, and four of them appear together as priests under Dubricius. The best that can be said for the chronology at this point is that in no case does a man appear as a priest *after* he has been a bishop. Between this group and Grecielis and his successors there is little relation—they are simply stuck end to end— save that Ubeluiu and Comeregius are made contemporary with the father and grandfather of Morcant, Berthguinus's king.

The element of hazard and the freaks of planning in the early witness lists are made very clear in A. Anscombe's articles in the *Celtic Review* (VI–VII, 1909–12), in which he attempted to put them in chronological order. But the most remarkable result of his analysis is the place it gives to Oudoceus. Fifteen of Oudoceus's twenty witness lists contain abbots from the three Glamorgan houses of Llancarfan, Llantwit and Llandough; they also appear in nine charters of Bishop Berthguinus, but not in those of any other early bishops. A closer view of the witness lists shows that there are no links between Oudoceus and his fellow-saints, and also that the forger must originally have meant Berthguinus to succeed Oudoceus directly, although in his final scheme they are divided by ten names. It is not only the abbots who join them together: most of Oudoceus's charters refer to King Morcant, who is made contemporary with Berthguinus, although four attach him to Mouric, Morcant's grandfather; and Berthguinus appears as witness to two of

---

[1] No. 28, ed. Faral, *op. cit.* I, iii, 56; ed. E. Phillimore, *Y Cymmrodor*, IX (1888), 181–2 and cf. no. 29. The name of Mouric has fallen out of the Harl. copy, but is supplied in the version in the Jesus MS. of the Welsh pedigrees (*Y Cymmrodor*, VIII (1887), 85, no. 9).

Oudoceus's charters. There are two possible explanations of this state of affairs: either bishops 4–13 are later additions, and the series originally ran straight from Oudoceus to Berthguinus; or Oudoceus has been moved from his original place. Two facts suggest that the latter is the true explanation. Several of the intervening bishops appear as priests in Dubricius's charters; and so if the bishops are later additions, these charters must also be, which seems hardly likely. In addition, St Oudoceus is very properly not included among the saints of Llandaff in the days of Dubricius and Teilo and in his own charters; but what is not so proper—indeed is very hard to explain—is that he does not achieve this position until Berthguinus, from which time he is fairly consistently present. It looks as if Oudoceus was originally placed much later in the episcopal list, immediately before Berthguinus, spanning the reigns of Mouric and Morcant.

Canon Doble has argued (in his study of 'Saint Oudoceus') that the saint is a conflation of the eponym of Llandogo on the Wye and the Bishop Eudoce of the Llancarfan charter cited above; and he has suggested that to fill a gap in the Llandaff pantheon Eudoce–Oudoceus was moved back several centuries. This hypothesis fits extraordinarily well with the evidence we have been considering; and it certainly looks as if the forger had composed the charters for most of his early bishops, or at least made a considerable start, before he effected the translation. This is further support for the view that charters and *Lives* (Teilo excepted) are all part of a single project. Since St Oudoceus was already hailed as one of the saints of Llandaff in a bull of 1128 (*LL*, 30 ff.— unless, of course, his name is an addition to the original bull), it may be that the composition of the book was well under way by this date, even though, as we have seen, it was not completed until after 1134.

APPENDIX II

NARRATIVES OF THE LUCIUS LEGEND

What follows is a skeleton of the narratives in Geoffrey of Monmouth's *HRB* (c. 1138: IV, 19; G, 328–30; F, 144–5), the letter of the chapter of St David's to Pope Honorius II (1125–30: Gerald of Wales, *De Invectionibus*, II, 10, ed. W. S. Davies, *Y Cymmrodor*, XXX (1920), 143 ff.), the *De primo statu Landavensis ecclesie* (after 1120: *LL*, 68–9), and the *De antiquitate Glastoniensis ecclesie* of William of Malmesbury (1129–39: for reasons expounded at length by Armitage Robinson, *loc. cit.* (above, p. 214, n. 1), I quote from the *Gesta Regum*, ed. Stubbs, I, 23–4), and Bede, *Hist. Ecclesiastica*, I, 4 (ed. C. Plummer, I, 16). These are not designed to give a coherent narrative in each case, but merely to show the verbal relationship between the narratives. Words which each passage has in common with the passage succeeding are shown in italics; words in the *De primo statu* derived from Bede are underlined. The problems raised by these passages are discussed above (pp. 207–8, 230, n. 4).

They all ultimately derive from an error in the *Liber Pontificalis* (cf. W. Levison in *Bede, his life, times and writings*, ed. A. Hamilton Thompson (Oxford, 1935), 135 n.; the passage is quoted in *LL*, 26).

GEOFFREY OF MONMOUTH: [Lucius.]... epistulas suas *Eleutherio papae* direxit, petens ut ab eo *christianitatem* reciperet.... Siquidem beatus pontifex... duos religiosos doctores, *Faganum et Duvianum*, misit ad illum, qui... abluerunt ipsum baptismate sacro et ad Christum converterunt.... Fuerant tunc *in* Britannia *XXVII*I flamines, nec non et tres archiflamines.... Hos etiam... eripuerunt et, ubi erant flamines, *episcopos*, ubi archiflamines, *archiepiscopos* posuerunt. Sedes autem archiflaminum in tribus nobilioribus civitatibus fuerant, Londoniis videlicet, atque Eboraci, et in Urbe Legionum... super Oscam fluvium ... [and *ibid*. IX, 15; G, 458; F, 247]: In cuius [sc. *Dubricii*] loco sacratur David....

THE CHAPTER OF ST DAVID'S: Innotescimus... ecclesiam nostram esse metropolitanam, et fuisse a primordio Christianitatis, quam *Lucius* totius regni Britannie tenens monarchiam, delegatis sibi a beato papa *Eleutherio*, Fagano *et* Duviano *predicatoribus*,... *anno* dominice *incarnationis cxl°* [? *vi* omitted] *suscepit*, et ad propagandum Christiane fidei sacramentum totidem in regno suo cum xx et vii *episcopis*, quot scilicet in tempore gentilitatis iuxta eorum ritum extiterant, reformavit archiepiscopatus, quorum ecclesie nostre in textu historiarum reperitur numero quidem tercius, sed regni provinciarum positione primus.... [David] electione... tocius regni occidentalis *Britannie* assumptus, ac deinde a sancto Dubricio antecessore suo... archipresul consecratus....

DE PRIMO STATU LANDAVENSIS ECCLESIE: Anno ab incarnatione Domini CLVI. *Lucius Britannorum rex ad Eleutherium* duo*decimum* apostolice sedis *papam* legatos suos scilicet Elvanum et Meduuinum *misit*, implorant *ut*... Christianus fieret, quod ab eo impetrauit... [there follows a reference to Brutus, from Nennius] placuit eosdem legatos baptizari et... ordinari... predicatores reversi sunt... quorum sancta predicatione Lucius et totius *Britannie* primates baptismum susceperunt et secundum iussum beati Eleutherii pape... episcopos ordinavit... [and shortly after:] super omnes autem Britannos dextralis partis Britannie beatum Dubricium summum doctorem... archiepiscopum consecraverunt.

WILLIAM OF MALMESBURY: Tradunt bone credulitatis annales, quod Lucius rex Britannorum ad Eleutherium, decimo tertio loco post beatum Petrum papam, miserit, oratum ut Britannie tenebras luce Christiane predicationis illustraret.... Venerunt ergo, Eleutherio mittente, predicatores Britanniam, quorum in evum durabit efficacia, quamvis longe situs etatis consumpserit nomina... [he goes on to say that they built a church at Glastonbury].

BEDE: [*Heading*: Ut Lucius Brittanorum rex, missis ad Eleutherium papam litteris, Christianum se fieri petierit.] Anno ab incarnatione Domini C^{mo} L^{mo} VI^{to} Marcus Antoninus Verus XIIII ab Augusto regnum cum Aurelio Commodo fratre suscepit; quorum temporibus cum Eleuther vir sanctus pontificatui Romanae ecclesiae praeesset, misit ad eum Lucius Brittaniarum rex epistolam, obsecrans, ut per eius mandatum Christianus efficeretur; et mox effectum piae postulationis consecutus est; susceptamque fidem Brittani usque in tempora Diocletiani principis inviolatam integramque quieta in pace servabant.

ADDENDUM

Since this chapter was in proof, I have by the kindness of Mr R. W. Southern seen his forthcoming article on 'The Canterbury Forgeries', due to appear shortly in *English Historical Review*. He argues—I think convincingly—that the Canterbury forgeries date from *c.* 1121 not *c.* 1072, and so played no part in the first primacy dispute of 1072; and also that Lanfranc played a more considerable part in the first dispute than I had supposed. This means that some sentences on pp. 211 and 214 above need revision, and that some of the documents quoted on p. 214, n. 5, are later than Rhigyfarch. But it remains probable that Rhigyfarch was aware of developments in Canterbury; and I do not think the rest of the argument is affected.

V

The Distribution of Irish Scriptoria and Centres of Learning from 730 to 1111

BY KATHLEEN HUGHES

The Irish scribe at work in the earlier Middle Ages is a familiar figure. He may be seen in the Old Irish poems, sitting under the green wood,[1] with the sun flickering pleasantly over his manuscript.[2] He often speaks directly to his readers, asking prayers of their kindness[3] or complaining of his poor equipment[4] and physical discomfort.[5] He might write in his own hut,[6] or in one of the monastic buildings used as a scriptorium,[7] and he was treasured by the monastic authorities, who were proud of the books he wrote and of the tradition of learning which went with them. Great Columcille is venerated in the Old Irish *Amra* as teacher and scribe: 'Faig ferb fithir. Gaiss gluasa gle. Glinn-si us salmu'; and the glosses explain:

> He, the tutor, used to sow the word of teaching.
> He was swift to interpret the glosses.
> He corrected the psalms with obelus and asterisk.[8]

Many texts dating from the later Middle Ages record, in poetic imagery, the power of books and learning,[9] and the saints'

---

[1] Thurneysen, *Old Irish Reader* (Dublin, 1949), 39.

[2] *Zeit. für celtische phil.* VIII (1912), 175.

[3] E.g. 'Diarmait scripsit: orate pro illo peccatore'. Stokes and Strachan, *Thesaurus Palaeohibernicus* (Cambridge, 1901–3), II, p. xv.

[4] 'Thin ink, bad vellum, difficult text', *ibid.* xxi, xxii.

[5] 'Oh, my hand!' 'Alas, my chest, O holy virgin!' *ibid.*

[6] Stokes, *Félire Óengusso* (London, 1905), 202.

[7] 'Huic autem monasterio [i.e. Devenish] aliquid secretum adiacet monasteriolum quod scola dicitur.' *Acta Sanctorum ex Codice Salmanticensi* (ed. C. De Smedt and J. De Backer, Edinburgh and London, 1888), col. 894.

[8] Bernard and Atkinson, *Irish Liber Hymnorum* (London, 1898), I, 173, translated, II, 67.

[9] Wild animals are tame to carry books—a fox carries Ciarán's (Stokes, *Lives of the Saints from the Book of Lismore* (Oxford, 1890), ll. 4044–57) and a stag acts as his lectern (*ibid.* 4036–41). Books are unharmed by water, *ibid.* 4356–60. Bede speaks of the healing properties of Irish books, *H.E.* I, i.

eagerness to possess them.[1] Writing at the beginning of the period chosen for this study, Bede describes the generosity of the Irish in providing hospitality, masters and books for foreign students, and in the twelfth century, soon after its end, Giraldus comments on a Gospel Book at Kildare, with its full-page illuminations and numerous miniatures:

> If you look at them carelessly and casually and not too closely, you may judge them to be mere daubs rather than careful compositions. You will see nothing subtle where everything is subtle. But if you take the trouble to look very closely, and penetrate with your eyes to the secrets of the artistry, you will notice such intricacies, so delicate and subtle, so close together and well-knit, so involved and bound together, and so fresh still in their colourings, that you will not hesitate to declare that all these things must have been the result of the work, not of men, but of angels.[2]

Since Giraldus, a long succession of antiquaries and historians have pursued their interest in Irish scriptoria and centres of learning, and today the Irish scribe is still a popular figure, perhaps best known to the Irish public in the person of the seventeenth-century scribe Michael O'Clery, who decorates a postage stamp of the Republic. In spite of this general familiarity, the student who formulates more precise questions about Irish scribes and scriptoria finds it harder than he expects to answer them. Who were the scribes? Were they a special group of persons? Were they anchorites, and to what extent were they influenced by the religious reform of the eighth and ninth centuries? Where were the scriptoria? At what monastic centres are they to be found? What is the general picture given by their distribution? Do certain scriptoria rise and decline, and is it possible to advance any reasons for such changes? What are the conditions under which the manuscripts were written and which govern their production?

The evidence from which these questions may be answered is mainly of two kinds. There is the testimony of the manuscripts themselves. The preparation of insular vellum and ink, the use of paint, the genesis of insular decoration, the influences which

---

[1] Cuimíne's dearest wish was to have a church filled with books (*Lismore*, p. 304). Baithín makes a vow not to forsake learning, and his tutor blesses him, 'God Himself for thine instruction'. Plummer, *Bethada Náem nÉrenn* (Oxford, 1922), I, 180, trs. II, 173.

[2] Ed. J. J. O'Meara, *Proc. Roy. Irish Acad.* LII (1949), 151–2, trs. *Topography of Ireland* (Dundalk, 1951), 67.

governed the way in which Irish books were put together, are subjects which would clearly provide essential evidence if our last question, on the conditions under which the manuscripts were produced, is to be considered adequately. To the question at what scriptoria were the manuscripts written the extant manuscripts do not always provide a decisive answer. Where traditional ascriptions exist, it is not always clear whether they record the place where the manuscript was written or where it was kept. A study of the palaeographical evidence involves technical problems which require an expert discipline and are outside the competence of this paper. Dr Lowe, in his *Codices Latinae Antiquiores*, has provided an invaluable guide to Irish manuscripts. The interpretation of their evidence has, in the last decade, been hotly disputed. M. Masai's thesis of an Anglo-Saxon origin for 'Irish' illumination[1] has provoked convincing opposition from Mlle Henry, who argues that an Irish style had developed in the seventh century independently of Anglo-Saxon influence;[2] it must also be modified in the light of Herr Nordenfalk's article 'Before the Book of Durrow'.[3] For our purposes the palaeographical evidence is technical, controversial and scanty.

The other great body of evidence on Irish scribes and scriptoria, and the one on which this paper is mainly based, is contained in the annals. The validity of conclusions based on such material will necessarily depend on whether the combined annals give a comprehensive and representative idea of Irish monastic learning, or whether they only give the history of certain narrowly selected houses. The *Ulster Annals*, surviving in an extensively interpolated fifteenth-century manuscript,[4] draw on much earlier material and are particularly well informed on the events of Leth Cuinn, the northern half of Ireland. The *Annals of Inisfallen* provide the earliest manuscript tradition, with their first section, to 1092, in a hand of the late eleventh century; internal evidence shows that the compiler's main interests were in Munster, for which his entries are sometimes unique.[5] The *Annals of Inisfallen* therefore provide

---

[1] *La miniature dite irlandaise* (Brussels, 1947).
[2] *Gazette des Beaux Arts*, xxxvii (1950), 5–34.
[3] *Acta Archaeologica*, xviii (1947), 141–74.
[4] Ed. W. M. Hennessy, *Annals of Ulster*, Dublin 1887–1901. Abbreviated as *AU*.
[5] Ed. S. Mac Airt, *The Annals of Inisfallen*, Dublin, 1951. Abbreviated *AI*. For its dating see especially pp. vii, xxii–xxiv, xxvi–xxvii. T. F. O'Rahilly, *Early Irish History and Mythology* (Dublin, 1946), 503.

a vital addition to the Ulster chronicle. *Chronicon Scotorum* is a Clonmacnoise compilation, and from the early tenth century its account is independent of *AU*.[1] It represents the interests of one of the most important of Irish monastic houses, in a strategic position on the borders of Connacht and Meath. These three records have been supplemented by the so-called *Annals of Tigernach*,[2] a text closely related to *Chron. Scot.*, and by the *Annals of the Four Masters*, compiled in the seventeenth century from earlier materials, and particularly useful for the tenth and eleventh centuries, where their entries are much fuller than those of *AU*.[3] The combined annals supply a chronicle for Ulster, Meath, Leinster, Connacht and Munster. They are sufficiently complete, and after 730 sufficiently reliable, for us to conclude that almost all scriptoria of repute gain some notice in the annals.

The opening date of 730 has been dictated by the nature of the material, not because it marks the beginning of Irish scriptoria. All the Irish annals for the early Christian period share a common source, which is generally considered to have been a chronicle compiled in Ulster in the early eighth century. O'Rahilly would date its compilation to the decade 730–40, MacNeill to *c.* 712.[4] Both scholars consider (without giving convincing arguments) that Bangor was probably the place where it was drawn up. There is little evidence in the annals on monastic centres of learning before 730, so it seemed wiser to begin the present study at this date and thus avoid controversy on how the earlier entries should be handled. In the four centuries which follow, the constitutions and customs of the Church in Ireland are predominantly Celtic, until, after a long and gradual development, the reforming synods of Cashel (1101), Rath Bresail (1111) and Uisnech (1111) brought the Irish Church into conformity with the ecclesiastical organisation and usages of the Continent.

The Irish annals are the obvious source to consult in an inquiry into Irish scriptoria, and scholars have already recorded their impressions on the evidence. H. J. Lawlor, in four brief pages of his introduction to the *Psalter and Martyrology of Ricemarch*,

---

[1] O'Rahilly, *Early Irish History*, 258. Text ed. W. M. Hennessy, Rolls Series, 1866. Abbreviated *Chron. Scot.*

[2] Ed. Stokes, *Revue Celtique*, xvi (1895), 374–419; xvii (1896), 6–33, 116–263, 337–420; xviii (1897), 9–59, 150–303, 374–91. Abbreviated *A. Tig.*

[3] Ed. J. O'Donovan, 2nd ed., Dublin, 1856. Abbreviated *AFM*.

[4] O'Rahilly, *Early Irish History*, 253–4. MacNeill, *Ériu*, vii (1914–16).

sketches the picture which the annals give of the monastic schools up to the end of the eleventh century, though without differentiating between the various kinds of learning which the annals distinguish. Flower, again all too briefly, indicates his view of the relationship between the scribal and anchoritic movement. To him, probably more than to any other single scholar of this century, we owe our understanding of the Irish manuscript tradition. His work on the *Catalogue of Irish Manuscripts in the British Museum* provides evidence mainly for the later Middle Ages; his critical perception and imaginative insight interpret the complex evidence of the earlier period in essays on the 'Two Eyes of Ireland',[1] on Irish high crosses,[2] and in *The Irish Tradition.*[3] But, so far as I know, no one has made a detailed study from the historical evidence of the annals of the distribution of schools and scriptoria, their relative rise and decline and the influences governing these changes. The conclusions which arise from such an examination demand that we should reconsider the association between the scribes and the religious reform of the eighth and ninth centuries.

The annalists distinguish carefully between the various types of learning of the men whose obits they record. Among the earliest in time is the *sapiens, suí, doctor*, descriptive titles which continue right through our period, indicating familiarity with the Latin language and with theological studies. To these may be added the poets and historians, who become fairly frequent from the end of the ninth century.

Scribes' obits are occasionally entered before our period begins, and they continue into the tenth and eleventh centuries. Undoubtedly there were scribes whose names never entered the annals, as we may see from the notes which they wrote in surviving manuscripts. The annal entries must imply a comparatively highly organised scriptorium. From their spacing, often at intervals of a generation,[4] we must conclude that the Master of the Scriptorium was given an obituary notice and that probably, now and then, a specially distinguished 'fellow' was allowed in. The 'scribe' of the annals was, then, usually Master of the Scriptorium and probably also in charge of the monastic school. But after the early tenth

---

[1] *The Church of Ireland, 432–1932*, ed. Bell and Emerson (Dublin, 1932), 66–75.

[2] *Journal of the Warburg and Courtauld Institutes*, XVII (1954), 87–97.

[3] Oxford, 1947.

[4] E.g. Finglas 796, 812, 838, 867; Duleek 872, 907, 920, 929 (*immatura etate*), 961.

century his obit is rarely recorded, and his place as Master of the Schools is taken by the 'man of learning', the *fer-léginn* or lector. Was the change merely one of name?[1] The Four Masters refer to Torbach of Armagh (obit 808) as scribe and lector, and their Mochta *fer-léginn* of 876 is probably identical with Mochta *scribnid* who died in 889. But, in spite of the very occasional identification of scribe and lector in these seventeenth-century annals, the bulk of the evidence seems to suggest that some genuine difference of emphasis in function is implied.[2] The golden age of the scribes was the great period of Irish book production, as the surviving manuscripts witness. After the mid-tenth century the emphasis ceases to be on transcription and illumination. Only the two greatest of all the Irish houses, Armagh and Clonmacnoise, maintained both 'scribes' and 'lectors' at the end of the tenth century. Armagh's last scribe is recorded in the annals at 1006; in the later ninth and tenth centuries there are obits of both scribes and lectors. At Clonmacnoise both scribes and lectors were known in the tenth century, and the frequency of the obits at the end of the century suggests that the lector's office was not identical with that of the scribe.[3] Elsewhere, after the earlier tenth century, it is as Master of the Schools rather than Master of the Scriptorium that the learned man achieves eminence. By the eleventh century the lector's office was an important appointment; it might be the stepping-stone to higher things, as it was for Dubdáleithe, raised to the abbacy of Armagh in 1049, or at Emly in 1052, where the lector assumed the abbot's seat.[4] But in this century there are no more records of personal virtuosity in the scriptorium: instead of the *scriba optimus* of the earlier annals, we have the occasional outstanding administrator, who proves his value in the schools.

[1] Colgan thought so, *Trias Thaumaturga* (Louvain, 1647), 632.
[2] This seems to be Lawlor's view, *Psalter of Ricemarch* (London, 1914), p. xii.
[3] Lectors, 977, 987, 999; scribes, 989, 994.
[4] Muiredach of Armagh (obit 1010) was intended for the abbacy, but died before his higher appointment. Armagh had 'chief lectors' who died in 1046, 1056, 1102; Kildare in 1041. This must imply a large school.

THE DISTRIBUTION OF SCRIPTORIA, AND THE CONDITIONS GOVERNING THEIR RISE AND DECLINE

The art of transcribing manuscripts was one of the radical innovations which the introduction of Christianity brought upon Ireland. For some centuries secular learning continued its tradition of oral transmission, but from the beginning the scribes were busy copying the Latin texts which were introduced into Ireland or compiled in the monasteries. But we know very little about these early scriptoria, and one of the great problems of Irish illumination has been that the *Book of Durrow*, which Lowe dates to the mid-seventh century, indicates the final stages in the development of an elaborate technique, whose earlier phases it is difficult to trace. When we come to the second quarter of the eighth century, the annals provide a remarkable spate of scribes' obits. No less than eight of the sixteen scribes recorded in this century are named within this short period:

724 Caech-scuili of Derry
725 Colmán Banban of Kildare
    Colmán Uamach of Armagh
    Rubín son of Broccán of Tehelly
730 Mac-Onchon of Kildare
    Cochul-Odhor of Bangor
    Mac-Concumba of Clonmacnoise
732 Ferdomnach of Armagh
739 Cuana of Trevet
742 Cudgile of Louth

The distribution supports the known connection between Anglo-Saxon and Irish scriptoria—Derry and Bangor on or near the north-east coast, Armagh, Louth and Trevet easily accessible from the eastern coast, Tehelly and Clonmacnoise and Kildare on the main routes westward from the Bay of Dublin. Lowe has pointed out the similarity of English and Irish manuscript traditions, their vellum, different from that used in Continental scriptoria, their ink still black and fresh, their similar punctuation and abbreviations.[1] But, though the places in which these scribes died, and presumably worked, suggest traffic with Great Britain, their markedly Irish names provide no evidence in favour of M. Masai's thesis that the so-called 'Irish' illumination was executed in the schools of Northumbria. On the contrary, they prove that by the first half of

---

[1] E. A. Lowe, *Codices Latinae Antiquiores* (Oxford, 1934–), II, pp. xii ff.

the eighth century Ireland possessed well organised scriptoria of her own.

From the late eighth to the early tenth century, the period when the expert writers and illuminators were most active, the distribution of houses is widened. Nevertheless the scribes are still concentrated in the centre of Ireland and on the coasts. The annal entries show them thickest in a rectangle from Carlingford Lough (near Dundalk) to a little south of Dublin Bay on the east coast, with Roscommon and Roscrea as its westward corners—in more precise terms between the Slighe Dhála and the Slighe Assail.[1] There are outlying pockets in the central north and south, and along the northern and southern coasts. Always they remain on or near the great routes. In the last quarter of the eighth century and the first quarter of the ninth a number of monasteries, for which no later scribes' obits are recorded in the annals, possessed working scribes. Such are Letuba 773, Cill Cuilinn and Kilmanagh 785, Loch Cré 807, Linn Duachail 808, Airecul-do-chiaroc 810, Aghaboe 813, Kilmoone 814, Lann-Ela 817, Trim 821; and some of these houses sank into comparative obscurity later. After about 825 the period of numerous small scriptoria is passing, a growing tendency towards concentration is evident, and the centres shift. Bangor has three scribes' obits in the eighth century, Armagh, Clonmacnoise, Kildare and Trevet each have two; but this balance is not permanently maintained. Trevet slips out of the race after 888 with three scribes in all, and only one lector's obit in the eleventh century (*AFM*, 1004); Kildare's fourth and last scribe of the annals died in 862, though from 962 to 1126 she has a fairly steady series of *fir-leginn*. Bangor's learned men cease altogether in the tenth century; her sixth and last scribe to be recorded in the annals 'rested happily at Rome' in 929. Armagh and Clonmacnoise are left with a record of ten and eleven scribes, scriptoria flourishing throughout the tenth century and great schools maintained until the end of our period. Other houses which made a promising early start were Finglas, with four obits between 796 and 867, and Kildalkey with obits at 837 and 868; but the Northmen were beginning to settle at Dublin from the 840's, and scriptoria at Kildalkey and Finglas, both in exceptionally exposed positions, must have suffered acute disorganisation. The height of

---

[1] For ancient Irish roadways see the map by Colm O Lochlainn in *Féil-sgríbhinn Eóin Mhic Néill*, ed. J. Ryan (Dublin, 1940).

the religious reform movement, with which Finglas under her Abbot Duiblitir is identified, coincides with the period of rapid expansion in the number of scriptoria. Later in the ninth century certain houses secured an undisputed lead. What reasons lie behind this change in the pattern of distribution?

Heavy expenses were incurred in running a scriptorium, and it cannot be accidental that the monasteries which were most successful in establishing themselves as learned societies and publishing houses had access to wider sources of income than those which fell out of the production race. Irish churches drew their income partly from their own lands and endowments; the law tracts carefully regulate the conditions under which the layman may grant land to the church so that no injury results to his *fine*. A church fortunate enough to possess the relics of a powerful patron and to be recognised as his chief foundation also had a right to certain dues from the other houses of the confederation. The annals constantly refer to the circuit which, after his installation, a new abbot of a mother house made to all the churches in his *paruchia*. There were also gifts and dues from the laity, to which the church was entitled by customary law.[1] In addition to these sources of income, the leading church of a province and the local king often made a *rapprochement*. The king assisted the church in the enforcement of its *lex* throughout the whole province over which he ruled.[2] It is sometimes recorded that the patron's relics were carried round to add a supernatural sanction to the law: 'Commotatio martirum Petir ocus Phoil ocus Phatraicc ad legem perficiendam' clearly links the *lex* with the circuit of the relic shrine. In this period relics have legal and financial, as well as religious significance, and the occasion seems to have been used to obtain the saint's tax.[3] The double purpose of the *lex* is suggested in the Irish word which the annalists use to translate it, for *cáin* has the sense of 'tribute', as well as 'law'.[4] The 'fulfilment' of the law

[1] *Corus Brescna, Ancient Laws of Ireland*, III, 18–20.

[2] Fergus, king of Connacht, promulgates the law of Ciarán and Brendan; Felim, king of Munster, promulgates the law of Patrick in Munster; Domnall Mide promulgates the law of Columcille. See index to *AU* for other illustrations.

[3] 'It is probable that the chief feature of many of these promulgations of laws was the levying of a cess.' Kenney, *Sources*, 237. Cf. F. Ó Briain in *Féilsgríbhinn Eóin Mhic Néill*, 458: 'The alleged judicial title under which the tax was claimed was termed the "lex" of the saint whose relics they carried.'

[4] Meyer (*Contributions to Irish Lexicography* (London, 1906), I, i, 302) gives examples from the *Book of Leinster* and elsewhere.

almost certainly involved payments to the church, and the king was concerned in it. The alliance between the community which guarded the patron's relics and the ruling house which co-operated in its levies was therefore of the utmost importance to ecclesiastical finances.

We can trace these alliances in the history of the individual houses which we are considering, and it quickly becomes evident that there is a close connection between financial success and the stability of a scriptorium over several generations. Whereas in the late eighth and early ninth centuries, the period of the anchoritic reform, a considerable number of houses record the obit of a single scribe, only a few maintained a succession of scribes, and these were exceptionally wealthy and powerful. Kildare, Clonmacnoise, Armagh, Bangor and Clonard finally established an undisputed pre-eminence. It is worth considering whether these monasteries had any particular financial advantages, and to what extent the fortunes of their scriptoria are affected by their material prosperity or depression.

Two of our earliest scribes' obits, at 725 and 730, are for Kildare. Kildare under the patronage of Brigit, 'the queen of the south, the Mary of the Gael', was from the earliest times the leading church of Leinster.[1] The site may, even in pre-Christian times, have had some specially sacred character.[2] From the sixth to the twelfth century, the ruling house of Leinster provided candidates for the abbatial succession of Kildare.[3] Consistent dynastic control by ruling families cannot be demonstrated for many houses,[4] but it can be abundantly proved that kings and coarbs of great monasteries allied themselves for mutual advantage. A saint like Brigit, 'patron of all the Leinstermen', in alliance with a provincial king, could draw on wide sources, and the history of Kildare shows her special advantages. Already in the seventh century she was eminent in dignity and power—Cogitosus describes a comparatively splendid church and double monastery—and by the eighth century she

[1] Even Armagh did not attempt to dispute superiority here. In the *Book of the Angel* Patrick recognises it: 'O mea Brigita, paruchia tua in provincia tua apud reputabitur monarchiam tuam: in parte autem orientali et occidentali dominatu in mea erit.' Stokes, *Vita Tripartita* (London, 1887), II, 356.

[2] Kenney, *Sources*, 356–8, and the references which he cites.

[3] F. Ó Briain in *Féil-sgríbhinn Eóin Mhic Néill*, 455–7, 460–2.

[4] Killeevy is one of those for which it can be shown. This is a house which must have had written records, on which Cotton Cleop. A. II was based, but no scribes' obits are recorded in the annals.

must have possessed some of the best established and most tenacious traditions in Ireland. As a scriptorium and centre of learning Kildare developed early, and continued in splendour into the ninth century, when some of the Irish scholars of the Carolingian renaissance may have come from Kildare.[1] Although no more scribes are recorded after 862, a series of lectors from the mid-tenth century maintained the reputation of her schools.

The scribal traditions and the financial stability of Kildare seem to have developed together. Does the history of other great Irish centres of learning suggest that this was a common phenomenon? Clonmacnoise seems to have emerged rather later than Kildare or than Bangor as one of the most powerful and most learned monastic cities in Ireland. Ciarán's *Lives*, probably going back to a ninth-century original, tell how the founder died during the great plague of 549 in the thirty-third year of his age, and the Irish recension explains that his early death was due to the jealousy of his fellow-saints.[2] Before his death he foretold that disasters would come upon the monastery, and advised his monks: 'Haste ye to other quiet places, and leave my relics here like the dry bones of a stag on a mountain. For it is better for you to be with my spirit in heaven, than beside my bones on earth, and stumbling withal.'[3] The legend of his death may suggest that the period which followed it was one of some obscurity in the history of the monastery, though the annals provide an uninterrupted list of abbots. There is certainly no reliable evidence for seventh-century manuscript traditions at Clonmacnoise as there is at Bangor or Kildare.

Clonmacnoise began to develop in the seventh century as the great church of Connacht. Memorial slabs and inscriptions and later poems record the burial of seventh-century kings of Connacht,[4] and if burial with a great saint provided spiritual privileges for the layman it also brought financial privileges to the saint's heirs.[5] During the eighth century the material fortunes of Clonmacnoise were steadily improving. Two abbots of the previous century had been of the Corcu Mogha (obit 613, 664) a *daer-tuath* of the Uí

---

[1] Flower, *Irish Tradition*, 35–40.

[2] *Lismore*, ll. 4472–6. *Félire Óengusso*, 204.

[3] Plummer, *Vitae Sanctorum Hiberniae* (Oxford, 1910), I, 215.

[4] Petrie, *Christian Inscriptions*, ed. M. Stokes (Dublin, 1872), I, 5–7, 76–81, 83.

[5] *Corus Brescna* (*Ancient Laws of Ireland*, III, 65) discusses how the financial profits of burials are to be distributed in special cases.

Máine, and a third from the Conmaicne Mara. Both these septs were tributaries of the kings of Connacht, and branches of the Uí Máine and the Conmaicne continued to supply abbots.[1] But in the second half of the century abbots are also coming for the first time from the Uí Fiachrach (obit 789) and the Uí Bríuin (obit 770, 799), from whom the kings of Connacht were derived. Meanwhile Clonmacnoise was helping herself in her upward struggle to power by battles with the neighbouring cities of Birr[2] and Durrow; out of the last, in 764, she certainly came victorious. And no doubt she made the most of the 'visio terribilis hi Cluain mac Nois' which occurred in 786 and resulted in 'poenitentia magna per totam Hiberniam'. Throughout the period she was receiving economic support from the kings of Connacht. In 744 Fergus mac Ceallaigh proclaimed the *lex Ciaráin* and the *lex Brendain*, but the *lex Brendain* is not mentioned again, and in 788 it is 'the law of Ciarán over Connacht' which is recorded. Muiris, king of Connacht, made a hosting in 814 with Forchellach, abbot of Clonmacnoise, over the southern Uí Maine, and raised Ciarán's *lex* over Cruachan, the plain of Roscommon, where the kings of Connacht kept their chief royal residence.[3] From the eighth century the fortunes of Clonmacnoise were closely linked with the kings of Connacht. The Uí Fiachrach and the Uí Bríuin continued to supply occasional abbots,[4] and their kings, with kings of other powerful groups in Connacht, had right of burial in Clonmacnoise.[5]

By the late ninth century Clonmacnoise was sufficiently well established, with Ciarán as patron of the three divisions of Connacht, to allow her abbots to hitch their waggon to the rising star of the Uí Maelsechlainn of Meath. Maelsechlainn, king of Meath and Ireland, the founder of this royal line, died in 862, and his son Flann Sinna ruled from 879 to 916. At the end of the ninth century the bishop of Clonmacnoise, Cairbre Crom, had a vision in which King Maelsechlainn appeared to him beseeching his

[1] Of the Sogain, obit 724; of the Síl Coirpre, obit 761, 784; of the Duíne Mór, obit 740. Professor Ryan lists the abbots of Clonmacnoise up to 799 in *Féil-sgríbhinn Eóin Mhic Néill*, 490–507.

[2] *AU* 760. In Ciarán's Irish *Life*, Brendan of Birr is made to prophesy: 'We shall take two habitations on two streams between chief cities, and the difference that shall be between the two streams shall be the difference between the size of the cities.' *Lismore*, ll. 4254–6.

[3] Hogan, *Onomasticon Goedelicum* (Dublin, London, 1910), 311.

[4] Obit 811, 829 (tanist abbot), 929, 964, 1089.

[5] Petrie, *Christian Inscriptions*, I, 82–3.

prayers. After Cairbre and twelve priests of Clonmacnoise had interceded for a year, Maelsechlainn escaped the pains of purgatory.[1] Here was a demonstration of the spiritual benefits which Ciarán and his heirs could confer which Flann mac Maelsechlainn was not slow to grasp. It was he who, with Abbot Colmán, built the stone church at Clonmacnoise, and Abbot Colmán erected a cross in honour of Flann.[2] The Clan Colmáin had a burial place at Clonmacnoise, and owed Ciarán certain services.[3] Clonmacnoise profited by her position on the borders of Connacht and Meath to secure support from both provinces. While her material fortunes were improving in the eighth century she was able to establish and maintain a scriptorium,[4] and her scribes continue throughout the ninth and into the tenth centuries. Suibhne of Clonmacnoise was famous enough to be noted in the *Anglo-Saxon Chronicle* as 'the best teacher among the Scots'.[5] In the tenth and eleventh centuries a steady sequence of lectors maintained her traditions of learning. Intellectually as well as materially she justified the prophecy that her founder Ciarán should be a golden moon to shed radiance from the Shannon over central Ireland.

A great scriptorium was not, of course, simply the result of wealth. Intellectual and spiritual stimulus were essential, but it seems that unless there was also material prosperity, it proved impossible to maintain a scriptorium over several generations. Wealth and learning enriched each other. A learned tradition brought prestige and popularity: financial stability allowed the production of expensive manuscripts. Clonard provides another example of a monastery where the rather late emergence of a scriptorium coincides with her material rise to power. The annals enter the obits of scribes in the ninth and earlier tenth centuries, and the record of her lectors and *sapientes* shows that she survived as a centre of learning for the next hundred years (her last lector is recorded in 1047). The development of Finnian's *paruchia* has been traced elsewhere:[6] his *Lives* suggest that it was based

---

[1] The annals record his apparition to Cairbre, but not its purpose. The full story is contained in *Martyrology of Donegal* (ed. Reeves, Dublin, 1864), 66.

[2] Petrie, *Christian Inscriptions*, I, 42–4.

[3] Petrie, *op. cit.* I, 5. P. Grosjean edits 'Why the Clann Colmáin and Síl Aeda Slaine serve Cluain', in *Anal. Boll.* LXIX (1951), 96–102. Cf. Register of Clonmacnoise, in *Jrnl. Kilkenny Arch. Soc.*, new series, I (1857), 444–60.

[4] Scribes' obits 730, 768, 798.   [5] I.e. the Irish.

[6] K. Hughes, *Irish Historical Studies*, IX (1954), 13–27.

originally on Laginian interests, though it is clear that by the mid-ninth century Clonard had become the leading church of Meath, and was in close alliance with the Uí Maelsechlainn kings of Meath. The change of orientation and interests may date from the 'conflict' in 775 between Donnchad, king of Meath, and the *familia* of Clonard. This was followed by the circuit of Finnian's relic shrine and payment of his tax in 776, and in 787 by a visitation of part of his *paruchia*. At the end of the eighth century Clonard was exerting herself financially for the first time on record. The obit of her first recorded scribe occurs at 830. In 851 and 859 her abbot Suairlech, 'bishop and anchorite, the best doctor of religion of all Ireland', attended the royal assemblies of Armagh and Rahugh at the head of the clergy of Meath, together with Maelsechlainn, king of Ireland and Meath, the congregation of Patrick and the chief men of Leth Cuinn. Clonard was now probably at the height of her prestige, and the alliance with the Uí Maelsechlainn continued. The scribe Colmán Conaillech, who died in 926, was also abbot of both Clonmacnoise and Clonard, and was in close touch with King Flann, who built the great church of Clonmacnoise. Clonard remained associated with the kings of Meath into the eleventh century. Her connection with them undoubtedly improved her prestige and finances, and coincides with the development of her scriptorium.

The evidence for Duleek shows that the decline of her learned tradition synchronises with the collapse of the royal house of Bregia. Duleek, within the kingdom of Bregia, had some reputation as a centre of learning in the ninth and tenth centuries, with scribes' obits at 872, 907, 920, 929 and 961. But after 961 not a single scribe, lector or learned man of any kind is mentioned; her school and scriptorium seem to have disappeared. It is significant that at the end of the tenth century the Bregia dynasty was suppressed by Maelsechlainn II, king of Ireland and head of the Clann Colmáin of Meath.[1] Duleek's decline may be in part the result of this suppression. Nothing is known of Duleek's sources of income, but the extinction of an independent local dynasty may well have affected her financial stability. The kings of Meath were actively linked with Clonard and with Clonmacnoise, and it is very probable that Duleek was unable to maintain its former prestige in the face of such competition.

[1] E. MacNeill, *Phases of Irish History* (Dublin, 1919), 236.

Armagh and Bangor, the two great learned centres of the north which remain to be discussed, show some unique features. Of all the great monasteries, the influence of Armagh by the ninth century was the most spectacular, the more so when one recalls that there is no early evidence that Patrick was universally recognised as patron of Ireland. Armagh was within the territory of the Cenél Eoghain, which, until the end of the eighth century, competed with the Cenél Conaill for the Uí Néill kingship of the north. By the time that the annals are giving the kind of information which we need to trace the contacts of Armagh, it is clear that the monastery was closely associated with the Uí Néill kings. Flaith-bertach of the Cenél Conaill, king of Ireland 728–34, died at Armagh, having resigned his kingdom for the monastic life. His successor in the high-kingship, Aedh Allán of the Cenél Eoghain, had the coarb of Patrick, Congus, as his *anmchara* or spiritual adviser, and it was Congus who instigated Aedh Allán to war with Aedh Roin of Ulaidh in revenge for the profanation of Cill Cunna, a church within the territory of Cenél Eoghain. In 737 the annals for the first time imply Patrick's spiritual overlordship of the whole island with the entry 'Lex Patricii tenuit Hiberniam'. The *lex* followed a royal conference at Terryglass in north Munster between Aedh Allán and Cathal, king of Munster. After 789 the Cenél Eoghain become the dominant people of the north; they control the northern Uí Néill kingship, and until the early eleventh century they and the southern Uí Néill (of Meath) share the succession to the high-kingship. Throughout the ninth and tenth centuries Armagh and the northern Uí Néill kings are close allies. In 804 Abbot Condmach was heading a *congressio senatorum nepotum Neill*, successfully pleading for clerical exemption from hosting obligations. Two years later Aedh Ordnidhe, king of Ireland (797–819), was promulgating Patrick's *lex*. A man was killed in 870 in Armagh 'ante ianuam domus Aedho regis Temhro', so presumably Aedh, king of Ireland (862–79), was either in residence or had a permanent residence at Armagh. The coarb of Patrick, on his circuit of Cenél Eoghain in 993, conferred the rank of king on Aedh mac Domnaill in the presence of the congregation of Patrick. This is one of the few references in the annals to the financial support afforded to Armagh by the people in whose territory she lay—for the circuit has financial significance. Earlier in the century the Cenél Eoghain gave 'the full of the finnfadhach of silver for the blessing of

Patrick and his coarb'. Presumably dues must have been collected from the home territories of the Uí Néill from an early period.

From the early eighth century, then, Armagh was in close touch with the Uí Néill kings and succeeded in establishing Patrick's claims to spiritual overlordship. The annals show that towards the end of the eighth century she had widened the area from which she could draw her income, to include Connacht. The first specific reference to the law of Patrick in Connacht is in the year 783, when Abbot Dubdáleithe and King Tipraite promulgated it over Cruachan (the plain of Roscommon). Between 799 and 836 it was issued five times; thereafter a circuit of Connacht is only twice mentioned (in 959 and 1107). In Munster Patrick's *lex* is first mentioned in 823, when it was imposed by Bishop Airtrig and by Felim, son of Crimthann, king of Munster. There is independent evidence that Felim initiated material support of a particular kind for part of the *familia* of Patrick. The Egerton copy of the *Vita Tripartita* concludes by enumerating the members of Patrick's household, and adds: 'This is the number that should be in Joseph's company (probably to be identified with the abbot of Armagh in 936) and it is the number that should be at the king of Cashel's table down from the time of Felim son of Crimthann, king of the two provinces of Munster.'[1] There are irregular records of visitations of Munster down to the end of our period, when the abbot made a circuit and obtained 'seven cows and seven sheep and a half ounce from every cantred of land in Munster, besides many valuable gifts as well', and when King Muirchertach Úa Briain 'gave Cashel of the kings as an offering to Patrick and to the Lord'.[2] Armagh's political power and financial resources were therefore developing in the eighth century, and in the ninth they continued to be greater than those of any other monastic foundation in Ireland. Does her scriptorium show any similar expansion?

The scriptorium of Armagh was one of the earliest to emerge. Obits of scribes are recorded for 725 and 732, and the literary evidence shows that original work was produced there earlier than this. In the later seventh century Tírechán had set to work to provide hagiographical justification for the claims of Armagh over churches in northern Connacht and Meath, and Muirchú's *Vita* marks an important stage in the development of the Patrician

---

[1] Ed. Stokes, *Vita Trip.* I, 264–6.
[2] *A. Tig., Revue Celtique*, XVIII, 21 = *AU*, 1101.

legend. In the eighth century her learned administrators were probably formulating the claims contained in the *Liber Angeli*,[1] which they put into effect in 737, when 'the law of Patrick took Ireland'. In the ninth century her scriptorium was clearly active. The obits of scribes at 808, 829, 846, 852, 861, 893 provide a regular and unbroken sequence. Ferdomnach, the third in this series, wrote the *Book of Armagh*, as he claims in a colophon, at the dictation of Torbach, scribe and abbot, who died in 808. Further contributions to the Patrician legend (of which the *Vita Tripartita* was the most important) were made throughout this period up to the death of Joseph, abbot, scribe and bishop, in 936.[2] After this the sequence of scribes is broken, and only one further scribe is recorded in the annals. But the learned tradition at Armagh was continued in her schools. She has a separate Master of the Schools a century before most of the other houses.[3] After 879 her *fir léginn* are regularly recorded, and the office becomes one of particular importance in the eleventh century. The evidence shows that Armagh's pre-eminence as a centre of studies throughout the whole of our period goes hand in hand with unusual financial stability and political power.

Of the Irish houses with exceptional scribal records which we set out to consider, there seems to be, in the cases of Kildare, Clonmacnoise, Clonard, Duleek, and Armagh, a definite correlation between book production and wealth. The last monastery of our group, Bangor, in her rise and decline provides the greatest problem of all. On the shores of Belfast Lough, she was accessible to influences from Great Britain until the Viking menace became acute at the end of the eighth century. She was thus in an excellent position for the very early development of a scriptorium, and her Antiphonary is one of our earliest surviving Irish manuscripts.[4] During the eighth century more scribes' obits are recorded for Bangor than for any other Irish house, but in the ninth century the weakness of her position becomes apparent. The obit of her last scribe is recorded in 929, her last learned man (*suí*) in 951, not a

---

[1] Kenney, *Sources*, 335–7.

[2] *Ibid*. 319ff. on the Patrician documents. The scribal period, up to 936 at Armagh, is the period during which almost all the important texts appear to have been compiled.

[3] Following *AFM*, 808. Clonmacnoise is the other house with an early lector, Colgu, at 789.

[4] The list of abbots from Comgall (obit 602) to Crónán (obit 691) proves its provenance.

single *fer-léginn* is given, and after the mid-tenth century her reputation as a centre of learning and religion lapses until the reforms of St Malachy.

It has been suggested that this decline was due to the Viking raids. No doubt the Vikings had a disrupting influence. Comgall's relics were temporarily removed to Antrim in 824,[1] but the raids of 823-4 were the only occasion on which Bangor was intensively plundered. Her history must be compared with that of Armagh, raided eight times between 830 and 943, on two occasions with very heavy losses,[2] and Clonmacnoise, plundered by the Northmen five times between 922 and 953. In spite of such disturbance both these houses show remarkable vitality as centres of learning. The explanation for Bangor's failure to develop in the ninth century and her collapse in the tenth may be found rather in the narrow limitations of her financial resources. Comgall was patron of the Dál nAraidhe, the people living to the east of Lough Neagh. His neighbour immediately to the west was Finnian of Moville, patron of the Ulaidh (i.e. of the Dál Fiatach). The Dál nAraidhe and the Dál Fiatach both provided candidates for the kingship of Ulster until the late tenth century; after this the succession was confined to the Dál Fiatach.[3] Ulster had once been a great kingdom, but had contracted before the steadily expanding power of the Uí Néill, in the central north. The possible range of Bangor's financial resources was from the first a narrow one, and it was still further limited by the encroachments of Armagh. The churches of the eastern province were no match for Armagh's men of affairs and her flair for big business. By the time the *Vita Tripartita* was composed at the end of the ninth century, Armagh was claiming Patrician foundations within the territory of Dál nAraidhe.[4] Comgall's efforts at expansion are by comparison pitiful. Patrick founded churches in Uí Tuirtri (the territory to the west of Lough Neagh), but Comgall in his *Life* could not even persuade its chieftain to

---

[1] *The Four Masters* indicate a removal: 'It will be true; By the will of the supreme King of kings; My stainless bones shall be taken From beloved Bangor to Antrim.' The conclusion of Comgall's *Life* (written, according to Kenney, either in or before the tenth century or after the restoration, *c.* 1125) suggests that his relics are at Bangor.

[2] 869 (when *AU* says that 1000 people were lost), and 895 (710 captives taken).

[3] Reeves, *Ecclesiastical Antiquities* (Dublin, 1847), 353 ff., lists ten kings of Ulster from the Dál nAraidhe between 527 and 978. O'Rahilly, *Early Irish History*, 347, indicates the same number, though he does not quote Reeves.

[4] Stokes, *Vita Trip.* I, 164.

sell him corn.[1] Comgall wished to found a monastery on Rathlin Island off the coast of Antrim, but was prevented by thirty impious men; Columcille's successors, however, succeeded in establishing themselves here. Bangor in the sources has a reputation for great austerity, but her abbots were no match for the politics and propaganda of Armagh. Comgall refused the gold and silver offered by a king of whom he disapproved: 'Ut quid vult peccator peccata sua super nos effundere? Habeat ipse iniquitates suas, et fructum earum.' His disinterested severity contrasts sharply with the legendary Patrick's grasping determination to secure privileges[2] or with his methods of inducing the conversion of the king of Cenél Eoghain.[3] Cut off from the intellectual stimulus of Great Britain, patron of a small and after the tenth century an insignificant people, hemmed in by the Uí Néill and Armagh, it is not surprising that, after Patrick's legend reached its crest, c. 900, and his claims advanced to their full height, Comgall's foundation must shrink. Bangor was a great scriptorium and a centre of ecclesiastical studies, but only for about two centuries. Comgall's *Life* pictures him in the simplicity of an early scriptorium and provides a vivid comment on the inelegance and illegibility of the poorer type of *scriptura hibernica*. One of the boys in his school wrote so badly that it was impossible to tell whether the letters were made by man's hand or bird's claw. Comgall blessed his hand, the crabbed script was corrected, 'et in ipsa arte auctor et doctor in vita sua fuit'.[4]

IRISH SCRIPTORIA AND THE ANCHORITIC REVIVAL

The greatest Irish scriptoria from the seventh to the early tenth century, as we have seen, are to be found in a handful of the wealthiest monasteries in Ireland, founded under the patronage of some of her most venerated saints. A prosperous house did not necessarily enjoy the prestige of learning, but a school of writing

[1] *Vita Trip.* I, 168; Plummer, *Vitae Sanctorum Hiberniae*, II, 10–11.

[2] On Cruachan Aigle the angel comes to Patrick: '"God gives thee not what thou demandest; it seems to Him excessive, and obstinate and great are thy requests." "Is that His pleasure?" saith Patrick. "It is", saith the angel. "Then this is my pleasure", saith Patrick, "I will not go from this Rick till I am dead or till all the requests are granted to me." Then Patrick abode in Cruachan in evil mind....' In the end he received his demands. *Vita Trip.* 112–20.

[3] *Ibid.* 150–2.

[4] Plummer, *Vitae SS. Hib.* II, 13. See Lowe, *op. cit.* IV, 457, for a ragged Irish minuscule.

could not be maintained in the face of financial decline and collapse. What then is the relationship between the scribal movement, centred in these old churches, and the anchoritic reform which often led to the establishment of new communities? Flower, writing in 1932, suggested that there is a definite connection between the two contemporary movements. Here and in an article published posthumously, which uses the same evidence, he assumed the identity of scribes and anchorites.[1] Other scholars have followed Flower in this identification.[2]

The scribe of the annals and the scribe of the hermit poetry can rarely be identical. Where we can trace the scribe in the annals, he is usually at work in a wealthy environment, with a good deal of expensive equipment about him—vellum, ink, sometimes paints and gold leaf, exemplars to copy and adapt, and a building in which to practise writing and illumination. The conditions of the scribe in the contemporary hermit poetry are very different.

A hedge of trees overlooks me; a blackbird's lay sings to me (an announcement which I shall not conceal); above my lined book the birds' chanting sings to me.

A clear-voiced cuckoo sings to me (goodly utterance) in a grey cloak from bush fortresses. The Lord is indeed good to me: well do I write beneath a forest of woodland.[3]

The anchorite's 'secret little hut in the wilderness' cannot be identified with the monastic scriptorium.

But Flower surely intended no such identification. He points out how the anchorites, who had always existed within the Irish Church, gained consistency, acquired the character of a movement, under the leadership of Duiblitir and Máelrúain, the abbots respectively of Finglas and Tallaght, the 'two eyes of Ireland'. It is perhaps not fanciful for us to see here the difference between the scribe and the man who was pre-eminently a religious teacher. In later tradition it is Máelrúain the teacher who is best remembered in the work of his disciples. In the later eighth century Duiblitir, scribe and abbot of Finglas, was probably the more influential of the two. It was certainly he who headed the scribes and anchorites

[1] For references to Flower's work see above, p. 247.

[2] K. Jackson, *Early Celtic Nature Poetry* (Cambridge, 1935), 96; Henry, *Irish Art* (London, 1947), 168.

[3] *Thes. Pal.* II, 290, translated Gerard Murphy, *Early Irish Lyrics* (Oxford, 1956), 5.

at the synod of Tara in 780, where Flower suggests that a penitential may have been drawn up. And it is noteworthy that whereas Finglas maintained a scriptorium for a century, with four scribes' obits about a generation apart, the annals record only one scribe for Tallaght. It is not impossible that some of the religious texts associated with Máelrúain were compiled in other monasteries of Máelrúain's 'unity'.

Máelrúain's anchorites grouped themselves into a confederation. The most important of them are listed in a tract in the *Book of Leinster*, with Máelrúain's name and twelve others, headed 'The Folk of the Unity of Máelrúain'.[1] For us the significance lies in the distribution: three of the men belong to Tallaght, one each to the counties of Westmeath, Kildare and Clare, two to Cork, and no less than five to Tipperary. Munster provides a weighty element in this pattern of distribution. One of the Tipperary anchorites is Feidlimid mac Crimthann, king of Cashel. A similar tract, again in the *Book of Leinster*, provides a list of the folk of the 'unity' of Feidlimid.[2] 'There are twenty-four about Feidlimid son of Crimthann', it begins, 'who have one request in heaven and one entreaty upon earth', and it goes on to enumerate Máelrúain's 'unity', adding eleven other names. Some of these men are unidentified, but the emphasis on a Tipperary grouping is unmistakable. Feidlimid himself, king of Cashel from 820 to 845, may have offered some material protection and support to the group. He was a powerful king, and the annals are packed with his exploits —battles, burnings, plunderings of monastic property—from his accession until the notice of his death as 'rex Muman, optimus Scotorum, scriba et ancorita'. The compiler of the 'unity of Feidlimid' was especially interested in Daire Ednech and in Druim Abrat. After giving the twenty-four names and cursing all opposition, he goes on:

They used to be together in Daire Ednech, no false order, practising devotion without extravagance, at cross vigil in Lent. They come precisely to Daire Ednech to work their miracles, until their journeying arrives in the east, on the flagstone in Tallaght.... They used to come hither to Druim Abrat, these saints whom we expect; in this place they used to practise with renown the eight hours.

[1] *Book of Leinster*, facs., 370 a. Flower lists its contents in the 1932 article already cited, 70 ff.
[2] I am indebted to Fr Brendan O'Dwyer, O.Carm., for bringing this list to my attention. It is found in *Book of Leinster*, facs., 374 c.

Daire Ednech is Daire na Flann or Derrynavlan in Co. Tipperary,[1] and Druim Abrat may be the Árd Fínáin on the river Suir.[2] So this account of Feidlimid's unity bears out the emphasis on Munster as a centre of the movement on which Flower commented in his study of the 'unity of Máelrúain'. If we compare the anchoritic 'unities' with the distribution of scribes' obits from the annals, we find a different scatter. The scriptoria are located over the whole of central Ireland eastwards from the Shannon and round the north-east coast, spreading in the ninth century to the south coast with Lismore (856), Roscarbery (866), and Cork (876, 891), and in the north to Airecul-do-chiaroc (now Errigal, Co. Tyrone, 810), Clones (840), Connor (865), Clogher (869) and Devenish (984). There is no parallel between the distribution of the scribes and of the *Book of Leinster* 'unities', and no support here for any identification of scribes and anchorites.

Anchorites are, however, to be found in many houses other than those listed in the 'unities'. The annals distinguish carefully between men who are scribes, or scribes and anchorites, or anchorites only,[3] and if their evidence is to be trusted (and it is hard to see where we could find better), in the overwhelming majority of cases the scribes were not anchorites. Of the eighty-six scribes whom I have been able to attribute to specific houses in Ireland during our period, twenty-two only are called anchorites, and twenty-one of the scribes come from houses for which no anchorites at all are recorded in the annals. The conclusion is inescapable that the identity of scribes and anchorites has been too readily inferred.

What then is the connection between the scribal golden age and the anchoritic movement? It cannot be accidental that the two are contemporary, and that a number of men are associated with both. The anchorites, in spite of considerable diversity among themselves,[4] were united in pursuit of a stricter obedience, tighter discipline, and more rigid (though not more extreme) asceticism. Often they established themselves near to some ancient foundation.

---

[1] Hogan, *Onomasticon Goedelicum* 327.   [2] *Ibid.* 357, 41.

[3] E.g. 851 'Forannan, scribe, bishop and anchorite'; 1005 'Dunchadh, *ferléginn* of Clonmacnoise, and its anchorite afterwards...'.

[4] In using the word 'movement' this diversity between the practices of various anchoritic leaders should not be forgotten. See the tract which recounts the teaching of Máelrúain and Máeldithruib, ed. Gwynn and Purton, *Proc. of the Royal Irish Acad.* XXXIX (1911), C. 115–79, especially ch. 5, 6, 23–4, 33, 81.

The *Rule of Columcille*, which probably dates from the ninth century,[1] begins 'Be by yourself in a retired spot near a chief monastery', and the *Rule of Fothad 'na canóine'* has a section 'on the céile Dé, or the clerics of the enclosure'. The *Céile Dé*, or Culdees, were a part of the anchoritic movement of religious revival. There were groups of Culdees at monasteries such as Clonmacnoise and Armagh, living separately from the main body. From the account of the customs of Máelrúain and Máeldithruib it is clear that the anchorites, at least in some cases, were supported or partly supported by the ancient foundations to which they were attached. Máeldithruib of the anchorites of Terryglass accepted part of the produce of the 'old church',[2] Elair of Loch Cré was supported by Roscrea,[3] and an anchorite of Slane from the 'patron's fruits'.[4] Of the twenty-two scribes whom the annals call anchorites, four are from Armagh, three from Clonmacnoise, two each from Bangor and Finglas and nearly all the rest from long-established and prosperous communities.[5] The anchorites who were also scribes were no doubt able to use the amenities of the monastic scriptorium. Many other anchorites are named in the annals,[6] and it is hardly possible that those were all scribes. The religious reform of the late eighth and ninth centuries stimulated intellectual and artistic life and led to the production of liturgical and devotional texts. But the evidence suggests that the anchorites became scribes through their association with the great scriptoria of the period, and that the majority of the anchoritic settlements developed no distinguished scribal traditions.

Irish scribes writing *c.* 800, at the height of the anchoritic revival, were not 'new' men; they had a respectable ancestry. The 'Cathach of St Columba' is dated by Lowe to the second half of the sixth century. In the following century a style with distinctly Irish characteristics is discernible in a number of Bobbio manuscripts,[7] and the establishment and continuance of such a style implies a fairly highly developed and organised scriptorium. The script of

---

[1] *Zeit. für celtische Philologie*, III, 28.
[2] Ed. Gwynn and Purton, *op. cit.* ch. 4.   [3] *Ibid.* ch. 4.   [4] *Ibid.* ch. 77.
[5] From Kildare, Duleek, Lismore, Tehelly, Clones, Roscarbery, Trim, Kilmoone. Cill-achaidh, Laragh-bryan and Glen-uisean have comparatively few entries in the annals.
[6] I have noted seventy others, but my list of anchorites is not complete.
[7] Henry, *Gazette des Beaux Arts*, 6th ser., XXXVII (1950), 5–34; Lowe, *C.L.A.* IV, pp. xx–xxv.

Luxeuil, an earlier foundation of St Columban, as it is first seen in a manuscript of 669, shares some of the peculiarities of the insular manuscripts from Bobbio.[1] The Antiphonary of Bangor and the *Book of Mulling*, both written at the end of the seventh century by more than one scribe, indicate an organised scriptorium with scribal traditions. The scriptoria of Ireland were ancient institutions when the ascetic revival started. It seems manifestly unlikely that the new movement should have completely captured the scriptoria, or that the scribes should all have become anchorites. If it is legitimate to seek a parallel in twelfth-century England, we might note that although the ascetic Cistercians exercised a great influence on religious life and thought, wrote and transcribed manuscripts and practised a new building style, the old Benedictine scriptoria at St Albans, Bury, Canterbury, Winchester and Durham, far from being eclipsed, at this time produced some of their finest work. The Irish anchoritic foundations did not supersede the learned traditions of the older houses; the two existed side by side. Some of the old foundations welcomed groups of anchorites to live in close touch with the monastic city, some of the new anchoritic communities developed scriptoria of their own. Religious enthusiasm poured new life into the old institutions. At the height of the revival there were scribes in a number of houses, but they were evidently unable to support a scriptorium for long, and soon a handful of the old churches, great centres of wealth and power, secured an undisputed leadership in book production. Anchoritic enthusiasm needed to combine with financial stability if a firmly established scriptorium was to be maintained. Finglas and Tallaght might be, for a short time, the 'two eyes of Ireland', but Armagh remained her 'head' and Clonmacnoise her 'dignity' until the end of our period.[2]

IRISH SCRIPTORIA IN THE LATER TENTH AND ELEVENTH CENTURIES

In the later period, after the mid-tenth century, the word 'scribe' rarely occurs in the annals, and other terms are used to describe men who pursue learning. From the late ninth century onwards

---

[1] Lowe, *Rev. Bénédictine*, LXIII (1953), 139–40.

[2] A tract in *Yellow Book of Lecan*, 414 b. 25, and *Book of Ballymote*, 65 b. 11, gives such appellations to a number of Irish monasteries besides these three. I owe this reference to Fr O'Dwyer.

the obits of poets and historians become common. Owing to the nature of the words used to describe these men, it is not always easy to decide what place they should have in a consideration of monastic centres of learning. *Fili* denotes a member of the bardic order, and is nearly always applied to seculars who are associated with a province, or with Ireland as a whole.[1] It is, however, very occasionally used in connection with a monastery, as of Flann Mainistrech (obit 1056), who was distinguished not only for his literature and history, but also in the art of the *fili* and in poetry (*hi filidheacht ocus i nairchetal*). *Éices*, scholar, learned man, poet, may also mean a member of a bardic retinue[2] and in the annals is applied to seculars.[3] *Ollam* is the word used to describe the highest rank of the bardic order, and the ollav is eminent in secular poetry within the province and not attached to a monastery.[4] *Ollam* occasionally describes an expert in any art[5] and is so used of Colcu, abbot of Cenn Etigh (obit 884), 'doctor of eloquence (*ollamh aurlabhraidh*) and best historian that was in Ireland in his time'. The historian (*senchaidh*)[6] or chronicler (*chronicidh*) of the annals is more often than not attached to a monastery. Fochladhe Mide, abbot (*AU*, 871), Colcu of Cenn Etigh (*AFM*, 884), Daniel of Cluain Coirpthe (*AU*, 918), Eochaidh of Armagh (*AI*, 1005), Flann Mainistrech (*AFM*, 1056) and his son Feidlimid (*AFM*, 1104), Tigernach Ua Braein of Clonmacnoise and Roscommon (*AFM*, 1088) and possibly Erard Mac Coisse, 'ard chronicidh na nGaoidheal', who died at Clonmacnoise in 1023, were all monastic historians, though there seem to have been one or two historians mentioned in the annals who were outside the monastic world of learning.[7]

[1] E.g. *AFM*, 1064: 'Ua Lonáin, airdfhile ocus aird seanchaidh na Mumhan'; *AI*, 896: 'Flann rí filed nErend.'

[2] Joynt and Knott, *Dictionary of the Irish Language* (Dublin, London, 1932), fasc. E, 70–1.

[3] E.g. *A.Tig.*, *Rev. Celtique*, XVII, 353 = *AU*, 999: 'Cellach Húa Máel-Corgais, priméces Connacht.'

[4] 'Muiredach na tengadh o Slebin, ollam tuaisceirt Erenn, o Feraib Roiss occisus est', *A.Tig.*, *Revue Celtique*, XVII, 361 = *AU*, 1022. 'Cennfaeladh ollamh Mumhan', *AFM*, 1048. 'Murchadh hua Carrtaigh, primdruith ocus primollam Condacht', *A.Tig.* XVII, 406 = *AU*, 1067. 'O Mail Girig, ollam Ulad, *A.Tig.* XVIII, 10 = *AU*, 1088. [5] *Dictionary of the Irish Language*, fasc. N–O–P, 138.

[6] *Contributions to a Dictionary: S*, ed. E. G. Quin and others, col. 177, for examples of use of the word. Josephus is called *primshenchaide na nEbraide* in the *Passions and Homilies*.

[7] *A.Tig.* XVII, 364; *AU*, 1024: 'Cuan hua Leochan, primsenchaidh Erenn ocus a prímeolach.' *AFM*, 1064: 'Ua Lonan airdfhile ocus aird seanchaidh na Mumhan.' Possibly also the entry at *AFM*, 884, of Maelmora, poet and historian.

The period from the later ninth century to the early twelfth, the age of the poets and historians, is one in which the vernacular was being used increasingly for monastic writings. Sometimes the annal entries record competence in both Irish and Latin. The author Máel Ísu Úa Brolchain was 'skilled in wisdom and piety, as well as in poetry of both languages'. Some of our earliest surviving memorials of the Irish Church were written in Latin in the seventh century; Muirchú's *Life* and Tírechán's *Memoir of Patrick* belong to this group, so do Cuimíne's and Adamnán's *Lives* of Columcille, Cogitosus's *Life of Brigit* (and perhaps the *Life of Ita* may go back to a source of similar antiquity). But most of our pre-Norman saints' *Lives* go back to materials put together in the period from the ninth to the twelfth centuries, and are written in either Latin or Irish. Armagh was drawing together its Patrician legend at the end of the ninth century with the *Vita Tripartita*, the most famous text of the group, and at Clonmacnoise a *Life of Ciarán* was compiled which became the exemplar of the four extant *Lives*. Finnian of Clonard's legend seems to have been established in the ninth century, and his Irish *Life* may go back to materials of this date.[1] The originals of the *Lives* of Molúa and Abbán are dated by Kenney to the ninth century, and he tentatively gives tenth to twelfth century dates to a number of other *Lives*.[2] The annals were being continued in the north, and also at Clonmacnoise and at Emly. Altogether monastic historians of the period seem to have been busy.

From the late ninth century, as the entries of the *Annals of Inisfallen* become fuller, more evidence is made available on western Irish centres of learning. A considerable number of the secular bardic poets are from Munster and Connacht, and Cenn Etigh and Clúain Coirpthe are among the earliest monastic houses where historians are mentioned. All the same the western houses, with the exception of Clonmacnoise, do not seem to have appointed an official Master of the Schools (*lector, fer-léginn*) before the eleventh century. As early as the ninth century there are lectors at Armagh and Lusc, and obits are recorded from a number of eastern houses

---

[1] Hughes, *English Historical Review*, LXIX (1954), 353–72; *Irish Historical Studies*, IX (1954), 13–27.

[2] Tenth-century: Probus's *Patrick, Navigatio Brendani*, Irish *Life of Senán*, story of Colmán Mac Dúach, and possibly the *Life of Comgall*. Eleventh or twelfth century sources for the *Lives* of Findchú of Brigown, Crónán of Roscrea and possibly the Irish *Moling*.

in the tenth century—Downpatrick, Slane, Fore, Clonard, Tallaght, Kildare, Glendalough, Leighlin and Timahoe, as well as from Clonmacnoise. But obits for the western monasteries appear for the first time in the eleventh and twelfth centuries at Cork, Lismore, Emly, Ardfert (Co. Kerry), Kilmallock (Co. Limerick), Tuaimfinnlocha and Tomgraney (Co. Clare), Killaloe, Roscrea, Roscommon, Devenish and Tory. The anciently established centres, Armagh, Clonmacnoise, Kildare, continued their traditions of learning. Other foundations in the east of Ireland gained, it would seem for the first time, considerable reputations as monastic schools—Monasterboice, with her school of historical writing under Flann and his son, and her library housed in the bell tower,[1] or Glendalough with her lectors and her abbot Úa Manchán, a noted brehon.[2] But the western houses were now contributing more and more to the total, and were able to continue the native tradition of learning after the Anglo-Norman invasion. It is from Munster and the Shannon that some of the most important religious compilations come in the later Middle Ages.

For the Latin learning of the earlier period Continental contacts were essential: it is not accidental that Irish learned foundations were on the coast or on routes orientated to the east. Irish and Anglo-Saxon scripts and illumination were both enriched by fusion into the insular style. The Irish anchoritic reform stimulated book production, especially of liturgical texts, but scriptoria were established, not in anchoritic settlements, but in monasteries which had wealth and power. Though financial stability could not create a scriptorium, a centre of learned writing could continue for generations only in a milieu of economic prosperity. The monastic compilers and transcribers added to their patron's possessions by issuing texts which popularised his shrine. A monastic scriptorium, like a modern publishing house, needed funds to maintain it, but it brought in returns. We may legitimately think of the material splendour of Armagh, as well as of her intellectual and cultural eminence, when we read the proverb first provoked by Congus, her scribe and abbot—'the fruit of Congus' pen'.[3]

[1] In 1097 the tower was burned 'with its books and many treasures'.

[2] Kenney would date the first version of Coemgen's *Life* to the tenth or eleventh century.

[3] *Torad penne Congusa.* List of coarbs, ed. Lawlor and Best, *Proc. Roy. Irish Acad.* xxxv (1919), C, 321.

Evidence for Welsh scriptoria during the Celtic period is scanty, and we have to rely to a dangerous degree on Irish analogy. The *Annales Cambriae* record no scribes' obits, Welsh manuscripts are few,[1] and not many of these can be assigned to any particular centre. In North Wales, in the kingdom of Gwynedd, antiquarian speculation was recorded.[2] The genealogies of the early tenth century bear out Giraldus's claim that the court poets kept the pedigrees of the princes 'in their ancient and authentic books',[3] and a century earlier Nennius, the pupil of Elfoddw 'archbishop in the region of Gwynedd', had been able to consult a small library. But until the very end of the Celtic period there is little evidence for flourishing scriptoria in Wales on the Irish scale. It may be that Welsh scriptoria were once as active as Irish, though it is now almost as though they had never been. But it is possible that Wales was in a less favourable position than Ireland for the development of fine books. The Irish clearly gained much from their contact with Anglo-Saxon scriptoria. In the eighth century their scribes' obits are distributed along the routes converging on Dublin Bay and the coasts northward. While English and Irish were exchanging experiences with generous freedom, Wales clung to its separateness from England; Offa's Dyke is an enduring testimony of the suspicion between the Welsh and English. At this period Welsh scriptoria were probably not accessible, as were the Irish, to the stimulus of Anglo-Saxon competition.

Thus it was Ireland which contributed most to Welsh developments. Yet even here, if the Irish annals may be relied on, the contact was less than might be expected. In the eighth century no scribes' obits are recorded from south-east Leinster or around Wexford harbour, the area which we know to have been in intimate contact with Wales. This was the period also of the Irish anchoritic revival, and St David's, the greatest ascetic centre in Wales, can hardly have been untouched by it; but no eighth-century record survives of St David's as a publishing house, or as a learned community.[4] With one notable exception there is no early evidence for important scriptoria in south-east Leinster or south-west Wales,

---

[1] W. M. Lindsay, *Early Welsh Script* (Oxford, 1912), lists a possible twelve.
[2] Cf. above, pp. 32 f.   [3] *Desc. Kambriae*, I, 3.
[4] Cf. above, pp. 123–4, 161. After 810 the St David's entries in the *Annales Cambriae* become more frequent, and records must have been kept there: until this time the emphasis of the entries is much more clearly on Gwynedd. Asser, who is known to have had some connection with St David's, died in 908.

and the provenance of the *Book of St Chad*, dated by Lowe to the eighth century, is a matter of dispute. It certainly came to be associated with the church of St Teilo, presumably Llandeilo Fawr.[1] If it is from a Welsh scriptorium—and this is by no means established—it argues a high degree of accomplishment and sophistication, and it bears out the relationship between the experienced scriptorium and the monastery of wealth and power, which we have seen was normal in Ireland.

For the Irishman, Wales was one of the main roads which led to Rome, and learned Irish were frequenting the court of Merfyn in the ninth century.[2] Some Irish scribes may have been welcomed as long-term visitors in Welsh scriptoria. One of our few Welsh manuscripts, the ninth-century Cambridge *Juvencus*, glossed in Welsh and Irish, was partly written by a scribe with an Irish name, who asks 'a prayer for Nuadu'. The similarity between Welsh and Irish systems of abbreviation show that both countries belong to the same manuscript tradition. But though Irish and Anglo-Saxon manuscripts found their way to the Continent, there is no evidence that Wales took any considerable part in this big book-export business.

It is not until the eleventh century that the surviving manuscripts clearly reveal an active Welsh scriptorium, and Llanbadarn Fawr emerges as a place of learning and book production.[3] The three manuscripts connected with the Sulien family are in Latin, but it is perhaps worth noting that Giraldus, who could understand and write Welsh, considered the vernacular of Ceredigion to be the most supple and clearest in expression of all the Welsh dialects.[4] We may argue back from the evidence of Norman sources to show that, in the same period, Llancarfan, and possibly Llanilltud Fawr, must also have maintained scriptoria, since the surviving sources for the southeast seem to have been preserved largely by these two schools.

In so far as there is evidence of Welsh monastic scriptoria, we may say that they appear to have existed in some of the wealthy *clas* churches;[5] in particular, towards the end of the Celtic period,

---

[1] Bowen, *Settlements*, 57–8. Cf. p. 125 above.
[2] Cf. above, pp. 94 ff.   [3] Cf. above, pp. 126–8.
[4] 'Lingua praecipua uti et laudatissima plerique testantur', *Desc. Kamb.* i, 6.
[5] Of the 'seven bishop houses' which are in Dyfed, mentioned in the Welsh Laws, 'the abbots of Teilo, Teulydawc, Ishmael and Decuman should be ordained scholars (*yscolheigion*)'. A. W. Wade-Evans, *Welsh Medieval Law* (Oxford, 1919), 121, transl. 263.

at Llanbadarn Fawr, Llancarfan and Llanilltud Fawr.[1] It is possible that the absence, at an earlier period, of scribal records from south-east Leinster, and of stimulating contact between Anglo-Saxon and Welsh scriptoria, may indicate a much poorer scribal tradition in Wales than in Ireland. Giraldus, with all his contempt for the Irish, comments on their magnificent books;[2] in his enthusiasm for the Welsh he admires the music which 'charms and delights the ear with its sweetness', the exquisite eloquence of the bardic order, the ecstatic utterances of the seers. Of Latin learning among the ancient Welsh, of Welsh publishing and Welsh artistry in vellum he is significantly silent.[3]

[1] And wherever the *Annales Cambriae* were compiled.
[2] Above, p. 244.
[3] Father Paul Grosjean, S.J., Bollandist, and Professor Francis Wormald discussed chapter III with me in a first draft, and Professor Wormald chapter V. I am especially indebted to them both for help and advice.

VI

The Sources for the Life of St Kentigern

BY KENNETH HURLSTONE JACKSON

St Kentigern, the patron saint of the cathedral of Glasgow and reputed founder of the Christian Church in the British kingdom of Strathclyde in the second half of the sixth century, is a shadowy figure. Our information on him is meagre, and almost all comparatively late; indeed the only notice of him that can be called early is the mention of his death in 612 in the *Annales Cambriae*.[1] However, so little is known about the history of Strathclyde and of the Church there that even these late sources of information are commonly regarded as important historical documents. The present article is an inquiry into what seems to have been the nature of the material used by their compilers, and some conclusions on their value as history will be drawn.

One of the oldest extant is a fragmentary *Life of St Kentigern* consisting of a preface and the first eight chapters of what must have been a much longer work.[2] The anonymous author tells us that it was composed at the request of Herbert, bishop of Glasgow (1147–64), in emulation of Symeon of Durham's *Life of St Cuthbert*. He speaks of himself as 'a cleric of St Kentigern's'; and says that he had travelled through many lands, which he had found venerating each its own patron saint, but that when he came to Scotland[3] he considered it neglectful in this respect, and hence set about composing the *Life*, 'from the material found in a little volume (or, 'little volumes')[4] of his miracles, and from what was

---

[1] *Conthigirni obitus.* The *Annales Cambriae* were drawn up in their present form in the middle of the tenth century, probably based on an earlier edition about a century older, which itself apparently made use of some Strathclyde material put together in the eighth century. Cf. above, p. 47.

[2] Edited by A. P. Forbes, *The Lives of S. Ninian and S. Kentigern* (The Historians of Scotland Series, v; Edinburgh, 1874), 243–52; transl. 123–33.

[3] *Ad regnum Scottorum.*

[4] Forbes prints *codicello*, but the MS. itself reads *codicell-*, with the mark of suspension drawn through the *ll*. This suspension may mean *codicellis* or *codicello*; the former is perhaps slightly more probable palaeographically, but the latter seems to suit the context rather better. Cf. H. Ward in *Romania*, XXII, 505. I wish to thank Mr J. MacQueen for pointing out the reading and sending a photostat.

told me orally by trustworthy people'.[1] It appears from this that the author was not himself a Scot but a foreigner, who had come to Scotland and was settled there in the middle of the twelfth century as one of the clergy of Glasgow Cathedral. It would hardly be too speculative to suggest that he was a Norman priest brought there by David I when, as Earl of Cumbria, he refounded and reorganised the diocese of Glasgow on Norman ecclesiastical lines about 1115; or that he came there somewhat later as a consequence of this reorganisation. We learn further that at the prompting of his bishop he set himself to bring the diocese, formerly the national church of Strathclyde, into line with the general practice in other countries, i.e. in Norman western Europe, by providing it with an up-to-date edition of the legend of its founder. For his sources he used a 'little volume' or 'little volumes' on the miracles of Kentigern, and oral tradition—which would be in the main that handed on by the clergy, though popular folk-lore need not be excluded.

The 'Herbertian Life', as it will be called here, seems to have continued in use at Glasgow for about 30 years. It was then superseded by a new one,[2] written by Jocelyn, a monk of Furness Abbey in northern Lancashire. He tells us that he compiled it for his namesake Bishop Jocelyn of Glasgow (1175–99). As Jocelyn was taken from Furness by John de Courcy and established at Down in Ireland in 1185, it is likely that he wrote the *Life* before then; say about 1180. In his preface he says that he searched diligently in Glasgow for a recorded *Life*, more authoritative, more clearly reliable, and in a more cultivated style than the one used by the church there ('quam vestra frequentat ecclesia'), which was commonly thought to be uncouth in diction, obscure by reason of its ill-composed style, and even containing at the beginning 'something contrary to sound doctrine and to the belief of the Church'. He found, he tells us, a *codicilus*, 'a little volume', composed 'in the Scottic style', abounding in grammatical faults but containing a fuller account of Kentigern's deeds ('diffusius tamen vitam et actus sancti pontificis continentem'). Considering that the one contained a perverse and heretical episode, and the other

---

[1] Or, 'by the faithful'; the passage in the MS. reads: 'de materia in virtutum eius codicell- reperta et viva voce fidelium mihi relata.'

[2] Edited by Forbes, *op. cit.* 159–242, transl. 33–119. Pinkerton's edition in his *Vitae Antiquae*, 191 ff., is from the Cotton Vitellius C. VIII MS., also used by Forbes, and offers no variants of any interest.

was obscured by barbarous language, he decided to combine material from both accounts, 'restoring' it[1] and improving the style where this was 'barbarous'—'barbarice exarata Romano sale condire'.[2]

The *Life* which was current in Glasgow when Jocelyn began his researches can surely only be the one compiled for Bishop Herbert and for the use of the Glasgow church some thirty years before.[3] The episode 'doctrine et catholice fidei adversum', which stained Jocelyn's source with its 'relatu perverso et a fide averso', must refer to the obscure and extraordinary account given by the Herbertian *Life* of Kentigern's conception and birth by a virgin. It would seem to have been part of his traditional and semi-popular 'legend'[4] that he came of a virgin birth, a motif—'the Fatherless Child'—which is known elsewhere in early British semi-learned popular lore.[5] The Herbertian author does not question its truth, but struggles at considerable length to find a scientific physiological explanation of it; but to Jocelyn the story was shockingly blasphemous and heretical, and he tries to gloss it over.[6] None of our other sources for the life of Kentigern has anything comparable, and the probability is strong that Jocelyn is referring to the Herbertian *Life*. The other book on which he drew, the *codicilus*, can scarcely be anything but the *codicellus* (or one of the *codicelli*)[7] known to the Herbertian author, which would seem to have become lost in the interval, and was rediscovered in Glasgow by Jocelyn in the course of his 'diligent' search there. The bishop's request that he should seek in the city for such a *Life* very likely implies that it was known or believed still to exist. The fact that this book did *not* contain the story of the virgin birth is important.

[1] *Redintegrando.*
[2] A specimen of Jocelyn's 'Roman salt' is 'turba ergo mutuo verborum turbine turbam turbabat' (c. 3); and another, 'ephebum, qui juxta putrabilem putride carnis pulchritudinem, ei videbatur vernans venusto aspectu' (c. 36).
[3] [On this point see now pp. 347ff.]
[4] 'Populus stultus et insipiens, in diocesi Sancti Kentegerni degens, ipsum de virgine conceptum et natum adhuc astruere non veretur' (Jocelyn, c. 1). This bears witness to the existence of oral tradition, of the kind which the Herbertian author says he used.
[5] Nennius, *Historia Brittonum*, c. 41.
[6] Jocelyn himself has something of a struggle with it, though he attempts to be very discreet, and ends by saying 'Sed quid hiis immoremur? Sane absurdum, et ab re arbitramur diutius indagare quis quomodo sator terram araverit vel severit' (c. 1).   [7] Cf. p. 273, n. 4.

Now, Jocelyn speaks of this book as being *stilo Scottico dictatum* and obscured *sermone barbarico*. Does this mean that it was in Gaelic (whether of Irish or Scottish provenance), as some have thought? It must be allowed that there is nothing inherently impossible about the existence of a Gaelic *Life* of Kentigern in the eleventh or twelfth century. In Ireland, *Lives* of the Celtic saints were certainly being composed in Irish by this time—the so-called 'Old Irish Life' of St Columba is an instance; and the Gaelicising of Strathclyde which must have been a consequence of its absorption into the orbit of Gaelic Scotland on the death of Owen, the last king, in or about 1018, and which is abundantly proved by the Gaelic place-names found there,[1] must surely have led to an interest on the part of the new Gaelic overlords in the national saint of Strathclyde which might well have resulted in the production of a *Life* in Gaelic. Further, *sermone barbarico* could point only to Gaelic[2] (or Cumbric, which is improbable), if we render it 'in a language other than Latin'.

Nevertheless the *codicilus* can hardly have been in Gaelic, though pretty certainly of a Gaelic background, as we shall see. Jocelyn's words clearly imply that it was in Latin. He could not describe it as *per totum soloecismis scatentem*, 'abounding all through in grammatical errors', if it was in Gaelic; and *barbarice exarata Romano sale condire* must mean 'to season with the salt of a good European Latin style that which was composed in an uncouth one', not 'that which was composed in a non-Latin language'. Again, *stilo Scottico* means naturally 'in the Gaelic style of Latin' rather than 'in Gaelic'; the Latin of early medieval Irish writers is of course notorious for its peculiarities, many of them of Gaelic origin,[3] and these could only seem 'barbarous' to a man like Jocelyn. We must therefore interpret *sermone barbarico* as 'in uncouth diction', a meaning which the phrase can perfectly well bear. Finally, it must be at least doubtful whether Jocelyn could read Gaelic at all, though the close connection of his monastery with the Church in the Isle of Man, and his own residence at Down, where he composed a *Life of St Patrick*, suggest that it is possible.

[1] Cf. *Antiquity*, XXIX (1955), 88.
[2] 'Gaelic' is used here throughout in the sense of 'the Goedelic language of Ireland and Scotland', which was one language at this time. To call it Irish would appear to beg a geographical question which it is better to avoid here.
[3] Cf. G. Brüning, *Zeitschr. für celtische Phil.* XI, 229 ff.

In point of fact, the charge of inelegance brought against the style of one's predecessors, and made by Jocelyn against the Herbertian *Life* as well as the 'Scottic' book, is a natural device intended to justify the production of a new *Life*, and one that can be paralleled at this very period. Ailred of Rievaulx, writing his *Life of St Ninian* about 1165, uses very much the same phrases about his source. In his prologue he says, 'But those who lacked the skill to compose in a decorative and artistic fashion because of the barbarity of their native land (*ob barbariem natalis soli*) did not defraud posterity of an account of those who were worthy of imitation, though writing in a more simple style';[1] that hence the *Life* of Ninian had previously been obscured by its *sermo barbaricus*; and that he proposes to bring forth from its *sermone rustico* into the light of Latin diction that which had been composed by his predecessors *nimis barbarico...stilo*. In the preface, Ailred calls his source *liber de vita et miraculis eius barbario scriptus*.[2] Some of these words could be taken to refer to a work in the vernacular, and have been so taken; but none of them *must*, and 'those who lacked the skill to compose in a decorative and artistic fashion', 'writing in a more simple style', and using 'a very barbaric style', are clearly the authors of a Latin document which Ailred chose to think uncouth.[3] It looks very much as if Jocelyn, who appears to echo Ailred, was actually imitating him here. It may be worth while adding that if the 'little volume' was in the vernacular it would be unique among *Lives* of the saints composed in Scotland.

We must reckon, then, with the existence of some kind of account of the life and miracles of Kentigern written by a Gael, whether of Scotland or Ireland, and older than about 1150. The period during which such a *Life* is most likely to have been composed is between about 1018, when Strathclyde was absorbed into the greater entity of Gaelic Scotland, and about 1115, when David I refounded the diocese, after which any new *Life* would almost certainly be in Norman Latin. During this time it is evident that there was a considerable influx of Gaelic population into Strathclyde. Just as the landed estates were probably largely taken over by a class of Gaelic overlords, so the chief control of the Church would fall into

[1] Forbes, *op. cit.* 137. [2] *Ibid.* 140.
[3] This source being, of course, the lost eighth-century *Life* also used by the author of the *Miracula Nynie Episcopi*; see W. Levison in *Antiquity*, xiv (1940), 280ff. This was evidently in Latin, as is shown by the fact that in giving an Anglian place-name (*Fearres Last*) it explained it in Latin.

the hands of 'Scottic'[1] clerics. One may compare what seems to have happened (perhaps only gradually) to the Church in what had been Pictland after the establishment of the line of Kenneth Mac-Alpine. The incomers could not, of course, dispossess Kentigern of his position as founder of the Church in Strathclyde; and having adopted him instead, they would be bound to wish to produce a written *Life* of the national saint, for their own information and because it was their custom. The 'Scottic' branch of the Celtic Church had been addicted to writing saints' *Lives* from very early times, and the practice was growing in Ireland in the eleventh and twelfth centuries.

The fact that almost nothing is known about the Church in Strathclyde between Kentigern's time and David I's reconstruction ought not to blind us to the probability that such a Church existed.[2] It is true that the account given in the 'Inquisition' of David I suggests great confusion, disorganisation, and lack of manpower in the Strathclyde Church in the eleventh century, but we should not therefore conclude that Strathclyde was as good as pagan, and had been so for centuries. Under its native kings, when it was a powerful kingdom, this is incredible. In the eleventh century, with the upheavals caused by the change of kingship and the influx of Gaelic overlords, disorganisation is to be expected, but that the Church should have ceased entirely to function here, any more than elsewhere in Scotland, is not likely. The period was one of decay in the Scottish Church everywhere, but the decay was

[1] This word is used here throughout referring to the people and kingdom of Gaelic Scotland north of the Forth and Clyde; as well as to the people of Ireland in some contexts. The kingdom itself is called Scotia.

[2] Two points are often made. Bede's words telling how 'plurima pars Scottorum in Hibernia et nonnulla etiam de Brettonibus in Brittania' (*H.E.* v, 15) in 703 or 704 were converted to the Roman Easter are generally taken to refer to the Britons of Strathclyde, since those of Wales cannot be meant. Bede uses a similar phrase of the Britons who regained their liberty from Northumbria after Nechtansmere (*H.E.* IV, 24), where Strathclyde must be intended. The Britons of Western Wessex and Devon were also converted to the new Easter about this time (*H.E.* v, 18), but it is less probable that Bede means them. The other passage is the reference to 'Sedulius episcopus Britanniae de genere Scottorum' who took part in a council at Rome in 721 (cf. Forbes, *op. cit.* p. xcii), which is often taken to point to a Strathclyde Briton, through the loose association of *Britannia* and *Scottus*. But the words patently mean 'a bishop from Britain, of the race of the Gael', i.e. an Irish or Scottish Gael from the Columban Church in (northern) Britain; cf. Bede's use of *Scotti Brittaniae* referring to the Gael of Dál Riada. In any case Sedulius is a well-known Latinisation of an Irish name, but is not anywhere else used of Britons.

perhaps exaggerated by the new Normanising church party; one must allow for the fact that it was necessary to make the re-organisation of *c*. 1115 seem a revolutionary and desperately needed measure. Indeed we know that there were bishops of Glasgow in the eleventh century, since two were consecrated between 1055 and 1060. The reason for the blank in our knowledge of the Strathclyde Church is simple—for lack of documents, we know very little about any of the history of Strathclyde at any period. I suggest therefore that the 'little volume' in Scottic Latin was a product of the Gaelic occupation of Strathclyde in the eleventh century. If it was the book, or one of the books, known to the Herbertian author, as it surely must have been, it would seem to have continued in use at Glasgow until it was superseded by his own compilation.

The latter, and Jocelyn, are our two chief sources for the story of St Kentigern, but they are not the only ones. Another is an office of St Kentigern in a breviary of the late thirteenth century, printed by Forbes.[1] This consists of nine short prose *lectiones* interspersed with verse canticles. The prose parts deal only with the story of the bringing up of St Kentigern by St Servanus. It is impossible to compare this in detail with the Herbertian *Life*, since that *Life* breaks off where this episode has only just begun; but the version in the Edinburgh breviary differs in certain important respects from that given by Jocelyn, as will appear below, and in ways which strike one as older and more original. The verse canticles are very brief and allusive, but are drawn at random from all parts of the story of Kentigern, and unlike the prose they do seem to depend upon Jocelyn's version of the *Life*, as we shall see. It would seem that the *lectiones* of the Office were derived from an early prose version of the tale of Servanus and Kentigern, and the compiler went to Jocelyn's account of the whole of Kentigern's life for the source of his canticles.

The other important remaining source for the story of St Kentigern is the Breviary of Aberdeen, of the beginning of the sixteenth century, which contains accounts of Kentigern's own life[2] and that of Theneuu his mother.[3] These are again offices consisting, like

---

[1] *Op. cit.* xcivff. The MS. is called the Sprouston Breviary, and is now classed as 18. 2. 13b in the National Library of Scotland; the office of Kentigern is on ff. 35b–38b. An opinion by Bannister in National Library MS. 18. 1. 9, p. 11, dates it late thirteenth century, probably *c.* 1300.

[2] Maitland Club, 1854; *Breviary of Aberdeen*, Winter, pt. 3, ff. xxviiff.

[3] *Op. cit.* (1852), Summer, pt. 3, ff. xxxivff.

that in the Edinburgh breviary, of prose *lectiones* and verse canticles, the verse parts being very brief and allusive, and the prose only a summary by comparison with the much fuller versions of the Herbertian *Life* and Jocelyn. The *lectiones* in this Office of Kentigern agree with those in the Edinburgh breviary, as against Jocelyn, in the points referred to above, and are therefore more nearly related to them than to him; but there is reason to think that the compiler of this Office also knew Jocelyn's *Life*, as we shall see. The Office of St Theneuu on the other hand is taken from the Herbertian *Life*, as the many close verbal resemblances clearly show, as well as the identity of content (granting that the Office is a summary).[1]

Lastly, there is a version of the *Life of St Kentigern* given in Capgrave's *Nova Legenda Anglie*,[2] and reprinted in the *Acta Sanctorum* of the Bollandists.[3] It is attributed to *auctor anonymus*, but is pretty clearly nothing but a paraphrase summary of Jocelyn, cutting out many of Jocelyn's verbosities but tending to preserve more when they are given by Jocelyn as Kentigern's own words. The similarities of phrasing are close throughout; and the only passage in this version not found in Jocelyn as we know his text is the brief note in its c. 41 (which should appear in Jocelyn between his c. 41 and c. 42) about a miraculous mill which Kentigern built on the Clyde, which would not grind stolen corn and would not work between Nones on Saturday and Mass on Sunday. This passage must presumably have dropped out in the MS. from which our copies of Jocelyn derive, and it is not found in any other account of Kentigern.[4]

In what follows, one must bear in mind that the Offices in the

[1] Since the present study was written the article by Mr John MacQueen, 'A Lost Glasgow Life of St Thaney', has appeared (*Innes Review*, VI, 125 ff.). Mr MacQueen likewise regards the Office of St Theneuu as derived from the Herbertian *Life*, but at one remove, not directly, through a lost intermediate source which he thinks was a *Life* compiled at Glasgow. I find myself in general agreement with the possibility of an intermediate source, though some of the arguments are more weighty than others. [2] 207 ff.

[3] 13 January, II, 98 ff. According to T. D. Hardy, *Descriptive Catalogue of Materials* (Rolls Series, XXVI, 1862–71), I, i, 208, this version is found in British Museum Cotton. Tiberius E. 1, f. 17 b, and in Bodleian Tanner, 15 vell. folio, fifteenth century.

[4] The hymn mentioned by Forbes, *op. cit.* pp. c–ci, is in the Edinburgh University MS. now classified as Dc. 7. 63, f. 156 b, of the early sixteenth century, and is edited in the *Registrum Episcopatus Glasguensis* (Bannatyne Club, 1843), I, p. xcix. This hymn offers nothing of any interest, and the fact that it is late is indicated by the words 'sacramenta praebuit Merlino precanti', which are probably based on Bower, see p. 329, n. 2 below.

two breviaries are only summaries and that the Herbertian *Life* is a fragment; also that Jocelyn, who seems to list his sources conscientiously, mentions only two, one apparently the Herbertian *Life* and the other the Scottic 'little volume', as we have already seen. It is important then to consider what his attitude to his predecessors may have been, since his *Life* is the only complete and full narrative of Kentigern that we have. The Herbertian author impresses one as a man who honestly and patiently repeated in detail all he had heard, and did his best to account for it, no matter whether he cared for or fully understood the very strange and very Celtic character of some of the matter, or was interested in the intimate local knowledge of places doubtless quite unknown to him which it displays. Jocelyn on the other hand takes very little interest in all this; so little that it might be argued that he did not use the Herbertian *Life* at all, though I think it will become clear that he must have done so.[1] In any case, local legend and the names and nature of places and people in this Celtic and Scottish setting seem to have meant comparatively little to him, and he mostly passes them over in a very cavalier fashion, just as he glosses over the peculiar story of Kentigern's conception. He is more concerned to glorify his hero, and it is significant, as we shall see, that his tendency is to remove or alter anything which might be interpreted as discreditable to him.

According to the Herbertian *Life*, c. 1, 'King Leudonus, a semi-pagan man, from whom the province which he ruled in northern Britain got the name of Leudonia, had a daughter, with a step-mother, who was called Thaney' ('rex...Leudonus, vir semi-paganus, a quo provincia quam regebat Leudonia nomen sortita in Brittannia septentrionali'). She was wooed by 'juvenis quidam elegantissimus, Ewen videlicet filius Erwegende, nobilissima Brittonum prosapia ortus.... In gestis histrionum[2] vocatur Ewen filius regis Ulien.' The only reference to Kentigern's parentage in the *lectiones* of the Edinburgh breviary is the statement that he was 'nobilissima inclitorum regum Britannie gentis prosapia illustris', and 'natum in provincia que ab avo suo Leudono rege Leudonia denominatur'. It would seem that its source did not know, or more probably did not choose to say, who Kentigern's own parents were, though it does say that he was of the line of the kings of Lothian.

---

[1] [Cf. now pp. 347 ff. below.]

[2] On this reading cf. Ward, *Romania*, XXII, 506.

The *lectiones* in the Office of Kentigern in the Breviary of Aberdeen begin by saying that he was 'nobilissima Scotica prosapia, patre Eugenio Eufurenn regis Cumbrie, matre vero Teneuu filia Loth regis Laudonie ortus'. The use of the adjective Scotica for the country south of the Forth, and the form *Loth*, which is evidently due to the influence of Fordun and through him of Geoffrey of Monmouth, are late features, consonant with the date of the Breviary, but are no doubt secondary. All these details seem to derive ultimately from a common source, presumably the hypothetical original *Life of Kentigern*, on which see p. 332 below; the supposed story of Servanus and Kentigern discussed below (pp. 295 ff.) would know them as part of the common stock of information on him. Jocelyn, c. 1, only says 'His mother was the daughter of a certain king, of a most pagan creed, who ruled the northern part of Britain' ('regis secta paganissimi in septentrionali plaga Britanniae principantis'), and he has nothing whatever to say about his father. This is because he wishes to suppress so far as possible the whole story of Kentigern's conception, and if he mentioned the father at all he would have had to tell how he begot Kentigern. All he does is to admit that he was conceived 'de humano complexu'. The Office of Theneuu in the Breviary of Aberdeen says that the king of Leudonia, which is the northern part of Britain, had a daughter Theneuu, and that Kentigern's father was 'Euuen Cumbrie regis filius de nobilissima Britonum oriundus prosapia, iuvenis quidam elegantissimus', where the resemblances are even more striking.

The etymology and history of the name *Lothian* is full of difficulties, and need not be discussed here. In any event, *Leudonus* looks suspiciously like an artificial eponym for the province, and it is most improbable that he was a historical person. The girl's name is *Thaney* in the Herbertian *Life*, *Taneu* in Jocelyn (c. 4; he does not mention her by name at this point); *Teneuu* in the Office of Kentigern and *Theneuu* in her Office in the Aberdeen Breviary. Now this must be a perfectly genuine form, though the spellings in *Th-* and *-y* are corruptions of a characteristic Norman-Latin type. The copies of the Herbertian *Life* used by Jocelyn and the Breviary no doubt had better readings than the one in ours. It may well be the Cumbric[1]

---

[1] 'Cumbric' denotes the language of the Britons of Strathclyde and north Britain in general in the Dark Ages. What little is known of it suggests that it was very similar indeed to contemporary Welsh.

equivalent of the Middle Welsh adjective *teneu* or Cornish *tanow*, 'slender',[1] and the writing of *-eu* for older *-ou* would indicate a MS. source of not much earlier than about 1100 if it were Welsh; however, as the *pronunciation* with *-eu* is older, and as we are dealing with Cumbric, not Welsh, one cannot be positive. On the other hand in medieval Welsh tradition, which often preserves very faithfully indeed the correct form of early northern British names, she is known as *Denyw*[2] or *Dinw*[3] (where *D-* must be a generalisation of lenition of *t-*). This would be a derivative from the same stem as the adjective *teneu*; and since such a derivative is more probable as a name than the bare adjective would be, it may be right. If so, *Taneu* is a (perfectly possible) spelling for *Taniu*,[4] which would be an earlier form of *Teniu*; and this may imply an ultimate written source which, to judge Cumbric from our knowledge of Welsh, is not very likely to be later than the ninth century if it is a purely written form, or even the seventh to eighth if it represents pronunciation. In this case *T(h)eneuu* would be a Norman-Latin spelling derived from *Teneu* meaning *Teniu*. There is too much that is uncertain here to lay any great weight on it, but at least it is clear that Jocelyn and the Breviary preserve a better spelling than the version of the Herbertian *Life* that has come down to us, and that the girl's name is a genuine Cumbric one.

The passage on the name of Kentigern's father in the Herbertian *Life* is specially important. The man referred to is one of the most famous characters in the medieval Welsh traditions about the Britons of the North, traditions which certainly have some historical basis. In medieval Welsh poetry he is *Ywein*, *Ewein*, or *Owein* (these are all spellings of one single pronunciation), son of Urien. According to the *Gododdin* poem he was one of the very few northern heroes who escaped from the disastrous British defeat at

---

[1] *Taneu* for *teneu* (without vowel-affection) would be a quite possible by-form in Middle Welsh; but Cumbric may have had a form which would not have had vowel-affection in any case (i.e. *taneu*), like Cornish *tanow*. Cf. my *Language and History in Early Britain* (Edinburgh, 1953), § 164 and p. 376.

[2] Cf. Williams in *Transactions of the Cumberland and Westmorland Antiquarian and Archaeological Society*, n.s., LI, 87.

[3] Wade-Evans, *Vitae Sanctorum Britanniae* (Cardiff, 1944), 320 (the twelfth-century *Bonedd y Saint*). In the same source, however, she also appears as *Tynoy* (*op. cit.* 321). The whole tradition of the name seems curiously corrupt.

[4] Cf. *Language and History*, p. 283, n. 2. The *-eu* in this case, for *-iu*, would represent a quite different diphthong from that in the Welsh *teneu*, Cornish *tanow*.

Catterick about A.D. 600; and in other very early Welsh sources his father Urien, king of 'Reget',[1] was a doughty opponent of the Angles of Bernicia in the second half of the sixth century. These traditions were handed down in Wales partly in the form of popular tales in a mixture of prose and verse, with which professional story-tellers entertained chiefs and retainers alike, in the familiar Celtic manner. It is highly probable that such stories were current in the vernacular in Strathclyde as well as Wales, especially those dealing with Cumbric national heroes, and it seems certain that by *gesta histrionum* the Herbertian author meant exactly this. If so, he or his source was familiar with a body of saga concerning Urien and his sons in Cumbric, doubtless very similar to that popular at the same time in Wales, of which we still have fragments.

In the ninth century these names would have been pronounced something like *öüyein* and *ürvyen* (*ö* and *ü* meaning the sounds so written in German, and *y* being consonantal), and in Old Welsh documents deriving from about that time they are therefore spelt *Ougen* (for *Ougein*) and *Urbgen*, since *b* in Old Welsh means *v* and internal *g* before *e* or *i* means consonantal *y*. Somewhat later the first became approximately *eüyein*, probably as early as the late tenth century; and with the loss of *y*, still later *əwein* (where *ə* is roughly the sound of *e* in *hammer*). The form *eüyein* is spelt in late Old Welsh *Eugein*, and *əwein* would be spelt *Euein*; both might be written with *-en* in the second syllable, and in Cumbric this may well have been the actual pronunciation. *Eu-* instead of *Ou-* would probably not be expected in Old Welsh spelling before about 1100, but the sound it represents was in existence at least a century earlier, and there is no reason to doubt therefore that *Eu-* might be written in Cumbric as early as say 1000. It follows then that the *Eugenius* of the Office of Kentigern in the Breviary of Aberdeen represents a written form which may belong to the eleventh century, and the *Ewen* of the Herbertian *Life* and *Euuen* of the Office of Theneuu go back to the later *Euen*, with *w* or *uu* for consonantal *u* due to Norman-Latin spelling habits and therefore perhaps to the Herbertian author or a later copyist.

As for *Ulien*, this may well be genuine. In Welsh, *ürvyen* became *üryen* at some time in the late Old Welsh period, which

[1] On the whereabouts of this kingdom, evidently somewhere in south-west Scotland and north-west England, see *Antiquity*, XXIX (1955), 82.

would be spelt *Urien* in the twelfth century and probably *Urgen* or *Urien* in the eleventh. Since both branches of the Celtic languages, the Goedelic and Brittonic, had a sporadic tendency to interchange *r* and *l* in certain circumstances, there is nothing contrary to the genius of a Brittonic dialect like Cumbric in such a development as *Ulien* here. It seems evident that in *Ewen filius Ulien* the writer was reproducing the spoken form of both names in the eleventh century, presumably in the *gesta histrionum*. This still does not explain the *Erwegende* of the Herbertian *Life* and the *Eufurenn* of the Aberdeen Office of Kentigern. The context in the Herbertian *Life* seems to make it clear that *Ewen filius Erwegende* represents the form the writer found in his written source, and that the words *in gestis*, etc., which are in fact a kind of parenthesis, are a comment or gloss: 'This is the person whom we all know in the popular tales as Ewen son of Ulien.' The *-de* in *Erwegende* is obviously wrong, and the parallel of *Melconde* discussed below suggests that it is not part of the name, but here may well be simply the Latin preposition *de* (*de nobilissima...prosapia ortus*), wrongly written as being the end of the name by some late scribe to whom it was in any case unknown and barbarous, but whose Latinity was better than the author's. We have then *Erwegen* and *Eufurenn* to reconcile. It has just been noted that in the ninth century the name was pronounced approximately *ürvyen*, written *Urbgen* in Old Welsh; however a spelling *Urugen*, with *v* written *u*, might be possible in Cumbric. But, as with some other compound names in Old Welsh, a by-form with the old composition vowel preserved would be quite in order and in fact exists; it would be pronounced *ürvəyen*, and this is what is meant by the *Urbeghen* and *Urbagen* of certain MSS. of Nennius.[1] I suggest that what lies behind *Erwegen* and *Eufurenn* here is *Uruegen*, wrongly spelt in the original source as *Euruegen* or *Eruegen*, owing to the scribe's eye falling on the preceding name as he wrote. The *fu* would be a spelling for the sound *v*, as is sometimes the case in medieval Welsh MSS., due to a later copyist, who metathesised the *v* and *r* and perhaps also substituted the more common form of the name in *-en* for the less common *-eyen*. The hypothetical erroneous *E(u)ruegen* would be more archaic than *Ulien* and might well be as old as the ninth century or even older, though it could equally well be later; at any rate it struck the person responsible for the comment '*in gestis*' etc. as being obsolete

---

[1] Cf. my *Language and History*, p. 648.

or strange. The result of all this is that behind the Herbertian author and the Breviary of Aberdeen we seem to see someone who was familiar with Strathclyde oral saga in the eleventh century, and was using an older written source of Strathclyde provenance which might (but need not) go back to the ninth century or beyond. Incidentally it should be noted that this son of Urien was a popular figure in Welsh (and evidently Cumbric) story who attracted all kinds of tales and legends to himself, and that there is no positive reason to think that he was really the father of Kentigern. A saint had to have a royal father, and 'Euen son of Uruegen' would be an obvious candidate in the eyes of a Cumbric compiler of a *Life*. Indeed it would be absurd chronologically, since Kentigern, who died in 612 according to the *Annales Cambriae*, would presumably have been born about 540 or 550, which would make Urien's son a younger contemporary of the man whose father he was reputed to be.

The Herbertian *Life* and the documents derived from it now continue with the story of the conception and birth of Kentigern and the punishment of his mother.[1] It describes how the girl's father, annoyed by her refusal to marry Ewen, sends her to be servant to a swineherd, who is secretly a Christian. He had been converted in *Scocia* by St Servanus, disciple of Palladius the first bishop of the *Scotti* who was sent in 430 by Pope Celestinus and worked as a missionary in *Albania*. Having told in physiological detail the strange tale of how Ewen, after having employed a procuress in vain, disguised himself as a girl and how Thaney conceived by him though a virgin, the *Life* describes how she was sentenced to death by stoning according to the law, was taken to the top of a hill or mountain (*mons*) called Kepduf, put in a wagon, and thrown from the top, but reached the bottom miraculously unhurt. The wagon, pushed down backwards, turned round as it ran, and its pole stuck in the ground, whence 'straightway there began to gush forth a most limpid spring which has not ceased to well to the present day'; and in the same way the ruts made by the wheels in the rock 'still present a great miracle to those who see them'. When the king failed to kill his daughter in this way he decided to set her adrift in a boat and leave the judgment of life or death to God.

---

[1] On the fact that the Office of Kentigern in the Aberdeen Breviary knew of the tale, and on the significance of this, see p. 333.

She was brought to the strait which is distant from the mount of Kepduf about three miles, namely to the river-mouth which is called *Aberlessic*, that is, 'the River-mouth of the Stench'; because at that time the abundance and luxuriance of fish caught was so great that the multitude of fish thrown out of the boats on to the sand was too troublesome for men to carry away; and such a rotten smell broke out from the fish left on the shore of the river-mouth, whose putrefying juices clotted the sand, that the stench of this noxious foulness was accustomed to drive back more quickly than they came many who approached there.

The king now pursued the swineherd, intending to kill him; the latter dodged into a marshy place, where he killed the king with a spear. A 'great royal stone' was erected as his memorial, crowned with a smaller carved stone, 'which remains there to the present, distant about a mile from the mount of Dumpelder, on the south side'. Meanwhile the girl was put into a boat (*in laubo*), defined as a skiff made of hide, and set adrift; she was carried out into the high sea beyond the Isle of May. As she left the shore all the fish followed her, so that fish were never caught on that coast any more, and the river-mouth which had been so rich in fish became barren to the present day. But the fertility was transferred to the part of the sea where they followed her; and now fishermen come from far and wide, Englishmen, Scots (*Scottici*), Belgians, and Frenchmen to fish there, and find harbour in the Isle of May. Next morning the boat was washed up on the sand at Culross (*prope Collenros*), which sailors reckon to be thirty miles from the Isle of May in *Scotia*. Having come to land, the girl gave birth to a son.

Such is the account given by the Herbertian *Life*, c. 1–8. Jocelyn is briefer, partly because he wishes to suppress so far as possible the whole story of the lover and the virgin conception. He has nothing to say of Ewen or the swineherd, though of course he admits the pregnancy and its discovery; he repeats the story of the death sentence and how the woman was thrown from the hill (*mons altissimus*), which he calls Dumpelder (var. *Dunpelder*), without harm to herself. He does not mention the wagon, the spring, or the ruts. For the story of the setting adrift he only says, 'Finally it was decreed by the common connivance of the assembly of spiteful men and enemies of the name of Christ that the poor pregnant woman should be put alone in a boat and left to the ocean', and that the king's servants set her adrift 'in a very small boat of hide, made according to the custom of the Scots (*iuxta morem Scottorum*), without any means of rowing'. The boat was carried 'towards the opposite shore', and she landed safely at Culross (*Culenros*) and there gave birth to a son. Jocelyn says nothing of the killing of the king, his monument, the story of *Aberlessic* and the fish, the origin of the good fishing grounds round the Isle of May, or the distance thence to Culross.

As for the Office of St Theneuu, it tells how Euuen woos her and is refused, how her father gives her the choice of marrying Euuen or being given to the swineherd *perpetuo stuprandam*, how Theneuu chooses the latter, and how the swineherd (secretly a Christian) treats her with honour. No mention is made of his conversion by Servanus. Euuen, his procuress having failed, dresses as a woman and rapes her. Her pregnancy being discovered, Theneuu is condemned to be stoned, is taken in a wagon to the top of a hill (*in montis summitate*), and thrown off, but descends unhurt; the wagon sticks in the ground, and 'a most limpid spring welled forth, which has not ceased to flow to the present'. The shafts of the wagon dig up the rock, and leave a perpetual sign. The father, thinking she is a witch, has her taken to the sea near by, 'to the haven (*portus*) which is called by the common people *Aberledy*, where a very great number of fish is accustomed to be caught'. She is put in 'a boat made with osiers and pitch and covered with hide, without any rudder, sail, or oar', and carried to the Isle of May, where she is borne up by a crowd of fish against the current, comes to Culross (*ad Culros*), and gives birth to Kentigern.

In all this episode, the detailed knowledge of Lothian shown in the Herbertian *Life* is remarkable. It sounds like the work of someone who knew the geography of the place intimately, together with its religious 'local legends' and its etymological place-name stories. He did not attempt to disguise the story of the virgin birth, which as Jocelyn himself bears witness was a matter of popular folk-lore; on the contrary he dealt with its blasphemous implications not by suppressing it but by attempting a 'scientific' explanation. Jocelyn on the other hand deliberately ignores Ewen's part in it, including the story of the swineherd which belongs to it; and, having no interest in or knowledge of Lothian himself, and assuming none in his readers, he leaves out almost the whole of these matters. The Office of Theneuu also suppresses the story of the virgin birth, but otherwise keeps fairly close to the Herbertian *Life*, except that it is obviously summarising and hence omits some passages not likely to be of general interest. The resemblances in wording are often so close that it is clear it is paraphrasing the Herbertian *Life* itself.[1]

Certain matters here must be considered in detail. The reference to the swineherd being converted by Servanus is of course left out by Jocelyn, and the author of the Office of Theneuu did not think it important enough to include in his summary. That Scotland is meant here by *Scocia*, not Ireland, is proved by the synonymous use of *Albania*. In fact the old Gaelic kingdom of Scotland north of the Forth is intended, as distinct from Lothian, as appears below, though this does not necessarily imply a source older than the cession of Lothian in 975 or 1018. The story of Palladius as missionary to the Scots of Scotland is of course a misunderstanding of his mission 'ad Scottos in Christum credentes', i.e. to the Irish; it can be traced back to the ninth century in Nennius, and led to the invention of a Scottish 'Saint Paldy'. Its presence here is due to someone to whom *Scotti* already meant Scots rather than Irishmen, perhaps the Herbertian author himself;[2] and in any case the association of Servanus with Palladius is a gross anachronism.

The Herbertian *Life* calls the hill Kepduf as against the Dumpelder of Jocelyn, but in c. 7 it speaks of Dumpelder without however identifying it with Kepduf; still, it seems likely that the same place is meant. Dumpelder is Traprain Law near Haddington, as Watson shows,[3] and the etymology he proposes for the element *-pelder*, namely Welsh *pelydr*, 'spearshafts', may well be right; the *Dun-* would be a Gaelicisation of Cumbric *Din-*, and the name would have been in Cumbric *Din Pelidr*. We may suggest, however, that *pelydr* here is to be taken rather in one of the other possible meanings of the word—'staves, beams', and that the whole name is really 'The Fort of the Beams', referring perhaps to a wooden stockade which may once have crowned the ramparts of the Dark Age hill-fort on Traprain Law. However that may be, someone with a knowledge of Brittonic seems to have thought of spear-

[1] Or, if MacQueen is correct (see p. 280, n. 1), a lost source directly derived from the Herbertian *Life*. Some of the parallels he quotes suggest this.

[2] There is no reason to think it was introduced by the compiler of the Servanus–Kentigern material described below (pp. 295 ff.), who probably did not know the story of the swineherd, as we shall see. The Herbertian author or his source may have asked himself how the swineherd could have been a Christian, and the answer would be to hand in the person of Servanus, of whom of course he knew. Evidently the legend of Palladius in Scotland was already current there in the twelfth century.

[3] W. J. Watson, The *Celtic Place-Names of Scotland* (Edinburgh, 1926), 345.

shafts in this connection, since in c. 7 the Herbertian *Life* makes the swineherd, when he kills Leudonus close to Dumpelder, 'snatch up a javelin and throw it by its finger-loop from behind the king so that it transfixed him'. Anyone familiar with Celtic methods of story-telling, and with the *Lives* of the Celtic saints, will realise that the javelin is introduced here solely to account for the place-name; though, as very often happens, this is not explicitly stated.

Kepduf is unquestionably Gaelic, not Cumbric. *Kep* is early Gaelic *cep*, 'block, stump', a loanword from *cippus*, and it is not uncommon in Lowland place-names, used of prominent hills—the Kips in the Pentlands are an instance. The second element is early Gaelic *dub*, 'black', pronounced *duv*; and the whole appears to be derived from an oral source, not a written one, since *Kepdub* would otherwise be expected. 'The Black Block' would be an excellent name for Traprain Law, with its grim dark cliffs over which the woman was thrown in the story. As a matter of fact there is a small spring just below the hilltop on the south side, above the cliffs, and there are rib-like formations in the rocks on this side which might perhaps have suggested cart tracks to the eye of faith. It may well be, then, that *Din Pelidr* was the Cumbric and *Cep Dub* the Gaelic name for Traprain Law. We must remember that there are numerous Cumbric place-names in Lothian to the present day; that up to the seventh century the language of the whole of Lothian was Cumbric; that very likely for some centuries later it may have been spoken, especially in the more remote hills and glens, by the descendants of the Britons; and that in any case Strathclyde, with its solid population of Cumbric speakers, was not very far away. Hence the survival of a Cumbric name for this striking landmark is not at all unnatural. On the other hand, when Lothian was ceded to the Gaelic kingdom of Scotia, in the second half of the tenth century or early in the eleventh, there must have been a consider-able immigration of speakers of Gaelic, perhaps especially of a land-holding aristocracy, as is very clearly shown by the evidence of many place-names and personal names; and these people could hardly fail to give a name in their own language to such a place as Traprain Law. Moreover, in *Dumpelder* the Cumbric *din* was replaced by Gaelic *dun*, with the same meaning, as happened in other Lothian place-names, such as *Dunbar*.[1] This coexistence of

---

[1] Cf. my *Language and History*, p. 320. Or the *Dun* in both might be Anglo-Saxon, but in any case it cannot be Brittonic.

speakers of Cumbric and Gaelic, not to mention also Anglian, in Lothian in the Dark Ages is an important clue to the history of the St Kentigern story, as will appear.

It is of course not certain that *Kepduf* is Traprain Law. Watson [1] very oddly attempts to identify it with Kilduff, about $4\frac{1}{4}$ miles north-west of Traprain Law. But Kilduff is a low flattish hill from which it would be quite impossible to throw anyone, in a wagon or otherwise, and one which could not conceivably be called a 'Block' nor spoken of as *mons*, whether *altissimus* or not. Besides, the name is early Gaelic *Caill Dub*, 'Black Wood', not 'Black Block'; and both elements, *caill* and *dub*, are extremely common in place-names. It is likely that Watson's real reason for this identification was the matter of the distance of Kilduff from Aberlady, which is discussed below. In any case the Herbertian author was once again using here some source which had an intimate knowledge of the district and its *mirabilia*, as well as its place-names and their pronunciation, and one which was not anterior to the Gaelic occupation of Lothian. The story of the javelin may suggest that its composer knew Cumbric, as well as Gaelic, or at least the local legends of a Cumbric-speaking peasantry. The fact that Jocelyn omits so many local details simply means that he was a foreigner indifferent to such matters, and that he had no sympathy with the Celtic fondness for place-name stories and local legends.

The tale of 'The River-Mouth of the Stench' is another characteristic Celtic place-name legend. *Aberlessic* has always been identified, on geographical as well as (mistaken) linguistic grounds, with Aberlady, and we can see this already as early as the sixteenth-century Breviary of Aberdeen. Watson,[2] noting that the two names cannot be the same, suggests that the story has got muddled here, and that two different river-mouths are involved. *Aber*, 'river-mouth', is of course a Brittonic[3] word, and for the second element he compares Cornish *lesic*, 'herbaceous, bushy'.[4] In Aberlady (thirteenth-century *Aberleuedi*, etc.) he proposes to see a Brittonic cognate of the Gaelic stem *lobh-*, 'to rot'. The story of the fish would therefore belong to Aberlady, and Watson suggests that *Aberlessic*, which would have to be a different place, may have been the mouth of the Gosford Burn about a mile south-west of Aberlady. If Watson is right, it would mean that someone in the line of those

---

[1] *Loc. cit.*   [2] *Op. cit.* 460.   [3] And Pictish.
[4] The Welsh *llusog* which he compares is a different word.

who handed down the story of Kentigern, who knew the neighbourhood but did not know Cumbric, confused the two names; and either gave *Aberlessic* under the wrong impression that it meant 'River-mouth of the Stench' and was the scene of the casting adrift (really Aberlady), or correctly gave *Aberlessic* as the place but interpreted its meaning wrongly by using a place-name legend belonging to Aberlady.

There are several unsatisfactory features here. The source for this whole story is likely to have been the compiler of the tale of Kentigern's conception, and we have seen that there is some reason to think that he did understand Cumbric. Certainly we must clear our minds of all association between the names *Aberlessic* and *Aberlady*; but the Gosford Burn is a tiny stream with nothing at all at its outflow that could be called an *aber*, which always implies some sort of very distinct inlet. The burn simply trickles into the sea on a perfectly blank and straight stretch of coast, and the place could not possibly call for a name in *Aber-*, nor indeed for any name at all. Again, the Cornish comparison is not entirely convincing,[1] and the Brittonic cognate of *lobh-* is a pure hypothesis, made even less plausible by the difficulty of explaining the *-dy*. In fact *Aberlady* and *Aberlessic* may quite possibly be Pictish, given by settlers from across the Forth, for the element *aber*, well known in Pictish names as in Welsh ones, is exceedingly rare in Scotland south of the Forth, and most of the few instances are on the south shore of the Forth immediately facing Pictland. It looks as if the Britons of southern Scotland, like their Cornish and Breton relatives but unlike the Welsh and Picts, made little or no use of this word in forming place-names. It is perfectly possible therefore that *-lessic* is some word meaning 'stench', or a corrupt form disguising something of the sort, either in Pictish or in Cumbric, two languages about which little is known; or at least that popular etymology—never very exacting by scholarly standards—thought it recognised such a word.

Where then is *Aberlessic*? The reason for looking for it exclusively near Aberlady is doubtless the unconscious influence of the incorrect idea that *Aberlessic* is an early form of *Aberlady*; and it is perhaps possible that Watson was led to identify Kepduf with Kilduff because Kilduff is in fact just over three miles from

---

[1] The authority for a Cornish *lesic*, 'herbaceous', is not very good, though such a form is quite possible.

Aberlady Bay, whereas Traprain Law is about 7½. But with the river-mouth at Aberlady already pre-empted by the name *Aber-leuedi*, and the outflow of the Gosford Burn not suitable to be called an *aber*, there is really no reason at all why we should look to Aberlady Bay. Everyone seems to have forgotten that about 3½ miles north-*east* of Traprain Law there is another river-mouth, which has every qualification to be called an *aber* and besides has very extensive sands—the mouth of the Tyne near Tynninghame, whence the crest of Traprain Law is clearly visible, towering over the low hills between. I suggest that this is Aberlessic; that whatever *lessic* really means local Celtic tradition chose to see in it a word meaning 'stench', and provided the story of the fish on the sands as a popular etymology; and that if so, the probability that Kepduf is Traprain Law, not Kilduff, is greatly strengthened. Anyway, it is clear that once more we see behind the Herbertian author a source with intimate knowledge of Lothian and its Celtic local traditions, and probably at least some acquaintance with the Cumbric language. Of course Jocelyn omits all this as of no interest, perhaps also in this case because he was offended by the 'stench'. Jocelyn seems to have been a bit of a prude, and one suspects that if he had been a nineteenth-century *littérateur* straying into the realms of folk-lore he would have called the legend of Kentigern's birth a 'wild tale' and would have suppressed much of it—as in fact he did. Indeed the uncouthness of which he complains may have lain as much in the content as in the style. The Office of Theneuu shows that it knew the story of the fish (from its source the Herbertian *Life*), but like Jocelyn it does not trouble its readers with the etymological explanation. The fact that it calls the place *Aberlady* is of no significance considering its late date, by contrast with the Herbertian *Life*. It simply made the same identification that others have made.

Next comes the killing of the king by the swineherd. Here again we evidently have our Lothian man at work, for there is in fact still a standing stone, about nine feet high, at the foot of Traprain Law, about half a mile south of the summit,[1] which is obviously the one meant, though the carved stone mentioned is now missing. What is the purpose of introducing this story? The Herbertian *Life* makes the king give his daughter into the power of the swineherd,

[1] It has been moved, to its present position by the hedge, from where it originally stood in the middle of the field.

but why does it say of him that he counted her death as nothing unless the swineherd perished by a like fate (c. 7)? It is not explained, but a careful reading of the whole suggests that he did not know that Ewen was the father of the child, and believed that the swineherd, to whom he had merely bound his daughter as a servant to humiliate her, was the guilty party—hence his eagerness for his death. The Office of Theneuu seems to have misunderstood the motivation here, for it makes the king give her to the swineherd *perpetuo stuprandam*, and hence has to cut out the story of the king's anger, which would have no rational basis; in addition to which this brief summary would have been likely to omit such matters in any case. Of course Jocelyn leaves out the whole, because it belongs to the episode of Ewen, which he has practically suppressed.

The punishment of setting a wrongdoer, especially a woman, adrift in a small boat, without rudder, oars, or food, is familiar in early Irish literature,[1] and the 'Scottic' background of this part of the *Life* is now coming to the fore. The boat is described as a skiff made of hide in the Herbertian *Life* as we have it, but it looks as if something has dropped out in the course of the transmission, since both Jocelyn and the Office of Theneuu point to the Herbertian *Life*'s originally having had a fuller description. Jocelyn notes that the hide boat was made *juxta morem Scottorum*, 'in the Gaelic manner', and that there were no oars; while the Office of Theneuu describes the boat as a frame of wicker covered with hide and caulked with pitch—a very exact description of the typical Gaelic sea-going coracle—and says there was neither rudder nor sail nor oar. The close personal acquaintance with the neighbourhood continues in the Herbertian *Life*; someone knew that fish were abundant in the mouth of the Firth in his day, and that foreign fishermen flocked there; and was familiar with Culross, by its correct early Gaelic name *Culennros* ('Hollywood'), and knew that it was reckoned to be thirty miles from the Isle of May by sailors.[2] Jocelyn of course leaves out the fish, as he did the story of *Aberlessic*; the Office of Theneuu has nothing to say of the local story of the fishing grounds round the Isle of May, in accordance with its regular policy in summarising, but again betrays that it knew the fishy story. It seems to envisage a shoal of fish bearing up the coracle with their mass and swimming it up the firth to Culross.

---

[1] Cf. M. E. Byrne, 'On the Punishment of Sending Adrift', *Ériu*, XI, 97 ff.
[2] It is actually nearer forty modern miles.

Our sources now enter on a new and probably originally separate episode in the life of their saint, namely the association of Kentigern with Servanus. Unluckily the Herbertian *Life* breaks off when this section has hardly begun, and the Office of Theneuu derived from it ceases with the arrival of Theneuu at Culross, barely mentioning the discovery by Servanus. We depend therefore entirely on Jocelyn for our knowledge of what was in the Herbertian *Life*; but fortunately two new sources come to our aid here, the nine prose *lectiones* in the Edinburgh breviary, dealing with this very episode, and the beginning of the Office of Kentigern in the Breviary of Aberdeen. One must first ask why it is that Kentigern and Servanus are associated at all. Servanus was certainly a popular saint in the district immediately north of the Firth of Forth, in Fife, Clackmannan, and south-eastern Perthshire, where there are or were several dedications to him and other associations with him, Culross being one of the chief. In his *Life*[1] (thirteenth century) Adamnán gives him 'Fife, and from the Mount of the Britons[2] to the mount called Okhel'. The 'Mount of the Britons' must surely be Dumbarton (*Dún mBretan*, 'the Hill-fort of the Britons'), and 'the mount called Okhel' is of course the Ochils. A passage in the *Book of Ballymote*[3] calls him 'the venerable ancient who holds Culross in Strathearn in the (district of the) Comhghill[4] between Mount Ochel and the Firth of Forth'. It is not very easy to make geographical sense of these two passages, but it may be remarked that while Strathearn certainly does not include Culross or anything south of the Ochils it does stretch from the Ochils in the south-east to the neighbourhood of Balquhidder (east of Loch Lomond) in the west; that at the time when the *Life of Servanus* was compiled this seems to have coincided roughly with the northern part of the bishopric of Dunblane, which reached from the Ochils (where Servanus had his well-known church at Dunning) in the east to the upper Forth and almost to Loch Lomond on the west, where it marched with the bishopric of Glasgow, the inheritor of the territory of the older kingdom of Strathclyde of which Dumbarton was the capital; that in the Middle Ages Culross belonged to the bishopric of Dunblane as a detached portion; and that it is therefore perhaps not extrava-

---

[1] Edited by Skene, *Chronicles of the Picts and Scots* (Edinburgh, 1867), 412 ff., from the same MS. as one of the two copies of Jocelyn.
[2] *A monte Britannorum.*   [3] F. 214. a. 21.   [4] Name unknown.

gant to suggest that Culross had at one time some territorial connection with Strathearn (possibly it belonged to the mormaers of the district) and was therefore regarded as part of Strathearn though not in it. At any rate it would make good sense if we could paraphrase the passage in the *Book of Ballymote* as follows: 'Culross in the bishopric of Dunblane,...between the Ochils and the Forth.' Servanus was of course associated particularly with the 'culdees' of the island in Loch Leven, an association which can be traced back at least to the first half of the eleventh century, and probably to the period 842–5. Nothing is really known of him, or when he lived. His name in its Gaelic form is Serb ('Bitter'), Anglicised as Serf; Servanus is evidently an attempt to render it with a Latin approximation;[1] and whatever his origin may have been it is evident that he was fully adopted as the saint of this district by the Gaelic Church in Scotland from the ninth century on. The Herbertian *Life* makes him a disciple of Palladius, which would put him a century before Kentigern's time, and the *Life of Servanus* treats him as a contemporary of Adamnán (d. 704) and of the Bruide, king of the Picts, who reigned 697–706, a century after Kentigern.[2] One may suggest that the reason why Kentigern is brought into association with Servanus is twofold. First, they were the two chief saints of two bordering districts, southern Scotia and Strathclyde, and that in itself was enough reason for the compilers of *Lives*. Secondly, there was a chapel at Culross,[3] Servanus's chief place, dedicated to Kentigern, and such a hint would be all that was necessary to clinch the matter.

At any rate, chapters 4 to 8 in Jocelyn, all nine *lectiones* of the Edinburgh breviary, and the beginning of the Aberdeen Office of Kentigern are devoted exclusively to the story of the relation between Servanus and Kentigern; of which the beginning only is preserved also in the Herbertian fragment. As we shall see, there are features about the *lectiones* which seem to indicate that they are not derived from Jocelyn but from a more primitive source, and

---

[1] Watson believed that this was really his name, and that he was a Briton, since the Latin name Servanus is found in Welsh, as *Serwan* (*op. cit.* 332), but there seems to be no supporting evidence for this.

[2] Perhaps by confusion with the Pictish King Bruide who is said to have dedicated the island of Loch Leven to Servanus and his culdees, between 842 and 845.

[3] Aberdeen Office of Kentigern: '(Culros) in quo loco insignis capella in eius honore usque in hodiernum diem dedicata est.'

some hint that they do not even come from the Herbertian *Life*. We may suggest, then, a fairly early document, drawn up in a Gaelic context with knowledge of the local geography (perhaps at a monastery of St Servanus such as Loch Leven), which consisted only of the Servanus–Kentigern episode; and that this was used and summarised by the *lectiones* of the Edinburgh breviary and incorporated independently into the Scottic 'little volume' (or one of the 'little volumes' if there were more than one),[1] whence it passed naturally into the Herbertian *Life*, and to Jocelyn, as well as into the Aberdeen Office of Kentigern. The story of Kentigern's virgin conception, and of his mother being thrown from Traprain Law, did not form any part of this, though it did probably include a mention of both his parents, as we shall see.

The following is a summary of the Servanus section, episode by episode, as it appears in the various sources. According to the Herbertian *Life*, when Thaney gave birth to Kentigern they were discovered by some herds, who went to St Servanus where he was teaching his disciples, and told him of it. The saint cried, '"*A Dia, cur fir sin!*" quod sonat Latine "O utinam sic esset!"'; adding, 'Thank God, for he shall be my dear one' ('hic enim erit carus meus'). He had already had a premonition of this, as he had heard the Gloria in Excelsis being sung in Heaven, which reminded him of the birth of Christ. The *Life* then breaks off with a sermon by Servanus on virginity, 'seeing that the birth of the servant was in a certain respect similar to the birth of the Lord'. Jocelyn, no doubt following the Herbertian *Life* when it was complete, tells much the same story but omits the phrase '*a Dia cur fir sin*' and its Latin gloss, and 'Thank God, for he shall be my dear one', as well as of course the sermon. When the shepherds bring the news to St Servanus, he rejoices; 'and hence he said in his native tongue (*patria lingua*) "Mochohe! Mochohe!" which means in Latin "My dear one, my dear one" (*care mi, care mi*)'. Servanus baptises mother and child, calling the former *Taneu* and the latter *Kyentyern*, 'which means Head Lord' (*capitalis dominus*). The boy is brought up by Servanus, who loved him much; 'and hence he was accustomed to call him in his native tongue (*patria lingua*) Munghu, which means in Latin "Dearest Friend" (*Karissimus amicus*)'. The Aberdeen Office of Kentigern suggests that some at least of all this was in the Scottic *Life*[2] which lies behind the 'little volume';

[1] Cf. p. 273 n. 4.   [2] See p. 277.

perhaps all of it (except the sermon, which derives from the virgin birth legend), considering that the Office is only a summary. Servanus, warned by angels ('angelica monicione preventus') and summoned by his shepherds, finds and baptises the pair; the woman's name is not mentioned, but he calls the boy 'Kentigernum hoc est capitalem dominum', and he brings him up honourably at Culross ('apud Culros honorifice educavit'). The *lectiones* in the Edinburgh breviary are very short here; Servanus, 'angelica ammonicione edoctus', adopts Kentigern and fosters him honourably at Culross ('apud Colenros honorifice nutrivit'), and loves him more than his other disciples.

The whole passage is of considerable importance. The words *a Dia cur fir sin* are Gaelic, meaning 'O God, may that be true!' Here is a positive proof of the 'Scottic' nature of some of the matter behind the legend of Kentigern, though it is difficult to see why this particular phrase is preserved. For the rest, we are dealing with a feature very characteristic of Celtic Latin material— the attempt to find an etymology for one's hero's name. Before discussing this, it would be as well to set out the facts about the name Kentigern. It is a Brittonic one, and in the language of the Roman period would have been *Cunotegernos* or *Cunotegirnos*, consisting of *tegernos* or *tegirnos*, 'lord', and the element *cuno-*, very common in Celtic names, always with an honorific sense. The only plausible etymology is the stem *cun-*, 'hound';[1] and if this seems strange, we must remember that for the early Celtic people the hunting dog was a highly admired animal, and that our instinctive feeling that 'dog' as applied to humans is insulting is probably of Hebrew origin. For the Celts, *cuno-* must have had something of the overtones that 'lion' has for us. *Cunotegernos* meant therefore 'Hound-like Lord', and one may compare the *Maelgwn*, 'Princely Hound', discussed below. In Kentigern's own time the name would have been pronounced in Cumbric and Welsh something like *cöndeyern, cöndeyirn, cöndiyern*, or *cöndiyirn* (with *ö* and *y* as described above, p. 284), and the spelling of it in the notice of his death in the *Annales Cambriae*, s.a. 612, *Conthigirni obitus*, means this last, though at the time the *Annales* were com-

---

[1] It has often been said, and denied by competent Celtic scholars, that *cuno-* in place-names and personal names means 'high'. In fact there was no such word; see *Journal of Roman Studies*, XXXVIII (1948), 56. The note on the name Kentigern in Forbes, *op. cit.* 326, is wrong all through.

piled in their present form commoner spellings in Brittonic Latin would have been *Cintegern, Centegern, Cintigern, Centigern, Cinti-girn*, or *Centigirn*. After the loss of the intervocal consonantal *y* spelt *g*[1] and the consequent contraction it became pronounced approximately *cəndeirn* (*ə* as above), which is spelt in Middle Welsh *Cyndeyrn*. The *Kentegernus* and *Kentigernus* of our Latin sources are of course the above *Centegern* and *Centigern*, spelt with *k* before *e* in the common Norman-Latin manner.

Now, what does Jocelyn mean by saying in his chapter 33 (which may best be discussed here): 'It was often declared by the king that it was not without significance that he was called Kentegernus by St Servanus, but rather with good reason, since by the will of the Lord he should become the head lord (*dominus capitaneus*) of them all, since *ken* means "head" (*capud*) in Latin, and the Scottic (*Albanice*) *tyern* means "lord" (*dominus*) in Latin'? It is clear, and was recognised by Skene,[2] that the second is a Gaelic etymology; Middle Irish *cenn* is 'head', and *tigerna*, the cognate of the Brittonic word, is 'lord'; pronounced approximately *kyenn* and *tiyernə*. Jocelyn spells the former as *ken* and the latter as *tyern* (where *y* means *yy*, the vowel plus the consonant). But Skene regarded the first as being Brittonic ('Welsh'), under the influence of the mistaken belief that Welsh *Cyn-* means 'chief'. In fact it is quite obvious that this too is 'Scottic', and the spelling *Kyen* proves it; for the *ye* would be inexplicable in Brittonic, and *Kyen* (where the *y* was intended as the consonant) is nothing but a rendering, rather better than *ken*, of the true pronunciation of Middle Irish *cenn*, namely *kyenn*. There is no Brittonic word meaning 'head' which is anything like *kyen*. Obviously then the etymology of the name as *capitalis dominus* in Jocelyn and the Aberdeen Office of Kentigern and *dominus capitaneus* in the former is not a Cumbric but a Gaelic one, and the whole thing comes from a 'Scottic' source—just as *a Dia cur fir sin* does—where a meaning for the hero's name was naturally looked for in Gaelic. Very likely the Cumbrians of Strathclyde had their own views on the etymology of the name *Centegern*, but if so we have no record of them.[3]

[1] Probably lost in the ninth century; but it continued to be written for some considerable time, cf. my *Language and History*, §78.   [2] See Forbes, *loc. cit.*

[3] *Capitalis* and *capitaneus* are as it were almost a pun; *cenn* is *caput*, 'head', as is expressly stated, and *capitalis dominus* and *dominus capitaneus* are 'head lord' in the sense of 'chief lord'. If the name in British had been *Cintutegernos*, 'First Lord', therefore 'Chief Lord', as suggested by Watson (*op. cit.* 169), the

Nevertheless we have a record of their ideas about the meaning of his nickname. Kentigern's other name is of course *Mungo*, in medieval sources *Mungho* or *Munghu*, as given by Jocelyn in c. 4, and also c. 7 (the reading of the Cotton MS.; the *Munhu* of the Dublin MS. is inferior). Jocelyn himself guarantees that this was the popular form of the saint's name in Strathclyde in the twelfth century, since he says in c. 4, 'Munghu,...by which name the common people have become accustomed frequently to call him even to the present day, and to invoke him in their need'. Jocelyn tells us that it means 'Karissimus amicus', and it is obvious that his 'Mochohe! quod Latine dicitur Care mi' is in some way another version of the same name and the same interpretation—just what, will be considered below. The Herbertian author does not give the name itself, but the fact that he must have known it and its supposed meaning seems indicated by his otherwise rather pointless 'hic enim erit carus meus'. Doubtless it was present in his source, and very possibly even the original Herbertian *Life* as used by Jocelyn, but became dropped subsequently in the course of copying. The two breviaries have no space for such things.

Now, *Munghu* is not Gaelic but Brittonic. Skene, as quoted by Forbes,[1] derived it from Welsh *mwyn*, 'gentle', 'dear', and *cu*, 'dear', which in composition would be *mwyngu*. There are serious objections to it. In the first place, a name consisting of a compound of two adjectives would be abnormal, though admittedly not in a title suffixed to a proper name, as this might conceivably be. Then, the regular spelling with *u* instead of *ui* and with voiceless *ngh* instead of *n* plus voiced *g* would be inexplicable, and *Muingu* would be needed if the etymology *mwyngu* were correct. Lastly, there was evidently a current belief that the meaning was *carus meus*, which does not suit *mwyngu* very well. Students of Celtic Christianity are of course familiar with the custom in the early Irish and Scottish Church of calling monks by pet-names, consisting of an abbreviated or otherwise mangled form of their real name, prefixed by *mo*, 'my', less often *do*, 'thy'. So Laisrén was Mo Laisse, Lugaid was Mo Lua. The same thing was done in the early British Church, where however *dy* and *t'*, 'thy', were the

---

meaning (though not the etymology) proposed by the Gaelic etymologiser would, by a coincidence, have been right for Brittonic. But this would have given *Cynteyrn*, not *Cyndeyrn* in Welsh (which Watson failed to realise), and so will not do.　　　　　　　　　　　　　[1] *Op. cit.* 327.

normal thing, and 'my' is rare, in the form *M'* before vowels[1]—
examples before consonants are almost entirely lacking and are not
certain.[2] We do not know what form the word for 'my' took in
Cumbric in, say, the tenth century, but in Welsh it was pronounced
mə or *və* (with *ə* as above), causing the nasalisation of certain
following consonants, and hence when it preceded a word beginning
with *c-* the *c-* became a voiceless *ng* which is written in Welsh *ngh*.
When 'my' qualified a word the stressed vowel of which was *ü*
(spelt *u*) there was a tendency for the *ə* to become assimilated to it;
hun or *hunan* is 'self', and while 'myself' in early Middle Welsh is
regularly spelt *vy hun*, *my hunan*, etc. (*y*=*ə*), the form *mu hunan*
does occur in archaic verse. *Munghu* is obviously a nickname, and
it is surely far more in keeping with all we know of the Celtic
Church that such a name should be one of these common com-
pounds with a possessive as the first element and a broken-down
form of the full name as the second, than that it should be an
adjectival compound which does not suit the spelling. The unstressed *u* in the old British form of Kentigern's name, *Cunotegernos*, was very likely evolving towards some sort of *ö* during his
own lifetime, so that while it would perhaps have been pronounced
cundeyern in his youth it would become something like *cöndeyern*
later. These pet-names usually distort the real name very greatly,
and it would be not in the least surprising if the rather indeter-
minate unstressed vowel of the first syllable was rendered *u* or *ü* in
the pet form, where it was stressed. This is nothing compared to
what happened with the names of the Irish saints Carthach and
Crónán, whose nicknames were *Mo Chuta* and *Mo Chua* respectively. It will not seem unreasonable to suggest, therefore, that
Munghu is a Cumbric ecclesiastical nickname, where the saint's
name is reduced to *Cu*; *c*, being preceded by *mə*, regularly and
normally becomes *ngh*; and the unstressed *ə* gives *u* under the
influence of the stressed *u*, exactly as in early Welsh *mu hunan*.[3]

We now have to explain *Mochohe*. This again is clearly a monkish
pet-name in 'my', and the *ch* alone, not to mention the first *o*,
proves that it is Gaelic not Cumbric. It must consist of Gaelic *mo*
'my' and *Cohe*, in which the *h* can only be a spelling-device to

---

[1] Cf. Henry Lewis, *Zeitschrift für celt. Phil.* xx, 138ff.
[2] *Ibid.* 140.
[3] The above etymology of *Munghu* has been hinted at already very briefly by
Mr Carney in *Éigse*, vi, 110.

separate two vowels in hiatus, so that we start with *Coë* as the reduced form of some as yet undetermined full name. Mr Carney[1] regards this *Mo Choe* as the same as the name *Mo Chua*, earlier *Mo Choe*, and apparently thinks this means that there was some special link[2] between Kentigern and one of the Irish saints Mo Chua, namely the brother of Guaire, king of Connaught in the seventh century. But this is scarcely necessary; there were many Irish saints Mo Chua and several whose names are spelt Mo Choe, abbreviations formed from various real names beginning with *C-*.[3] I suggest then that *Mo Choe* (spelt *Mo Chohe* in Jocelyn's source to indicate hiatus)[4] was the nickname of Kentigern in a Gaelic context just as Munghu was in a Cumbric context, and that it was similarly formed from *cundeyern* or *cöndeyern*. There is in fact what may be interpreted as some positive evidence for this. The church of Kilmahoe in Kintyre is *Cill Mo Chotha* in modern Gaelic, where the *th*, which is not pronounced, is simply a spelling-device to separate the two vowels in hiatus as the *h* is in *Mo Chohe*, so that in early Irish and Scottish Gaelic the name would have been *Mo Choë*, giving the later Scottish Gaelic *Mo Choä* (spelt *Mo Chotha*). There is also Kirkmahoe in Dumfriesshire, in Kentigern's own diocese. Watson[5] attributes both to Mo Choe of Aendruim in Ireland (d. 497), though without any evidence. But the church at Kirkmahoe is dedicated to Kentigern,[6] and Watson mentions two men in Dumfriesshire in 1296 bearing names which go back to an early Gaelic *Gille Mo Choi*, 'Servant of St Mo Choe'. There is therefore every reason to say that Kentigern bore a characteristic Celtic ecclesiastical nickname which took the form Munghu in Cumbric and Mo Choë in Gaelic.

Moreover it is evident that this name was popularly etymologised as meaning 'My Dear' in both languages, since it is rendered *care mi* and *karissimus amicus* by Jocelyn and is obviously intended by *carus meus* in the Herbertian *Life* (which in itself supports the view that *Munghu* contains the Cumbric for 'my'). Now Welsh *cu*

---

[1] *Loc. cit.*

[2] Identity of person? Or merely influence of the one legend on the other? The argument is not clear to me. [See now Appendix II below, pp. 355 f.]

[3] Watson apparently regarded *Mo Chua* and *Mo Choe* as different names (*op. cit.* 162), but *Mo Choe* is probably a more archaic form of *Mo Chua*, which is itself a contraction of an older, intermediate, *Mo Chuä*.

[4] [See now Appendix, p. 347.]

[5] *Loc. cit.*　　　　　　　　　　　　　　[6] Forbes, *op. cit.* lxxxix.

means 'dear, beloved', and it must be that the 'common people' who, Jocelyn tells us, called upon him in need by the name Munghu, his nickname, believed that the *Cu* it contains was this word. There is no early Irish word *coe* meaning 'dear', and in saying that Mo Chohe meant *care mi* Jocelyn's source was presumably following the popular interpretation of Munghu, though it may also have been thinking of the early Irish *coí* meaning 'affection, friendship'.[1] The upshot of all the above is to supply further evidence that the Herbertian author and Jocelyn were using a story about the birth of Kentigern and his fosterage by Servanus which derives from a 'Scottic' source,[2] though Jocelyn (and doubtless also the Herbertian author, who fails us here) knew the Cumbric form of his nickname and its popular etymology. Incidentally the fact that Jocelyn makes Servanus use both a Gaelic and a Cumbric form of the name and calls both *patria lingua* need cause no surprise. Jocelyn would not know the difference or care about it, and by *patria lingua* he means simply 'in the vernacular' —any vernacular.

The rest of the material belonging to the story of the association of Kentigern with Servanus is less illuminating. Since the evidence of the Herbertian *Life* is now completely lacking, our only sources are the *lectiones* of the Edinburgh breviary, the Office of Kentigern in the Breviary of Aberdeen, and Jocelyn's *Life*. There are four episodes. First, the story of Servanus's pet robin. According to the prose parts of the Edinburgh breviary, when Kentigern and Servanus's other pupils were playing, Kentigern accidentally tore off the bird's head. Servanus was told, and Kentigern, frightened of the consequences of his anger, quickly fitted the head to the body, and the robin miraculously came to life again. The Office of Kentigern in the Breviary of Aberdeen gives more briefly exactly the same story, in wording which is clearly connected; it omits the other pupils. Jocelyn, who tells the story very verbosely, introduces certain alterations which are characteristic of him. Wishing to remove from his hero the taint of even accidentally killing the bird, he makes the other disciples tear off its head in play; and, being envious of Kentigern, they lay the blame on him though he had taken no part in the affair. Kentigern then performs the miracle. It is significant that the canticles in the Edinburgh

---

[1] Kuno Meyer, *Contributions to Irish Lexicography* (Halle, 1906), 400.
[2] *A Dia cur fir sin*; *Mochohe*; *Kyentyern*.

breviary disagree with the prose *lectio*, and agree with Jocelyn, in making the envious boys kill the bird. It has already been noted that these canticles, unlike the prose, seem to derive from Jocelyn.

The second episode, in the Edinburgh breviary, tells how the fire in Servanus's refectory, which had been sent down from Heaven, used to be tended by the pupils in turn to prevent its going out; and one night, when it was Kentigern's turn, the fire went out while he slept. When he woke he asked the others what he should do, but they only mocked at him, because they hated him. He went out to a thicket and plucked some frozen green branches, laid them on the hearth, and blew on them; they at once caught fire. And still, it says, green brushwood from that thicket catches fire as quickly as if it were very dry, 'as the inhabitants of the place assert to the present day'. The Aberdeen Breviary tells the same, but more briefly, omitting the story about the reputation of the wood. Jocelyn, who always strikes one as a bit of a prig, once again wants to have his hero quite blameless, and instead of making the fire go out through Kentigern's own negligence, he describes the envious fellow-pupils secretly putting out all fires in the monastery and in the neighbourhood on the night when it is Kentigern's turn. He differs also in that Kentigern works the miracle while he is outside, and lights his way home with the burning bough. The local people say that even to the present day the greenest branch taken from that hazel wood will catch fire like the driest wood. Here again, then, the *lectiones* in the two breviaries agree against Jocelyn (except where the Aberdeen Breviary omits something), and it is Jocelyn who is responsible for the difference. It is notable that local tradition is appealed to here. The canticles in both breviaries agree with Jocelyn in making the fire be put out by Kentigern's fellow-pupils.

The third episode is that of the cook. In the Edinburgh *lectiones* Servanus's cook dies, and Servanus, who has a party of reapers at work, says that one of the boys must prepare food for them. The envious pupils shuffle the task on to Kentigern, who refuses it; and Servanus tells him he must either do it or bring the cook back from the dead. Kentigern prays, an angel appears, and brings the cook back to life; and he prepares the food for the reapers. He lived seven years, and when he died the story of his revival was inscribed on his grave; and this inscription remains to the present, though now covered with stones placed on top, at *Lokencheinoch*.

The Breviary of Aberdeen has exactly the same tale, more briefly, but does not mention the death of the cook nor the inscription. Jocelyn leaves out the reapers and the order given by Servanus, and changes the story in such a way that on the death of the cook the disciples and servants persuade Servanus to demand that Kentigern should raise him from the dead; the envious ones pretend that Kentigern is holy enough to do this, but hope that he will fail. Servanus hesitates at first, but at last asks it. Kentigern prays, and the cook comes forth from the grave, without any angelic intervention. He tells how he had seen God judging the dead, and how the wicked were punished and the righteous rewarded. He lived seven years, and when he died the story of his revival by Kentigern was engraved on the lid of his tomb. There is no mention of 'Lokencheinoch', but such a local detail is exactly the sort of thing Jocelyn would leave out. Here once more, then, the two breviaries agree except in so far as that of Aberdeen is summarising; and Jocelyn disagrees, secondarily, because he wants his hero to appear blameless of the sin of refusing an order of his teacher's. It is evident that the motif of the inscription formed part of the original tale, and very likely the unidentified place-name too (presumably somewhere near Culross); and this again is another example of a local legend current at the time the Servanus–Kentigern material was compiled. Probably some early Christian tomb was actually pointed out, perhaps being known to have had a visible inscription at one time, which local ecclesiastical tradition claimed as that of Servanus's cook. It is to be noted that, whatever the place-name is,[1] it appears to be Gaelic, not Brittonic, which is in keeping with the Gaelic background of the whole Servanus cycle.

The fourth episode tells how Kentigern finally deserted Servanus. The ninth *lectio* in the Edinburgh breviary describes how an angel warns Kentigern to leave his master, which was the cause of another miracle. Kentigern crossed 'the river which divides Scotia from the kingdom of the Britons', the tide being down so that it was passable for him ('recedente pelagi estu sibi tunc transmeabilis extiterat'); and having crossed, he saw Servanus coming up in pursuit. He prayed that the tide should come in again and fill the river so that it could not be crossed ('equoreo reumate retrogradente repletus transiri penitus non posset'). This miracu-

---

[1] *Lok=loch*? Or *loc*, 'monastery'? The *en* very likely the Gaelic definite article.

lously occurred at once, and the river, overflowing with the tidal water, flooded its banks ('fluvius marinis redundans aquis ubertim transgreditur ripas'). Servanus was unable to cross, and after complaining in vain to Kentigern, he bade him farewell and returned to his monastery. And, the story continues, to confirm the truth of the miracle, at every flow and ebb of the tide the shore still retains this feature to the present day, though such is not found to occur on any other shore. The Breviary of Aberdeen says that Kentigern was warned by an angel to leave his master; and coming to the river Forth ('ad fluvium qui Forth dicitur') and crossing by a ford ('vadum transiens'), he prayed God to make the water impassable to his master; which at once took place, the flood-tide coming in ('fluctu marino redeunte'). Servanus was unable to proceed, and having said farewell to his disciple he returned. Nothing is said about the flooding of the banks or the state of the tides there at the present day, but this is evidently for the sake of brevity.

Since Jocelyn's account differs in certain important respects, it would be best to discuss first just what picture the two breviaries envisage. The familiarity with local conditions observed in all the Servanus–Kentigern episode, and the circumstantial nature of the description of the present scene, make it probable that the author not only knew the district but was describing some actual spot on the Forth which he believed to have been the place; and it might not be impossible to trace it at the present day. Clearly, Kentigern crosses the Forth where it is fordable at low tide but not at high tide, and the miracle consists of two parts: (1) that the flood-tide came in with supernatural rapidity, and (2) that ever since then the tidal river overflows its banks at this point at high tide. Now, where was this supposed to have taken place? Obviously not across the Firth of Forth itself, which could never be forded at any state of the tide; besides which, the Firth could not be spoken of, in the *present* tense, as dividing Scotia from the kingdom of the Britons.[1] It is evident that some point on the *river* Forth, in the tidal part of it but where it is fordable at low tide, is intended. Somewhere in the general neighbourhood of Stirling would suit this; the river is tidal about as far as its junction with the Teith a short distance above Stirling, and below the town for several miles it was very liable to flood its banks at high tides until the present embank-

[1] The Firth divided Scotia from Anglian Lothian from the ninth century.

ments were made.[1] There must have been a Roman crossing of the river somewhere close above Stirling, though no traces of it have been discovered; but Kentigern's route from Culross to Carnock (see below) suggests that he would naturally be thought of as having forded the Forth at the lowest possible point. There is in fact a place less than two miles below Stirling on the north side of the river called Manor Ford where what was believed to be a paved ford across the Forth actually existed at one time,[2] though the banking up of the river and deepening of the channel has destroyed it. The reference to dividing Scotia from the kingdom of the Britons is very interesting, since it suggests that the boundary between the kingdoms of Gaelic Scotia and British Strathclyde was on the line of the river Forth near Stirling; and this is very likely to have been the case. The upper Forth, higher than this, formed the boundary between the bishopric of Glasgow (i.e. the inheritor of the kingdom of Strathclyde) and that of Dunblane in later times; lower down, St Andrews took in both sides of the Firth, but this extension into Lothian is not older than the twelfth century, and before then it is by no means impossible that the bishopric of Glasgow, and therefore Strathclyde, reached to the river Forth near Stirling, including much of the modern county of Stirling. In any case, it is to be noted that the original of the Servanus–Kentigern episode would seem to go back to the period when Strathclyde still existed as an independent *regnum Britannorum*.

The story in Jocelyn has some very interesting differences. When Kentigern decided to leave he came to the Forth ('ad Frisicum litus'), where the river *Mallena*, flooding its banks at high tide, prevented his passage. However, the waters of the sea and the river were miraculously divided, as the Red Sea for the Israelites and in other Biblical precedents, and stood on either hand, and he crossed on dry ground. After this he then crossed 'a small arm of the sea by a bridge which the inhabitants call The Bridge of

[1] Cf. *The (Old) Statistical Account of Scotland*, VIII (Edinburgh, 1793), 597.
[2] The *New Statistical Account of Scotland*, VIII (Edinburgh, 1845), 222, says 'near the farmhouse of Manor...the Manor Ford...formed of loose stones, remains to the present day'. I owe these references, and much help with the question of the crossing of the Forth, to the kindness of my friend Mr Angus Graham, Secretary of the Royal Commission on Ancient and Historical Monuments, Scotland. He informs me that 'ford' is applied locally to the kind of natural geological formation in the bed of the Forth described below, p. 309; and it is of course possible that Manor Ford was really one of these, as 'loose stones' perhaps suggests.

20-2

Servanus' ('brachiolum marinum per pontem qui ab incolis Pons Servani vocatur'); and the water flowed back from where it had been heaped up, filled the channel of the Mallena, and even over-flowed the bridge. Servanus, in hot pursuit, was prevented by the Mallena from passing, and could only call and complain to Kentigern across the water, but the latter refused to return. Ever afterwards the bridge was covered by the sea, so that it was impassable, and the Mallena, having changed its course, flowed into the river *Ledo* instead of separately into the sea, and both now run into the sea together. As before, the canticles in the Edinburgh breviary agree with Jocelyn against the prose *lectiones*, saying 'the bed of the Ledo is stunned, belching forth the waves of the Mallena'. Taking this passage at its face value, and understanding 'sea' in the sense of 'tidal part of the Forth', it looks as if Jocelyn envisaged a river Mallena, which flooded its banks at high tides, running into the Forth; and the 'small arm of the sea' should be close to the Mallena, since if not, when Kentigern had crossed it he would have been out of shouting distance from Servanus.

Now Jocelyn clearly failed to understand his source, because Mallena (better, *malina*) and Ledo are in fact not river-names at all but rare medieval Latin terms for 'high tide' or 'spring tide' and 'low tide' or 'neap tide' respectively; evidently then he was following an account (presumably the Herbertian *Life*) which made use of these terms in describing the scene, but he mis-understood it—perhaps it was not very clear or legible—and created a confluence of two rivers[1] (and then proceeded to make the whole thing far more impressive by inventing a second miracle in imitation of the crossing of the Red Sea). Besides, the reference to a local legend of Pons Servani is not likely to have been intro-duced by Jocelyn, whereas it is characteristic of the lost Servanus–Kentigern document which lies behind all this. We may reasonably suppose therefore that the names of the tides and the reference to the Bridge of Servanus were in the lost original (and doubtless the Herbertian *Life*) but were dropped by the breviaries in the process of summarising. It seems likely that this original made Kentigern cross the tidal part of the river Forth at low tide by some ford or

[1] Forbes, *op. cit.* 328, suggests that Jocelyn meant the confluence of the Forth and Teith. But Jocelyn is not likely to have had anywhere definite in mind, since he probably did not know the country; and in any event this place will not suit, since though the Forth is barely tidal up to this point it could not have overflowed its banks regularly here.

bridge later known as Pons Servani, and before Servanus could catch up he had prayed for a miracle and the high tide came in before its time, flooding its banks; since when the 'bridge' remained impassable and the banks were always flooded at specially high tides. At the time when the whole story was composed there must have been something at the Forth near Stirling—it could have been a paved ford, the remains of a Roman bridge, or a natural formation—which local folk-lore called 'St Serf's Bridge', and by which it was no longer possible to cross the river. The paving of the 'ford' at Manor, if it really was man-made, would perhaps hardly have gone back to the Dark Ages, and it is not likely that anyone would build a bridge at a place impassable at high tides; it is at least worth while suggesting another possibility.

At Throsk, nearly three miles below Manor Ford and about one mile above Alloa, there is a place where a peculiar natural narrow spit of rocks, bare at low tide, runs out from the south bank, pointing straight towards Alloa and reaching much of the way across the river bed. It is not fordable right across now, but before the river was banked up it might have looked more so; and in any event a natural feature of this sort, passable or not, is just the kind of thing that attracts a local legend of the 'bridge' variety, like the many 'Devil's Bridges', and if not crossable these legends explain why. This would suit the route from Culross to Carnock even better, and would account for the story that the place could no longer be crossed, whereas Manor Ford would not. Besides, the river at present divides its channels near this point round a number of low flat 'islands', little more than grass-grown mud-flats, and if this was the case in the Dark Ages the story may have included some reference to a shift in its bed which would explain Jocelyn's garbled mention of it. It may be added that the parish church of Alloa was dedicated to St Kentigern, a dedication which can be traced to the time of James IV;[1] if it was as old as the twelfth century or older, it is a further argument for looking for the bridge in this neighbourhood.

However the whole is to be interpreted, we seem again to have the two breviaries agreeing against Jocelyn, whose account is padded out and glorified; and further evidence that the original Servanus–Kentigern story was compiled by someone who knew the central and upper Forth district—and in this case, a hint that the

---

[1] Cf. Forbes, *op. cit.* xc.

date was while the kingdom of Strathclyde retained its independence, i.e. before 1018.

From this point on, the *lectiones* in the Edinburgh breviary fail us; the canticles are drawn in part from later episodes in the life of Kentigern, but, as we have already seen, these derive from Jocelyn. Our only source apart from Jocelyn (and the Capgrave version which is itself an abbreviation of Jocelyn) is the summary account in the Breviary of Aberdeen; which however remains important, since it is independent of Jocelyn, at any rate in part, and doubtless more original. Kentigern now continues his journey, which brings him to Glasgow. It is to be noted that anyone travelling from Culross to Glasgow and intending to cross the Forth by a ford or bridge, not by boat, would take very much the route that Kentigern did take. He would follow the north bank of the Firth and the river till he could cross it, somewhere near Stirling, and would then turn south, skirt the massif of the Fintry and Kilsyth hills on the east, via Bannockburn, and would then head south-west for Glasgow. The Aberdeen Breviary tells how Kentigern, having crossed the Forth, comes that night to the house of a man called Fergusius, who dies; Kentigern lays his body in a wagon drawn by untamed oxen, and giving them their head, follows them to 'the place called *Glascu*', where he buries it and himself dwells according to divine command. Jocelyn as usual is fuller, and contains certain details likely to be original and omitted by the Breviary, as well as much verbosity which is presumably due to himself. The sick man is *Fregus*, living 'in villa cui vocabulum est Kernach'; the untamed animals (which have become bulls in Jocelyn) are told by Kentigern to carry the body to the place God provided for it, and they go straight to 'Cathures que nunc Glasgu vocatur' by a way where there is no path, followed by Kentigern, who buries the body in a cemetery consecrated long before by St Ninian. The canticles of the Edinburgh breviary follow Jocelyn here too, in making the wagon pulled by bulls. The name of the old man is obviously the Gaelic *Fergus*, corrupted in Jocelyn. *Kernach* was plausibly identified by Forbes[1] with Carnock, south-east of Stirling; this again is a Gaelic name. *Cathures* is not otherwise known, and is unclear, but it is possible that we should see in it the early Gaelic *cathir* 'city' or 'monastery' plus a defining name which may be corrupt.[2]

---

[1] *Op. cit.* 329.   [2] *Cathir Esa*, 'The City or Monastery of the Waterfall'?

Here in Jocelyn there follow some twenty chapters of material which has an entirely Cumbric and Welsh character, not Gaelic at all. It contains points of great interest for the background of the Kentigern legend, and I shall examine these, leaving aside many events which throw no light on the history of that legend. In Jocelyn c. 11–12, Kentigern, having buried Fregus, lives with two brothers *Telleyr* and *Anguen*. He establishes his cathedral see 'in the town called *Glesgu*, which means "Dear Community" (*cara familia*), which is now called *Glasgu*'. For the former the British Museum MS. reads *Deschu* and for the latter *Glaschu*. The name *Telleyr* is not recognisable, but *Anguen* with its *gu* must be a Brittonic name, and probably comes from a Cumbric written document, since if the source was oral *Anuen* would probably appear. The use of *gu* as a graphic device for the sound *w* is characteristic of Old Welsh, Cornish, and Breton,[1] and the evidence of this and other passages in the *Life of Kentigern* suggests that the same practice was followed in written Cumbric; which is what would be expected. The passage on the name of Glasgow appears to be corrupt. The *D-* of the British Museum MS. is doubtless a miscopying of *Cl-*, and it looks as if the exemplar read 'Clesgu, quod interpretatur Cara Familia, que nunc vocatur Glasgu'; where *Clesgu* was an original error for *Clasgu*. At any rate the gloss *cara familia* shows that the glossator was thinking of Welsh (or rather, Cumbric) *clas*, 'monastic community', and *cu*, 'dear'. The British Museum MS. has Gaelicised forms, the Gaelic for Glasgow being *Glaschu*. The real etymology of the name is quite uncertain, and 'Dear Community' would be *Clas Cu*, not *Clasgu*; this is no doubt a popular etymology. In any event it is Brittonic, and points, like *Anguen*, to a Cumbric source.

In Jocelyn's *Life*, c. 14, Kentigern used to take ascetic cold baths, and afterwards he would sit to dry himself on top of a hill called *Gulath*. Skene,[2] followed by Forbes, compares *Penren Wleth* in a poem in the *Book of Taliesin*, says that *gwleth* means 'dew' in Welsh, and identifies the place with the 'Dew or Dowhill in Glasgow'. This is full of misapprehensions. *Penren Wleth* means 'the Promontory of Gwleth', and Glasgow has no capes or headlands. The poem shows that it was an important landmark and boundary, something like Kintyre or Land's End, not a monticle

---

[1] See my *Language and History*, §49.
[2] *The Four Ancient Books of Wales* (Edinburgh, 1868), II, 404.

in Glasgow. The Welsh for 'dew' is *gwlith*, not *gwleth*, and it is not likely to have been spelt with *e*. The etymology of Dow Hill can have nothing to do with dew. Finally, the *Life* reads *Gulath*, not *Gulith* or *Guleth*. The meaning is unknown, but once more a Cumbric written source is indicated by the *Gu-*.

Jocelyn, c. 21–2: 'A certain tyrant called Morken' becomes king of Cumbria. He scorns and oppresses Kentigern and refuses his requests for food for his monastery; but the river Clud floods miraculously, and carries the king's barns of corn downstream, where they are washed up just by Kentigern's monastery. Later the king, having kicked Kentigern, dies very suitably of gout, and is buried at the royal manor (*in villa regia*), which was called after him *Thorp Morken*. Ever since, his descendants have suffered from gout. This is not mentioned in the prose *lectiones* in the Breviary of Aberdeen, but the canticles tell how a '*regulus*' refused him corn and how the *Cluda* washed it down to the saint's place; and how, after kicking Kentigern, the *regulus* was seized with gout, which was transferred to his descendants. There is nothing to show whether this is derived from Jocelyn or not. Here again we are in a definitely Brittonic context. The king's name is no doubt the Old Welsh *Morcant* or *Morcan*; and *Clud* is the correct Middle (and Modern) Welsh form of the name Clyde (it occurs again in c. 36). The source of this tale is not very likely to be older than the late ninth or early tenth century, the period of the Scandinavian settlements in Galloway and Cumberland, since *thorp*, 'outlying settlement', in names is usually of Scandinavian origin; though it is possible that it might be from Anglo-Saxon *throp*, with the same meaning, in which case it would still not be earlier than the occupation of south-eastern Scotland by the Bernicians in the late seventh century. On the other hand the tale appears to give a *terminus ante quem*, for it seems clear that at the time when it was written there still existed in Strathclyde a noble family, recognised as being such, which traced its descent back to Morken. It does not seem very probable that this would have been the case much later than the absorption of the kingdom into Scotia early in the eleventh century. As to Morken, scholars have usually identified him with the Morcant who fought together with Urien against the Angles, and betrayed him to them, in the latter part of the sixth century.[1] Such an identification is methodologically very unsound,

---

[1] Nennius, *Historia Brittonum*, c. 63.

though it follows a pattern only too often used; that two men of the same name living about the same time must necessarily be the same person is, in the absence of any supporting evidence, most uncertain. In fact the Old Welsh genealogies give two Morcants among the descendants of Coel Hen about this time, one the grandson of the other, and there is nothing to show which, if either, is the Morcant of Nennius or the Morken of Jocelyn. All that we can safely conclude is that the name Morcant may have been current among the nobles of Cumbria in the sixth and seventh centuries. All this is on the assumption that Morken was a real person. If on the other hand, as seems very probable, the story was a late invention fathered on to some character of popular 'historical' tradition, it is likely enough that the inventor meant by him the Morcant who betrayed Urien, since this Morcant was known (and notorious) in Welsh heroic saga in the ninth century, and no doubt in Cumbric too.[1]

Jocelyn, c. 23–31: Morken's relatives plan revenge on Kentigern, but he escapes and makes for St David's in South Wales. Passing through Carlisle (Karleolum), he undertakes missionary work, and sets up a cross at a place *Anglice Crosfeld, id est Crucis Novale*, 'in which place a church, built in modern times, is dedicated to St Kentigern'. He meets and lives with St David (Dewi), and is befriended by the king Cathwallan, who gives him a site called *Nautcharvan* where he founds a monastery. He is led by a white boar to a place on the banks of the river Elgu, from which river the town there takes its name. He and his followers begin to build a monastery, but they are stopped by a heathen prince Melconde Galganu, who appears to be a subject of King Cathwallan; he orders the monastery to be pulled down, but is struck blind. He then repents, and when Kentigern has restored his sight and baptised him, he helps in the building of the monastery. An account of its constitution is given. One of the members is a novice called Asaph. When Kentigern is recalled to the north, Asaph becomes his successor as abbot and bishop. Kentigern leaves by the north door of the church, which was ever afterwards

---

[1] Mrs N. K. Chadwick suggests to me that if Owein son of Urien was father of Kentigern the hostility of 'Morken' to him, unmotivated in the *Life*, would be explained, assuming that 'Morken' is Nennius's Morcant—there would be a family feud. This would argue for the identification; or rather for the identification in popular tradition, since Owein cannot really have been Kentigern's father (cf. p. 286).

kept closed except on St Asaph's day. So far Jocelyn. The only reference to all this in the Office of Kentigern in the Breviary of Aberdeen is the passage quoted on p. 315, and the canticle which says that 'King Melchon, a quarrelsome man, became suddenly blind; to whom at the prayer of the bishop his sight was restored; seeing which, Wales (*Vallia*) and its prince believed in Christ'.

The whole story in Jocelyn is much longer than this, but these are the incidents relevant to the question of sources. It is notable that the Brittonic names here are curiously corrupt, partly through mere error but partly also because the narrative has passed through the hands of Norman-Latin writers, if not originally composed by them. *Karleolum* is the Normanised form of the Cumbric name, familiar as such in the French Arthurian romances; in genuine pre-Norman Brittonic Latin it would have been something like *Cairliuel*.[1] *Dewi* is the Welsh form of St David's name, in a spelling not older than the twelfth century. Cathwallan[2] is of course the well-known name written in late Old Welsh *Catuallaun* or in early Middle Welsh *Cadwallawn*.[3] The *th* for *t* or *d*, and especially the *-a-* for *-au-* in the final syllable, are Normanisations. *Nautcharvan* is a scribal error for *Nantcharvan*, itself showing Norman Latin *ch* for *c*; in late Old or early Middle Welsh, of the twelfth century, the name would be spelt *Nantcarban* or *Nantcarvan*. It is the famous South Welsh monastery of Llancarfan. *Elgu* is an error for *Elgui*, which would be an eleventh- or twelfth-century Welsh spelling of the river name *Elwy*, and the town referred to is Llanelwy, the Welsh name of St Asaph. *Melconde Galganu* is the reading of the Dublin MS.; the British Museum MS. reads *Melcoinde Galganii*. This is exceedingly corrupt, and the *-de* does not belong to the first name, exactly as with *Erwegende*, as the reading *Melchon* in the Aberdeen Breviary suggests. Without doubt this is the sixth-century king of North Wales scolded by Gildas for his sins under the form *Maglocunus*; the Old Welsh of it is *Mailcun*, Middle Welsh *Maelgwn*, and he was a favourite (or notorious) character in the *Lives* of the Welsh saints and

[1] Cf. *Luel* in Bede's *Life of Cuthbert*, c. XXVII.
[2] The name occurs twice, both times in the genitive; the Dublin MS., followed by Forbes, reads *regis Cathwallain* and *regis Cathwalain*, but for both the British Museum MS. has *regis Cathwallani*. This is the better reading; the Dublin MS. has miscopied *ni* as *in*.
[3] Forbes absurdly identifies it with *Casswallawn*.

in medieval Welsh historical and literary tradition, where he was Maelgwn Gwyned (Old Welsh *Mailcun Guined*), associated particularly with Deganwy (Old Welsh *Decannui*). *Melcon* and *Melchon* are Normanising corruptions of *Mailcun*, and *de Galganu* is presumably a perversion of *Deganui* (compare *Elgu* for *Elgui*), though it might be possible that it is for *de Guined*.[1]

The names in this episode point therefore to a Norman-Latin source giving Norman-Latin forms of Brittonic names, and with characteristic Norman-Latin corruptions; the whole thing smells strongly of the twelfth century, and indeed the see of St Asaph was not founded, or refounded, till 1143.[2] The probability is that it was introduced into his *Life* by Jocelyn himself, who at Furness may have been in touch with North Wales.[3] The Office of Kentigern in the Breviary of Aberdeen knew of the story, both in the prose *lectiones* and in the canticles. The words 'cum autem beatus Kentigernus ex iussu angeli de Vallia revenit ad Glasgu, et ibi sanctum Aseph suum discipulum pro regimine ecclesie sue post se relinquens in Vallia', in the *lectiones*, and the brief reference to the blinding of king 'Melchon' in the canticles, show this. It can hardly have known it, however, in any source older than the second half of the twelfth century; not, for instance, in the Scottic *codicilus* or the like; and one can only assume therefore that it learned of it directly or indirectly from Jocelyn. This sixteenth-century book may well have made some use of him or of material derived from him (cf. p. 340). The form *Vallia* which they give as the name of Wales is certainly late, not older than the twelfth century, and this bespeaks a late source for this particular passage, though Jocelyn

---

[1] Or perhaps *Degeingl*, 'of *Tegeingl*', the cantref in Gwynedd in which St Asaph lies. But it is not likely that Maelgwn would be called 'of Tegeingl' when this was only part of his dominions. 'Of Deganwy' is natural, as he lived at that place. Cf. *regis Dyganwy*, p. 317.

[2] Cf. Owen Chadwick in *Studies in Early British History* (edited by N. K. Chadwick; Cambridge, 1954), 176.

[3] [Since the above was written a very interesting article by the Rev. S. M. Harris (*Journal of the Historical Society of the Church in Wales*, VI, 5 ff.) has shown that the connection of St Kentigern with St Asaph is an artificial Norman invention of the twelfth century, and that genuine Welsh tradition knows nothing of it. It is noteworthy that as early as 1125 a bishopric at St Asaph was apparently already being mooted, with the proposal that it should be subject to York, not Canterbury; see *op. cit.* 6, and p. 318, n. 2 below. Mr Harris would appear to agree with the present writer that Jocelyn's tale of Kentigern in Wales is bogus from start to finish.]

does not use the word himself.[1] As regards the content of Jocelyn's tale, it has the look of a spurious invention making ignorant use of names well-known in native tradition. *Cathwallan* is doubtless the ancient national hero Cadwallon Llawhir, king of North Wales and father of Maelgwn. Maelgwn himself died in 547, according to the *Annales Cambriae*, and could therefore just have been a contemporary of the young Kentigern, but his father could not; nor would Cadwallon have been able to grant land to Kentigern in South Wales, which was outside his kingdom. The famous monastery of Llancarfan was founded by St Cadog, according to the firmly established Welsh tradition. The whole story of Kentigern's visit to St David and his founding of Llancarfan is transparently a late and bogus attempt to give him credit by linking him with the man who had become regarded by the twelfth century as the chief saint of Wales, and by impudently taking the credit for Llancarfan from St Cadog. As for Kentigern's relation with St Asaph, this must be of a similar nature. That the patron of the monastery of Llanelwy was St Asaph is the native tradition as far back as it can be traced (twelfth century), and Kentigern in our narrative is once again a cuckoo in the nest. However, the narrator bows to the facts by making Asaph his successor, and is embarrassed to explain why the north door of the church was opened annually on St Asaph's day when, as he declares, this ceremony was performed in commemoration of Kentigern's having left by it. The story of Kentigern's missionary labours round Carlisle, and the setting up of a cross at *Crosfeld*, is intended to explain the presence of a number of churches in northern Cumberland dedicated to the saint,[2] dedications which probably date from the period between the early tenth century and 1092, when this district was part of Strathclyde again and (after 1018) of Scotland, and of the bishopric of Glasgow; or as late as 1133, when it was taken from the bishop of Glasgow and formed into the new bishopric of Carlisle. They bear witness to the natural popularity of his cult there at the time. Indeed the author of this passage clearly states that the church at *Crosfeld* was only

---

[1] The canticles in the Edinburgh breviary, which have already been noted as based probably upon Jocelyn, also bring in this name; they begin 'In septentrionali Uuallia' (i.e. in Cumbria); but by the time this breviary was written Wallia was a well-known form for Wales and the Brittonic country in general.

[2] There is no need to discuss here the theory, a favourite with some writers, that all dedications to a Celtic saint necessarily mean that the church was actually founded by him. Cf. Owen Chadwick, *op. cit.* 175 f.

built 'in modern times'. *Crosfeld*, glossed *Crucis Novale*, 'the Field of the Cross', is of course 'Cross Field', but where this was is unknown.[1]

This story of Kentigern at St Asaph must be taken in conjunction with another document, also printed by Forbes,[2] apparently dating from 1256 but with its place-names in modernised spelling. The language is characteristic medieval feudal charter Latin, and it purports to be an account of the lands and privileges given to Kentigern 'in tempore cujusdam regis Dyganwy nomine Malgini'. Kentigern, it says, came from the east to Llanelwy with 300 priests, knights, and servants, and was ordained bishop by Maye, king of Powys (who is unknown), and Malginus gave him Llanelwy, with various estates which are listed. Later a quarrel arose between Malginus and one Kedicus, who took sanctuary at Llanelwy. Malginus came in pursuit and was blinded; he begged pardon of Kentigern, who restored his sight; and in gratitude he granted the church extensive rights of sanctuary and further estates. This is fairly typical of the Welsh *Lives* of the saints as an account of how a saint worsted a king and obtained lands from him, though its list of the lands is far fuller than normal in the main body of Welsh *Lives* composed about 1100, and the language is characteristically feudal. It is certainly later than Jocelyn's time, yet it seems to bear witness to the existence of a story at St Asaph, not (or not wholly) derived from Jocelyn, that the monastery was founded by St Kentigern and that it received benefactions from Maelgwn of Deganwy after that king had been blinded as the result of a quarrel with Kentigern, and then cured.[3] The whole story of the connection of St Kentigern with St Asaph is obscure and evidently spurious, though some have thought it genuine.[4] It seems to derive ultimately from St Asaph itself, and can scarcely have been invented

[1] Identified by Forbes with Cross Fell, a mountain almost 3000 feet high, *op. cit.* lxxxviii and 349. *Field* and *fell* are of course two quite different words. Cross Fell seems to be a comparatively late name; cf. *English Place-Name Society*, xx, 243. [2] *Op. cit.* lxxixff.

[3] The account just summarised evidently does not derive from Jocelyn, but bears independent witness to the existence of the legend at St Asaph.

[4] The dedications of Llanffinnan and Llanidan in Anglesey to SS. Ffinnan and Nidan have been regarded as evidence for the existence of a cult of Kentigern in Wales (cf. E. G. Bowen, *The Settlements of the Celtic Saints in Wales* (Cardiff, 1954), 76). But quite apart from the general unreliability of the evidence of dedications, the whole idea that these people had any connection with Kentigern is without real foundation (cf. Watson, *op. cit.* 286, 337).

entirely by Jocelyn, since it contains more knowledge of Welsh matters than he is likely to have possessed. The evidence analysed above would tend to show that he got his information from some Norman-Latin document of the middle of the twelfth century[1] coming from Wales and containing an earlier and considerably different account of the legend of Maelgwn and Kentigern, but one built up late and using no genuine traditions. Why the monks of St Asaph should wish to take the credit from their patron Asaph and give it to Kentigern, if that is what happened, remains a mystery.[2]

Jocelyn, c. 29–33: While Kentigern was in Wales, a new king arose in Cumbria, Rederech, who had been baptised in Ireland, and he attempted to restore Christianity in his kingdom, where it had languished after Kentigern's flight. He summoned Kentigern to return. He did so, and Rederech came to meet him at *Holdelm*. Kentigern there preached a sermon against idols: Woden,

whom they, particularly the Angles, believed to be the chief of the gods, from whom they derived their origin and to whom they had made sacred the fourth day of the week, he declared with probability to have been a mortal man, king of the Saxons, a pagan by creed.

The place where he preached at Holdelm miraculously became a hill, which remains to the present. Kentigern's work now prospered in Cumbria, and the people were baptised. Rederech,

having taken off his royal robes, bending his knees and joining his hands, did homage to St Kentigern by the consent and counsel of his nobles, and handed over to him the lordship and princedom over all his kingdom, and desired that he should be called king, and he himself ruler of the fatherland, as he knew that the emperor Constantine the Great had done with Saint Silvester. Whence the custom grew up, through the passage of many years, as long as the kingdom of Cumbria lasted in its own proper state, that the prince was always subject to the bishop.

(Here follows the passage already referred to, explaining the name Kentegernus from '*Ken*' and '*tyern*'.) The queen, called Languueth (Dublin MS., and Langueth in c. 36; BM. MS.

---

[1] After 1143; cf. p. 315.

[2] [A mystery which may possibly be solved by the proposal to put the new see of St Asaph under York; see above, p. 315, n. 3. The reason for this move seems obscure, but it is thoroughly in keeping with medieval ecclesiastical politics that those who supported it should put it about that the monastery and bishopric were originally founded by one who was a famous ornament of the northern British Church, over which York certainly claimed supremacy.]

Languoreth), having been long barren, bore a son who was baptised Constantine, who grew up a holy man and succeeded his father as king, subject like him to the bishop; and 'subdued all the barbarian nations bordering on his own people, without bloodshed', and after death was called by many, and is to the present day, St Constantine. Returning to Kentigern's work, Jocelyn adds that he built churches in Holdelm and ordained priests, and placed his episcopal see there for a time, but afterwards moved to Glasgow. The Breviary of Aberdeen gives a much shorter account, differing materially. When Kentigern returns to Glasgow, King Redrath comes out to meet him, with so large a crowd of followers that the saint could be scarcely seen or heard when he preached to the people. By a miracle, the ground on which he stood rose up into a small hill, so that he was visible and audible to all; and here there is consequently a notable chapel (*insignis capella*) dedicated to him, close by Glasgow (*iuxta Glasgu*).

This passage is one of the most interesting, and in some ways probably the most genuine, in the whole of Jocelyn. Rederech is certainly a historical person, king of Strathclyde in the latter part of the sixth century. His name in British would have been *Rodercos*, in his own day pronounced something like *röðerch* (*ð* = *th* in 'this'; *ch* = *ch* in 'loch'); later pronounced *rhəðerch*, spelt in Old Welsh *Riderch* (or *Rederch* would be equally possible), Modern Welsh *Rhydderch*. In Nennius he is Riderc(h) Hen, 'Riderch the Old', one of the kings of the northern Britons who fought the Angles of Bernicia (Urien and Morcant being two others).[1] His real existence is guaranteed by Adamnán's *Life of Columba*, I, viii, where 'King Rodercus son of Tothal[2] who ruled at the Rock of the Clyde' (i.e. Dumbarton) sends a message to Columba. The spelling *Rederech* seems to indicate a genuine (Cumbric?) pronunciation, with an epenthetic vowel between the *r* and *ch*, which is quite possible. The Redrath of the Aberdeen Breviary is corrupt. The name *Languueth* or *Languoreth* is unidentified, but the *-gu-* is Brittonic and points to a written source, which may be as late as the twelfth century. The account of Rederech doing homage is of course derived from late feudal custom, not Celtic, and someone—

---

[1] Nennius, *Historia Brittonum*, c. 63.
[2] *Filio Tothail*, where *Tothail* is genitive of *Tothal*, the Archaic Irish form (later *Tuathal*) of the British name *Tudwal*. In the Old Welsh genealogies Riderch Hen is son of *Tutagual*, an Old Welsh spelling of the name.

doubtless Jocelyn himself—is drawing here on his knowledge of the usual feudal ceremony. But the strange story that the kings of Strathclyde were 'subject' to the bishop as long as the independent kingdom lasted, i.e. till 1018, has the air of representing some fact, whatever it really means,[1] which was remembered in Glasgow after it ceased to exist. Probably too the son and successor Constantine may derive from some genuine Strathclyde tradition, though his subduing the neighbouring barbarians, by whom the Bernicians are presumably chiefly meant, with or without bloodshed, is hardly warranted by the history of northern Britain at the time. The Old Welsh genealogies do not mention any son of Riderch, and the historical line of the kings of Strathclyde traced themselves from a collateral branch. As to his being a saint, there were various saints Constantine in the Celtic church;[2] in south-western Scotland the churches of Govan and Crawfordjohn in Lanarkshire, and Kil-chousland in Kintyre, are dedicated to a Constantine, and in the twelfth century there was another at Colmonell in Ayrshire. It is likely that these dedications played some part in creating the character of a holy king Constantine of Strathclyde.

The story of Kentigern at *Holdelm* is of interest. The place is no doubt Hoddom in Dumfriesshire, where there was an Anglian monastery during the period of Northumbrian supremacy in south-western Scotland, late seventh to late ninth century, noted for its school of stone carving in the eighth and ninth centuries. Hoddom is adjacent to Abermilk, the church of which is dedicated to St Kentigern. Whether this dedication is anterior to the Northumbrian conquest and the establishment of the Anglian monastery at Hoddom, the latter being attracted by the sanctity of Kentigern's name, or whether it dates from the re-occupation of Dumfriesshire by Strathclyde in the tenth century, and therefore at any time between then and Jocelyn's day, can scarcely be determined for certain. On general grounds the second may be more probable; apart from the fact that an early dedication to Kentigern is perhaps not very likely to have survived more than two centuries of Northumbrian supremacy (though this should not be pressed), it is evident that the revival of the cult of Kentigern

---

[1] Perhaps that the kings paid taxes to the bishops; cf. A. O. Anderson, *Early Sources of Scottish History*, 1, 365. But Professor W. Croft Dickinson suggests to me that it may only mean that the kings were consecrated by the bishops and vowed to rule subject to the law of God.

[2] See Anderson, *op. cit.* 1, 92 f.

in the twelfth century, which is witnessed by the production of the two *Lives*, was leading to the foundation of churches dedicated to him in Cumberland and south-western Scotland. The dedication of Abermilk might well date from this period, perhaps attracted by the previous ecclesiastical distinction of Hoddom, and if so, the attribution of the 'local legend' about the hill to this district would be of recent manufacture. That this last was in fact the case seems indicated by the Breviary of Aberdeen, which, deriving no doubt from some older source,[1] places the scene of the miracle, and the chapel, close by Glasgow.[2] In any case the story that Kentigern actually converted some of the inhabitants, including Angles among them, from the worship of Woden is a plain anachronism. The people of Bernicia could not have occupied Dumfriesshire in Kentigern's time, and therefore would not be worshipping Woden there; still less could they have taught his cult to the Britons. Evidently some much later writer wanted to say that Kentigern converted the Britons of Hoddom from the worship of Celtic pagan gods, but not knowing the names of any,[3] and not being very particular, he had recourse to a well-known Germanic god, though he had the grace to admit the necessity of Angles being present. This shows plainly that the story does not come down as a genuine tradition from Kentigern's own time, and supports the view that the whole concept of Kentigern's see at Hoddom is a late and spurious invention, derived from dedications like that of Abermilk and from the one-time ecclesiastical fame of Hoddom. It is not improbable that the whole matter of the introduction of Hoddom and Woden into the older story seen in the Breviary of Aberdeen is the work of Jocelyn himself.

Jocelyn, c. 34: Kentigern continues his missionary work, driving out idolatry from 'the country of the Picts which is now called Galloway'. He goes into the country north of the Forth (*Albania*) where he converts the people from idolatry and heresy and builds and dedicates many churches, ordaining priests, consecrating bishops, and founding monasteries. He sends out missionaries to

---

[1] On what this source may have been, see p. 340.

[2] Moreover it gives an explanation for the miracle of the hill, which is lacking in Jocelyn. Mrs N. K. Chadwick refers me to the similar story in the *Life of St David* (A. W. Wade-Evans, *Vitae Sanctorum Britanniae* (Cardiff, 1944), 165–6), and suggests that it may be a hagiographical commonplace.

[3] As he would not; no traditions of Celtic gods *as such* seem to have survived in Britain in the Dark Ages.

the Orkneys, Norway, and Iceland. This being done, he returns to Glasgow. The whole of this passage is obviously late and spurious, and it is significant that none of it appears in the Breviary of Aberdeen. It is now generally agreed that 'the Picts of Galloway' are an invention of the twelfth century.[1] The missionaries to Scandinavian lands are a bogus and preposterous piece of fancy. As for the mission and foundations in 'Albania', there are a handful of church dedications to Kentigern beyond the Forth,[2] but probably few serious historians would still subscribe to the view that such must be the work of the saint to whom they are dedicated—much less to the extravagant claims put forward by some for supposed foundations by disciples of Kentigern in Aberdeenshire and elsewhere.[3] One may guess that the Kentigern dedications in the north are due to the twelfth-century revival of his cult already mentioned, dating perhaps from the period when David I, formerly earl of Cumbria, became king of all Scotland and introduced many southern influences to the north. That Jocelyn should know of these dedications and claim them for Kentigern himself is typical, and the one extravagance led to the other.

The remainder of the *Life* is almost entirely an appendix reciting his miracles, as is often the case with *Lives* of saints. Jocelyn, c. 36, tells a story traceable in an inchoate form as far back as the adventure of the ring of Polycrates in Herodotus III, 41–3, which is well known as an international popular tale.[4] Rederech's queen Langueth[5] has a lover, to whom she gives a ring previously given her by the king. Rederech is told of this, and slips the ring from

---

[1] Cf. F. T. Wainwright, *The Problem of the Picts* (Edinburgh, 1955), 40–4.

[2] Cf. Forbes's list, *op. cit.* xc.

[3] Cf. the note on Watson, above, p. 317, n. 4, and Watson himself, *op. cit.* 324.

[4] It is no. B. 548. 2. 1 in Stith Thompson's *Motif-Index of Folk-Literature* (first edition); cf. no. N. 211. 1. A very large number of highly varying stories based on the motif of the lost ring recovered from the fish, from many parts of the world and many periods of time, are to be found mentioned by Thompson or in other sources to which he refers. I have not been able to consult quite all of these, as a few were unobtainable by me, but none that I have seen among them throws any special light on the particular development seen in the *Life of Kentigern* (the Irish sources discussed below were, of course, unknown to Thompson and the others). The most useful bibliographical sources, from which the rest may easily be traced, are: R. Köhler (ed. J. Bolte), *Kleinere Schriften* (Berlin, 1900), II, 209; A. Wünsche, 'Die Sage vom Ring des Polycrates', *Beilage zur Allgemeinen Zeitung*, 1893, nos. 179, 180, 185, 188; P. Saintyves, 'L'Anneau de Polycrate', *Essais de Folklore Biblique* (Paris, 1923), 365 ff.; W. Clouston, *Popular Tales and Fictions* (Edinburgh, 1887), I, 398 ff.

[5] So spelt here.

the man's finger while he is asleep and throws it into the river. He then asks his wife for his ring; in distress, she sends to her lover for it, and he cannot produce it. The king charges her with adultery, and imprisons her under sentence of death. She begs Kentigern to intercede. He tells her messenger to fish in the Clyde (*Clud*), and he catches a salmon inside which the ring is found; he brings it to the queen, and she is set free. In the Breviary of Aberdeen this episode comes immediately after Kentigern's arrival in Glasgow from Culross, and before the mention of his return from Wales; it is probably out of place there. Its account, much shorter than Jocelyn's, differs from him in only two points; it calls the queen not Langueth but *regina de Caidzouu*, and it makes Kentigern send one of his own people to fish for the salmon, instead of telling the queen's messenger to do so. The king is not mentioned by name. It is clear that this is independent of Jocelyn; once again, the Breviary differs from him. *Caidzouu* is the modern Cadzow, a place close by the Clyde near Hamilton. A third version, different from the other two, is given by Camerarius[1] (1631), who says he found it in a fragmentary MS. in the Glasgow cathedral library. The queen loses her ring accidentally, observing which the king suspects her chastity and demands it back; the injured queen begs Kentigern's help, and the miracle follows. Here the motif of the adulterous love-affair is lacking, but has probably been suppressed at some stage; the suspicion of unchastity points to this. The Glasgow MS. is now unknown, but it can scarcely have been a copy of the Herbertian fragment, since the only MS. copy of this now extant, of the beginning of the fifteenth century, seems to show that it was already reduced to the first eight chapters over 200 years before Camerarius saw his Glasgow fragment.

This tale was evidently current in Ireland before Jocelyn's time.[2] Something very like it is told of St Brigit in Cogitosus's Latin *Life* of that saint, which belongs to the middle of the seventh century;[3] and, somewhat differently, in Irish *Lives* of Brigit which may go

[1] D. Camerarius, *De Scotorum Fortitudine* (Paris, 1631), III, 82.

[2] References, see T. P. Cross, *Motif-Index of Early Irish Literature* (Indiana, 1952), 407.

[3] A nobleman wishes to get a certain woman as his handmaid and mistress. He gives her a brooch to keep, but steals it away and throws it in the sea, so that when she is unable to produce it he can enslave her. The woman appeals to Brigit, and while they are talking a fisherman comes by. One of his fish is cut open and the brooch is found. See the Bollandists, *Acta Sanctorum*, February 1, p. 139.

back to the ninth century.[1] There is however an even closer version in the heroic romance *Táin Bó Fraích*, a (probably) eleventh-century redaction of a story some two or three centuries older,[2] though it is here clearly corrupt and does not hold together well. The princess Findabair gives Fraech as a love-token a ring given her by her mother. Her father discovers it in Fraech's purse and throws it in the water (intending to ask it of Findabair); but a salmon swallows it, and Fraech, who has seen this, catches the fish, hides it, and tells Findabair of it. The following night the father demands the ring, saying that Findabair shall die if she cannot produce it. She pretends not to know where it is, and is condemned to death; but she sends for the salmon, and shows the ring. The story is thus well established in Ireland before Jocelyn's time, whereas there is no evidence for it in Britain so early as this except in Jocelyn. The inference from this will be discussed below.

Jocelyn, c. 37: A king of Ireland, who has heard reports of Rederech's fame, sends a minstrel[3] to his court at Christmas time to find out whether they are true. He entertains the company by playing the lute and the harp, and the king offers him gifts, which he refuses, saying that Ireland abounds in gold, silver, clothes, and horses; and he asks for a dish of fresh blackberries[4] instead. This is taken as a joke, but he is serious, and insists; 'and getting up, he declared that he would retire from the company and carry off the king's honour, as the common saying is' ('et regis honorem, ut vulgo dici solet, asportare'). Rederech asks help of Kentigern, who tells him to go and look under a certain bush on which the king had thrown off his cloak while hunting the previous summer so that he could follow the hounds more easily, and had never troubled to retrieve it; and he will find the blackberries there. This is done,

[1] A poet gives a silver brooch to his maid to take care of it; his wife throws it in the sea to get her into trouble; the poet is about to kill the maid for losing it, but Brigit by a miracle catches a salmon with the brooch inside it. In *Broccán's Hymn* (W. Stokes and J. Strachan, *Thesaurus Palaeohibernicus* (Cambridge, 1903), II, 345), a composition dating probably from the ninth century, but with perhaps tenth to eleventh century interpolations and alterations. The same tale is found in the appendix to the 'Old Irish' *Life of St Brigit* (C. Plummer, J. Fraser, and P. Grosjean, *Irish Texts*, I, 1931, p. 17), which *Life* M. O'Brien suggests may be as old as the ninth century (*Irish Historical Studies*, I, 341); but the appendix seems later.

[2] Text, ed. M. Dillon, *Táin Bó Fraích* (Dublin, 1933), see 6 ff.; translated by the same, *Études Celtiques*, II, see 6 ff. [See now Appendix II below.]

[3] Or 'entertainer'; Latin *joculator*, wrongly rendered 'jester' by Forbes.

[4] *Mora*; not 'mulberries' here, as Forbes wrongly gives it.

and the minstrel is persuaded, by the miracle, of Rederech's generosity and Kentigern's holiness. None of this is in the prose *lectiones* of the Breviary of Aberdeen, but there is a reference to it in the canticles ('et dumus insolitas brume dat tempore bachas'), which may or may not come from Jocelyn.

Even if there were not external reason, as we shall see there is, for suspecting a Gaelic origin here, there is strong internal evidence for it. Translating *joculator* and *hystrio*, as the man is called, into Celtic terms and noting that he plays the lute and the harp, and regards gold, silver, clothing, and horses as regular and common-place pay for his repertoire, we deduce that this is an early Irish *senchaid*, a high-class professional story-teller, sage, and entertainer. But one other feature clinches the matter. What does 'honorem, ut vulgo dici solet, asportare' mean? The answer is to hand in Old and Middle Irish, where the phrase applied to a poet or other learned man who, by the composition of a satire or otherwise, puts shame upon a chief for ungenerosity or other ignoble vices, is *berid enech*, 'carries off the honour'. This is a frequent concept in Irish literature; though there is a corresponding formula in Welsh it seems to be very rare there. *Ut vulgo dici solet* must therefore really mean 'as the saying is in the vernacular', and the vernacular in question is probably the Middle Irish of Ireland or Scotland, rather than Cumbric.

The story is of course built round the popular international folk-motif known as 'strawberries in winter',[1] most familiar for its occurrence in the wonder-tale called 'The Three Little Men in the Wood' in Grimm;[2] but it belongs to a special sub-type for which there is clear evidence in Ireland.[3] In various versions of the *Life of St Ciarán of Saighir* it is told that one day he found a bush of blackberries, and covered them so that they might remain when wanted; or only that he specially noticed them. Next April (or at Easter) the queen of Munster fell in love with the king of Ossory and was repulsed by him; she feigned sickness and said she would only be well if she could get blackberries to eat. The king asked Ciarán for help, and the latter took him to the bush, where he gathered blackberries. The queen ate them—they had the scent of

[1] See Stith Thompson, *op. cit.* no. H. 1023. 3.

[2] Grimm no. 13; =Aarne and Thompson, *The Types of the Folk-tale* (Helsinki, 1928), no. 403.

[3] For references, see Cross, *op. cit.* 344. Add to these C. Plummer, *Vitae Sanctorum Hiberniae* (Oxford, 1910), I, pp. 78, 224, 251.

wine and taste of honey—and was cured. The various *Lives* of Ciarán are all late as they stand, but appear to derive from some early source.[1] The general motif of a saint miraculously producing plants or fruits out of season when requested is found in other *Lives* of Irish saints;[2] but by far the closest parallel to the story in Jocelyn is found in the Irish *Tromdám Guaire*.[3] The daughter of the poet Senchán has a desire for ripe blackberries in early spring, and Senchán tells King Guaire of this. Marbán, poet and wonder-worker, instructs Guaire how to find them. He says that one day when the king was hunting with a hound on a leash, the hound dragged him forwards and a bramble-bush caught his cloak so that it was torn off. Marbán had found it and spread it over the bush, on which were many red blackberries, so that through the wondrous powers of God and of himself they were unharmed by bad weather or storm; and what was red then is black now, and what was black then has the taste of honey now. The blackberries are fetched and given to the girl. Here, apart from the close general similarity, the passage about the king leaving his cloak on the bush while hunting is so alike in both the *Tromdám* and in Jocelyn that there must be some especially close connection; and the fact that it is told of Guaire (who was famous for his generosity) and of Rederech (who was known as Rhydderch Hael, 'Rhydderch the Generous', in Welsh tradition), as an illustration of their liberality which caused them to go to any trouble to grant even the most outrageous requests, is a further striking likeness. What the explanation may be will be considered below, but for the moment it is enough to note that the tale of the blackberries is well established in early Irish story. *Tromdám Guaire* is probably not older than the thirteenth or fourteenth century as we have it, but any direct influence from Jocelyn's *Life* is improbable.[4]

Jocelyn, c. 39–40: St Columba of Iona, hearing of Kentigern's fame, comes to visit him. He is described as 'the holy abbot Columba, whom the English call Columkillus'. They exchange croziers, and the one which Columba gave Kentigern was long preserved at the church of St Wilfrid at Ripon, and revered for the holiness of both saints. The Breviary of Aberdeen also has the

---

[1] Cf. J. Kenney, *The Sources for the Early History of Ireland* (New York, 1929), I, p. 316.   [2] References, see p. 325, n. 3.

[3] Edited by M. Joynt (Dublin, 1931); see p. 15.

[4] [See now Appendix II, p. 355.]

story of the visit, but not the 'English' name Columkillus or the exchange of croziers. Both give certain other events here, such as the theft of Kentigern's ram and the miracles following it, but these need not be described here as they throw no light on the history of the text. The Breviary makes Columba come when he hears of Kentigern's return from Wales, but in Jocelyn it occurs later.

Adamnán's *Life of St Columba* has no mention of this visit, nor have other early and reliable sources such as Bede. Visits paid by one saint to another are a commonplace in the *Lives*, and it would be natural that anyone writing of Kentigern should wish to dignify him by making him meet the most celebrated figure in the Celtic, and especially the Scottish, Church in his day; the inventor of the story did not scruple to treat Columba as the party anxious to pay his respects to Kentigern rather than *vice versa*. But this particular passage has two very unusual features. Columba's name was of course Colum Cille in Irish; why does the story say that it was the *Angli* who call him this, not the *Scotti*? And what is the English church of Ripon doing here? The only solution which makes any sense is that this version of the episode must have reached the Kentigern legend from an English source. We may guess that there was, preserved at Ripon, one of the typical Celtic saints' croziers (*bachall*), which was believed to be a relic of Columba and Kentigern. Such a connection between the English Church and the diocese of Glasgow is not unnatural considering that in the eleventh century Glasgow was ecclesiastically subject to the archbishop of York, so that the Church in Yorkshire may well have taken a certain proprietary interest in Kentigern. Ripon was of course an important centre in the Northumbrian Church, having been the seat of a bishopric in the seventh century. *Angli* instead of *Scotti* seems to prove that this episode does not come from a 'Scottic' source, and taken in conjunction with the crozier at Ripon makes it appear virtually certain that it derives from northern England, very likely from Ripon itself. Perhaps Jocelyn, a monk of a monastery likewise subject to the archbishop of York, and not so very far from Ripon, may have heard of the crozier in England.[1]

[1] For connections between Ripon and Iona compare the reference in the ninth or tenth century Chartres MS. of Nennius's *Historia Brittonum* to the date of the Adventus Saxonum: 'sicut Libine abas Iae in Ripum civitate invenit vel reperit'. This is perhaps Slébine, abbot of Iona 752–67, and it has been suggested that he visited Ripon to see the crozier, which would carry the story back to the eighth century. Cf. F. Lot, *Nennius et l'Historia Brittonum*, 28 ff.

Jocelyn, c. 45: At Rederech's court there was a fool called Laloecen. When Kentigern died he was inconsolable, and when asked to explain his grief, he said that King Rederech and one of the nobles of the land called Morthec would not long survive him but would die within the year. This prophecy came true. It is well known that this brief passage constitutes an exceedingly broken-down version of the story of Lailoken or Myrddin, the Merlin of Geoffrey of Monmouth and Arthurian romance. There is no need to elaborate this here, as it has been fully discussed elsewhere.[1] The point is that there was a legend current on both sides of the North Channel, traceable as far back as Adamnán's *Life of St Columba* at the end of the seventh century, about a man the nature of whose death was foretold on three different occasions by one and the same person, but in three quite different ways; and in the sequel the prophet, suspected of being unreliable or insane, is vindicated when the man is mortally hurt in all three ways in rapid succession. In some versions (including the story of Lailoken) the prophet and he of whom the prophecy is made are the same person. In Ireland and in Strathclyde this motif was incorporated into another tale, that of the man who went mad in a battle, fled to live in the wilds like a beast, and was befriended and eventually buried by a saint. The latter can be traced back to the ninth century in Ireland in the legend of Suibhne the Madman, and the association of the 'Three-fold Death' motif with it is at least as early as the eleventh. A twelfth-century Irish version of the Suibhne story contains in it a brief narration of the Threefold Death but told of another Wild Man (called Alladhan), located in Strathclyde. As for Strathclyde material proper, the chief source for the story of Lailoken is a

---

[1] See H. M. and N. K. Chadwick, *The Growth of Literature* (Cambridge, 1932), I, 108 ff.; K. Jackson, *The Motive of the Threefold Death in the Story of Suibhne Geilt* (in J. Ryan, *Essays and Studies Presented to Eoin MacNeill* (Dublin, 1940), 535 ff.); J. Carney, *Éigse*, VI, 83 ff.; K. Jackson, *Éigse*, VII, 112 ff. [See now also Carney, *Studies in Early Irish Literature and History* (Dublin, 1955), appendix B. It would not be relevant here, nor would there be space, to discuss his contentions. I remain quite unconvinced that the legend of the Wild Man in Ireland has been proved to have been borrowed from the Lailoken–Myrddin story. The argument (*op. cit.* 389) that a special association between the word *geilt* and the kingdom of Strathclyde is demonstrated by a passage in which *Glaisdig* is translated by Prof. Carney 'of Glasgow' will not recommend the theory to Celtic scholars. I may add that, in commenting on his words about *Mullach Edin, I remarked that the name has *Éid*- not *Eidh*-; the correction of the spirant to a stop has escaped his notice, and he would apparently now think that the Gaelic of 'Edinburgh' is *Dún Éidheann* (*op. cit.* 390).]

passage known as Lailoken fragment A found in the same MS. as the incomplete Herbertian *Life*, and before it. Here the saint who befriends the Wild Man Lailoken is Kentigern himself, and Lailoken visits Glasgow and interrupts the saint's services by shouting prophecies. Having foretold his own threefold death that day (which comes true), he prophesies that the noblest king of the Britons, the holiest bishop, and the most distinguished chief, will die that year. It is very possible that this fragment once formed part of the Herbertian *Life* itself when the latter was complete.[1] An almost identical version, slightly influenced by Geoffrey of Monmouth's Merlin[2] and omitting the Threefold Death, is told in Bower's *Scotichronicon*, III, 31, and the two are clearly closely related. The Lailoken fragment B, also in the MS. of the Herbertian *Life*, has no connection with Kentigern, and simply tells two stories about Lailoken, the second being the Three-fold Death. In Welsh poetry of the twelfth century the Wild Man is Myrdin, a prophet, living in the forest of Celydon in Scotland as a result of having gone mad in a battle (Arfderydd, near Arthuret, dated 574 by the *Annales Cambriae*), and in terror of Ryderch. There is no mention of Kentigern. In his *Vita Merlini* Geoffrey of Monmouth adopted this, making 'Rodarchus' however a friend of 'Merlinus'; he also introduced the motif of the Threefold Death, with Merlinus foretelling it of another, which is not found in the extant Welsh poems.

There is plenty of evidence therefore for the legend of the Mad Prophet, the Threefold Death (whether of the prophet or of another), and the association with a saint, in Ireland and Strath-clyde, as well as for parts of it in Wales, by the twelfth century, and there are indications that parts are much older. Jocelyn is obviously giving a version of a legend which was well established in his day. Whether it formed part of one of his main sources, such as the Herbertian *Life* itself, or whether he learned of it independently as a separate tale, it would seem that he thought the whole much too 'wild', and watered it down in such a way that very little is left, and most of what is left is different. Lailoken foretold the death within the year of the noblest king of the Britons, the holiest bishop, and the most distinguished chief, but did not name them, nor is the prophecy fulfilled in the story. Jocelyn's Laloecen, when Kenti-

[1] Cf. H. M. and N. K. Chadwick, *op. cit.* 109.
[2] The Wild Man is called Merlinus, a form due to Geoffrey of Monmouth.

gern is already dead, foretells the death within the year of Rederech and 'one of the nobles of the land, called Morthec', and this comes true. It seems likely that the more original form was that the Wild Man foretold the death in the allusive fashion that Lailoken uses, and that within the year Rederech, Kentigern, and 'Morthec' (of whom nothing is known) actually died. Why Jocelyn brings this motif in in such a truncated form, *after* the death of Kentigern and therefore minus one of the three prophecies, does not appear; but it is at least obvious that he was using material which was well established in Cumbria in his day as a popular legend, both in association with Kentigern and without him.

The above analysis of our information on the *Life of St Kentigern* should make it possible to glimpse some of the chief sources. In the first place, scattered at various points through much of the story, there are a number of names which are indisputably Brittonic; several of them are known elsewhere as those of characters or places in Strathclyde history, saga, and legend, and there is no reason to doubt that these and the others are genuine Cumbric forms, though sometimes more or less disguised by later scribes.[1] Moreover, they are in a spelling so similar to that of late Old Welsh, Old Cornish, and Old Breton that we are quite justified in regarding them as Old Cumbric. The Celtic Church in Strathclyde must have shared a common orthographic tradition with that of Wales, Cornwall, and Brittany.[2] It is probable that some kind of written document or documents of Strathclyde origin, with the names in Cumbric forms, lie behind parts of Nennius and the *Annales Cambriae*, and here in the Kentigern material we have further positive evidence for the use of writing applied to native tradition in Strathclyde. In the absence of other definitely Cumbric written matter, the only criterion for dating the forms of the names must be the analogy of Welsh, Cornish, and Breton, and this would indicate that they are not later than the early part of the twelfth century, and that most of them might belong to any period back as far as the eighth or ninth. The -*eu* in *Taneu*, if this means -*eu* not -*iu*, and the *eu*- in *Ewen* and *Euuen*, would imply in Welsh a date scarcely older than the late eleventh century, but since Old Welsh orthography probably lagged about a century behind pronuncia-

---

[1] Taneu, Ewen, Erwegen, Ulien, Kentegernus, Munghu, Anguen, Glasgu, Gulath, Clud, Morken, Rederech, Langueth or Languoreth, Laloecen.

[2] On this cf. my *Language and History*, pp. 72 ff.

tion in this matter it is hard to be positive, and they might well be as early as the beginning of the century; besides, we are dealing with Cumbric, not Welsh. *Ulien*, quoted from '*gesta histrionum*', suggests a late oral form belonging to the writer's own day, and again probably not older than the eleventh century, but behind *Erwegen* and *Eufurenn* there appears to lie a spelling which may be as old as the eighth or ninth century, though it too could be as late as the eleventh as a written literary form. It has already been noted that if Jocelyn's *Taneu* means *Taniu*, this form without vowel-affection is not likely to be later than the ninth century if it is a purely written one, or even than the seventh–eighth if it is a pronunciation-spelling; but this is very uncertain. Lastly *Kentegernus* with its internal *g* would suggest a source hardly later than the ninth century if it was written down from an oral source, but as a purely literary spelling it could be much later.

These points of spelling by themselves are rather indecisive, because ambiguous, but they suggest that a date somewhere around A.D. 1000 might suit. There are certain features of the content of the parts which manifestly belong to the Cumbric source or sources which may help a little. Riderch as king of Strathclyde about 600 and Morcant as a prominent noble were too well known in later 'historical' saga for it to be safe to assert that the account of them goes back to Kentigern's own time. *Thorp Morken* cannot be older than the late seventh century, and is probably subsequent to the late ninth or early tenth, perhaps very much so. The episode of Kentigern at Hoddom converting the natives from the worship of Woden, if it did form part of the original, cannot be any earlier than the end of the seventh century and may be quite late; in fact, as we have seen, there is reason to think that it was not in the original and that it is an alteration made perhaps by Jocelyn himself. On the other hand the story of the gout hereditary in Morken's family can scarcely be significantly later than the Gaelic occupation of Strathclyde after 1018. The note on the kings of Strathclyde being 'subject' to the bishops 'quamdiu regnum Cambrinum in suo statu perduravit' must be later than 1018 but need not be much later. Indeed, considering that it does not seem very probable that a *Life of Kentigern* of a purely Cumbric character would be put together in Glasgow after the church there had recently been taken over by an incoming Gaelic clergy, it may be that the Latin words just quoted are an interpolated gloss; so that the hypothetical Cumbric Latin *Life* would really go back before the events of 1018, though hardly much before. However, this is speculation; perhaps the church at Glasgow retained its Cumbric character for a generation or more. Taking everything into consideration, the writer is inclined to suggest that we must reckon, as a prime and basic source, with a Latin *Life of Kentigern* drawn up in a Cumbric context, not a Gaelic one, in Strathclyde in the eleventh century at a time when Brittonic traditions were still strong there, and quite possibly even before the fall of the independent kingdom. This lost document will be called here A.[1] Whether its compiler had any considerable older written material to draw on seems very doubtful. It is quite likely that all he had was the oral tradition of the clergy of Glasgow, plus possibly the written form of the names of the saint, his mother, and his father, with perhaps a brief statement of a few of the supposed facts of his life;[2] and that he eked these out from his imagination and from the common stock of hagiographic folk-lore, in the usual manner. Very likely it was he who was responsible for the comment on *Ewen filius Ulien*.

It has already been suggested[3] that behind the 'little volume' used by Jocelyn lies a *Life* compiled in a Gaelic context before about 1150, probably between 1018 and 1115; and this was doubtless represented by the *codicellus* (or *codicelli*) used by the Herbertian author, which (or one of which if there were more than one) was also employed by Jocelyn, called by him a *codicilus* composed in the 'Scottic' style. Our older, lost, source A in some form must have constituted the ultimate nucleus of this *Life*; but it evidently contained other material too, some of which fairly certainly and some probably was not part of A. It is pretty clear that someone, very likely a cleric at one of St Servanus's monastic foundations,[4] compiled an account of Kentigern's '*enfances*' with the idea of bringing together these two famous Celtic saints, whose territory was contiguous; the more so since Kentigern had a chapel at Servanus's own Culross, which may have given the initial idea. This lost document will be called here B. The originator of it would know of Kentigern from the general popularity of his

[1] For a stemma of the sources discussed in the following pages see p. 342 below.
[2] Cf. J. F. Kenney's words (*op. cit.* 300f.) on the nature of the sources generally available to the compilers of Celtic saints' *Lives*.
[3] See p. 277.   [4] Culross, or Loch Leven?

legend in Strathclyde, not necessarily from A, but rather from A's own sources; and this would include no doubt the names of his parents and grandfather, the Lothian connection, and very likely some vague tradition that his mother 'got into trouble' and was sentenced to death for fornication, though he evidently had not heard of the belief in the virgin conception, nor of the throwing from Traprain Law. B would then have introduced the characteristically Gaelic motif that she was punished by being set adrift in a coracle, and that she was washed up at Culross, thus bringing Kentigern into the orbit of Servanus. If so, the *lectiones* of the Edinburgh breviary, which simply say that Kentigern was born in the province called Leudonia after his grandfather Leudonus and brought up by Servanus at Culross, have chosen to suppress this episode so discreditable to their hero; indeed the wording cries out that something has been hushed up here.[1] The *lectiones* of the Office of Kentigern in the Aberdeen Breviary however do betray a knowledge of the affair, and indicate much more clearly than the Edinburgh ones what was probably originally in B—that when she became pregnant her father set her adrift in a boat so that she might be drowned, and she landed at Culross.[2] B continued certainly as far as the farewell between master and pupil at the Forth, and quite probably down to Kentigern's safe arrival at Glasgow. The compiler had a good knowledge of the country north of the Firth of Forth and round the river basin in the neighbourhood of Stirling, which is what would be expected of a cleric of St Servanus. The setting is entirely Gaelic, as is natural in that case; the names and other features are all Gaelic[3] except of course those of Kentigern and his parents, of his grandfather, and of the province called after him. The compiler also knew enough to be aware of the Brittonic nickname Munghu and its meaning,

[1] The suppression of the names of his father and mother would be a natural consequence of this, as they were so closely linked with the question of how he came to be born.

[2] 'Quam pater imprengnatam ad mare submergendam in veteri cimba ex Laudonia transmisit que...usque Culros...proiecta terram applicuit.' They also mention that Servanus baptised him there, and give the etymology *capitalis dominus*.

[3] *A Dia cur fir sin*; the etymology *Kyentyern* = *capitalis dominus*; *Mochohe*; *Lokencheinoch*; and probably also belonging to it, *Kernach, Fergusius*, and *Cathures*. The first four of these at least are essential parts of B, and the Breviary of Aberdeen probably witnesses independently that the etymology is older than Jocelyn.

as well as the corresponding Gaelic form Mo Choë, which he seems to have interpreted in his mind as meaning 'My Dear', just as Munghu was popularly interpreted. The Gaelic background of the whole shows very clearly again in the miracle of the robin, Servanus's pet, an episode particularly characteristic of the Irish *Lives* of the saints and its treatment. In short, B is an independent document hailing from the Scottic church of St Servanus; and, as we have already seen,[1] it appears to belong to the period *before* the Scottic occupation of Strathclyde about 1018 (probably tenth to early eleventh century),[2] so that it is perhaps older than A though doubtless not older than A's sources. B is perhaps represented most closely, though only in a very summary form, with omissions, by the prose *lectiones* in the Edinburgh breviary, which, betraying no knowledge of any other information, are perhaps derived directly from a copy of the original B. Since B was distinct from A, and the story of Kentigern's conception was not in the Scottic *codicilus* used by Jocelyn, as we have seen,[3] it would appear that A originally began with Kentigern at Glasgow itself (= Jocelyn, c. 10, minus the first four words), preceded by the mention of his parentage and perhaps by some reference to the questionable nature of it (which was very likely part of the legend from the beginning), but not by the story of the virgin conception and Traprain Law.

The ultimate basis of Jocelyn's *codicilus* must surely have been A in some form, as already noted, since a *Life* containing fuller details than the Herbertian one is not likely to have omitted it. Indeed if we read *codicello* not *codicellis*, implying that the Herbertian author had only one MS. source, the same as Jocelyn's, it is certain that it did contain A. In any event, a version of B must also have appeared in the Scottic *Life* which constituted the *codicilus*, and so became known to Jocelyn, whether the Herbertian author learned of B from this, or from some other *codicellus* if he knew others. What else did the Scottic *Life* include? It has already been proposed that it was a Latin work produced in Glasgow by the clergy of the new Gaelic church there, after the kingdom of the Scots had absorbed that of Strathclyde;[4] since it is secondary to A, already dated beginning of the eleventh century, it may be described in broad

---

[1] Cf. pp. 309–10 above.
[2] The reference to the *Frisicum litus* (see p. 307 above) may suggest a comparatively early date. Cf. P. Hunter Blair, *The Origins of Northumbria* (Gateshead on Tyne, 1948), 22–3.   [3] Cf. pp. 274 f. above.   [4] P. 277.

terms as belonging to the middle of that century. The stories of
the ring in the salmon and the miracle of the blackberries have
characteristically Irish features. The former was familiar in Ireland
at this time; the latter was well established there, and there must
be some close connection between the version in the *Life* and that
in *Tromdám Guaire*. Besides, the words *honorem asportare* point to
a Gaelic origin. Both these motifs must have been current as
popular tales among the Gaelic-speaking immigrants in Strathclyde. Miraculous stories of this type, full of folk-lore and popular
motifs, are absolutely characteristic of Irish saints' *Lives*, and are
very much rarer and less well-developed in the Brittonic ones. If
the Herbertian author used only one *codicellus*, the same as
Jocelyn's *codicilus*, it would seem certain that all this obviously
Gaelic material, which will be called here C, was included in that
MS.; if more than one, C may have been learned by Jocelyn from
the Herbertian *Life*, not from the *codicilus*. It is likely however
that wherever the Herbertian author got it, C was in Jocelyn's
codicilus, the 'Scottic' nature of which would make this probable;
the compiler of this 'Scottic' *Life* may have got it from oral or
written sources. The story of the Wild Man probably came in in
the same way at the same time, and may be said also to belong to
C. Whatever its ultimate origin, this was very likely a well
established popular tale in Cumbric Strathclyde, belonging to the
saga of the Battle of Arfderydd, before the Gaelic immigration ever
took place, but it would be quite at home in an Irish saint's *Life*,[1]
and would certainly have appealed to anyone who liked the other
two tales. Quite possibly our Glasgow Gaelic cleric who compiled
the 'Scottic' *Life* was responsible for this too, taking it however
from local Cumbric lore, not from Gaelic; and if so, the connection
of the Strathclyde Wild Man with the Strathclyde saint may be due
in the first place to him. There is in fact reason to think that the
tale was actually part of the Herbertian *Life* ('Lailoken A'), and it
remains in Jocelyn in the form of an expurgated debris.

As has already been shown,[2] the Scottic *codicilus* evidently did
not contain the story of Kentigern's conception by a virgin, which
must have reached the Herbertian author therefore from some

[1] In fact Suibhne, the corresponding Irish Wild Man, is closely linked with
the legend of an Irish saint, Moling, and one would say that this is a necessary
part of the story, if it were not that the fragmentary Welsh versions of the
Strathclyde Wild Man (Myrdin) have nothing comparable.

[2] See pp. 274–5.

other source. This episode, which is described here as D, must now be examined. It is quite clear that it is the work of someone with an intimate personal knowledge of the Lothian scene; of its local legends and *mirabilia*, of its place-names and the popular etymologies supposed to explain them, and of minute details such as the exact distance of one place from another. Such a person must have been a native or at least a resident of Lothian. The context of the whole story is purely Celtic, and moreover for the most part Brittonic. The names Dumpelder and Aberlessic, the etymology *Ostium Fetoris* and the typical etymological tale implied in the motif of the swineherd killing the king with the javelin, these things belong to the Brittonic population of Lothian. There is, however, reason to think that the whole has passed through Gaelic hands, or in other words if this is a Brittonic tale it is told by someone who knew Lothian when it had already been annexed by the Gaelic kingdom to the north, and therefore after the later tenth or early eleventh century. This is indicated by the name *Kepduf*. It would follow that the actual compiler of D was a member of the Gaelic overlord class which held Lothian in the eleventh and twelfth centuries, doubtless himself a cleric; but one who was in touch with the local and probably oral lore of a Brittonic peasantry. That such a peasantry should still exist in Lothian at this time may seem surprising, but not incredible. It is true that the district was occupied by the Angles in the first half of the seventh century, but in spite of the many Anglian place-names there is no real reason to suppose that a peasant population speaking Brittonic may not have lingered on for centuries, especially in the more remote valleys; and the considerable number of Brittonic place-names, especially in the western part of the whole area, suggest this. One should bear in mind that Lothian was co-terminous on the south and west with Strathclyde itself, where a vigorous Brittonic kingdom, with unquestionably a Cumbric-speaking population, survived to the beginning of the eleventh century, all through the period when Lothian was under the English. Watson[1] has pointed out how Eddleston near Peebles, right in the Anglian country and less than five miles south-west of the present boundary of Lothian, bore the extremely Brittonic name of Penteiacob[2] in the eleventh century, becoming Gillemorestun, a Gaelic–English hybrid, in the twelfth;

---

[1] *Op. cit.* 135.
[2] 'Iago's Outhouses'; the rendering given by Watson, *loc. cit.*, is inaccurate.

one cannot but feel that a name like Penteiacob, with its exactly correct Brittonic form so well preserved, was in use among people who still understood what it meant, and still spoke Cumbric after four centuries of Anglian rule.

Our Gaelic cleric with Lothian connections would naturally be someone with a special interest in St Kentigern—probably a member of Kentigern's religious community. He might of course be a Lothian man who joined the church of Glasgow, but one looks for some particular connection of that community with Lothian, and there is one which strikes the eye at once. In his c. 41, Jocelyn tells us that Kentigern lived for eight years at *Lothwerverd* (variant *Lothwerwerd*), where he set up a miraculous cross, 'incredibilem dictu, nisi posset explorari visu et tactu,...de sola arena maris'. This description shows that it was of sandstone, and that it was still extant when this account was written down; indeed it describes, clearly speaking of the present time, how the sick and especially lunatics are often found cured next morning if they are bound to the cross the previous evening. *Lothwerverd* is Loquhariot,[1] some fifteen miles from Traprain Law and about three-quarters of a mile from Borthwick church in Midlothian. There is a reference to St Kentigern's Well at Loquhariot in 1534,[2] and the church itself is dedicated to St Kentigern, a dedication which can be traced back to the first half of the fourteenth century.[3] The wonder-working cross of the saint there in the eleventh or twelfth century, the dedication at least as old as the early fourteenth, and the well there in the sixteenth, show that this place had special associations with St Kentigern. It is possible of course that these go right back almost to his own time, before the Anglian conquest, and that though Lothian became part of the bishopric of Lindisfarne in the seventh century, such of the Brittonic population as survived kept his memory alive there. There does not seem to be any obvious reason for the site to become dedicated to Kentigern any later, since Lothian passed from the bishops of Lindisfarne (or rather of Durham, the inheritors of Lindisfarne) directly to those of St Andrews, and did not become part of the diocese of Glasgow. If we envisage a Gaelic priest living at Kentigern's church at

---

[1] Cf. Watson, *op. cit.* 150.   [2] Watson, *loc. cit.*
[3] *Liber Ecclesiae de Scon* (The Maitland Club, 1843), 33; a confirmation by the bishop of St Andrews of a gift by David de Lyn 'deo et ecclesie Sancti Kentegerni de Lochwerweth'.

Loquhariot, or a native of the district who became a 'cleric of Kentigern' at Glasgow, who knew an account of Kentigern's conception, as it appears we must, we should remember that Loquhariot would be an outpost of the saint's cult area. When the clergy of Glasgow began to take a revived interest in writing up the life of their founder, our Loquhariot man in Glasgow would be pleased to supply all the information he could, from the local traditions handed down by a Brittonic peasantry and from his own personal familiarity with the neighbourhood.

How, then, did D get into the Herbertian *Life*? If we read *codicellis* in the passage discussed on p. 273, it may very well be that the author of this work had two manuscript sources and only two: Jocelyn's *codicilus* and a MS. of D. In that case, everything said above on the assumption that he had several, unknown, MSS. would have to be greatly restricted; apart from D, his only other MS. would be the *codicilus* used by Jocelyn, so that in effect the result is the same as the picture so far envisaged for the reading *codicello*. Otherwise, D would simply be one of several MSS. known to the Herbertian author, on the assumption that *codicellis* is correct. But if we read *codicello*, we must suppose that D was from the 'materia...viva voce fidelium mihi relata'. In that case we must assume that he learned of D from our Loquhariot Gael by word of mouth, very likely at Glasgow; and therefore that this episode was compiled in the middle of the twelfth century. We have already seen (p. 290) that the spelling Kepduf suggests an oral source. The 'wild tale' that Kentigern was born of a virgin was believed by the common people in Kentigern's diocese, as Jocelyn witnesses, but we have been unable to find clear evidence for it in any written source before this; very likely if it was known at all to the authors of A, B, and the 'Scottic' book they ignored it for the same reasons as Jocelyn. The Herbertian author was less squeamish, and welcomed it all; though he did his best to offer a rational 'scientific' explanation for what would otherwise seem a blasphemous parody. It has been suggested above that he found already in his *codicellus* (or *codicelli*) an account of the punishment of the girl as a fornicatress by setting her adrift in a coracle, derived from B; if so, he inserted the Lothian episode as a kind of doublet. The fact that the passage about Aberlessic implies both D and B may mean that the tale of the setting adrift, invented north of the Forth, had already become current in Lothian by this time; or quite possibly the composer of D, hearing from the Herbertian author of the sending afloat from the shore of Lothian, remembered the popular etymology of Aberlessic and decided on his own that this was where it took place. The close verbal coincidences between the Herbertian author's account and that in the Office of Theneuu in the Breviary of Aberdeen show that the latter is a summary of this part of the Herbertian *Life*.[1]

Our next major source for the *Life*, designated here E, appears to be a Norman-Latin document of Welsh origin concerning the legend of the foundation of St Asaph by Kentigern. That this comes from Wales and not from Cumbria seems proved not only by its character and content, including the names, and its general similarity to the *Lives* of Welsh saints which were being drawn up about 1100, but also by the fact that we have independent, thirteenth-century, evidence for the currency of this legend at St Asaph, without any trace of northern British connections apart from the figure of Kentigern himself. Perhaps the clergy of St Asaph's had heard about Kentigern through contacts between the Church of Wales and that of Strathclyde, though it remains a mystery why they should have superimposed him upon their own St Asaph.[2] It would be naïve to suppose that the tradition is genuine, considering the general nature of our sources for St Kentigern. The whole story has the look of a Welsh production of the twelfth century, and as we see E in Jocelyn it has passed through Norman-Latin hands rather ignorant of Welsh historical tradition. Consequently it is in any case not likely to be older than the early part of the twelfth century, and in fact it is doubtless later than 1143.[3] The scanty references to it in the Office of Kentigern in the late Breviary of Aberdeen must therefore be due to the compiler's having known directly or indirectly of Jocelyn's work.

Such are the five main sources which seem to have gone to the building up of the extant material on the *Life of St Kentigern*. One or two minor ones, apparently inserted by Jocelyn himself and treated here all together as F, may perhaps be glimpsed; apart of course from much else—such as the episode of the followers of

---

[1] Either directly or perhaps more probably at one remove, see p. 280, n. 1.
[2] [But see now p. 318, n. 2.]
[3] Cf. pp. 315, 318 [or perhaps rather, as early as about 1125; see pp. 315, n. 3 and 318, n. 2].

St Columba who stole Kentigern's ram[1]—where there is no definite evidence touching its ultimate source and which is therefore disregarded in this study. One is the motif of the exchange of croziers, which as we have already seen was quite possibly learned by Jocelyn from an English source—he may even have seen the one preserved at Ripon, where he might have noted also that they called Columba Columkillus. The mention of Kentigern's activities at 'Crosfeld' and of the recent building of the church there 'in modern times' may be due to Jocelyn's own personal knowledge of north-western England and its ecclesiastical history in the eleventh century. It has been pointed out above that the note on Kentigern converting the 'Picts of Galloway', and his missions to 'Albania', the Orkneys, Norway, and Iceland, have a twelfth-century look about them which suggests that here again we have the work of Jocelyn himself, if not of the Herbertian author. The remark in his c. 1 on the 'stupid and ignorant' people living in Kentigern's diocese suggests that Jocelyn made some use of popular tradition during his stay at Glasgow.

What is the relation of the Office of Kentigern in the Breviary of Aberdeen to these sources? We have seen[2] that it contains material which is unlike Jocelyn in being more primitive, nearer to the version of the *lectiones* of the Edinburgh breviary, which appear to derive closely from B. In other points[3] the Breviary differs from Jocelyn without necessarily being more primitive, though the story of the miracle of the hill is altogether better in the Aberdeen version than in Jocelyn. Elsewhere[4] it agrees with Jocelyn without there being anything to show whether the agreement is or is not due to a common source, though again the absence in the Breviary of the exchange of croziers in the story of St Columba's visit may suggest that it did not get the story from Jocelyn, who very likely added the motif of the croziers. On the other hand there are certain points in which the Breviary, especially in its canticles, does seem to have been influenced by Jocelyn. The idea that the fire at Culross was put out by Servanus's pupils[5] is found in the canticles both in the Edinburgh breviary and in that of Aberdeen, whereas the prose

---

[1] This story is in the Office of Kentigern in the Breviary of Aberdeen, both prose and verse, as well as in Jocelyn and the canticles of the Edinburgh breviary; it may therefore have formed part of the Scottic *Life*, and indeed its general character is typical of Irish *Lives* of saints.

[2] See pp. 303, 304, 305, 306.   [3] See pp. 319, 323, 327.

[4] See pp. 325, 326 f.   [5] See p. 304.

lectiones in both make it go out through his own fault. It has already been suggested that Jocelyn was responsible for this piece of priggishness, and that here as elsewhere the Edinburgh canticles derive from him; the same may well be the case with the Aberdeen ones in this instance. Again, the mention of the visit to Wales in the *lectiones* of the Breviary of Aberdeen and to the blinding of 'Melchon' in its canticles must come directly or (perhaps more probably) indirectly from Jocelyn.[1] It looks, then, as if the Office of Kentigern in the sixteenth-century[2] Aberdeen Breviary was drawing much of its material from some comparatively early source, very likely some version of the Scottic *Life* which presumably lies behind the Scottic *codicilus*, but that it knew Jocelyn's *Life*, at first or second hand, and was to some slight extent influenced by this. The Aberdeen Breviary, which is of course only a skeleton summary, nevertheless throws valuable light on the nature of the 'Scottic' compilation.

In concluding this study of the sources for the *Life of St Kentigern*, an attempt at constructing a tentative stemma may now be offered (p. 342). The query 'Other MSS.?' is present on the assumption that the correct reading of the contraction *codicell-* is *codicellis* not *codicello*; if the latter, it is unnecessary. Even if the former, it may still be superfluous, if we take it that D was a written source (cf. p. 338).

Finally, it is perhaps worth asking what is the value of the *Life of St Kentigern* as a strictly historical source for events in Scotland, ecclesiastical or other, in the fifth to sixth centuries. The answer is clearly, very small. One may reasonably accept that Kentigern was a real person, founder of the church at Glasgow and missionary in Cumbria; and the date of his death in the *Annales Cambriae*, 612, may well be approximately correct. Whether he really came from Lothian; who his parents were; how much truth there is in the story of a pagan reaction under Morken, Kentigern's consequent exile in Wales, and his recall owing to the accession of an enthusiastic Christian king Rederech; whether Rederech was really followed by a pious and successful son Constantine; whether Kentigern ever really met Columba—on all these questions we are ignorant. There is perhaps only one detail which is pretty certainly

---

[1] See p. 315.

[2] The fact of its lateness is emphasised by the modernised forms of many of the names, such as *Culros* for older *Culenros*, or the use of a later corruption like *Loth* in place of *Leudonus*, doubtless derived from Fordun.

genuine and is significant and interesting for the history of Strathclyde, and that is the curious story that the kings were 'subject' to
the bishops as long as the kingdom lasted—whatever that really
means. The mention in Jocelyn, c. 11, that while Kentigern was
bishop the kingdom, and bishopric, stretched from sea to sea 'like

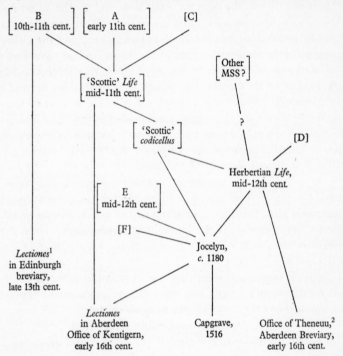

[B
10th-11th cent.] [A
early 11th cent.] [C]

['Scottic' *Life*
mid-11th cent.]

[Other
MSS?]

['Scottic'
codicellus]

?

[D]

Herbertian *Life*,
mid-12th cent.

[E
mid-12th cent.]

[F]

Jocelyn,
c. 1180

Lectiones[1]
in Edinburgh
breviary,
late 13th cent.

Lectiones
in Aberdeen
Office of Kentigern,
early 16th cent.

Capgrave,
1516

Office of Theneuu,[2]
Aberdeen Breviary,
early 16th cent.

[1] The canticles in the Edinburgh breviary fairly certainly derive from
Jocelyn.
[2] Perhaps derived from the Herbertian *Life* through a lost intermediary: see
p. 280, n. 1.

the rampart built by the Emperor Severus...(which) reaches as
far as the river Forth and...separates Scotia from Anglia'[3] is
doubtless true, but it tells us nothing new; and it can scarcely be
derived from a contemporary document, nor probably from one
older than the middle of the ninth century, when Pictland gave
place to Scotia. The fact would have lasted in popular and learned
memory in Strathclyde for many centuries.

[3] I.e. the Antonine Wall. At its eastern end it was probably the boundary
between Scotia and Lothian. This note may have been in A.

APPENDIX

The above article was already completed, typed, and accepted by the editor, when two works bearing on St Kentigern came to hand, one after the other. As both of them contain theories in contradiction to some of the views put forward above, theories with which I disagree but which cannot merely be passed over in silence, it is necessary to discuss them, as briefly as possible. It seems simpler to deal with them here, in the form of an appendix, rather than to disarrange the thread of the argument by introducing comparatively minor but lengthy and distracting matters of controversy into the body of the article.

I

First Mr John MacQueen's extremely interesting and ingenious article 'Yvain, Ewen, and Owein ap Urien', in the *Transaction of the Dumfriesshire and Galloway Natural History and Antiquarian Society*, XXXIII (1956), 107 ff. This is a scholarly contribution to the problem, and the fact that I find myself in disagreement with a number of his conclusions does not by any means imply that I regard it as without value. Mr MacQueen sets out the following theory: A *Life of Kentigern* was composed in Glasgow in the first half of the seventh century. In the first half of the eighth century Baldred, the East Lothian Anglian cleric, used this in compiling a new *Life*, into which he introduced East Lothian traditions, from written or oral sources; Mr MacQueen calls this the 'Glasgow Cathedral *Life*'. At some time before about 800 a third *Life* was put together, 'in the Scottish style' (=our 'Scottic' *Life*), which derived directly from Baldred; and this was the basis of the now fragmentary Herbertian *Life*. Of Jocelyn's two sources one was the Scottic *Life* but the other was Baldred's, the 'Glasgow Cathedral' *Life*, and *not* the Herbertian one, which he did not use at all; this last is independent of Jocelyn, and drew on some material which was not available to him.[1] It follows that matters common to the Herbertian *Life* and to Jocelyn must have been in the Scottic *Life*.

The above account differs materially from my own in the following respects, among others: (1) it dates the Strathclyde basic source (=my A) first half of the seventh century instead of early eleventh. (2) It states (*a*) that Baldred composed a *Life* based on the foregoing in the first half of the eighth century, and (*b*) that the East Lothian traditions were introduced by him. (3) It dates the Scottic *Life* second half of the eighth century instead of mid-eleventh. (4) While agreeing that the Scottic *Life* was one of Jocelyn's two sources it disagrees in denying that the Herbertian *Life* was the other. Some of Mr MacQueen's other ideas

---

[1] Mr MacQueen says that the Herbertian *Life* has no demonstrable connection with Baldred but seems to be based at least partly on the Scottic work (*op. cit.* 121). But if the Herbertian *Life* derives from the Scottic and the Scottic from Baldred, the connection appears clear enough.

have already been dealt with, by anticipation, above, and need not be reopened.

St Baldred, apparently a personage of outstanding importance in the early Anglian Church in Lothian, is well attested historically, since Symeon of Durham refers to him as dying in 756, and his source for this may have been early and good; however he mentions no connection with Kentigern. The first and only document which does this is the Office of Baldred in the Breviary of Aberdeen, of the beginning of the sixteenth century, which says that Baldred was Kentigern's suffragan and that he 'commended to memory his teacher, the most blessed Kentigern, and the sanctity of his life' ('beatissimum Kentigernum praeceptorem suum suaeque vitae sanctitatem...commendabat memoriae'). Mr MacQueen takes this to mean that there was a tradition, known to the authors of the Breviary, that Baldred wrote some kind of account of Kentigern (*op. cit.* 116). It is chronologically impossible that Baldred could have been a pupil and suffragan of Kentigern, and one might well consider that this discredits the whole passage, but Mr MacQueen would explain it as meaning that the existence of a *Life* of Kentigern by Baldred was later wrongly taken to imply that he had been his pupil.

But even if the words *commendabat memoriae* can bear the meaning 'handed down to posterity', i.e. 'wrote a *Life*', ascribed to them (which, especially in the whole context, is at least doubtful) there is no evidence on this point older than the early sixteenth-century Breviary. That some of its many sources were old does not prove or necessarily make it probable that this was the case here. According to Mr MacQueen, it followed Bower (writing about sixty years previously) in some details concerning Baldred, though admittedly it did not get this supposed reference to a *Life* from him; Symeon may have heard of Baldred from an almost contemporary source; and Baldred was pretty certainly a historical person. True, but these things are scarcely relevant. As Mr MacQueen himself says, of this very late reference to a sixth-century saint dating almost a millennium after his time, 'Had this stood in isolation, its value would, of course, have been very small'. But the point is, it does stand in isolation, and therefore *has* very small value— one may say, virtually none at all.

Under its twelfth-century dress, the entire story of Kentigern is coloured through and through with the characteristics of Celtic hagiography, and has little that could appeal to an English cleric living long after the synod of Whitby and the death of Cuthbert, and doubtless familiar with the recent models of Bede's sober *Life of Cuthbert* and *Ecclesiastical History*. Nor does it seem very likely that Baldred would go out of his way to 'hand down to posterity' one of the heroes of a Church which was in his day notoriously hostile and unsympathetic to his own, in a province conquered from the Britons within the memory of men living in his youth. In the later Middle Ages, when these rivalries were forgotten, and the Church had been for centuries the Church of all Scotland, it is likely enough that the clergy of Lothian would claim Baldred, to whom a number of their churches were dedicated, as pupil and successor of the great bishop, of Lothian origin, whose legend was by now one of the most famous in the Scottish Church, and might even assert that some one of the accounts of Kentigern then extant was Baldred's work.

It is argued further (*op. cit.* 118 ff.) that the story of Kentigern's uncanonical consecration in Jocelyn, c. 11, is also due to Baldred; that it is reminiscent of the eighth century and Bede's style, not of the twelfth century and Jocelyn's; that Baldred must have got the story from Glasgow since the consecration took place there; and that the source for the tale must be seventh century since Baldred wrote in the early eighth.[1] Also that the episode in c. 27 about Kentigern's visit to Rome, where he got his irregular consecration confirmed and regularised, is part of this.

On the contrary, one might well suggest that it all belongs essentially to the twelfth century, along with the passage in Jocelyn's c. 33 in which the Pope sent Kentigern the privilege of being subject to no bishop but only to himself direct. All this surely has reference to the famous struggle which rent the Church in Britain in the twelfth century, to decide whether the Scottish bishops were to be subject to and consecrated by the English archbishops or directly by the Pope—in other words, whether the Church in Scotland was independent of that in England—and to the Scottish attempt to have an archbishopric established for Scotland. It is doubtless included in the *Life of Kentigern* as a piece of propaganda on the Scottish behalf, and one can sense that Jocelyn or the anonymous Herbertian author was persuaded to insert it by the clergy of Glasgow for whom the *Lives* were written. From them too would come the story of Kentigern's 'Celtic' consecration. The nature of this and other aspects of the Celtic Church would be well known still in the twelfth century, both by direct tradition (it may well have lasted in Glasgow to a recent period) and from various sources like Bede, as well as from the almost contemporary practice in Ireland. The whole tale would be inserted in the twelfth century partly to explain the direct papal consecration and partly also in defence against claims, actual or anticipated, by enemies[2] of the newly reconstituted Glasgow see that, as its founder must have been consecrated in the 'Celtic' manner, it could not have been canonical. The tone of the end of the passage suggests twelfth-century Glasgow clerics apologising for the well-known barbarity of their ancestors, admitting that such a practice would not be acceptable now, but nevertheless defending it and the validity of the consecration. The hypothesis that any or all of this comes

[1] This seems a little difficult to follow. If Baldred did write a *Life* and used a Glasgow source, how can we tell that the former was not as late as, say, 750, and the latter composed, say, about 740?

[2] Perhaps the clergy of St Andrews? There must have been a struggle in the early part of the twelfth century, between Glasgow and St Andrews, for the lands in Lothian and the Merse abandoned by the bishops of Durham. Glasgow succeeded in asserting its claim to Tweeddale and Teviotdale, but St Andrews carried off the rest.

from Baldred and the eighth century strikes the present writer as untenable.

Then, there is the theory (*op. cit.* 117) that the local Lothian tradition called D in our scheme is likewise due to Baldred, and that otherwise its presence is incomprehensible. If we believe, on *other* grounds, in a *Life* by Baldred, such a view would be an obvious inference (if *not* on other grounds, it would be an argument in a circle). Not believing it, and already having explained the presence of D in a different way above, there is no necessity to say more, except to remark that the occurrence of the Gaelic form *Kepduf* is positive proof that the Lothian traditions come from a source some centuries younger than Baldred's time. Besides, it is much more likely that D's purpose was to emphasise Kentigern's claims on Lothian as having once been subject to Glasgow (cf. p. 345, n. 2, above) than that Baldred would go out of his way to stress this.

Mr MacQueen seems to hold also (*op. cit.* 118) that certain other points in Jocelyn relating to English affairs come from Baldred, including apparently the stories of *Crosfeld*, of Hoddom, and of the crozier at Ripon. But it has been pointed out above (pp. 316 and 320 f.) that at least the first two of these are likely to be quite late; and a different interpretation has been offered for the third. The other two matters indicated (the reference to the Roman Wall and that to the English conquest, Jocelyn, c. 11 and 27) are such as might have been learned of by Jocelyn from almost anywhere; on the former see p. 342 above, where it appears that it cannot be as old as Baldred's time.

If the theory that Baldred composed a *Life of Kentigern* seems to have very doubtful foundation, the hypothesis of a Glasgow *Life* belonging to the first half of the seventh century is even more tenuous. The grounds for it appear to be mainly inferential[1]—that there must have been a nucleus of Glasgow origin, and since Baldred (and through him the Scottic *Life*) used this it must have been very early. The only positive evidence proposed seems to be the supposition that certain passages in Jocelyn emanating from Glasgow must date from within living memory of Kentigern. Apart from the story of his consecration there are said to be several other passages which *on other grounds* may be regarded as early and which claim to preserve records of Kentigern's actual conversation; this version (the Glasgow source is meant) must therefore have been written down within thirty years at most of Kentigern's death, and part at least of Jocelyn's *Life* must therefore date from between 600 and 650[2] and must have a very high historical value indeed (*op. cit.* 120). As the other grounds in question are not specified, one can merely note that the only two references given (Jocelyn c. 14 and 17) appear to be to stories of Kentigern's ascetic practices—stories which are of the most hackneyed sort in *Lives* of the saints, and which can scarcely be accepted as evidence of early date, much less as true and

---

[1] Cf. *op. cit.* 114, 115.

[2] The dating here and on p. 115 seems a little contradictory.

quasi-contemporary records. No doubt the Strathclyde source (my A) contained a small amount of comparatively early matter, just how much and how early being open to question (see pp. 330 ff. above); but anything so old as the first half of the seventh century, and in the form of a fairly detailed written *Life*, seems not only quite without proof but inherently improbable.

One reason for dating the hypothetical Glasgow original so far back is the opinion that the Scottic *Life*, itself derived from the former, was older than *c.* 800 (*op. cit.* 115). This depends on the view that the development of the name *Mochohe* into its later form *Mochua* is an example of that diphthongisation of Archaic Irish long *ō* to Old Irish *ua* which took place in the early part of the eighth century.[1] It is, however, in fact something quite different (see pp. 301 f. above), so that this argument for the earliness of the hypothetical Glasgow source, as well as of the Scottic *Life*, must be abandoned.

Then, there is the view that Jocelyn made no use of the Herbertian *Life*, and that this latter is *not* the Glasgow document which he says he used. It has always been assumed previously that it was, and that his two sources were this and the Scottic *Life*, as set out above, pp. 273 ff. In particular, the words *quam vestra frequentat ecclesia*, 'of which your church makes constant use', can surely only mean the Herbertian *Life*, put together some thirty years before for the use of the Glasgow clergy at the special request of their bishop, and avowedly intended as the latest in up-to-date hagiography.[2] It would require very strong arguments indeed to make one believe that another *Life* had superseded the Herbertian one in this short interval; especially as it is claimed that the document in question, Baldred's '*Life*', was an ancient one, dating from the first half of the eighth century—one which, if it ever existed, and survived at Glasgow in the twelfth century, would certainly itself have been outmoded by the Herbertian author.

The reasons in fact proposed for so thinking are as follows. First, the Herbertian *Life* lacks Jocelyn's words 'Mochohe, quod Latine dicitur Care mi', though it has the admittedly connected rendering 'carus meus'; that it is unlikely Jocelyn added the 'Gaelic tag' himself, even if he knew any Gaelic; and that therefore his source cannot have been the Herbertian *Life* (*op. cit.* 112 ff.). This point has already been discussed above, p. 300. Mr MacQueen and I are agreed that one of the sources of the Herbertian *Life* was the Scottic one; that *Mochohe* was in the Scottic *Life*; and that Jocelyn also used this *Life*. Mr MacQueen thinks the Herbertian author himself dropped the name, whereas it is suggested above that he himself kept it and that the omission came at a later stage. But this is of small importance here; assuming that Mr MacQueen is right, Jocelyn would very naturally insert the name

---

[1] Mr MacQueen's date, 'during the eighth century', is too late. If the premise were correct, the Scottic *Life* could scarcely be much later than *c.* 725; which would however agree ill with the theory that it derives from Baldred.

[2] Cf. p. 274 above.

from the Scottic *Life*, whether or not he noticed the implication in the wording of the Herbertian *Life* that its author had omitted it. There is no proof here that the Herbertian *Life* was not one of Jocelyn's two major sources.

Secondly, it is contended that since the Brittonic form *Munghu* is in Jocelyn but not in the Herbertian *Life*, he must have got it not from the Herbertian author but from some other written *Life*, of Glasgow, Brittonic, origin (*op. cit.* 114), i.e. from the original seventh-century Glasgow source via Baldred. But on this see above, pp. 297–303 and 333 f., where it is suggested that *Munghu* was in the Scottic *Life*—indeed since Mr MacQueen himself thinks the Scottic *Life* was based on Baldred, he too would doubtless admit that Jocelyn might have found it there. But in any case, *Munghu* was the pet form of Kentigern's name well known in oral use in Strathclyde, and Jocelyn could easily have found it there if not also in the Scottic *Life*.[1] Once again, this does not prove the existence of a Glasgow *Life* other than the Herbertian author's, or that the latter was *not* the one 'quam vestra frequentat ecclesia'.

Thirdly, Mr MacQueen holds that there were two distinct versions of the story of Kentigern's conception (*op. cit.* 121 ff.). One was that his mother wished to remain a virgin but that she conceived in some miraculous manner without the child having any father. The other was that her father wanted her to marry Ewen but she refused, and the father in anger bound her servant to a swineherd; that Ewen tried to persuade her by the intercession of a bawd, and that failing in this, he raped her in female disguise. Mr MacQueen calls these respectively A and B; to avoid confusion with our A and B they will be denominated here X and Y. It is claimed that Jocelyn knew only X, not Y; that the Herbertian author, which it is held has a mixture of both, got X from the Scottic *Life* and Y from some source unknown to Jocelyn; that X, and X alone, must therefore have been in 'Baldred' and the Scottic *Life*, and that it is the episode contrary to sound doctrine and the belief of the Church to which Jocelyn refers; and that Jocelyn, not having heard of Y, therefore could not have used the Herbertian *Life*.

There appears to be a serious contradiction here. Jocelyn says of his two sources that *one*, the Scottic *Life*, was full of solecisms, etc., and that it was the *other*, the one 'quam vestra frequentat ecclesia', that had at its beginning the episode contrary to sound doctrine and the belief of the Church (see p. 274 above). Words could hardly speak plainer, that if the episode in question is X, X was not in the Scottic *Life*; and this is one of the chief reasons for thinking that Jocelyn's other source was the Herbertian *Life*. Even assuming, with Mr MacQueen, that Jocelyn did learn X from a source other than the Herbertian *Life*, if it *was* in the Scottic *Life* Jocelyn could just as well have found it there as in 'Baldred'

---

[1] Mr MacQueen gives the view referred to and rejected above, pp. 300 f., that *Munghu* is *mwyngu*. It is scarcely probable that anyone who could write Latin would feel any need to interpret *carissimus*, especially by *amicus*, and the use of an unsupported superlative adjective would have caused no pangs of conscience to a medieval glossator (see *op. cit.* 113).

—i.e. there is nothing here to prove the tale as old as Baldred's time. In point of fact Jocelyn knew of X from popular oral tradition for one thing (cf. p. 275 above), as Mr MacQueen allows.

The Herbertian author's account is so confused and unclear that it is scarcely certain that he is really combining two separate tales, though it may be that he is attempting to reconcile them by pretending to give a physiological explanation of how Thaney was (or appeared to be) a virgin in spite of having been raped.[1] But that Jocelyn did not know and use the Herbertian *Life*, as he seems clearly to imply that he did, is quite another matter. He could not have got the legend of Kentigern's conception from the Scottic 'little volume', because, as we have just seen, he says plainly enough that it was not there. In my view, and that of all previous writers, the *Life* containing the heretical episode was the Herbertian one. Jocelyn toned it down, making some discreet play with it, attempting to condone the blasphemy; and, with his eye on the popular tradition of the 'Fatherless Child', which he may have been predisposed to treat as more original, he almost, but not quite, removed all reference to the story of Ewen. This version was discreditable to Kentigern, because it made him a bastard, conceived through a rape; and discreditable also to Thaney, in the form in which it is told by the Herbertian author, since he makes the rape a divine punishment for her presumption in wishing to imitate the Virgin. As we have seen, Jocelyn was a considerable prude, and he preferred to play down this unpleasant affair, though he could not resist the temptation to wander off into speculation. It is interesting to note that Mr MacQueen himself puts forward an analogous, though not identical, view when he proposes that Baldred rejected Y and substituted X, 'which better befitted...the dignity of a saint and his church' (*op. cit.* 131). Nevertheless Jocelyn betrays that he knew Y (and therefore, as I believe, the Herbertian *Life*), since he remarks that the conception was in fact 'by the embrace of man' (i.e. Ewen), and that it was owing to her presumptuous wish to be like the Virgin Mary, which comes from the Herbertian author rather than from the folktale of the Fatherless Child. Nothing proves, therefore, that Jocelyn's other source was not the Herbertian *Life*, nor that it was some Glasgow document now lost, whether proximately Baldred's work or another's.

Much of the rest of Mr MacQueen's thesis consists of a theory that the story of Kentigern's conception derives from popular tales which are variant versions of the Danae story; from three distinct ones at once, apparently, though the argument is not clear to me. This scarcely affects the article above,[2] and need not be discussed here, but it is by no means

[1] It would be a *petitio principii* to argue that the parallels with various versions of the Danae story which are claimed to exist lend any support to this.

[2] The motif of setting adrift in a boat is explained differently above, on purely Celtic grounds (p. 294). Such things are in any case commonplaces in the legends of the saints. Compare the story of the birth of St Dubricius (J. G. Evans and J. Rhys, *The Book of Llan Dâv* (Oxford, 1893), 78 ff.). The part played by the story of Moses in the bulrushes is only one item of many which need consideration.

349

a simple problem, and calls for a thorough and cautious critical examination along the well-established lines of modern folktale research. There is a good deal in it which I myself find unsatisfactory, though it has some attractive features.

II

The other work referred to above is Professor J. Carney's original *Studies in Early Irish Literature* (Dublin, 1955). His theory is that the episode of the 'Ring of Polycrates' in the Irish *Táin Bó Fraích* (abbreviated here *TBF*) is derived directly from a lost original *Vita* of Kentigern (abbreviated here *VK*); and, since he believes that *TBF* is as old as the end of the seventh century or the early eighth, he assumes (without, however, setting out any historical criticism of the Kentigern documents) that *VK*—apparently the whole of it—must be as old as the latter part of the seventh century, which would be almost within living memory of Kentigern himself. Also the motif of 'Strawberries in Winter' in Irish is held to come from *VK*.

The argument depends on the assumption that if two versions of a story exist, closely similar to one another in their plot, the one must be derived directly from the other. Now, it is well known nowadays that among peoples possessing a rich oral literature, stories—not merely their broad outlines, or single motifs, but complex tales preserving an intricate plot—migrate freely; and that before one can assert that version I is derived directly from version II, rather than both from a more distant third one now lost, it is necessary to produce some very strong and particular reason to think so. In the absence of such reason the only sound assumption is that though admittedly connected, and perhaps closely, the one known version cannot be proved to come straight from the other; that we have no right to claim that it does; and that the hypothesis of the lost common original must, as a matter of method, take precedence.[1] Identity of fundamental plot, even when long and complex, is not a 'strong and particular reason', as every folklorist knows. Professor Carney regards such caution as exaggerated and as a hindrance

---

[1] It might be argued that since Carney's *VK* is non-existent as such, it *is* a lost common original for the story of the Ring. But it is clear that he regards it as virtually identical here with c. 36 of Jocelyn, as Jocelyn projected back into the seventh century so to speak; and that if Jocelyn had written in the seventh century instead of the twelfth no *VK* would have been posited at all. In other words, practically speaking it *is* Jocelyn, as appears clearly from the words, 'Some general stylistic considerations show that Jocelyn has presented his early sources verbatim or nearly so' (*op. cit.* 79, n. 2). As we are not told what these considerations are, and what views Carney holds on the history of Jocelyn's sources, the point cannot be discussed. One may wonder, however, whether the considerations are the verbal resemblances between Jocelyn and *TBF* mentioned *op. cit.* 38 (and accounted for below, pp. 354f.); if they are, this is the familiar fallacy of assuming what one wishes to prove. Incidentally, Jocelyn himself would have been much incensed by such a slur on his modish 'Roman salt' (cf. p. 275, n. 2 above), which is certainly not the style of the seventh century.

to the study of literature (*op. cit.* 48);[1] others may perhaps agree with the present writer in considering it a fundamental of sound scholarship.

One might be the more ready to believe that *TBF* derives directly from *VK* if the literatures concerned were ones in which oral transmission had little place, and in which one could be confident that practically everything ever written is still extant; or if Strathclyde in the Dark Ages were believed to have had a flourishing literature and Ireland a meagre one. In fact the exact reverse of these propositions is the case. Early Ireland was certainly rich in oral tales, many of which have perished, whereas very little is known about the literature of Strathclyde in the Dark Ages. Carney does indeed hold that there was 'immense hagiographic activity between 650 and 700' in 'the greater Ireland... *including* Gaelicised Scotland' (*op. cit.* 79;[2] my italics). It would be interesting to know what evidence there is for this in Scotland, beyond Adamnán's *Life of Columba* and the lost one by Cumméne Ailbe; and in any case the point has no bearing on non-Gaelicised Scotland, including Strathclyde. In the circumstances, the burden of proof must be on those who hold it as a principle that when an identical tale is found in Ireland and in Celtic Scotland in the Dark Ages, the proximate source is less likely to be Ireland than Scotland.

To come now to the specific problem in hand. As we have already seen (pp. 323 f. above), the legend of St Brigit tells in various forms how a man gives a woman a brooch 'to take care of' (Cogitosus, *in depositum sibi commendans*; Broccán's Hymn, *dia tasced*, 'to keep it safe'; 'Old Irish' *Life of Brigit*, *i lláim cumaili*, 'into the keeping of a maidservant'). The brooch is stolen and thrown into the sea, unknown to the girl (Cogitosus: by the man, so that when she cannot produce it he can enslave her and make her his concubine; Broccán's Hymn: by the man's wife, so as to get the girl into trouble, evidently through jealousy of her; 'Old Irish' *Life*: by the man, to get her into trouble). The girl is in danger (Broccán's Hymn and the 'Old Irish' *Life*, the man is about to kill her), but by the miraculous intercession of St Brigit the brooch is found in a fish. In Jocelyn there are certain differences, and the story is more specifically sexually motivated. The queen has a ring which the king 'ei...in speciale signum conjugalis amoris commendaverat', and she gives it to her lover (*scil.* as a love-token). The king sees it on the lover's finger, steals it unbeknown, and throws it in the river; and then demands of his wife the ring which had been 'ad custodiam ei commendatus', charging her with adultery and threatening her with death. She appeals to Kentigern, by whose miraculous intercession the ring is found in a fish, and she brings this to the king. He is appeased (the reason is not

---

[1] Carney does indeed consider the theory of the lost common source in connexion with *VK* and *TBF*, but rejects it on the ground that it cannot have been a heroic tale (*op. cit.* 49). However that may be, it is not contended in this Appendix that it was a heroic tale; hence the probability of a lost source is not affected by assuming the question of its nature.

[2] Here and *op. cit.* 180, Kentigern is described as 'Gaelic-British', a phrase the meaning and application of which seem obscure.

made clear, but he was presumably persuaded that the ring he took from the lover and threw in the river was not after all the one he had himself given the queen). In *TBF*, Medb (or Ailill)[1] gives her daughter Findabair a ring *dia taiscid*, 'to keep it safe'; she gives it to her lover Fraech as a love-token (*do chomarthu*), saying that if it is missed she will say she has lost it. Ailill finds it in Fraech's purse and throws it in a river (the intention evidently being that when the girl cannot produce it she shall be punished), but it is swallowed by a salmon, observed by Fraech but by no one else; and he catches the fish and tells Findabair the ring is inside. Ailill demands it of his daughter, threatening her with death if she cannot bring it, but she sends for the fish and the ring is found. Fraech tells a rather thin story to explain how he got the ring innocently, in the attempt to conceal the fact that it was given him as a love-token.

We have here, then, a story, established in a simple form in the legend of St Brigit and traceable to the middle of the seventh century in Ireland, in which a brooch is given to a girl 'to keep', is thrown into the sea to get her into trouble when she cannot produce it, and is miraculously discovered in a fish. And, both in Jocelyn and in *TBF*, we have a modification, in which someone gives a woman a ring 'to keep' and she bestows it on her lover as a love-token; the first giver (or the equivalent) discovers this, suspects sexual misconduct, throws the ring in a river, and demands it of her with threats of death; but the ring is produced from the fish which swallowed it, and he is persuaded that his suspicions were unjustified. The story in Jocelyn holds together better than in *TBF* (which is, here and all through, a very broken-down and corrupted tale). For instance the father's threat to kill the girl is not explicitly motivated in *TBF*, though it obviously arises from his fury at her suspected fornication;[2] and the hero sees the salmon swallow the ring and catches it, which has less point than the miracle, though natural to a hero story as distinct from a saint's *Life*.

Now, in my view what has happened is this. An oral story, called here O, in the simple form seen in the Brigit material, was current in Ireland before the middle of the seventh century. Subsequently, the motif of the suspected sexual misconduct was added,[3] producing an Irish common source P, at some time between the later seventh century

---

[1] For the *mo mháthair* of LL Mr Carney proposes to read *m'athair*, 'my father', i.e. Ailill, with YBL.

[2] This explains his 'inexplicably harsh attitude' (Carney, 37). As regards the inexplicable harshness of punishing the loss of a ring with death, it is worth noting that the Brigit material shows that death or enslavement was to be the punishment for the supposed loss in the original story called here O, a few lines below.

[3] Among the manifold versions of the story of the ring in the fish referred to on p. 322 above, few have a definite and immediate sexual motivation, and those which have (e.g. *Sakuntala*, 'The Cruel Knight upon the Road', and some others) are nevertheless not connected with the motif of suspected sexual misconduct.

and the eighth to ninth.[1] A version of P became known in Gaelicised Strathclyde in the eleventh century, as already proposed; and *TBF* derives independently from P in Ireland, with a certain amount of corruption and unsuccessful rearrangement consequent on the effort to force a hagiographic[2] story into a heroic context. The idea that the ring was given for safe keeping, or at any rate to keep, seems inherent in all Celtic versions and was evidently in P. The king committed to the queen's charge (*ei...commendaverat*) a ring 'to keep safe' (*ad custodiam*), and she gave it to her lover, obviously as a love-gift or token; Medb (or Ailill) gave her daughter the ring 'to keep safe' (*dia taiscid*) and she gave it to her lover as a love-token (*do chomarthu*). The fact that the king committed the ring to the queen *in speciale signum conjugalis amoris* is, in my opinion, a minor secondary intrusive feature; the teller is anticipating the motif of the love-token which belongs properly to the relation of queen and lover.[3] In fact it may very well be that this giving of the ring to a wife or other woman 'to keep' is a feature much older than the lost tale O, and that the story reached Ireland in that form, for in one of the best known versions of the Ring of Polycrates, the tale of King Solomon's ring recovered from a fish, widespread in Jewish and Arabic lore,[4] Solomon lost his ring when he gave it to one of his wives 'to look after' in the evening 'while he visited an unclean place' or went to undertake a ritual washing. An oriental, Rabbinical, source for an early Celtic legend is inherently quite probable and can easily be paralleled, even in the Kentigern material itself.[5]

How does Professor Carney deal with these things, and how does his exposition demonstrate the existence of those *special* and *peculiar* similarities between *VK* and *TBF* without which, as already noted, the hypothesis of a lost common source ought not to be rejected as an explanation preferable to that of direct borrowing? Four points seem to be made (*op. cit.* 37 ff.). First, it is stated that the king gives the ring both as a love-token *and* for safe keeping; that this is a contradiction, and that the contradiction is echoed verbally in *TBF*. But I fail to see the echo. Medb (or Ailill) gives the ring to Findabair to keep, and Findabair gives it to Fraech as a love-token; this seems to me logical and natural.

[1] When, as the language of the text suggests, the first written version of *TBF* was probably redacted.

[2] Without prejudice to what may have been the *original* form of the 'ring-in-the-fish' story on Celtic soil. Incidentally the fact that the story is on the whole better preserved in Jocelyn than in *TBF* does not prove that *TBF* is derived from *VK* (cf. Carney, *op. cit.* 80–1).

[3] Quite possibly at an earlier stage (in the Scottic *Life?*) the queen gave the ring to her lover *in speciale signum amoris*, and a copyist transferred this to the king by error, and suited it to the new context by adding *conjugalis*.

[4] E.g. Wünsche, *op. cit.* p. 322 above, no. 179; G. Weil, *Legenden der Muselmänner* (Frankfurt, 1845), 271 ff.; Palmer, *The Quran*, II, 178.

[5] Cf. the writer's 'Motive of the Threefold Death', in J. Ryan, *Essays and Studies presented to Eóin Mac Néill* (Dublin, 1940), 548, n. 44; Carney, *op. cit.* 80, n. 1.

The king gives the queen a ring to keep, and she gives it to her lover (obviously as an expression of her love). If there is a contradiction, it is not in *TBF* but in Jocelyn; and it has just been suggested that even there it may be quite secondary. In any case one may note that in itself the giving of a ring as a love-token is not a *special* and *peculiar* feature; this has been done every day of the world since rings were invented. For Carney's second point, he finds it normal that the king should give the queen a ring, because according to him this act has (it appears to be understood, has *necessarily*) a sexual significance; and it seems that he implies that the giving of a ring by Ailill (as Carney emends the text)[1] to Findabair is therefore abnormal, because he is her father, and hence it is secondary. This, however, falls to the ground, since it is clear from all our Celtic sources that the giving of the ring 'to keep it safe' was the original form; and evident that in P the first giver gave it for this purpose, and only the second bestowed it as a love-token. It is important not to confuse the issue by limiting the senses of the verb 'give'. Thirdly, Carney considers it significant in both Jocelyn and *TBF* that a messenger is sent to fetch the fish, and that it is a salmon. I can see nothing significant, nothing peculiar, in sending someone, which seems to me perfectly natural; it may well have been in P, but it proves no more than that. As to the other, Carney seems to have overlooked the fact that the fish is a salmon in Broccán's Hymn and the 'Old Irish' *Life of Brigit*, and that this is also the case in a number of the many non-Celtic versions of the 'Ring of Polycrates', so that the resemblance here is not peculiar to Jocelyn and *TBF*. There can be little doubt that it was so in O, and it is very likely that it reached Ireland in that form. Fourthly, certain verbal similarities between *VK* (as seen in Jocelyn) and *TBF* are claimed to demonstrate the direct dependence of the latter on the former (*op. cit.* 38), and it is here that it is important to Professor Carney to believe that Jocelyn 'has presented his early sources verbatim or nearly so' (cf. p. 350, n. 1 above). But these few resemblances concern, not insignificant trifles (in which case the argument would have been good) but points in the construction of the plot; the plot is closely similar, so therefore in certain matters is the wording. Both stories have the giving of the ring as a love-token, therefore both say so. Both make the salmon fetched by a messenger, therefore both say so—and here, by the way, one wonders where the close verbal similarities lie between '"Go", said he, "to where I went into the water"' (Carney's translation) and 'praecepit nuntio...ad ripam prefati fluminis Clud pergere'. This is not a verbal similarity but a similarity of content. As to the one on which Carney lays most weight, the supposed echo of the king's 'ad custodiam ei commendatus' by Findabair's 'Gave it me to keep it safe' ('dia taiscid'), we have already seen that this must have been not merely in P

---

[1] However well-founded this emendation may be, the fact that Ailill is the would-be avenger does not necessarily make him the original giver. It is completely natural, and very human, that even though the mother gave the ring it should be the father who actually resented and proposed to punish their daughter's suspected misconduct.

but also in O,[1] and perhaps in the original non-Celtic source as well. The 'lost common original' carries the day here.

One may well agree that the story in *TBF* has 'undergone a process of adaptation' (*op. cit.* 49), for this is very obvious, since the whole story of Fraech hangs together very badly (cf. p. 324 above); and that it has parallels in Irish hagiographical material (as has also been noted above, *loc. cit.*). But nothing has been advanced to make plausible the theory that *TBF* is directly taken from a lost seventh-century original *VK*. Carney's recognition of the importance of the theme in the Brigit material really gives the case away. He derives the story in the *Life of Kentigern* from it, but will not allow that the version in *TBF* comes from it too. Yet he himself claims that in *TBF* there is another motif which does come from the *Life of St Brigit* (*op. cit.* 82–3). If so, an *a priori* case for influence from the legend of St Brigit on *TBF* by a more direct route than via Strathclyde is immensely strengthened.

As to the motif of 'Strawberries in Winter', Carney wishes to show that in Irish this too, as we see it in *Tromdám Guaire* (called here *TG*), comes directly from *VK*, and that the versions in the *Lives* of St Ciarán derive from *TG*. The close similarities have already been noted above, pp. 325 ff., but the evidence on which it is declared that the Irish story must come from *VK* can scarcely be taken very seriously. The theory that Kentigern and Marbán share an important motif in the matter of the white boar (Jocelyn, c. 26) has already been dealt with in *Éigse*, VII, 112 n., where I pointed out that this, as seen in Jocelyn, where in any case it is a mere passing incident, is a hagiographical commonplace, and that the situation is quite different from that of Marbán and his pet. The fact that the latter is called a swineherd and keeps a pet pig is, I believe, an expression of what I consider the probability that he was a Wild Man of the Woods, not a saint at all,[2] and parallel to Lailoken and Myrddin, not to Kentigern.[3] In any case, Kentigern's boar occurs in the episode in Wales which, as I think I have shown, dates from the twelfth century and had no original connection with Kentigern. For the theory that the name *Mo Chohe* must identify Kentigern with Marbán see p. 302 above; and one must emphasise that Guaire's brother *Mo Chua* was a quite different person from Marbán. Carney apparently believes that the period when *TG* borrowed all this from *VK* was at least as early as the tenth century (it is not clear to me whether he would push it back to the seventh, like the Ring story), because the famous dialogue of Guaire and Marbán is as old as that and Marbán is an adaptation from Kentigern (*op. cit.* 170). But this is an argument in a circle.

I see no convincing reasons to suppose that the story in *TG* comes from *VK*, though clearly there is some close connection, as already noted above, p. 326. Even if it did, it does not show that *VK* is as old

---

[1] Cf. Cogitosus's 'in depositum sibi commendans', and Broccán's 'dia tasced'.

[2] This explains the fact, noted by Carney, that there is no evidence for any St Marbán in Ireland.

[3] This has been hinted at already in my *Early Celtic Nature Poetry*, 121.

as the tenth century, much less the seventh, since the motif of the black-berries in connection with Guaire cannot be proved to be any earlier than *c.* 1100 in Irish, if that (cf. Carney, *op. cit.* 169). I hold rather that there is a close common source for it lying behind *TG* and Jocelyn, an Irish/Scottish-Gaelic one, belonging to the eleventh century, as already proposed, and that the 'Gaelic' character of Jocelyn's source has been demonstrated. The version of the same basic motif in the lost original *Life* of Ciarán is doubtless older, and would be an ancestor (whether collateral or possibly direct) of the Gaelic common source in question.

The reason why it was thought necessary to assume that the *Life of Kentigern* goes back to the seventh century is that Carney believes that *TBF* is the prime source for the epic of *Beowulf*, which he dates about 700. In his scheme, therefore, Cogitosus composed his *Life of Brigit* about 650; the motif of the Ring was adopted from it in Strathclyde in the later seventh century in a lost *Life of Kentigern*, with considerable modifications; this lost *Life* (including also the motif of the blackberries?) crossed the Irish Sea once again and shortly before 700 its version of the Ring story was transmogrified into *TBF*; which itself once more crossed back again to Britain and about 700 resulted in the Anglo-Saxon *Beowulf*. One may very well leave this last part of the theory to students of Anglo-Saxon literature who are competent to deal with it; but here one may remark on the extraordinary and violent amount of activity involved, and the short time in which such radical events are supposed to have happened.

The conclusion is, I believe, that nothing remotely like the *Life of St Kentigern* in the form we see it in Jocelyn existed so early as the seventh century, or probably before the eleventh; that the two motifs in question got into the Kentigern material in the eleventh century, as part of a secondary appendix of a hotch-potch of Kentigern's miracles[1] deriving from popular tales and 'religious folk-lore' of a predominantly 'Gaelic' background; and that the idea that the whole thing goes back almost to living memory of Kentigern himself is neither proven nor probable.[2]

---

[1] Compare the Herbertian author's description of the Scottic *codicellus* as containing *virtutes eius*, i.e. his miracles.

[2] In *Arctica, Studia Ethnographica Upsaliensia*, XI (1956), 226, Professor Carney argues that the spelling *Mochohe*, with -*h*- marking hiatus, supports an early date, quoting *rehe* in the mid-eighth century Würzburg Glosses. But the use of -*h*- as a hiatus separater, or between the elements of diphthongs, which is of Latin origin, occurs sporadically much later than this in Celtic words in Latin documents of Celtic provenance. Since so little is known of the early Irish orthographic tradition in Scotland it would be quite impossible to contend that the spelling *Mochohe* cannot be as late as the eleventh century, and that it constitutes an argument for an earlier date. Original hiatus has survived to the present day in Scottish Gaelic, and is marked usually by a vowel-separating -*th*-, not pronounced, though -*th*- is elsewhere pronounced *h*; the analogy is close. Compare the words above, p. 302, about *Cill Mo Chotha*, in the very same name.

ADDENDUM

It is remarkable that in the Irish Brigit material the object given is a brooch, not a ring, whereas in *TBF* and the *Life of Kentigern* it is a ring. Lest anyone should suppose that this constitutes a 'strong and particular reason' to derive the former from the latter, it should be noted that 'ring' was obviously in P. It was doubtless also in O, since the international tale in general has 'ring'; but was changed to 'brooch' in the Brigit stories (which evidently go back to a common sub-version of O). This suggests that P does not derive from O via the Brigit legend, but independently. The immediate common origin ('sub-version' of O) of the Brigit material would seem to have taken 'ring' in the sense of 'brooch', probably (as Mrs Chadwick suggests to me) because of the penannular form of the early Christian Irish brooch. The Latin life has *sentis*, 'thorn, brooch' (variant reading *fibula*, afterwards referred to as *gemma*), and the Irish material calls it *delg*, 'thorn, pin, brooch'.

Index

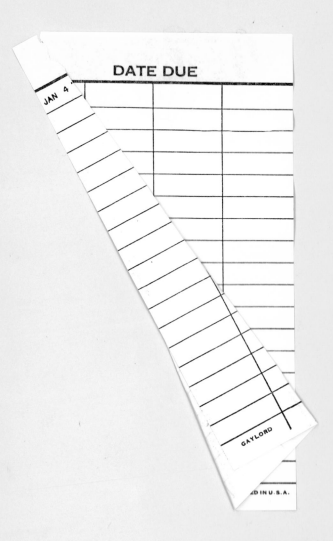

DATE DUE

JAN 4

GAYLORD

...ED IN U.S.A.